TITUS LIVIUS (LIVY), the historian, was born in Patavium (modern Padua) in 64 or 59 BC and died in AD 12 or 17 in Patavium, surviving therefore into his late seventies or early eighties. He came to Rome in the 30s BC and began writing his history of Rome not long after. There is no evidence that he was a senator or held other governmental posts, although he was acquainted with the emperor Augustus and his family, at least by his later years. He appears to have had the means to spend his life largely in writing his huge history of Rome, *Ab Urbe Condita* or 'From the Foundation of the City', which filled 142 books and covered the period from Rome's founding to the death of the elder Drusus (735–9 BC). Thirty-five books survive: 1–10 (753–293 BC) and 21–45 (218–167 BC).

J. C. YARDLEY has translated Livy's *The Dawn of the Roman Empire* (Books 31–40) and *Hannibal's War* (Books 21–30) for Oxford World's Classics, as well as Tacitus' *Annals*. He has translated Justin for the American Philological Association's Classical Resources series, Velleius Paterculus for Hackett, and Curtius Rufus for Penguin Classics. He is also the author of *Justin and Pompeius Trogus* (2003) and (with Waldemar Heckel) *Alexander the Great* (2004).

DEXTER HOYOS was born in Barbados, studied at Oxford, and taught Roman history and historians, and Latin, at Sydney University until his retirement in 2007; he is now an Honorary Affiliate of the University. He has published widely on Latin teaching and aspects of Roman and Carthaginian history, including *The Carthaginians* (2010) and, as editor, *A Companion to the Punic Wars* (2011). He introduced J. C. Yardley's translation of *Hannibal's War* for Oxford World's Classics.

OXFORD WORLD'S CLASSICS

*For over 100 years Oxford World's Classics have brought
readers closer to the world's great literature. Now with over 700
titles—from the 4,000-year-old myths of Mesopotamia to the
twentieth century's greatest novels—the series makes available
lesser-known as well as celebrated writing.*

*The pocket-sized hardbacks of the early years contained
introductions by Virginia Woolf, T. S. Eliot, Graham Greene,
and other literary figures which enriched the experience of reading.
Today the series is recognized for its fine scholarship and
reliability in texts that span world literature, drama and poetry,
religion, philosophy, and politics. Each edition includes perceptive
commentary and essential background information to meet the
changing needs of readers.*

OXFORD WORLD'S CLASSICS

——

LIVY

Rome's Italian Wars
Books Six to Ten

——

Translated by
J. C. YARDLEY

With an Introduction and Notes by
DEXTER HOYOS

OXFORD
UNIVERSITY PRESS

OXFORD

UNIVERSITY PRESS

Great Clarendon Street, Oxford OX2 6DP
United Kingdom

Oxford University Press is a department of the University of Oxford.
It furthers the University's objective of excellence in research, scholarship,
and education by publishing worldwide. Oxford is a registered trade mark of
Oxford University Press in the UK and in certain other countries

First published as an Oxford World's Classics paperback 2013

Impression:12

British Library Cataloguing in Publication Data

Data available

ISBN 978-0-19-956485-9

Printed and bound in Great Britain
by Clays Ltd, Elcograf S.p.A.

CONTENTS

For
Jann, Barbara, Camilla, Andrea, Elaine, and Jane

INTRODUCTION

Livy the Historian

LIVY, or in full Titus Livius, was born at Patavium in northern Italy (Padua today) in 59 BC, and so lived through the turbulent years of the fall of the Roman Republic into the calm and politically controlled era of one-man rule under Augustus and his successor Tiberius.[1] According to St Jerome's *Chronicle* he died in AD 17. He seems not to have held public office or done any military service. Apart from some essays, now lost, on philosophy and rhetoric, he undertook in his late twenties to compose an up-to-date history of Rome drawing on mostly Roman but also some Greek predecessors. He entitled it *From the Foundation of the City (Ab Urbe Condita)*: to all Romans their City was unique.

The history eventually amounted to 142 books, taking Rome's history from its traditional foundation-date of 753 BC down to the year 9 BC—a colossal achievement, much lengthier than Gibbon's *Decline and Fall*, for instance. Of it only the first ten Books and then Books 21–45 survive. Books 6–10 take the story of Rome from 390 BC down to the year 293. Evidence in the work indicates that Livy began writing in the early 20s BC, for around 18 BC he reached Book 28. A subheading to a surviving résumé (epitome) of the lost book 121 states that it was published after Augustus' death in AD 14: something that probably held true, too, for those that followed. The history ended at the year 9 BC.[2]

Livy's youth was a time of growing political instability, even though Rome had subdued and was still expanding an empire

---

[1] An epitaph at Patavium seems to commemorate him; it marks the tomb of Titus Livius son of Gaius, his wife Cassia Prima, and two sons (H. Dessau, *Inscriptiones Latinae Selectae* (Berlin, 1892–1916; henceforth *ILS*), no. 2919); we also know that he had a daughter.

[2] For Books 1–5 (the 'first pentad') see *Livy: The Rise of Rome*: translation, notes, and introduction by T. J. Luce (Oxford World's Classics, 1998). We have epitomes (*periochae*), put together in the late Roman empire, of all the Books except 136–7; they give an idea of what has been lost—although the *periochae* of surviving Books show how idiosyncratic and at times frivolous the anonymous epitomators could be. The epitomes are translated by J. D. Chaplin, *Livy: Rome's Mediterranean Empire. Books 41–45 and the Periochae* (Oxford World's Classics, 2007).

from the Atlantic to the river Euphrates, and Julius Caesar was about to launch his conquest of Gaul. Roman political life was degenerating fast into power-contests between dominant leaders even to the point of civil war in 49 BC. When Caesar triumphed, he was quickly eliminated, in 44 BC, by an alliance between disenchanted supporters and resentful ex-enemies. Fresh upheavals broke out, climaxing in prolonged and violent rivalry between the two remaining leaders—Caesar's former deputy Mark Antony and his great-nephew and adopted son Caesar Octavian. The outcome was victory for Octavian in 31–30, which made him master of Rome and the empire.

Taking the ceremonious name Augustus in 27, the new ruler set himself to restore peace, order, and confidence at home, to continue expanding the empire, and also to make it plain that he was not giving up his supremacy as *princeps* (first citizen). The renewal of Rome was accompanied by a remarkable literary and artistic flowering that came to be called the Augustan Age (although in fact it had begun in the still-stressful 30s), when poets like Virgil, Horace, and later Ovid composed masterpieces that became more or less instant classics, while at the same time taking care to laud the new ruler. Artists and architects created works like Augustus' emblematic Altar of Peace, dedicated in 9 BC, and the Augustan Forum, opened in 2 BC. The historians of the time were active too: for example writing on the tumultuous times that had recently ended (like the ex-consul Asinius Pollio, who also sneered at Livy, opaquely, for 'Patavinity') or, in our Patavian's case, undertaking the momentous project of telling a new generation Rome's history from its beginning.[3]

At the start, Livy had no idea that his work would fill 142 books. The first five, on Rome of the kings (Book 1) and then the fifth-century Republic, dealt with about 360 years; then Books 6–10 narrate the ninety-seven years from 389 to 293 BC. In the middle of Book 10 he pauses, almost in wonderment, to comment on how lengthy his narrative of the Samnite wars has so far proved—four books—and how more is still to come (10.31). He was undeterred: the next ten books, which did not survive Roman times, covered

---

[3] Livy's *Patavinitas*: Quintilian, *The Training of the Orator* 1.5.56, 8.1.3. The contexts make it clear that Pollio thought poorly of some of Livy's vocabulary choices and expressions, but other theories have been advanced.

only seventy-four years, and 21–30 (the famous 'third decad' on Hannibal's war) took the story through a mere eighteen, from 219 to 201. By the time he started on Book 31, Livy felt it necessary to tell his readers that he felt 'like someone who wades out into the sea after being initially attracted to the water by the shallows . . . and I foresee any advance only taking me into even more enormous, indeed bottomless, depths'. A task that he had thought would lessen in size as it progressed seemed instead to be expanding indefinitely.[4]

He was right. The epitomes that survive of the history show that the second half of his work, starting at Book 72, began with the year 91 BC, and the work from there to Book 133 gave an immensely detailed account of events down to 29 BC. Augustus' virtual monarchy brought about a change: if their epitomes are a guide, Livy's final books (134–142) narrated mainly foreign wars down to 9 BC—a sign, perhaps, of political discretion by an author now famous and enjoying the ruler's favour.

The complete history was too massive for most readers. Eighty years later the poet Martial joked that his library could not fit Livy in whole, and he welcomed an abridgement. Of this vast narrative only one-third survives. Book 10 ends with the year 293 BC; then 21–45 take us from 219 down to 167. Even these thirty-five Books fill six or seven volumes of Latin text.[5]

Structure and Chronology in Books 6 to 10

Book 6 opens with the year 389, the aftermath of the famous capture of Rome by a marauding army of Gauls. It takes the story down to 367, and then the narrative grows steadily ampler: Book 7 covers 366 to 342, Book 8 the years 341 to 322, Book 9 the period from 321 to 304, and Book 10 from 303 to 293.[6] Not only is Livy's narration fuller as it progresses from book to book, but the quality of information clearly improves, especially in Book 10: the numbers of enemy

[4] Livy 31.1, tr. J. C. Yardley, *Livy: The Dawn of the Roman Empire. Books 31–40* (Oxford World's Classics, 2000).

[5] Martial, *Epigrams* 14.190.

[6] This illustrates the 'landscape principle'—that more recent times receive fuller attention than those further back—noted by A. A. Barrett in J. C. Yardley and A. A. Barrett, *Velleius Paterculus: The Roman History*, translated with introduction and notes (Indianapolis and Cambridge: Hackett, 2011), pp. xxvii–xxviii.

casualties become somewhat more realistic (even if still not always credible), and place-names are not only more numerous but look more realistic, though with the same caveat. A great deal of the narrative throughout—well over half—relates the Romans' incessant wars with their neighbours, as the city expanded its dominance over further regions of the Italian peninsula. Another theme, likewise continuing from earlier books, is the struggle between Rome's oligarchic patricians and the plebeian majority over civil and economic rights and political power.

Both themes evolve steadily. In Book 6, Rome's military horizons extend only to regions within a few days' march: southern Etruria, eastern Latium, and, beyond this, the mountains and valleys of her old foes the Aequi, Hernici, and Volsci. In succeeding books, Roman diplomacy and warfare expand to Campania, the Sabines and Umbrians, all Etruria, Apulia, and—toughest enemies of all—the Samnites. Despite opponents' resilience, and occasional disasters like the famous affair of the Caudine Forks (9.1–11), Rome's fortune prevails over all. At home, patrician–plebeian confrontations bring a series of plebeian gains despite strong patrician resistance, from the easing of debt-burdens to laws that open consulships and pontifical priesthoods to plebeians. The politically dominant elite thus becomes a joint patrician–plebeian aristocracy, although social and economic tensions never die away.

A regular feature of Livy's history, like those of his predecessors (see pp. xii–xvi), is its 'annalistic', or year-by-year, structure: all events in a given year are narrated together before those of the next year begin. This was not a Roman peculiarity; Greek historians, including Thucydides, often used it too. The elaborate dating systems that Romans and Greeks employed, as well as the strong influence of the pontifical and other annals, dictated the format. In a detailed history it naturally produced rather jerky narrative sequences: a long war with the Samnites, for instance, had to be reported in yearly instalments, each taking its place alongside whatever other happenings the writer wanted to relate for that year. The risk of discontinuities, mistakes, and confused repetitions is obvious, and Livy's work is full of examples of them all.

The fact that each year was dated by the names of its consuls—a series that historians rarely correlated with other chronologies such as Olympiad years—could again lead to problems. Sometimes the same man held office more than once, like the famous Camillus (six times consular tribune and four times dictator), the hero Valerius Corvus (six consulships, two dictatorships), and the military eminences Fabius Rullianus and Papirius Cursor (five consulships each). Again, leading families' members over generations often bore very similar names—profuse sequences of Fabii, Valerii, Manlii, Claudii, and Cornelii, to mention only a few. Inevitably, uncertainties occurred about which year or which magistrate was associated with a given event.

For fourth-century events, two other difficulties need mention. The Gallic Sack of Rome, traditionally dated to 390 BC, actually occurred in 387 or 386—as Greek historians like Polybius knew (Pol. 1.6).[7] Matching post-Sack Roman dates to other established ones, including the chronological systems in Greek states and Greek historians, therefore required some juggling. Because it was necessary to bring the post-Sack decades into line with the year 367, when important political and economic reforms were enacted, Livy asserts (6.35) that over five years, 375–371 inclusive, plebeian tribunes backing reform not only were elected and re-elected but used their power of veto to prevent elections to any other offices, and so in the end got their way. Yet he has very little material to put into the so-called 'years of anarchy', filling the void instead (6.36–42) with a vivid depiction of patrician resistance to reform. The tribunes' agitation in reality probably lasted one to two years, and the years of 'anarchy' were some earlier annalist's chronological device.

The *Fasti Capitolini*, the Augustan-era lists of Republican consuls and other chief magistrates (see Glossary), present the other difficulty, the so-called 'dictator years' (equivalent to our 333, 324, 309, and 301 BC: see Glossary). Allegedly only dictators and their masters of horse held office in each of those years. This seems to be an invention, perhaps by the compilers of the *Fasti*, intended again to bring Roman chronology into line with other established dates. Such magistrate-deprived years were unknown to ancient historians and cannot have existed. The year we call 334 BC, for example, was actually followed by the year we call 332. Rather than disrupt long-standing conventions, however, modern scholars generally use the traditional

---

[7] *Polybius: The Histories*, tr. R. Waterfield, with Introduction and Notes by B. McGing (Oxford World's Classics, 2010), 6–7.

dates from 390 on, and employ a double numeral to designate the actual year before each fictitious 'dictator-year' (thus '334/333', etc.).[8]

Livy's Sources for Books 6 to 10

To write Rome's early history, Livy had to take information from past accounts and process it. By the fourth century BC, the complex of myths, legends, and facts for Rome's previous 350 years had shed the mythical element, and legends were shading into more reliable records. Even so the original records were varied, sometimes inconsistent, and vulnerable to exaggeration and invention. There were early items like inscriptions in public places, texts such as the famous Twelve Tables of Roman law (see Glossary), and interstate treaties incised on bronze plates. One surviving early verse epitaph commemorates the achievements of L. Cornelius Scipio Barbatus, consul in 298, a list that seems to contradict entirely what Livy and other sources report—raising pertinent questions about whom to believe (10.11, 12 notes).[9] We know, too, that early treaties with Carthage were stored on the Capitoline hill, where the second-century BC Greek historian Polybius saw them.[10]

Other basic records chronicled noteworthy events including omens, natural disasters, and treaties (though not their contents), accompanied by lists of office-holders, triumphs (these were religious as well as military ceremonies), and religious rituals. Everything was entered in year-by-year format. These records were kept by priests, who with few exceptions were senators. There were, for instance, the little-known 'Linen Books' which Livy's recent predecessors, Licinius Macer and Aelius Tubero, claimed to have read in the temple of Juno on the Capitoline.[11] The principal chronicle of events was supervised by the Chief Priest (*Pontifex Maximus*) until about 120 BC,

[8] On the chronology of early Rome, especially the fourth century, see e.g. T. J. Cornell, *The Beginnings of Rome: Italy and Rome from the Bronze Age to the Punic Wars (c. 1000–264 BC)* (London and New York: Routledge, 1995), 399–403.

[9] *ILS* 1; translated in (e.g.) N. Lewis and M. Reinhold, *Roman Civilization: Selected Readings*, 3rd edn.: vol. 1 (New York: Columbia University Press, 1990), 523; and online at: <wikipedia.org/wiki/Lucius_Cornelius_Scipio_Barbatus>.

[10] Pol. 3.26; just what building he means is not certain. Polybius was one of Livy's principal sources from Book 21 on but not for 1–10, because his *History* deals with the period from 264 to 146.

[11] Livy mentions these *libri lintei* on Macer's and Tubero's authority only in Book 4 (4.7, 13, 20, 23), even though he cites the two historians more than once in 6–10 as well.

and so came to be called the 'Pontifical Annals' or 'Chief Annals' (*Annales Maximi*). In its ultimately published form it took up eighty books (that is, book-rolls), which implies that its entries grew more detailed as the centuries wore on.

Such chronicles were not foolproof. With the Pontifical Annals, each year's entries were originally painted on white boards outside the Regia, the Chief Priest's official residence, so that reading and transcribing them could be difficult. Moreover, since many priests (especially Chief Priests) down the centuries belonged to powerful families, the records were at regular risk of tampering. Other records like the Linen Books were no safer.[12]

Less official or public Roman texts existed, too. The versatile Ap. Claudius Caecus (9.29 note), a controversial aristocrat of the later fourth and early third centuries, left behind writings on law, sententious aphorisms, and a famous speech delivered in old age.[13] Long-established leading families had their own traditions, religious and secular, handed down from generation to generation. Some of Livy's vivid accounts of notable deeds or episodes may draw, if indirectly, on such memories: for instance, how an insult to one daughter of Fabius Ambustus led her patrician father to back far-reaching moves for political and social reforms (6.34), and the tales of victorious single combats between aristocratic young Roman officers and huge yet easily beaten Gallic champions (7.9–10, 26). The relentless prominence of Q. Fabius Maximus Rullianus in Books 8 to 10, and Livy's clear admiration for him, may well be due in part to family tradition passed on by Fabius Pictor, the earliest Roman historian.

Various sources survived from other Italian states as well. Livy draws on local records or at any rate traditions of his home town Patavium for an episode in 302 that was still commemorated in his own day (10.2). Evidence from Etruscan cities and leading families survived into Roman imperial times, as the emperor Claudius and the encyclopedist Pliny the Elder attest. There survives, too, a number of intriguing epitaphs in Latin from the first century AD, that commemorate grandees of Tarquinii active in times before

---

[12] Cato, *Origins*, fragment 77P; Servius, *Commentary on* Aeneid 1.373 (the eighty books).

[13] The speech, made in 280, was extant in Cicero's time (*Brutus* 61). Ap. Claudius' most famous *sententia* was 'each man is the craftsman of his own fortune' (*faber est suae quisque fortunae*), still favoured in modern times for school mottoes, among other things.

Roman domination. Again, local records of Cumae, the old Greek colony near Neapolis (Naples), are reflected in Livy's Greek contemporary Dionysius of Halicarnassus, himself a historian of early Rome.[14]

Livy is aware that early records could be unreliable: 'I believe the historical record has been marred by funerary eulogies and false inscriptions on ancestral busts, with the various families all illegitimately appropriating to themselves military campaigns and public offices' (8.40). Every so often his narrative points out contradictions in his sources over who held office in a given year, or commanded in a military theatre. Cicero, too, complains (*Brutus* 61) that funeral eulogies from past times often invented triumphs, consulships, and other fabrications for the greater glory of the deceased.

There is not, in fact, much evidence that Livy consulted primary records himself. When he finds reason to cite sources, they are invariably previous historians: from Fabius Pictor around 200 BC to Macer, Tubero, Valerius Antias, and Claudius Quadrigarius of just a generation before Livy himself. For example, he is content to tell us what Macer and Tubero reported about items in the Linen Books.[15] He announces a treaty made with Carthage in the mid-fourth century (7.27) and its renewal in 306 (9.43), but says nothing of its contents— even though he could have made the effort to view it, as Polybius had done. When he cites his sources on a specific issue, even one that they recorded in divergent ways, again they are earlier historians.[16]

The predecessors were a mixed batch. To mention only those cited in Books 6–10, some belonged to ancient aristocratic families (Fabius, Piso, and Macer); certain others were aristocrats of less eminent ancestry (e.g. Cincius Alimentus and Tubero). They could make use

[14] Claudius' study of ancient Etruscan authors: *ILS* 212 (his speech in the Senate, AD 48). The Tarquinian *elogia* were collected and studied by M. Torelli, *Elogia Tarquiniensia* (Florence, 1975); on Tarquinii, cf. note to 6.4 below. Cumae's records: inferred from Dionysius of Halicarnassus' detailed account of the city's famous tyrant Aristodemus the Effeminate (Dionysius 7.2–12).

[15] He notes (4.23) that, though Macer and Tubero both claimed to have consulted the Linen Books for the consuls of 434, they gave different names: another sign of the problems posed by ancient, perhaps damaged, records.

[16] Fourth- and third-century Greek writers who at times mentioned events that Livy also narrates, for instance Duris of Samos (see note to 10.30), Aristotle, and Timaeus of Tauromenium, are never cited. Nor is Polybius, who (3.22–5) quotes and discusses the Roman–Carthaginian treaties of the fourth and third centuries. Probably Livy began to use him only when *From the Foundation* reached Hannibal's time.

not only of the various priestly annals but also, as just mentioned, of surviving family traditions. At the same time they were not above promoting their own ancestors' glory and playing down the achievements of the ancestors' rivals: this may partly explain Livy's constant sniping at the famous Ap. Claudius Caecus, a bitter enemy of Fabius Rullianus. Still other predecessors, of less distinguished background, were assiduous compilers of material and, often enough, equally keen to push a partisan point of view when narrating events both domestic and foreign: among them was another recent predecessor of Livy's, Claudius Quadrigarius, cited twice in Books 6–10 (see 8.19, 9.5).

These historians differed in various ways. The earliest, Fabius and Cincius, were Hannibal's contemporaries in the late third and early second centuries (Cincius was even a well-treated captive of Hannibal's for a time). In other words, no Roman wrote history during Rome's first half-millennium, although well before 200 BC speeches by leading men were written down and preserved.[17] By then, educated Romans could also read Greek, so Fabius, Cincius, and some subsequent Roman historians wrote their works in Greek in order to explain the Mediterranean's new superpower to the Hellenistic world, as well as to inform their fellow-Romans. Fabius Pictor certainly made an impact, to judge by a second-century BC painted inscription in the Sicilian city of Tauromenium, naming him—the sole non-Greek—in a list of historians, with a résumé of his account of Rome's foundation.[18]

Roman history in its own language was introduced by M. Porcius Cato, famous as Cato the Censor, who in a very long life from 234 to 149 held major offices (consul in 195, censor in 185), influenced state policy on issues domestic and foreign (including successful pressure for a third Punic war when in his eighties), championed old-style values against the seductive inflow of Greek culture—in which he himself was well versed—and in his later years opened the

[17] On the early Roman historians, the masterful chapter by E. Badian in T. A. Dorey (ed.), *Latin Historians* (London: Routledge & Kegan Paul, 1967) remains crucial; see also R. M. Ogilvie, *Early Rome and the Etruscans*, 2nd edn. (London: Fontana Press and Cambridge, Mass.: Harvard University Press, 1996), 1–29; E. Bispham in N. Rosenstein and R. Morstein-Marx (eds.), *A Companion to the Roman Republic* (Malden, Mass., and Oxford: Blackwell, 2006), 30–7; E. S. Gruen, ibid. 460–3. Ap. Claudius' speech is mentioned in note 13, and Pliny the Elder quotes from a funeral oration by Q. Caecilius Metellus for his eminent father, who died after 241 BC (*Natural History* 7.139–41).

[18] Fabius Pictor in list at Tauromenium: Frier (1976), 230–1.

illustrious roster of Latin historians with a seven-book work called *The Origins*. Uniquely, Cato not only wrote about Rome but also gave two books to the origins of other Italian peoples.

After Cato, Latin became the norm for Roman historians. Their works could be as concise as Cato's—L. Calpurnius Piso, consul in 133, wrote his history of Rome in seven books—or ambitious, like Piso's approximate contemporary Cn. Gellius who took some thirty books to reach 200 BC or thereabouts. In the half-century or so before Livy began to write, further annalistic histories appeared, notably those of Licinius Macer, Claudius Quadrigarius, and Aelius Tubero (as well as Valerius Antias, whom Livy cites in his first five books and often in Books 21–45, but not in our volume). Like earlier histories, they were uneven in quality, but Livy found them congenial to use. For example, his famous tale of how young Manlius slew the Gaul and earned the *cognomen* Torquatus is noticeably close to Quadrigarius' version, which happens to be quoted by the later writer Aulus Gellius, who was very interested in early Latin writers and often cites them (7.9–10 and notes); if we had more numerous extracts from these predecessors, we would probably find many other cases of close borrowing.

Livy on Fourth-Century Virtues and Vices

Romans always liked to believe that, just as they were morally superior to other peoples (even other Italians), so too their own past was morally superior to their present. Livy was not the first or last writer to depict the Romans of olden times as exemplifying the virtues of the ideal citizen, but his gallery of great Romans indelibly impressed readers' imaginations from his own time to ours. His first ten books might be seen as a paean to early Rome's simple and uncorrupted morality, represented both by eminent figures like Brutus the Liberator, Camillus, and Papirius Cursor, and also by a host of lesser figures in war and peace—an era that Livy clearly wishes readers to take to heart as a contrast to the regrettable sophistication of his own era (e.g. 8.10, 10.40, and notes). It is understandable that the ten books should inspire Machiavelli to set out a political philosophy of his own in the *Discourses on the First Decad of Titus Livius*.[19]

[19] Machiavelli's *Discourses* are translated by J. Conaway Bondanella and P. Bondanella (Oxford World's Classics, reissued 2008).

The Rome of Books 6 to 10 is blessed with a steady supply of hero-ically selfless leaders, through whom the struggling city-state of 390 BC becomes the mistress of nearly all Italy by 290. Livy singles out three for special praise, Camillus (7.1), Valerius Corvus (7.33), and Papirius Cursor (9.16); but others—Manlius Torquatus, Marcius Rutulus, Decius Mus father and son, and above all Fabius Rullianus—are no less admirable, as the long roster of their feats both military and civilian prove, together with Livy's generous assignment to them of vivid narrative and speeches.

The virtues that Romans extolled were firmly civic. Such personal attributes as humility, charity, and chivalry may have met with approval (from some), but were not part of the commonly laudable range; nor was a sense of humour. The admirable Roman was endowed with physical courage, moral firmness, religious reverence, a sense of justice, self-control and restraint, and—if a beaten enemy deserved it—mercifulness. He also possessed a paramount sense of duty, meaning obedience to lawful authority divine or human, and (as an extension of this) was devoted to his City and prepared to die for it. Livy's fourth-century Roman heroes embody these qualities, from Camillus, who displays all of them in various episodes and is complimented as Rome's 'second founder' (7.1), to Decius Mus father and son, whose enduring renown is due to each sacrificing his life in battle under the religious rite of *devotio*, to save his army and Rome (8.9–10, 10.28–29). In the lengthy story of Fabius Rullianus' clash with his superior at the time, Papirius Cursor, Livy paints a very sympathetic picture of Fabius—whose disobedience won Rome a great victory—yet comes down clearly in favour of Papirius' insist-ence on discipline and lawful obedience (8.30–35). Equally Roman, though, is Papirius' mercifulness towards his brilliant subordinate, whom he had the right to execute but instead dismisses with a warn-ing. Livy's admiration for such leaders colours his discussion of how Alexander the Great would have fared, had he lived to invade Italy: they would have been more than a match for him (9.18).

To depict Rome, all the same, as a community of uniformly excel-lent men and women would have been not only unattractively dull history but untrue to historical traditions. Livy has enough material, genuine or invented, to make fourth-century Romans more than cardboard icons. Camillus, 'the mainstay of Rome' during a very long life (6.3), nonetheless totally misjudges the political situation as an old man in 368, opposes the tide of reform, and finally has to admit defeat (6.38, 42). Manlius Torquatus, eventually to be another bulwark of the state, begins as a rough and ill-treated youth who reveals his noble qualities paradoxically, by defending his tyrannically unjust father against justified prosecution: filial duty triumphs over equity (7.4). Two other paragons, Fabius Rullianus and Papirius Cursor, have the bitter clash just mentioned because Fabius ignores the dictator's ban on engaging the enemy: facing capital punishment, he unleashes a savage attack on Papirius' pride and heartlessness (8.33). Later even Fabius' normally devoted colleague and friend, the younger Decius Mus, in turn has a dispute with him when both are again consuls, over who should have military command against the Etruscans (10.24). We might be forgiven for concluding that, with all his sterling virtues, Fabius could be a difficult man to get along with.

Livy's own conservative attitudes impel him to critical verdicts on some fourth-century matters. As in earlier books, he records and sometimes is sympathetic to the grievances of the plebeians—the overwhelming majority of the citizen body—who in 390 still had small say in government and were badly oppressed by debt. Yet actions to secure redress and reform for them usually draw Livian ire. The reformers Licinius and Sextius in the 370s–360s are sniffed at as manipulators (6.36) really seeking high office for themselves (6.39), though to be fair Livy gives them speeches of vigorous logic to press their demands. The great plebeian leader of the next generation, Publilius Philo, is characterized on his first appearance (8.12) as being more concerned for himself and his faction than for his country. The patrician Ap. Claudius' radical populist measures as censor in 312 are (it seems) so offensive to Livy that he offers minimal details about them—in one case only when reporting its annulment eight years later. There an accompanying comment makes clear his dislike of such measures (9.46 and note): 'from that time on' there were two sides in politics, honourable citizens (i.e. anti-populist) versus the 'Forum faction' (radical and bad, not to mention full of freedmen). Yet he himself has earlier reported how 'cliques and factions' were rampant among the ruling elite, and powerful enough to thwart investigation (9.26).[20]

---

[20] Still earlier, in fact, Livy has one of his admired heroes, Valerius Corvus, decry 'cliques that are common among the nobles' (7.32).

Cliques and factions are not the only features that make Livy's fourth-century Rome more human. In Books 6–10 a few notable Romans reveal serious character flaws—at any rate in Livy's telling. Marcus Manlius, the ex-consul and saviour of the Capitol during the Gallic siege in Book 5, succumbs to overweening ambition in Book 6 and plots a revolution to make himself master of Rome, only to be forestalled (6.11, 14–20). That he was so accused and suffered death for it is not to be doubted, and the charge itself may have been accurate. But of course the actual details available to historians must have been very limited. Undeterred, Livy relates the story in grand rhetorical style and with verbal and other colourings perhaps meant to call to mind the notorious conspiracy of Catiline in 63 BC (6.11, 16, 18 notes).

In Books 9 and 10 the much greater figure mentioned earlier, Ap. Claudius Caecus—builder of the Via Appia, statesman, orator, and author—receives repeatedly critical treatment from the historian. Livy detests his supposed currying of popular favour, including his alleged sponsoring of a 'Forum faction', and depicts him as headstrong, arrogant (arrogance being a standard Claudian family trait), quarrelsome, and a poor general into the bargain (9.29 note). In fact, not just Caecus but also various earlier Appii Claudii are forcefully portrayed by Livy as stereotypes of oligarchic high-handedness and even criminality. Given Ap. Caecus' lasting repute and the prominence of the family's descendants in Augustan Rome—the ruler's wife Livia and her sons among them—these portrayals are striking (to say the least).

Uglier incidents occur in reputedly virtuous fourth-century Rome. Rome's saviour M. Manlius plots sedition; a Roman army falls into vice and mutiny until recalled to its senses by Valerius Corvus (7.38–41); at Capua, now sharing Rome's citizenship, dissatisfied leaders plot betrayal (9.26). A Vestal virgin is convicted of unchastity—one of the worst offences possible at Rome, for Vestal *incestum* imperilled the safety of the state—and buried alive (8.15). Domestic crimes are also committed: nearly two hundred aristocratic wives are punished for the mass poisoning of their husbands (8.18); some years later, married women are fined for sexual offences—enough of them to pay for a temple to be built (10.31). Livy reports homosexual depravity, too, when a moneylender makes an assault on the virtue of a wellborn lad whose father owes him money (8.28 and note). The historian would argue, no doubt, that these were exceptional cases, far from the universal immorality of modern times that he laments in the Preface to the entire history.

Even uglier to modern readers might be a different feature that is a virtual staple in Livy's military narratives, but is reported with no sign of revulsion: the slaughter of colossal numbers of enemies all over Italy in Rome's victorious battles, with figures of tens of thousands killed each time. Fortunately, though, we can be certain that all such claimed carnage—the favourite figures are twenty thousand and thirty thousand—is the cheerful invention of annalists or family tradition (7.36, 8.30, and notes).

More agreeably, touches of dry humour occasionally lighten the march of fourth-century history. The spat mentioned earlier between the two daughters of Fabius Ambustus (6.34), one married to the plebeian Licinius Stolo and teased for it by her sister, the wife of a patrician, is the droll if rather improbable spur to Licinius' ultimately victorious reform campaign in the 370s and 360s. In Book 9, Livy tells the tale of how the city's guild of flute-players had a spat of their own with the authorities and how it was resolved by a ludicrous trick at their expense (9.30). In the same book he has a few, moderately humanizing, stories about that otherwise forbidding pillar of state, Papirius Cursor (9.16, about his cavalrymen and about the Praenestine praetor; 9.42 his 'stiff drink'); then in Book 10 we find two armies anxious to shirk battle because each is terrified of the other (10.35–6). So when Livy feels that he must record a boastful Gallic warrior 'even sticking his tongue out' at T. Manlius, because this was 'a detail that the ancient authors also thought worthy of mention' (7.10), he is censorious not because he is humourless but because he sees it as unbecoming to an epic-style duel.

Religion and Moralizing in Books 6–10

Unlike their modern counterparts in novels and television, Romans saw much of what they did as attended with religious significance or requiring ritual accompaniment—from marriages and births to public business and battles. Livy shares this concern, which for the fourth century BC is the more congenial to him (as it also will be in Books 21 to 45) because it brings out the pious scruples of olden-time Romans. His account naturally focuses on public rites and beliefs, which were varied, numerous, and sometimes bizarre to a modern reader but, to a Roman, essential. To end a plague, a dictator might be appointed for 'driving in a nail' into the wall of the temple of Jupiter on the Capitoline (7.3, 8.18, etc.). A temple could be built to commemorate a victory, fulfil a magistrate's vow—often made during battle to win divine aid—or to welcome a new cult to Rome (cf. 10.47 note). The Roman triumph, a military parade through the city displaying the booty and captives from a victorious war, emphasized the warlike power of Rome under the leadership of Jupiter (see Glossary, under 'Triumph'): Livy records dozens in Books 6–10.[21]

He is interested in smaller religious items as well, like the tale— plainly much adorned in the telling—of how the cult of Plebeian Chastity was begun as a counterweight to that of Patrician Chastity (10.23), and the famous story of how the young M. Curtius sacrificed himself for Rome by leaping on horseback into a chasm that had opened in the Forum, thus giving the gods their due and creating the Curtian Lake (7.6). It is instructive that he also mentions a different explanation for the lake; and though plainly feeling some scepticism, nonetheless declares that 'as things are we must accept tradition where the antiquity of events does not allow certainty'. The details of ceremonies and rites fascinate him: for instance, the ritual gestures and invocation to the gods performed by Decius Mus senior, and repeated by his son, as each general readies himself by the rite of *devotio* to die in battle for Rome (8.9, 10.28).

Omens, prodigies, and portents, and the Romans' reactions to them, receive plenty of mention. The Gallic sack of the city is blamed on the general who had fought without obtaining favouring omens (6.1); a dictator carefully delays his battle until midday so as to receive favourable ones (7.8); stones falling from the sky and a noon-time darkness require prompt consultation of the Sibylline Books, Rome's ultimate resource for dealing with signs of divine vexation (7.28).[22] When the opening vote at a meeting of the Comitia Curiata falls by lot to an ill-omened *curia*, the entire procedure is halted for

[21] T. J. Cornell gives a convenient list of the triumphs in the *Fasti Capitolini* (most of them also reported by Livy) in F. W. Walbank and others (eds.), *The Cambridge Ancient History*, 2nd edn. (Cambridge: Cambridge University Press, 1989), vii/2. 363-4. On triumphs generally, cf. M. Beard, *The Roman Triumph* (Cambridge, Mass.: Harvard University Press, 2007).

[22] The Sibylline Books are mentioned at 7.27, 28; 10.31, 47. They have no link, except the name, with extant 'Sibylline oracles' of Roman imperial times.

twenty-four hours until fresh auspices can be taken and, by implication, another *curia* be selected (9.38-9).

Livy's careful recording of the religious sides of Roman life throughout his work makes it clear that he took religion seriously. He registers performances of a rare ceremony called the *lectisternium*, noting that the one in 365 was the third, and in 326 the fifth, since Rome's foundation (7.2, 8.25). More than once in Books 6-10 he complains about what he and many of his contemporaries, including Augustus, saw as the scepticism and cynicism of modern educated Romans (8.11, 10.40). At the same time, he shows that even the pious Romans of the fourth century could draw the line at religious punctiliousness. The doughty Papirius Cursor knows how to deal with an unfavourable omen just before battle (10.40), and after victory pays Jupiter a cheerfully modest thanksgiving—not another temple but a thimbleful of honeyed wine, followed by a stiff drink for himself (10.42).

That Rome's fortune was guided by heaven—unsurprisingly, a widely held Roman view—is also believed by the historian, as he makes clear as early as his Preface. It would not be an easy ride: the Romans had to be continually tested, and Livy hints at this ongoing moral exercise every so often. Opening Book 7, for example, he notes that all was quiet at home and abroad that year (365 BC), 'but, so that there should at no point be relief from fear and danger, a virulent epidemic broke out' (7.1; cf. 7.27); there is to be no rest for the virtuous. If neither enemies nor epidemics are active, as in the year 300, then 'so that there should not be tranquillity in all quarters' the Romans fall into renewed plebeian–patrician strife (10.6). In turn, divine aid to defeat enemies and combat natural disasters is to be expected so long as the right rituals and prayers are employed, as in the examples mentioned above.

At the same time, alongside this confidence in heaven's favour comes his gloom and criticism of the present era. The characterization of a pious young officer in 293 as 'a young man born before that form of education that slights the gods' (10.40) is only one of several sniping comments about his own day. Asserting that Rome will no longer find it easy to raise ten legions in one go, as in the emergency of 349 BC, he feels he has to add: 'Such are the problems caused by the only things deriving from the growth of our power, riches and luxury' (7.25). A few pages later, when listing the great wars to come from the later fourth century on, he stresses the extreme dangers that those wars would entail 'so that the empire could be raised up to its present greatness, which is now barely sustainable' (7.29). Even some mild criticism of how his patron Augustus ran the state, by controlling who was elected to office, may be detected (6.41, 10.13 notes).

This downbeat attitude to modern times is in line with the Preface's famous summary of Rome's evolution. Virtue brought her to power and empire, but empire brought a collapse of moral discipline 'until the advent of our own age, in which we can endure neither our vices nor the remedies needed to cure them'. It has always been a common opinion, down to our own day, that the present is a values-free wasteland far decayed from the rectitude of the past. Livy himself, for just a moment, implicitly admits this relativism when Fabius Rullianus, under attack from his then superior Papirius Cursor, rages against his mistreatment: 'What a difference there was between the restraint of the ancients and today's pride and heartlessness!' (8.33)—in the year 325. All the same, neither Livy nor any of his equally pessimistic contemporaries accepted the relativism.

We might ask a reasonable enough question: why then should the gods trouble to sponsor the Romans' ascent to success, wealth, and power when, inevitably and foreseeably, these would corrupt and debase them? For Livy's older contemporary Sallust, it was the fault of Fortune—the Romans had achieved greatness through their virtues, only for Fortune to go mad and turn against them (*Conspiracy of Catiline* 10). Perhaps Livy offered the same explanation when he reached the same period that Sallust had narrated, for Fortune already plays its unpredictable part in the fourth century. It intervenes from time to time, usually in battles; is the reason why Alexander did not attack Italy (8.3); and afterwards Livy directly terms it 'a dominant force in all human activity and especially in the military sphere' (9.17, again discussing Alexander). That this does not completely fit in with the idea of divine care is another inconsistency left unexplored.[23]

Rome's Fourth-Century Enemies in Livy

Livy, a north Italian with pride in his home town (note the story of how his Patavian ancestors defeated Greek marauders in 302: 10.2),

---

[23] Other interventions of Fortune: 6.9, 12; 7.8, 23; 8.24, 29; 9.9, 17, 22; 10.13, 28, 36. Some, no doubt, are conventional literary expressions, but not all.

nevertheless treats the Italian enemies of Rome almost entirely from a patriotic Roman point of view, most of them with minimal specific characterization. For instance the Aequi, Volsci, Hernici, and Etruscans suffer defeat after defeat, incur heavy losses, and yet renew wars with irrepressible fervour in book after book. Livy is uninterested in their social or political structures, or in the identities of their leaders; his only, brief, rumination is on how the Aequi and Volsci could keep putting fresh forces into the field despite their many defeats (6.12).

It was not that information about such peoples, accurate or otherwise, was nonexistent—for example, as mentioned earlier, the later emperor Claudius (whom Livy himself had tutored when young) was able to write a lengthy work on the Etruscans—but that Livy writes from an insistently Rome-centred standpoint. He is just as aloof over the customs and institutions of the Apulians, Lucanians, and even the southern Greeks, despite all these communities' interactions, friendly or hostile, with Rome and despite his vignettes on Alexander of Epirus' and Cleonymus of Sparta's misguided interventions in the south (8.24, 10.2). On the Greeks of southern Italy he is content to pronounce one of the usual Roman clichés: 'a race stronger in speech than action' (8.22).

Only the Campanians and Samnites receive fuller comment, with contrasting portrayals. The Campanians (in practice Capua and its dependent cities) are a condescending stereotype, and not only in these Books: even though historically kin to their Samnite mountain-cousins, they are painted as luxury-loving, self-interested, slippery, and unreliable, virtually from the moment they present themselves to the Senate as suppliants for Rome's help against a looming Samnite threat (a crisis due to 'excessive luxury and its enervating effects': 7.32). They remain the same after becoming Rome's allies (8.3, 22; 9.25, 26); in fact even a century later, ungrateful and ambitious, they will be the first people to go over to Hannibal after his victory at Cannae (23.1–7). Yet in Livy's own day, Campania and its cities were all fully integrated members of the Roman state, with aristocrats in the Senate and holding magistracies—just like the cities of northern Italy. We may wonder what such readers thought of Livy's consistent denigration of their ancestors.

The Samnites, on the other hand, are indomitable and moral opponents. They release the Roman army captured in the Caudine Forks after imposing only a bloodless ritual humiliation and terms of peace; then send its generals home unharmed, after the Romans hand these over as scapegoats (9.1–11). Livy rather feebly decries the peace terms as 'arrogantly imposed' (9.12), but does nothing else to detract from the Samnites' dignity. The splendid military array of their soldiery is twice highlighted to emphasize Samnite mettle and resolve (9.40, 10.38). After years of incessant warfare and a multitude of Samnite defeats and losses, he admits his admiration for these unbowed folk who would still not be crushed for many more years (10.31): 'so far were they from tiring of the liberty that they had defended with unhappy consequences, and they preferred defeat to not attempting to gain victory'.

How Believable is Livy?

Livy is not a trained, still less a 'scientific', historian; indeed scarcely any Greek or Roman historian can be so described. Besides relying on literary predecessors (mostly recent) and largely avoiding such primary records as existed, he has only modest skills for analysing problems raised by the many discrepancies he found in his sources— or even for recognizing problems, such as the repeatedly huge numbers of Samnites regularly slain in battles, or his claim that Velia and Herculaneum were taken during the campaign of 293 in Samnium (10.45 and note: the only known cities with those names stand on the coast near Naples and Paestum).

When he does tackle a difficulty he does not always impress: for instance, in discussing the supposedly inexhaustible numbers of Aequi and Volsci (6.12), the differing versions of the army mutiny in 342 (7.42), and the puzzles about whether Fabius Maximus Rullianus or some other Maximus held offices in 302 and 299 (10.3 and 9). On many questions, of course, it was simply not possible for him to do more than set out the alternatives. There were two stories about how the Curtian Lake in the Forum gained its name, and he writes that 'I would have spared no pains if the truth could be reached by historical investigation', but that certainty was beyond reach (7.6). Similarly, Roman annalists were all too often at odds over who did what in a campaign, or where they did it. Livy is repeatedly reduced to simply setting out conflicting versions in his sources. Did the insubordinate master of horse Fabius Rullianus win a great battle, or two of them, and slay twenty thousand Samnites—or is the whole episode a fiction as 'some annals' implied (8.30)? Was it the consul Aemilius Paullus or the dictator Junius Bubulcus who operated in south Italy in 302 (10.2)? In domestic politics, did or did not the feisty Ap. Claudius Caecus prolong his censorship, against all convention, for five years and win election to the consulship while still holding it, as 'some annalistic works' claimed (9.34, 42)?

Livy's guesses are often as good as ours; and where his version differs from one in, say, Dionysius or the *Fasti Capitolini* or *Fasti Triumphales* we cannot assume that they are always right (e.g. 7.7, 9.44, 9.45, 10.3, 10.37 notes). Even items that at first seem mere colourful fiction may sometimes turn out to rest on some factual basis: for instance, the raven in the story of Valerius Corvus' duel with the Gallic warrior (7.26 note), and the report of Roman cavalry charging with unbridled horses for greater impetus (8.30 note). Nor need the betrayal of Neapolis' citadel Palaepolis by leaders named Charilaus and Nymphius be doubted (8.25–6), dramatized though it is with their speeches and even thoughts. Even the notorious clash between Livy's account of Scipio Barbatus' doings as consul in 298 and the details in Scipio's own epitaph is not so clear-cut a case against our Patavian as often thought (10.12 note)

On some matters Livy reveals shortcomings. Essentially (we may suppose) a man of peace with only an armchair knowledge of war, he has to rely on what his sources state—whether or not he fully grasps the issue. When Roman cavalry make no impression on the enemy with their charges, they dismount and charge on foot with alleged success, but it is an improbable tactic (7.7). Later the mountain-dwelling Samnites suddenly field a strong body of cavalry (9.22, 27), though such Samnite cavalry might is not attested elsewhere. He also is ready to add imaginative details to an episode (not to mention speeches, short or long) to heighten the vividness of the story, and again these are not always convincing. For example, a detached unit, surrounded by Samnites and planning to steal away by night while they sleep, nevertheless sounds the standard trumpet-call for the second night-watch (7.35). In Book 9 he embellishes the Roman debacle at the Caudine Forks not only with speeches and imaginative touches, but with detailed insistence on how the enforced peace terms were honourably rejected. Then he devotes much space to how the renewed war brought one smashing Roman victory after another.

These claims are not his own invention but a reworking of Roman tradition, which from early on found the shame of the Forks too bitter not to sugar-coat. Livy, intelligent though he is, accepts the claims even though his own narrative gives strong reason to suspect them (9.12, 20 notes).

Livian geography, too, can be wayward or confused. The hill-city of Luceria in Apulia is mysteriously placed on a plain (9.26), and Livy, along with some other sources, supposes Palaepolis—the citadel of Neapolis in Campania—to be a separate city (8.22). Elsewhere he goes along with the implausible idea that Etruscan Clusium was called 'Camars', even though the context, not to mention other evidence, is against it (10.25). In 293 a new invasion of Samnium supposedly opens with the capture of Amiternum (10.39): but the only Amiternum on record, the home-town of the historian Sallust, stood in the Sabine country north of Rome, a long way from any part of Samnium. Many obscure place-names occur, naturally enough, in his accounts of warfare across the peninsula—particularly numerous in Books 9–10 on the Samnite wars—and arguments over their genuineness, location, or both, are incessant.

One convention of ancient historiography had become firmly enshrined long before Livy: composing speeches, often elaborate (and often made up), for persons involved in the narrative. Livy's skill in composing speeches is one reason why Quintilian, Rome's master of oratorical training a century later, judges him outstanding in his depiction of emotions (*adfectus*).[24] The speech-writing convention is understandable, even if to moderns unusual, when the historian was close in time and sources to his topic, like Thucydides or Cato (who put his own speeches into his *Origins*). It feels stranger when speeches exploiting the resources of Augustan-era rhetoric are delivered by fourth-century and third-century Romans and Samnites, especially when they do so at some length: when, for instance, the treason-plotter M. Manlius in 384 BC delivers a rousing address to his followers, complete with echoes of the Catiline affair of 63 BC (6.18). Similarly, Ap. Claudius Crassus excoriates the overweening

---

[24] Quintilian 10.1.101: 'For [Livy] has a wonderful charm and transparency in narrative, while his speeches are eloquent beyond description; so admirably adapted is all that is said both to the circumstances and the speaker; and as regards the emotions, especially the more pleasing of them, I may sum him up by saying that no historian has ever depicted them to greater perfection' (tr. H. Edgeworth: Loeb Classical Library edn., 1922).

ambitions of the plebeian reformers (6.40–1); the elder Decius Mus accompanies a daring military exploit with no fewer than four speeches (8.34–6); and in telling of the Caudine Forks defeat and the Romans' response to it Livy gives nearly as much space to speeches by Samnite and Roman leaders as to the narrative (9.1–11). A modern reader may feel that such compositions, plainly with no basis in reliable records, are not just implausible but hold up the action. By contrast, for Livy and his Roman readers (and many later ones) they are desirable artistic creations in their own right, and furthermore vividly illustrate the speakers' characters and the issues addressed.

In the nineteenth and twentieth centuries, scholarly scepticism inclined to treat large amounts of his narrative as seriously untrustworthy because of such imaginative reconstructions, because so many details in his accounts of warfare and politics were hard to verify, suffered from topographical problems, or seemed merely copied from later well-attested events—M. Manlius' conspiracy judged a piece of Catiline-inspired imagination, Camillus' rescue of a rash younger colleague's troops (6.23–4) arguably invented from Fabius the Delayer's genuine rescue of his rash colleague during Hannibal's war. This suspicious attitude has eased, with the essential outline of many or most episodes now accepted, even if debates continue on how far the details in each (speeches apart) can be believed. Without Livy, indeed, our knowledge of what happened in fourth-century Rome and Italy would be seriously skimpy, for other sources are concise or deal with only limited periods or topics.

Books 6–10 offer an extraordinary spectrum of events, personalities, issues, and even trivia. Three digressions are especially interesting, and illuminate the range of the historian's concerns: the sketch of how stage entertainments began at Rome, taking their story down to the end of the third century (7.3); the description of the fourth-century legion, despite its flaws (8.8); and the counterfactual essay on how Alexander the Great would have fared had he lived to invade Italy (9.17–19—Livy's answer is: 'badly'). A surprising range of other information is given: debt and interest-rates problems (6.11, 14, 35; 7.16, 19, 21, etc.); a new tax on manumitted slaves (7.16); fines on transgressors of laws (7.16, 28; 10.13, 23, 31, 33, 47); coastal raiding by Greek pirate fleets (7.25, 26); the adventures and misadventures of Greek mercenary generals in southern Italy (8.17, 24; 10.2); road-building, including the famous Via Appia from Rome to Capua

(9.29, 44; 10.23, 47); the flute-players' story (9.30); an expedition to repress bandits (10.1); even a vignette of an Italian city bustling with workday tasks and children at school as a Roman army approaches (6.25).

The dozens of Romans holding civil and military offices in Books 6–10 are corroborated in the *Fasti Capitolini* and *Fasti Triumphales*, and many also by other authors who drew on sources partly or wholly different from Livy's. The basic framework of Roman actions at home and in the field, including political strife, the enactment of laws, performances of religious rites, temple-building, land-grants, and colony-foundations, are largely trustworthy, even though (as noted earlier) differences in the various sources sometimes complicate matters. These and other matters may not be precisely accurate in every case, but they illustrate the variety of information available to Livy from the sources that he followed and the constant richness of the narrative that he composed. Despite weaknesses and limitations, it is a historical work that is irreplaceable as well as a literary masterpiece.

Other Sources for the Fourth Century

Quite a number of other literary writings survive that mention topics or persons in fourth-century Rome. A few statements from near-contemporary Greek authors, like Duris of Samos (10.30 note) and Timaeus of Tauromenium in Sicily, are preserved in later writers, while important Greek authors of Livy's own time treated the period too. Diodorus, a Sicilian of the first century BC, reported some Roman events (as a rule briefly) in his world history *The Historical Library*, and the books dealing with the fourth and early third centuries (books 14–20) are among those that survive. Dionysius of Halicarnassus, active at Rome in Augustus' time, dealt with early Rome in his twenty-book *Roman Antiquities*; but only the first eleven books remain, down to the year 440, along with some useful later excerpts. The loss is the more regrettable because in *Antiquities* 1–11 he cites and uses Fabius Pictor, Cincius, and other predecessors a good deal more than Livy does in Books 1–4; no doubt he did the same in the lost second half.

At the end of the first century AD the Greek philosopher and biographer Plutarch included Camillus—his only biography of a fourth-century Roman—in his *Parallel Lives* of Greek and Roman leaders (pairing Camillus, a little paradoxically, with Themistocles). Livy is only one of his sources, so Plutarch's view of the great man is rather different, though still admiring. Narratives relevant to the period by the later Greek historians Appian and Cassius Dio (both of them Roman citizens, like Plutarch) are extant only in excerpts again: Appian's *Samnite Wars* and *Gallic Wars*, and the relevant parts of Dio's eighty-book *Roman History*. At least in Dio's case an epitome survives, compiled by John Zonaras, an eleventh-century Byzantine scholar, which shows that at times Dio reported details differing from—although not necessarily likelier than—those in Livy (8.7 note).

Surviving treatments in Latin are thinner. Most mention fourth-century matters only occasionally and depend heavily on Livy for them: for example, a much-read collection of 'notable deeds and sayings' by one Valerius Maximus in Tiberius' reign, and one of military stratagems by the rather later Julius Frontinus, a retired governor of Britain. Livy again is a major source for the early fifth-century AD *History against the Pagans*, by a Spanish deacon named Orosius. None of these adds more than a few items of use (and Orosius can mis-cite Livy: 10.30 note).

Writers using Livy as their chief source obviously do not contribute much independent information. Where they draw on other sources, questions inevitably arise about which version of events should be accepted—a regular challenge to scholars. In any case, whatever their qualities, an objective view of these other authors' contributions to the history of fourth-century Rome confirms our good fortune in having Livy.

NOTE ON THE TEXT AND TRANSLATION

THE text used for the translation is the Oxford Classical Text of Walters and Conway (see Select Bibliography). This, however, was published in 1919, and much work has been done on the text of Livy 6–10 since then, and as a result I have accepted what I feel to be superior readings in a number of places. These are gathered together in Appendix 1 ('List of Variations from the Oxford Classical Text of Walters and Conway').

I have attempted to produce a readable translation without straying too far from the original text, and I hope the work can be of use both to those with and without a knowledge of Latin. An obelus (†) indicates those points where the Latin text is thought to be defective, and the translation therefore tentative.

I have, as translators do, consulted a number of other translations, primarily Foster's Loeb (volumes 3 and 4), Betty Radice's Penguin, and the old, but still serviceable, Everyman version of Canon Roberts (now available online). My greatest debt, however, is to Stephen Oakley, whose magisterial four-volume commentary is an indispensable guide to anyone working on the text, history, scholarship, or any other aspect of Livy 6–10.

I have also profited greatly, yet again, from the comments and suggestions of Dexter Hoyos and John Jacobs, both of whom read the entire translation before and at the proof stage, and I cannot omit mention of Rob Crowe, whose computer expertise was a great help to me as we literally sweated over the proofs on vacation in Provence in August 2012.

J. C. Y

Apart from those mentioned by John Yardley above, we would also like to express our thanks to our Oxford editors, Jenni Crosskey, Jeff New, and Peter Gibbs, and also to Laura Gagné, who compiled our index (her third in the OWC series).

Finally, we wish to offer our special appreciation to Judith Luna and Oxford World's Classics for inviting us to complete Oxford's Livy series by preparing this volume.

J. C. Y., D. H.

SELECT BIBLIOGRAPHY

Texts and Commentaries

Conway, R. S., and Walters, C. F., *Titi Livi Ab Urbe Condita VI–X* (Oxford: Clarendon Press, 1919, and reprints).

Kraus, C. S., *Livy: Ab Urbe Condita Book VI* (Cambridge: Cambridge University Press, 1995).

Oakley, S. P., *A Commentary on Livy, Books VI–X*, 4 vols. (Oxford: Oxford University Press, 1997–2008): Vol. 1, General introduction and Book VI; Vol. 2, Books 7–8; Vol. 3, Book 9; Vol. 4, Book 10.

Livy and his Sources on Early Rome

Chaplin, J. D., *Livy's Exemplary History* (Oxford and New York: Oxford University Press, 2000).

—— and Kraus, C. S. (eds.), *Livy: Oxford Readings in Classical Studies* (Oxford and New York: Oxford University Press, 2009).

Dorey, T. A. (ed.), *Latin Historians* (London: Routledge & Kegan Paul, 1967).

—— (ed.), *Livy* (London: Routledge & Kegan Paul, 1971).

Feldherr, A., *Spectacle and Society in Livy's History* (Berkeley and Los Angeles: University of California Press, 1998).

Forsythe, G., *Livy and Early Rome: A Study in Historical Method and Judgment* (Stuttgart: F. Steiner Verlag, 1999).

Frier, B. W., *Libri Annales Pontificum Maximorum: The Origins of the Annalistic Tradition* (Rome: American Academy in Rome, 1979).

Jaeger, M., *Livy's Written Rome* (Ann Arbor, Mich.: University of Michigan Press, 1997).

Miles, G. B., *Livy: Reconstructing Early Rome* (Ithaca, NY: Cornell University Press, 1995).

Mineo, B., *Tite-Live et l'histoire de Rome* (Paris: Klincksieck, 2006).

Ogilvie, R. M., *A Commentary on Livy Books 1 to 5* (Oxford: Clarendon Press, 1965).

—— 'Introduction' (pp. 11–36) to *Livy: Rome and Italy* [Books 1–6], trans. B. Radice (Harmondsworth: Penguin Classics, 1982).

Rosenstein, N., and Morstein-Marx, R. (eds.), *A Companion to the Roman Republic* (Malden, Mass., and Oxford: Blackwell, 2006).

Yardley, J. C., and Barrett, A. A., *Velleius Paterculus: The Roman History*, translated with introduction and notes (Indianapolis and Cambridge: Hackett, 2011).

Walsh, P. G., *Livy: His Historical Aims and Methods* (Cambridge: Cambridge University Press, 1961).

The Early Roman Republic

Cambridge Ancient History, 2nd edn., edited by F. W. Walbank and others, Vol. 7, Part 2. *The Rise of Rome to 220 B.C.* (Cambridge: Cambridge University Press, 1989) [abbreviated *CAH* ²].

Cornell, T. J., *The Beginnings of Rome: Italy and Rome from the Bronze Age to the Punic Wars (c. 1000–264 BC)* (London and New York: Routledge, 1995).

Crawford, M. H., *The Roman Republic*, new edition (London: Fontana Press and Cambridge, Mass.: Harvard University Press, 2011).

David, J.-M., *The Roman Conquest of Italy*, trans. A. Nevill (Oxford: Blackwell, 1996).

Forsythe, G., *A Critical History of Early Rome: From Prehistory to the First Punic War* (Berkeley and London: University of California Press, 2005).

Harris, W. V., *Rome in Etruria and Umbria* (Oxford: Clarendon Press, 1971).

—— *War and Imperialism in Republican Rome, 327–70 BC* (Oxford: Oxford University Press, 1979).

Heurgon, J., *The Rise of Rome to 264 B.C.* (London: Batsford, 1973).

Mitchell, R. E., *Patricians and Plebeians: The Origins of the Roman State* (Ithaca, NY: Cornell University Press, 1990).

Ogilvie, R. M., *Early Rome and the Etruscans*, 2nd edn. (London: Fontana Press and Cambridge, Mass.: Harvard University Press, 1996).

Salmon, E. T., *Samnium and the Samnites* (Cambridge: Cambridge University Press, 1967).

Scullard, H. H., *A History of the Roman World, 753–146 B.C.*, 5th edn. (London and New York: Routledge, repr. 2002).

Sekunda, N., and Hook, R., *Early Roman Armies*, Men-at-Arms Series, 283 (London: Osprey, 1995).

Starr, C. G., *The Beginnings of Imperial Rome: Rome in the Mid-Republic* (Ann Arbor, Mich.: University of Michigan Press, 1980).

Other Works

Broughton, T. R. S., *The Magistrates of the Roman Republic*, 3 vols. (Philadelphia and Chicago: American Philological Association and Scholars Press, 1951–2, 1984).

Dessau, H., *Inscriptiones Latinae Selectae*, 3 vols. in 5 (Berlin, 1892–1916) [abbreviated *ILS*].

Hornblower, S., and Spawforth, A. (eds.), *The Oxford Classical Dictionary*, 3rd edn., revised (Oxford: Oxford University Press, 2003).

Potter, T. W., *Roman Italy*, Exploring the Roman World (London: British Museum Press and Berkeley: University of California Press, 1987).

Talbert, R. J. A., *Atlas of Classical History* (London: Routledge, 1985).
—— and others, *Barrington Atlas of the Greek and Roman World* (Princeton: Princeton University Press, 2000).

Further Reading in Oxford World's Classics

Livy, *The Dawn of the Roman Empire* (Books 31–40), trans. J. C. Yardley, introduction and notes by Waldemar Heckel.
—— *Hannibal's War* (Books 21–30), trans. J. C. Yardley, introduction and notes by Dexter Hoyos.
—— *The Rise of Rome* (Books 1–5), trans., with introduction and notes, by T. J. Luce.
—— *Rome's Mediterranean Empire* (Books 41–45 and *Periochae*), trans., with introduction and notes, by Jane D. Chaplin.
Polybius, *The Histories*, trans. Robin Waterfield, introduction and notes by Brian McGing.

A CHRONOLOGY OF EVENTS

All dates are BC.

753   Traditional date of foundation of Rome by Romulus.

578–535 Reign of Servius Tullius.

509   Foundation of the Republic.

496   Battle of Lake Regillus.

451–449 Rule of the Decemvirs.

396   Romans commanded by Camillus capture Veii in southern Etruria.

390   (traditional date; actually 387) Gauls defeat Romans at the River Allia, capture the city, but are defeated by Camillus.

BOOK 6

389   Camillus defeats Volsci, Aequi, Etruscans; retakes Sutrium in southern Etruria.

388   War with Tarquinii and with Aequi.

387   Four new tribes created in territory of Veii.

386   Camillus defeats Volsci, Latins, and Hernici; takes Sutrium and Nepete.

385   Satricum made a colony.

384   Treason and trial of M. Manlius. Plague and famine at Rome. War with Volsci. Revolt of Lanuvium.

383   Board of five for distributing Pomptine land, and of three for establishing colony at Nepete.

382   Operations against Volsci, Velitrae, Praeneste. Loss of Satricum.

381   Camillus defeats Volsci.

380   Quinctius defeats Latins, compels Praeneste to surrender, storms Velitrae. Complaints by tribunes over plebeian debt.

379   Volsci ambush Roman army. Fresh warfare with Praeneste and Latins. Colony founded at Setia.

378   Further agitation over debt. Serious warfare with Volsci.

377   Volsci driven from Satricum to Antium, which surrenders to the Romans. Tusculum retaken. Tax for building city wall arouses controversy. Reform proposals mooted by C. Licinius and L. Sextius.

376   C. Licinius and L. Sextius elected tribunes and propose reforms amid great opposition.

375–371 The supposed, but fictitious, 'years of anarchy', when only Licinius and Sextius are the elected officials.

370   Tusculum saved from attack by forces of Velitrae. Velitrae besieged.

369   Siege of Velitrae(?). (On this supposedly long siege see 6.36 note.)

368   Siege of Velitrae(?).

367   Camillus defeats Gallic raiders. Licinio–Sextian laws passed.

BOOK 7

366   Creation of praetorship and two curule aedileships.

365   Outbreak of virulent plague.

364   Plague rages on. *Lectisternium* held. Theatrical performances instituted.

363   Plague continues, and severe Tiber flood in Rome. 13 Sept.: dictator drives in nail in temple of Jupiter Optimus Maximus.

362   Young T. Manlius defends his tyrannous father against prosecution. Self-sacrifice of M. Curtius creates Curtian Lake in the Forum. Consul Genucius slain in battle with Hernici. Dictator Ap. Crassus routs them.

361   Further victories over the Hernici. Tibur at war with Rome. Gauls threaten Rome until T. Manlius kills their champion.

360   War with Tibur, and Roman victory outside the Colline gate.

359   New Tiburtine attack on Rome driven off. War declared on Tarquinii after raid on Roman territory.

358   Peace with Latins. Dictator Sulpicius defeats the Gauls. Hernici forced to surrender, but consul Fabius defeated by Tarquinienses. Raids by forces from Privernum and Velitrae. Creation of Pomptine and Publilian tribes.

357   Falisci at war with Rome. Consul Marcius forces Privernum to surrender. Interest rate set at 8⅓ per cent. Marcius' army enacts a law for tax on freeing slaves.

356   New war with Tibur. Consul Fabius defeated by Falisci and Tarquinienses; other Etruscans join the war. Dictator Marcius repels Etruscan raiders from Rome's vicinity. Political struggles over consular elections.

355   Successes against Tibur and Tarquinii. Renewed struggles over consular elections.

354   Tibur and Praeneste accept peace terms. Treaty with the Samnites. Continuing plebeian problems with debt.

353   Caere, Tarquinii, and Falisci at war with Rome. Caere granted 100-year truce. Volsci in arms against Rome and Latins.

352   Despite fears, no warfare in Etruria occurs. Five-man commission substantially eases debt problems.

351   Forty-year truce with Falerii and with Tarquinii.

350   Defeat of Gallic army raiding Latium.

349   Coastal raids by Greek fleets (from Sicily?). Latin allies become restive at Roman dominance. M. Valerius wins *cognomen* Corvus. Rout of Gallic army.

348   *Lectisternium* held. Treaty with Carthage.

347   Interest rate halved to 4⅙ per cent, with other debt-relief measures.

346   More Latin unrest. Valerius Corvus defeats Volsci and Antiates.

345   Defeat of Aurunci (Ausones). Consuls capture Sora from Volsci.

344   Serious prodigies. Trial and punishment of usurers.

343   Campanians appeal to Rome for help against Samnites. Rome goes to war with Samnites. Consul Corvus defeats Samnites at Mt Gaurus. Military tribune P. Decius Mus rescues consul Cornelius' army from entrapment. Corvus defeats Samnites near Suessula. Falisci (of Falerii) seek treaty. Embassy from Carthage to Rome.

342   Roman soldiers at Capua mutiny and march into Latium. Corvus settles the mutiny with concessions. Laws carried against lending at interest and holding a magistracy twice within ten years, and allowing two plebeians to be consuls in any year. Increasing unrest among the Latins. Privernates attack Norba and Setia.

BOOK 8

341   Privernates defeated and punished. Volsci defeated. Treaty with Samnites renewed. Latins and Campanians at war with Samnites, with Rome remaining neutral.

340   War with the Latins and Campanians. Manlius Torquatus executes his own son for military disobedience. Battle of the Veseris, with Decius Mus giving his life by *devotio* to secure Roman victory over Latins. Torquatus defeats Latins again near Trifanum. Surrender of Latins, Campanians, and Privernates.

339   Fresh revolt of Latins defeated at the 'Fenectan Fields'. Siege of Pedum. Dictator Publilius Philo carries reform laws.

338   Victories over Pedum and its allies. Total capitulation of Latins. Latin League abolished. Roman citizenship granted to Lanuvium, Aricia, Nomentum, and Pedum. Punishment of Velitrae, Tibur, and Praeneste. Roman colony placed at Antium. Campanians receive citizenship without the vote.

337   The Aurunci, Roman allies, attacked by the Sidicini. Vestal Virgin Minucia put to ritual death for unchastity.

336   Defeat of Ausones and Sidicini.

335   Corvus captures Cales in Campania.

334/333 Two thousand five hundred colonists settled at Cales.

('333' A 'dictator year' in the *Fasti Capitolini*; on 'dictator years' see Glossary.)

332   Census held. New tribes, Maecia and Scaptia, created. Unfounded rumours of Gallic war.

331   Poisons scandal at Rome, with scores of wives punished.

330   War with Privernum and its allies. Consul Papirius Cursor defeats Privernates. Consul Plautius accepts surrender of Fundi. Joint siege of Privernum.

329   Capture of Privernum. Privernates granted citizenship. Colony founded at Anxur/Tarracina.

328   Colony founded at Fregellae.

327   *Lectisternium* held at Rome. Publilius Philo besieges Palaepolis (Neapolis), which is supported by the Samnites. Publilius' *imperium* extended into following year, as the first 'proconsul'.

326   Abolition of debt-slavery. Operations in Samnium. Publilius takes Palaepolis.

325/324 Wars with Samnites and Vestini. Master of horse Fabius Rullianus defeats Samnites. Famous clash between dictator Papirius Cursor and Rullianus. Cursor defeats Samnites.

('324' A 'dictator year' in the *Fasti Capitolini*, listing Papirius and Fabius as holding office alone.)

323   Campaigning in Samnium and Apulia (alleged). Mysterious night-time panic at Rome. Trial and acquittal of the Tusculans.

322   Alleged victory over Samnites.

BOOK 9

321   Entrapment and surrender of consuls Postumius and Veturius in Caudine Forks. Samnites' peace terms allegedly rejected by Rome after army is released.

320   Fregellae taken by Samnites. Alleged (probably invented) victor-
      ies over Samnites. Three pairs of dictators and masters of horse
      in one year (two pairs ignored by Livy).

319   Romans retake Fregellae(?) and Sora(?).

318   Peace with Samnites continued, allegedly at Samnites' request.
      Consul Plautius captures Teanum and Canusium in Apulia.
      Creation of Oufentina and Falerna tribes.

317   Alleged Roman successes in Apulia and Lucania.

316   Roman attack on Saticula in Campania.

315   Saticula captured. Attack on Sora after it defects to Samnites.
      Romans defeated at Lautulae near Tarracina. Samnites raid
      Latium.

314   Romans capture Sora(?) (more likely Sora was taken in 312: see
      9.24, 29 notes), slaughter Ausones. Defection and recapture of
      Luceria. Consuls defeat Samnites in Campania. Colony founded
      at Luceria with two thousand five hundred settlers. Disloyalty at
      Capua investigated by dictator Maenius. His follow-up investi-
      gation at Rome into political cliques arouses bitter opposition.

313   Romans defeat Samnites, and take Fregellae, Nola, Atina (or
      Atella?), and Caiatia. Colonies established at Suessa and on
      island of Pontiae.

312   Colony established at Interamna (Liris valley). Busy censorship
      of Ap. Claudius, despite abdication of colleague: Senate member-
      ship controversially revised, Via Appia to Capua built and Aqua
      Appia to Rome, freedmen's sons enrolled among all the Roman
      tribes. Consul Valerius Corvinus captures Sora.

311   Laws passed for the sixteen military tribunes in army to be elect-
      ed, and for duumvirs to outfit a fleet. Consuls reject Senate list
      revised by censors. Samnites capture, then consul Junius retakes,
      Cluviae (or Rufrae) (see 9.31 note). Bovianum captured. Junius
      defeats Samnites. Etruscans besiege Sutrium but are defeated.

310/309 Victories of Fabius Rullianus over Etruscans and their Umbrian
      allies. Perusia, Cortona, and Arretium make a thirty-year truce
      with Rome. Marcius Rutulus captures Allifae in Samnium but
      is defeated in battle. Dictator Papirius Cursor defeats Samnites
      at Longula. Roman fleet ingloriously active along Campanian
      coast.

('309') A 'dictator year' in the *Fasti Capitolini*.)

308   Romans defeat Samnites, Marsi, and then Paeligni. A forty-year
      truce imposed on Tarquinii. One-year truce with rest of Etruscans.

New war with Umbrians; Romans compel their surrender. Ocriculum becomes a friend of Rome.

307 Consul Volumnius' (alleged) campaign against Sallentini. Proconsul Rullianus defeats Samnites and Hernici near Allifae. Samnites capture Caiatia and Sora in Campania.

306 Consuls defeat Samnites and subdue Hernici. Anagnia and other cities punished, but receive citizenship without the vote. Renewal of treaty with Carthage.

305 Samnites raid Plain of Stella in Campania. Drawn battle at Tifernum, then consuls defeat Samnites outside Bovianum. Recapture of Sora, Arpinum, and 'Cesennia'. Paeligni subdued.

304 Censors reassign freedmen's sons to the four city tribes only. Parade of Roman knights on 15 July instituted. Lowly-born Cn. Flavius becomes curule aedile, publishes the civil law and the calendar, dedicates temple of Concord. Consul Sempronius traverses peaceful Samnium (Livy); defeats Samnites (*Fasti*). Peace made with Samnites. Successful war with Aequi. Marsi and others seek peace.

BOOK 10

303 Colonies founded at Sora and Alba Fucens. Citizenship granted to Arpinum and Trebula (Suffenas?). Armed bands in Umbrian cavern suppressed.

302/1 Fresh but brief fighting against Aequi. Alleged campaign against Cleonymus of Sparta in southern Italy. Operations in Etruria and against Marsi. Roman army ambushed and routed by Etruscans. Dictator Valerius defeats Etruscans at Rusellae. Treaty with the Vestini. Patavium defeats Cleonymus' Greek marauders.

('301' A 'dictator year' in the *Fasti Capitolini*.)

300 Tribunes Q. and Cn. Ogulnius legislate to enlarge colleges of pontiffs and augurs. Consul Valerius carries law on right of appeal. Valerius subdues Aequi. Siege of Nequinum in Umbria.

299 Aniensis and Teretina tribes created. Nequinum taken; colony founded there as Narnia. Etruscans plan war, recruit Gauls as allies. Samnites again plan war.

298 Rome allies with Lucanians. Scipio Barbatus ravages Etruria. Fulvius Centumalus defeats Samnites, captures Bovianum(?) and Aufidena. Colony founded at Carseoli in Aequan territory.

297 Consuls invade Samnium. Fabius Rullianus defeats Samnites near Tifernum. Decius Mus routs Apulians at Malventum. Samnium ravaged.

296 Cult of Plebeian Chastity founded. Successful prosecution
of moneylenders and livestock-breeders. Romans capture Murgantia, Romulea, and Ferentinum in Samnium. Lucania subdued. Consuls defeat combined Etruscan and Samnite armies.
Fresh Samnite incursion into Campania defeated at the River
Volturnus. Grand alliance against Rome formed by Etruscans,
Samnites, Umbrians, and Gauls.

295 Married women fined for sexual offences. Temple of Venus
built near Circus Maximus. Defeat of propraetor Scipio near
'Clusium' (Camerinum?). Consuls engage allied coalition at
Sentinum in Umbria. Decius Mus devotes his life for Rome's
victory. Samnites raid northern Campania, but are defeated.

294 Further campaigning across Samnium. Samnite defeat at
Luceria. In Etruria, Romans defeat Volsinii and take Rusellae.
Volsinii, Arretium, and Perusia accept forty-year truce. Consul
Postumius triumphs against wish of most plebeian tribunes.

293 Censors register 262,321 citizens. Livestock-breeders fined.
Samnite armies defeated separately at Aquilonia and Cominium.
Bovianum, Saepinum, and other towns are captured. Romans
confront fresh opposition in Etruria, capture Troilum, and force
Faliscans to accept one-year truce.

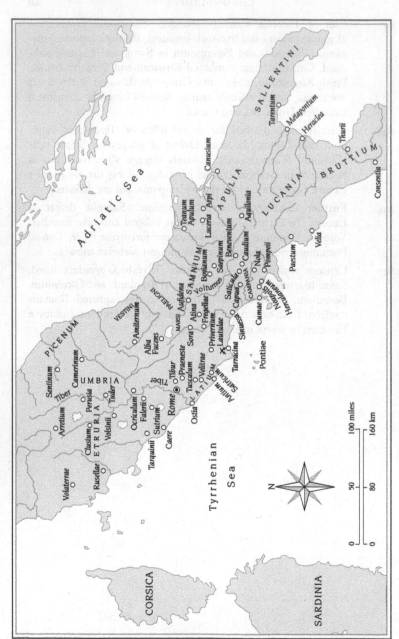

MAP 1. Italy in the fourth century BC

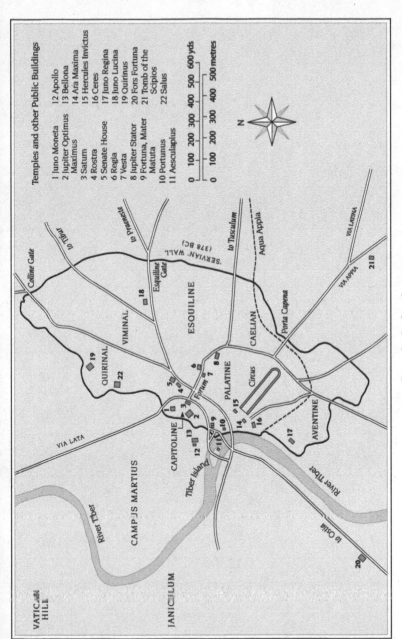

MAP 2. Rome in the fourth century BC

Temples and other Public Buildings

1 Juno Moneta
2 Jupiter Optimus Maximus
3 Saturn
4 Rostra
5 Senate House
6 Regia
7 Vesta
8 Jupiter Stator
9 Fortuna, Mater Matuta
10 Portunus
11 Aesculapius
12 Apollo
13 Bellona
14 Ara Maxima
15 Hercules Invictus
16 Ceres
17 Juno Regina
18 Juno Lucina
19 Quirinus
20 Fors Fortuna
21 Tomb of the Scipios
22 Salus

0   100   200   300   400   500   600 yds
0   100   200   300   400   500 metres

N

ROME'S ITALIAN WARS

BOOK SIX

1. I have now devoted five books to my account of the history of Rome from the city's foundation down to its capture, a history that began under kings and continued under consuls and dictators, decemvirs and consular tribunes, and was marked by warfare abroad and sedition at home. The events covered are unclear because they lie far in the past, rather like objects seen only with difficulty at a great distance. But there is also the added factor that writing, the only thing that keeps a reliable record of past events, was sparse and little used during the period, and also that whatever information was actually stored in the pontifical records and other public and private papers was for the most part destroyed when the city burned down.* The city was then reborn, from its original roots, as it were, with greater vigour and fecundity, and from that point on, from its second beginning, its history on the home front and in the military field will be presented with greater clarity and certitude.

The city's stability initially depended on the support it found in its leading citizen Marcus Furius,* who was also the prop responsible for its recovery, and the citizens did not allow him to lay down his dictatorship until a year had passed. It was decided that the holding of elections for the following year should not be in the hands of the tribunes* during whose term of office the city had been captured, and the state again had recourse to an *interregnum*. It was while the citizens were engaged in the endless and arduous labour of rebuilding the city that Quintus Fabius* was, as soon as he left office, impeached by the tribune Gnaeus Marcius for having contravened international law by opening hostilities against the Gauls, to whom he had been sent as an ambassador. However, a death so timely that most thought it suicide spared him the trial.

The *interregnum* then began, with Publius Cornelius as *interrex*, followed by Marcus Furius Camillus. Camillus held elections which led to the appointment of the following as military tribunes with consular power: Lucius Valerius Publicola (for the second time), Lucius Verginius, Publius Cornelius, Aulus Manlius, Lucius Aemilius, and Lucius Postumius.

These entered office right after the *interregnum*, and their very first act was to consult the Senate on matters of religion. One of their initial directives was for searching out such treaties and laws as could be found (which meant the Twelve Tables and a number of laws passed under the kings), some of which were even released to the general public, though those pertaining to sacred observances were withheld by the pontiffs, mainly so they could use superstition to keep the minds of the common people in check. Then began a discussion of days of ill-omen. July 18th was noteworthy for two disasters: it was the date on which the Fabii were cut down at the Cremera,* and on which the disastrous battle of the Allia,* which precipitated the city's destruction, took place later on. They called that date 'Allia Day' after the second disaster, †and banned the undertaking of any public or private business upon it.† Some people think that, because Sulpicius had not gained satisfactory omens on the 16th of July (and the blessing of heaven had not been gained when the Roman army was exposed to the enemy two days later), there was an injunction also against religious observances the day after the Ides (July 16th); and that the tradition flowed from this that the same taboo should also be observed for days following the Kalends and the Nones.*

2. But the citizens were not long granted peace to consider plans for reviving the state after its heavy fall. On one side their old enemies the Volsci* had taken up arms to wipe out the name of Rome, and on the other traders kept bringing word from Etruria of a war conspiracy that had been formed at the shrine of Voltumna* by the leaders of all its peoples. Fresh panic also arose with the revolt of the Latins and the Hernici who, following the battle at Lake Regillus,* had maintained their friendship with the Roman people for almost a century, their loyalty never in doubt.

So serious were the threats that beset the Romans on every side, and it was evident to all that the Roman name was in trouble, not only hated amongst her enemies but also despised by her allies. It was therefore decided that the defence of the state should be entrusted to the auspices of the same man who had been responsible for its recapture, and that Marcus Furius Camillus be named dictator. Appointed dictator, Camillus named Gaius Servilius Ahala as his master of horse, and after he had proclaimed a suspension of all business* he proceeded with the conscription of younger men, but without refusing to swear in, and form up in centuries,* any older men who still had some strength.

He conscripted and armed his force, and then divided it into three sections. One he deployed in Veian territory facing Etruria, and the second he ordered to establish its camp before the city with the military tribunes Aulus Manlius and Lucius Aemilius in command, Manlius of the first division, Aemilius of those sent to face the Etruscans. The third division Camillus personally led against the Volsci, and he proceeded with an attack on their camp not far from Lanuvium, at a place called Mecium.

The Volsci had set out for war because they felt contempt for the Romans: they believed that almost all their young fighters had been wiped out by the Gauls. However, simply hearing that Camillus was the commander had struck such terror into them that they surrounded themselves with a rampart and surrounded the rampart with piles of logs to prevent their enemy from getting through to their fortifications at any point. When Camillus observed this, he had fire thrown onto the barrier that faced them and, as it happened, there was a strong wind blowing in the direction of the enemy. Camillus thus not only opened up a way through by the fire but, as the flames headed for the camp, and there was heat and smoke, along with the crackling of the green wood ablaze, he also struck such panic into the enemy that his men had less difficulty in scaling the rampart that was defended by troops and entering the camp of the Volsci than they had experienced in crossing the barrier that had been consumed by the fire. The enemy were routed and slaughtered, and after the dictator took the camp by assault he awarded the spoils to the rank and file, a gift all the more appreciated by the men for being so unexpected, coming as it did from a man who was certainly no spendthrift.

In his pursuit of the fugitives Camillus plundered all the territory of the Volsci, finally forcing them to surrender after seventy years of conflict.* The conqueror then passed on from the Volsci to the Aequi who were also preparing to open hostilities. He surprised their army at Bolae, and with the first assault captured not just their camp but their city, too.

3. Although there was success of this order in the region where Camillus, the mainstay of Rome,* was in operation, a frightful threat was looming over another area. Nearly all of Etruria was up in arms and was blockading an ally of the Roman people, Sutrium.* Ambassadors from Sutrium appeared before the Senate with a plea for help in their desperate situation, and they took away with them a

decree stating that the dictator would bring assistance to the Sutrines at the earliest possible moment. However, the plight of the besieged inhabitants would not brook any delay of that hope; and the sparse population, worn down with fatigue, lack of sleep, and wounds received—the same men were continually under pressure—came to terms and surrendered the city to the enemy. It was at the very moment that they were leaving their homes in a pitiful column, sent off unarmed and with a single garment per person, that Camillus happened to appear with a Roman army.* The sad crowd threw themselves at his feet, and the words of their leaders, wrung out of them by dire necessity, were followed by tears from the women and children, who were being pulled along with them to share their exile. Camillus told the Sutrines to dispense with their lamentations: it was to the Etruscans he was bringing grief and tears, he said.

He then had the baggage set down and, leaving the Sutrines a small escort, told them to stay where they were, and ordered his soldiers to take up their arms and go with him. With his army thus in light marching order he set off towards Sutrium where, as he expected, he found complete lack of discipline, as happens when things are going well: the gates open, no sentry-post before the walls, the victor at large carrying their spoils out of the houses of the enemy. So it was that Sutrium was captured for the second time, and on the same day, with the victorious Etruscans massacred at all points and given no time to band together and form a unit, or to take up their weapons. Each individual headed for the gates in hopes of rushing out into the countryside, only to find that the gates had been closed (this had been the dictator's first command). Then some took up their weapons, and others, who happened to be armed when the attack had caught them unawares, called on their comrades to put up a fight alongside them. That, given the enemy's desperation, would have been a heated battle had not heralds been dispatched throughout the city giving orders for weapons to be put down, for unarmed men to be spared, and for no violence to be inflicted on any but those in arms. There were some who, when hope ran out, had determined to fight to the end, but even these threw down their arms at all points when given hope of surviving and, since circumstances had made it the safer course, surrendered themselves to the enemy unarmed.

The large crowd of prisoners was split up to be kept under guard, and before nightfall the town was restored to the Sutrines undamaged and spared all the devastation of war* because it had not been taken by force but had been surrendered on terms.

4. Camillus returned to the city in a triumphal procession as the conqueror in three simultaneous wars. Of the captives that he marched along before his chariot the largest number by far were Etruscans, and when these were auctioned off* so much money was raised that, after the married women had been reimbursed for their gold, three golden bowls were made from what remained. It is common knowledge that, before the burning of the Capitol,* these had been placed before the feet of Juno in the chapel of Jupiter and were inscribed with Camillus' name.

That year citizenship was granted to all those in Veii, Capena, and Falerii* who had deserted to the Romans in the course of these wars, and a land allotment was made to the new citizens. There was also a recall to Rome from Veii, by senatorial decree, of those people who, too shiftless to build in Rome, had taken over empty houses in Veii and moved there. This measure initially caused a stir, and people disregarded the order, but then a deadline was fixed, with a threat of capital punishment* for those not returning to Rome. That turned the whole defiant body into obedient individuals, each man fearing for himself. Rome was then experiencing an increase in population, and buildings were rising everywhere at the same time. The state assisted with expenses, and the aediles supervised the work as if it were in the public sphere, while private individuals, prompted by their desire to enjoy the property, themselves hastened the work to a conclusion. Within the year there stood a new city.

At the year's end there were elections for military tribunes with consular power. Those elected were Titus Quinctius Cincinnatus, Quintus Servilius Fidenas (his fifth term), Lucius Julius Iulus,* Lucius Aquilius Corvus, Lucius Lucretius Tricipitinus, and Servius Sulpicius Rufus. These led one of the armies against the Aequi, but not for a military campaign, since the Aequi admitted defeat. The motive rather was hatred, their intention being to devastate their territory so they should have no strength left for fresh schemes. The other army they led into the territory of Tarquinii,* where the Etruscan towns of Cortuosa and Contenebra were taken by storm. At Cortuosa there was no fighting at all: the Romans made a surprise attack and captured it with the first shout on the initial assault, and then the town was sacked and burned.

Contenebra withstood the attack for a few days, but the unremitting hardship, with no respite day or night, brought them to heel. The Roman army was formed into six divisions, each going into battle in rotation for six hours at a time; but the small numbers of the townspeople meant that the same men were exposed, exhausted though they were, to a fight that was ever being renewed. Finally they buckled, and the Romans were given an opportunity to penetrate the town. The tribunes wanted the booty to become state property, but the order came more slowly than the decision was reached. During the delay, the booty had already fallen into the soldiers' hands and could not be retrieved without causing resentment.

So that the city's growth should not be confined to private buildings, the Capitol was, in that same year, also given a substructure of dressed stone blocks,* a work that commands attention even in the splendid context of today's city.

5. By this time, while the community was preoccupied with construction, the tribunes were also attempting to increase attendance at their meetings with agrarian legislation.* The Pomptine area* was highlighted as a hopeful prospect, as it was now, for the first time since the power of the Volsci had been broken by Camillus, undisputedly under Roman control. The tribunes charged that it faced a greater threat from the nobility* than it had from the Volsci. The Volsci, they said, had merely made forays into it as long as they had the strength and armaments to do so; but the nobles were violently encroaching on it, attempting to take over state property and, unless it were sectioned before they took prior possession of the whole area, there would be no room for the plebs. This did not have much effect on the plebs. They were infrequent visitors to the Forum because of their preoccupation with their building, which left them drained by expense and thus unconcerned with land which they were incapable of providing with livestock.

The community was filled with religious anxiety, and even the leading citizens had at that time succumbed to superstition after the recent disaster; and so recourse was had to an *interregnum*. The post of *interrex* devolved (in succession) upon Marcus Manlius Capitolinus, Servius Sulpicius Camerinus, and Lucius Valerius Potitus. Potitus finally held elections to choose military tribunes with consular power, and declared the following appointed:* Lucius Papirius, Gnaius Sergius, Lucius Aemilius (his second term), Licinus Menenius, and

Lucius Valerius Publicola (his third term). These entered office at the conclusion of the *interregnum*.

That year saw the dedication of the temple of Mars, which had been promised in a vow in the Gallic war, by the duumvir for sacrifices Titus Quinctius. There was also the addition of four tribes* that were constituted from the new citizens, the Stellatina, the Tromentina, the Sabatina, and the Arniensis, and these brought the number up to a total of twenty-five.

6. The matter of the Pomptine land was raised by the plebeian tribune Lucius Sicinius before a popular assembly that was now better attended and more easily swayed into a craving for land than it had been. There was also some reference in the Senate to war with the Latins and the Hernici, but discussion was deferred* because of anxiety over a more serious war—Etruria was up in arms.

Power was again vested in Camillus as military tribune with consular powers, and he was given five colleagues: Servius Cornelius Maluginensis, Quintus Servilius Fidenas (his sixth term), Lucius Quinctius Cincinnatus, Lucius Horatius Pulvillus, and Publius Valerius. At the start of the year people's attention was diverted from the Etruscan war. A band of fugitives suddenly arrived in the city from the Pomptine lands bringing word that the people of Antium* were up in arms and that the Latin tribes had sent their military-aged men to this war. They added, however, that this was not state policy; the Latins, they said, had merely not forbidden the men to serve as volunteers wherever they wished.

The Romans had by now stopped considering any wars to be unimportant. The Senate therefore thanked the gods that Camillus held his magistracy, since he would certainly have had to be declared dictator if he were a private citizen; and his colleagues admitted that, when there was any urgent threat of war, the overall direction of affairs should rest with one man, and they had already decided that their *imperium* should be secondary to his. Nor, they added, did they regard deferring to such a man's authority as diminishing their own.

The tribunes were complimented by the Senate, and Camillus, overcome with emotion, personally thanked them.* He then declared that an enormous responsibility was being placed on his shoulders by the Roman people who had elected him for the fourth time; a great one by the Senate because that body had passed such judgement on him; but the greatest by the deference he was being shown by his

honoured colleagues. And so, if his industry and vigilance could be
heightened in any way, he would by challenging his own record make
every effort to ensure that he made permanent the opinion held of
him, very high though it was, and held with such unanimity by the
citizenry. As for the war and the people of Antium, he continued,
the situation was more threatening than perilous; nevertheless, his
advice was to show no complacency and at the same time to feel no
fear. The city of Rome was surrounded by envious and hostile neighbours, and so a number of generals and armies would be required.

'Publius Valerius,' said Camillus, 'I want you to be my partner in
command and strategic planning, and at my side to lead the legions
against our enemy, Antium. In your case, Quintus Servilius, I want
you to stay encamped near Rome with a second army that you will
have equipped and prepared, ready to act should there be in the
meantime any movement, as there was recently, on the part of Etruria
or else on the part of the Latins and the Hernici, this new concern
that we have. I am sure that you will carry out the assignment in a
manner worthy of your father and your grandfather, and of yourself
and your six tribuneships. A third army should be raised by Lucius
Quinctius, one made up of men discharged on medical grounds and
those beyond military age, to stand on guard for the city and its walls.
Lucius Horatius is to see to the provision of weapons, projectiles, and
grain, and everything else the crises of war may demand. As for you,
Servius Cornelius, we your colleagues appoint you president of this
state council,* and guardian of religious affairs, elections, the laws,
and all matters related to city governance.'

They all generously promised to apply themselves to the duties
of their particular sphere, and Valerius, who had been chosen to
share Camillus' command, added that in his eyes Marcus Furius
would be a dictator and he himself Furius' master of horse. Thus,
said Valerius, they should base their hopes for the campaign on their
estimate of their sole leader. The senators, in an outburst of joy, noisily declared that they certainly had sanguine hopes for the war, the
peace, and all matters of state. The state would never stand in need of
a dictator, they said, if it had men like them in office, men so united
in spirit, ready both to give and to follow orders, men who contributed their reputation to the good of all rather than using the common
good to gain a reputation for themselves.

7. Furius and Valerius declared a suspension of business, held a

levy of troops and then set off for Satricum.* There the people of Antium had mustered not only young Volscian warriors, hand-picked from a new generation, but also huge numbers of Latins and the Hernici, peoples whose strength was hardly diminished at all, thanks to the long peace they had enjoyed. A new enemy being added to the old had an unsettling effect on the Roman troops. Camillus was already deploying his line of battle when the centurions brought him the news that the men's morale had been shaken, that they had only half-heartedly taken up their arms, and that they had left the camp with hesitation and reluctance. Indeed, they said, there had also been remarks to the effect that they would be fighting one against a hundred, and that such numbers could barely be withstood if they were unarmed, and much less when they bore weapons.

Camillus leaped onto his horse and, turning to the battle-line and riding through the ranks, said:

'What is this despondency, men, and this unusual reluctance? Are you unfamiliar with the enemy, or with me, or with yourselves? What is the enemy if not inexhaustible material for honing your courage and winning glory? You, by contrast—and I say nothing of your capture of Falerii and Veii, and your slaughter of the Gallic legions in our captured land—you have recently won, under my leadership, a triple triumph for three victories, over these Volsci, no less, and over the Aequi and over Etruria. Or do you not recognize me as your commander because I gave you the battle-signal not as dictator but as a tribune? But I have no wish to hold supreme command over you, and in my case you should regard me as being nothing other than what I am. The dictatorship has never added to my courage, nor did my exile take it away. So we are all just the same as before and, since we are bringing to this war all the same attributes as we brought to those earlier ones, we may expect the same outcome from it. As soon as you have engaged, each man will do what he has learned to do and become used to doing. You will conquer, they will run.'

8. The signal was then given, and Camillus sprang from his horse, grabbed the nearest standard-bearer with his hand, and pulled him swiftly along with him towards the enemy, shouting 'Standard forward, soldier!'* Camillus' age* made him unfit for strenuous tasks, and when the men saw him wading into the enemy in person, the battle-cry went up and they rushed forward together, every one of them calling out: 'Follow the commander!' They say

that, on Camillus' orders, the standard was even hurled into the enemy lines and the front ranks urged to recover it, and that this was what started the Antiate retreat, with the panic spreading not only to the enemy front line but even to the reservists. Nor was it merely the dynamism of the soldiers, invigorated as it was by their leader's presence, that produced this effect; it was also the fact that nothing was more terrifying to the Volsci than the chance sighting of Camillus in person. Anywhere he went he took certain victory with him. This was quite clear to see from the following. His right wing was all but routed when Camillus suddenly seized a horse and rode up to it carrying an infantryman's shield, and, making it known that the rest of the force was carrying the day, he restored the battle's fortunes simply by showing himself.

A rout had now begun, but even flight was impeded by the large numbers of the enemy, and there still remained a huge multitude for the exhausted Roman soldiers to finish off in a lengthy bloodbath when, suddenly, a cloudburst with heavy winds broke off what was a clear victory rather than a battle. The signal to withdraw was then given, and the onset of night terminated the war for the Romans with no further action. The Latins and the Hernici left the Volsci and set off for home with a result appropriate to their wicked designs. When the Volsci saw themselves abandoned by the people on whom they had relied when starting the revolt, they left their camp and barricaded themselves within the walls of Satricum. At first Camillus started to surround the town with a mound and works for the usual assault procedure. He found, however, that his efforts were impeded by no counter-attack, and so assumed that there was insufficient courage in the enemy to justify his waiting in this case for a victory so slow in coming. He therefore exhorted his men not to exhaust themselves on a protracted undertaking as though they were attacking Veii—victory lay within their grasp! The men responding with intense enthusiasm, he attacked the walls from all directions and took them with scaling-ladders. The Volsci threw aside their weapons and capitulated.

9. The commander, however, had his mind set on something more important—Antium, which, being the capital city of the Volsci, had started the last war. But a city of such strength could not be taken without large quantities of military equipment, that is catapults and siege engines, and so Camillus left his colleague with the army and set

off for Rome in order to urge the Senate to destroy Antium root and branch. He was in mid-speech—I think the gods had willed that the state of Antium should last somewhat longer—when a deputation came in from Nepete and Sutrium* to request assistance against the Etruscans, noting that there was only a small window of opportunity for bringing them help. This was the direction in which fortune diverted the power of Camillus away from Antium. For these places face Etruria, serving, as it were, as barriers and also providing the gateways into it, and so the Etruscans were eager to seize them whenever they were planning some coup, and the Romans, too, were eager to get them back and defend them. The Senate therefore decided to make arrangements with Camillus for him to drop Antium and take on the Etruscan war, and the urban legions that Quinctius had commanded were officially assigned to him. Although he would have preferred the army in the lands of the Volsci, one that was tried and was familiar with his leadership, he did not demur; he merely insisted that Valerius share the command. Quinctius and Horatius were sent against the Volsci as Valerius' successors.

Furius and Valerius set off from the city for Sutrium, where they found that a part of the town had already been taken by the Etruscans, while in the other part the townspeople had blocked the roads and were having difficulty fending off the enemy assault. The arrival of assistance from Rome along with the name of Camillus (much celebrated amongst the enemy and allies alike) for the moment brought relief to the unpromising situation, and provided time for aid to be brought. Camillus accordingly split his army in two, and ordered his colleague to take his troops around and launch an attack on that part of the town that the enemy was holding. It was not that he had hopes of the city being captured with scaling-ladders, but rather that, with the enemy's attention diverted to that point, the hardship of the already battle-weary townspeople might be alleviated, and also that he himself might have an opportunity to enter the town without a fight. The action at both points taking place at the same time, the Etruscans faced terror on both sides: they could see that their walls were being violently attacked and also that the enemy was within those walls. In panic and in a single body, they hurled themselves out by the one gate that happened not to be guarded. There was a great massacre of the fleeing Etruscans, both within the city and in the fields. More were killed within the walls by Furius' men;

Valerius' soldiers were more lightly armed for conducting pursuit, and they did not end the slaughter before nightfall, which made it impossible to see.

With Sutrium recaptured and restored to the allies, the army was marched to Nepete which had capitulated and was now entirely in Etruscan hands.

10. It seemed that a greater effort would be required to recapture this town, not only because it was completely in the hands of the enemy but also because the surrender was the result of treason on the part of a group of the Nepesini. Nevertheless, it was decided that their leading citizens should be sent a communiqué urging them to break off relations with the Etruscans and themselves demonstrate the loyalty that they had begged the Romans to show them. The answer that came back was that they had no control over anything, and that the Etruscans held their walls and guarded their gates; and so, at first, raids on their farmlands were used to intimidate the townspeople. Then, when their respect for their terms of surrender proved more binding than their alliance, the Romans brought together bundles of brushwood from the countryside, and the army was led up to the walls. The ditches were then filled, the ladders moved up to the walls, and the town was taken with the first shout of the first assault. A proclamation was then issued to the Nepesini that they should lay down their arms, and instructions were given for the unarmed to be spared; the Etruscans were cut down, armed or unarmed. Those of the Nepesini who had been responsible for the surrender were also beheaded; the guiltless commoners had their possessions restored to them, and the town was left with a garrison. And so, having taken back from the enemy two allied towns, the tribunes marched the victorious army back to Rome covered with glory.

That same year a demand for reparations* was issued to the Latins and the Hernici, who were also asked why they had not in the past few years made the usual contribution of fighting men. The reply that came from the full council meeting of both peoples was that, in this matter, no blame attached to the state or its policies if a number of their young men had fought on the side of the Volsci. These men were paying the price for their wrong-headedness—none of them had returned. The reason for their not having provided soldiers, they said, had been the enduring threat from the Volsci; this was a curse clinging on to them that they had been unable to shake off even despite a long succession of wars. When this response was brought to the senators, they thought it offered them justification for war, but not a timely occasion.

11. The next year* the following men became military tribunes with consular power: Aulus Manlius, Publius Cornelius, Titus and Lucius Quinctius Capitolinus, Lucius Cursor (his second term), and Gaius Sergius (second term). The year saw a serious war abroad, and more serious discord at home, the war started by the Volsci, assisted by the insurgent Latins and Hernici, and the discord arising from a source where it was least to be feared, from a man of patrician pedigree and illustrious reputation, Marcus Manlius Capitolinus.

A man with a headstrong bent, Capitolinus looked down on the other leading men, but one of them he envied, a man outstanding for offices he had held and his military abilities, Marcus Furius; and he was angry that Camillus alone now enjoyed such pre-eminence as to regard those elected under the same auspices not as his colleagues but as his attendants. In fact, if anyone were willing to look at it fairly (his thinking went), the fatherland could not have been delivered by Marcus Furius from an enemy blockade if the Capitol and the citadel had not been first saved by Capitolinus himself. Moreover, Camillus attacked the Gauls while they were accepting the gold and feeling relaxed in anticipation of peace, whereas he himself had repelled them while they were armed and trying to take the citadel. Most of Camillus' glory should belong to the men who had won the victory along with him; in Manlius' victory no other living being had taken part.

Such thoughts swelled Capitolinus' head, and in addition brashness and lack of moderation were natural failings in his character. When he observed that his own influence amongst the senators was not as great as he felt it should be, he became the first of all senators to champion the popular cause, and to share his schemes with the plebeian magistrates.* Denouncing the senators and flirting with the commons, he was driven along by popular favour rather than by his use of judgement, preferring to have a grand reputation rather than a good one. Furthermore, the agrarian laws—which had always been the stuff of sedition* for the plebeian tribunes—were not enough for him, and he began to make inroads into the system of credit. He realized debt was a sharper stimulus, in that it not only carried the threat of poverty and disgrace but also terrified the free person with the

prospect of fetters and imprisonment.* (And debt had, in fact, been
contracted on a large scale thanks to what was, even for the rich, the
most ruinous activity, building.) And so the Volscian War, serious in
itself, and exacerbated by the uprising of the Latins and the Hernici,
was put about as a specious justification for seeking greater power;
but it was actually the revolutionary designs of Manlius that pushed
the Senate into appointing a dictator. Aulus Cornelius Cossus
received that appointment, and he declared Titus Quinctius
Capitolinus his master of horse.*

12. The dictator could see that a greater conflict faced them on the
home front than abroad, but he nevertheless held a troop-levy and
headed for the Pomptine lands, where he had heard that a muster of
their army had been called by the Volsci. This was either because
speed was essential for the war, or because he thought that he would
actually add strength to the dictatorship by victory and a triumph.

I do not doubt* that, apart from having had their fill in all these
books of the never-ending wars with the Volsci, my readers will also
have the same reaction as I did on conducting a thorough investigation of the historians living closer to the time of these events—amaze-
ment at where the Volsci and Aequi obtained their supply of troops
after so many defeats. But since the matter has been left in silence by
the ancients, what could I add to this subject other than an opinion
based on inference, as anyone else may do? It is probable that in
the intervals between wars, they often employed successive generations of young men—as happens these days in Roman recruiting—
to meet renewed hostilities, or else that armies were not always conscripted from the same tribes, though it was always the same nation
that undertook the war. Or possibly there was an infinite quantity of
free men in those areas where now there is left only an impoverished
'nursery' for military recruits and which only Roman slaves keep
from lapsing into desert.* At all events, as all the sources agree, the
army of the Volsci was huge, despite the toll recently taken on their
power by Camillus' leadership and auspices; and it had also been sup-
plemented by the Latins and Hernici, by some soldiers from Circeii,
and even by Roman colonists from Velitrae.*

The dictator pitched camp that day, and on the next, after taking
the auspices, he went forth and prayed for heaven's blessing with a
sacrificial victim. Then, in good cheer, he advanced to his men who
were now, at first light, taking up their weapons, as they had been

instructed, in preparation for when the signal for battle should be given.

'Victory is ours, men,' he said, 'if the gods and their interpreters can to any extent see into the future. So, as men full of confidence who are about to engage an enemy that is no match for them, let us set our javelins at our feet and arm ourselves only with swords.* I would not even want any running forward from the line; I want you to make a stand with feet firmly planted to receive the enemy charge. They will hurl their projectiles to no effect and, in disorder, they will throw themselves at you where you stand. That is when swords should flash, every one of you bearing in mind that there are gods— gods who are helping the Roman cause, gods who have sent you into battle with favourable omens. Titus Quinctius, you must take great care to hold back your cavalry until the very moment that the fighting starts; when you see that the lines are engaged at close quarters, strike the terror of your horses into them while they are grappling with another fear. Charge their ranks as they fight and scatter them.'

Cavalryman and foot-soldier fought as he had instructed them, and the commander did not disappoint his legions, nor fortune the commander.

13. The enemy hordes, relying on nothing more than their numbers, and weighing up the two battle-lines with their eyes, went into battle recklessly, and left it recklessly. They were resolute only up to the battle-cry, the discharge of projectiles, and the first clash of the engagement; they could not hold out when it came to the sword, the hand-to-hand fighting, and the sight of the inner fire that darted from their enemies' faces. First their front line caved in; panic hit the supporting troops; and the cavalry inflicted its own brand of terror on them. Next, the ranks were broken in several places; there was general disorder; and their battle formation seemed to be in turmoil. Then, when each man saw that as those in front fell death would be coming to him, they turned to run. The Romans were hard on their heels and, while the enemy retreated still retaining their arms and in close order, it was the infantry that had the task of giving chase. After it was observed that arms were being thrown down at all points, and that the enemy force was being scattered in flight all through the fields, the cavalry squadrons were unleashed, but given the signal not to hold back to kill individuals and thereby give the main body the opportunity to escape. It was sufficient, they were told, to scare them

with projectiles in order to slow them down, and to keep them grouped together until the infantry could overtake and systematically dispatch the enemy. There was no end to the flight and the pursuit until nightfall. On that same day the camp of the Volsci was also captured and pillaged, and the plunder was, apart from free persons, all handed over to the men. Most of the captives were Latins and Hernici, and not all were plebeians, men who might be thought to have fought as mercenaries; a number of aristocratic young men were also found, clear evidence that the assistance they had given the Volscian enemy was officially authorized. A number of Circeians were also recognized, and some colonists from Velitrae. All were sent to Rome, and when the leading senators interrogated them, they gave the same answers as they had given to the dictator, every one of them unambiguously exposing the defection of his people.

14. The dictator kept his army in camp, in no doubt that the senators would give the order for war with these peoples. Then a greater danger appeared on the domestic front, forcing them to have him summoned to Rome: the treason was growing daily, and the identity of its instigator made it more fearful than usual. For now it was not just a case of Marcus Manlius' speeches but of his actions, too. While these had the appearance of supporting the popular cause, they were at the same time seditious when the motive behind them was taken into consideration.

A centurion,* well known for his military record, was being led off after being condemned for debt. When Manlius saw him, he ran up to him in the middle of the Forum, accompanied by his crowd of supporters, and put his hand on him.* He loudly berated the senators for their arrogance and the moneylenders for their ruthlessness, and commented on the tribulations of the plebs and the fine qualities and misfortunes of this man. 'I certainly wasted my time saving the Capitol and the citadel with this right hand,' he said, 'if I must see my fellow-citizen and comrade taken away, a captive, to slavery and chains just as if the Gauls had been the victors.' He then paid off the creditor before the people and, with scales and bronze,* he set free the centurion, who called on gods and men to repay Marcus Manlius, his liberator and the father of the Roman plebs.

The man was immediately taken into the bustling crowd, and he himself increased the bustle by showing off his scars from the wars with Veii and the Gauls, and from other wars that followed.

While he was on campaign, he explained, and while he was rebuilding his ruined house, he had been overwhelmed by debt for, though
he had already paid back the capital many times over, the interest
payments always drowned the capital. The fact that he could see the
daylight, the Forum, the faces of the citizens—that was all thanks to
Marcus Manlius! All the benefits bestowed by one's parents, these he
had from him! To him, he said, he dedicated whatever remained of
his physical powers, his life, and his blood; and whatever the bond
that had tied him to his country and to the gods of the state and the
family, that now was a bond tying him to one man alone.

The plebs were roused by these words, and were already under the
spell of one man when another element was added, a more effective
ploy for creating general upheaval. Manlius put a farm in the territory of Veii, which represented the main part of his family fortune,*
in the hands of an auctioneer, 'so that' (he said) 'I may allow none of
you, citizens of Rome, to be hauled off after being found guilty of
indebtedness as long as anything at all remains in my estate'. This so
inflamed their spirits that they appeared ready to follow the champion of their freedom through anything, right or wrong.

In addition, Manlius made speeches at home,* like a man addressing an assembly, full of charges against the senators. One of these,
thrown at the senators with no distinction made between truth and
falsehood, was that treasures consisting of the Gallic gold were being
secretly hoarded by them, and that they were no longer satisfied with
seizing public lands—they wanted to appropriate to themselves public moneys as well. If that matter were brought into the open, he said,
the plebs could have all their debts discharged. Of course, when such
hope was offered them, it was felt to be a shameful injustice that when
money had to be gathered to ransom the state from the Gauls it had
been raised by taxation, but when that same gold was taken from the
enemy it had become the prize of a few. And so they kept asking
where this huge sum of stolen money was being concealed. Manlius
became evasive and told them he would make the disclosure at the
appropriate time, and now everyone's attention was focused on this,
with everything else forgotten; and it was clear that he would earn no
little credit if his information proved to be true, and no little resentment if it proved to be false.

15. Matters were left unresolved like this when the dictator, who
had been summoned from his army, arrived in Rome. The following

day he convened the Senate and, after probing to his satisfaction the sentiments of the members, he told the senators not to leave him. Then, attended by the large body, he set up his chair in the Comitium* and sent an attendant for Marcus Manlius who, summoned on the dictator's orders, signalled to his supporters that the fight was imminent and came to the tribunal with a huge retinue. On one side was the Senate, on the other the plebs, all looking at their respective leaders, just as if they had taken up their position in a battle-line.

Then, having succeeded in gaining silence, the dictator said: 'I wish that the Roman senators and I could reach an agreement with the plebs on everything else as easily as I am sure we shall on the subject of you and the matter on which I intend to question you. I see that, thanks to you, an expectation has been raised in the city that, with no damage to the creditors, money out on loan can be repaid from the Gallic treasures, which leading senators are supposedly hiding. Far from obstructing you, Marcus Manlius, I encourage you to free the Roman plebs from their debt and remove from their clandestine spoils those men brooding hen-like over state treasures. If you do not do so, either in order to have a share in that plunder yourself or because your information is false, then I shall order you taken into custody and no longer permit the crowd to be inflamed by you with groundless hopes.'

In reply Manlius said it had not escaped his notice either that it was not against the Volsci—enemies whenever that happened to be in the senators' interests—that a dictator had been appointed, nor against the Latins and the Hernici, whom they were driving into war with false accusations, but against him and the Roman plebs. Now the war, which was a sham, had been abandoned and an attack was being launched on him; now the dictator was holding himself up as patron of the moneylenders against the plebs; now grounds for an accusation that would ruin him were being sought in the favour he enjoyed with the common people.

'Does the fact that a crowd surrounds me for my protection offend you, Aulus Cornelius, or you, Conscript Fathers? Why does not each of you remove it from me with your own kind acts, by intervening, by setting your fellow-citizens free from prison, by forbidding those found guilty of indebtedness to be hauled off by creditors, and by using the excess of your wealth to help others in their time of need? But why am I encouraging you to spend your own money? Take what remains of the debt, but remove from the principal the amount that has been paid in interest. After that the crowd following me will be no more conspicuous than anyone else's.

'Perhaps you are wondering why I alone feel sympathy for my fellow-citizens? I can no more reply than if you should ask why I was alone in saving the Capitol and the citadel. At that time I brought such help as I could to the people as a whole; now I shall also bring it to individuals. And as far as the Gallic treasure is concerned, the matter is simple in itself, but your questioning makes it difficult. For why are you asking something to which you know the answer? Why are you telling us to shake out of you what you have in your pockets instead of putting it on the table yourselves—unless there's some chicanery involved? The more you insist on having your trickery exposed, the more frightened I am that you have even stolen our use of our eyes while we watched. So it is not a matter of my being obliged to give information on your plunder, but of your being obliged to bring it out into the open.'

16. The dictator told Manlius to have done with evasion, and pressed him to produce verifiable information or else admit to the crime of falsely accusing the Senate and exposing it to vilification over a non-existent theft. Manlius said he was not going to speak and give satisfaction to his enemies, at which point the dictator ordered him taken off to prison.*

Seized by the attendant, Manlius declared: 'Best and Greatest Jupiter, Queen Juno and Minerva, and all the other gods and goddesses that reside in the Capitol and citadel, are you allowing your soldier and guardian to be persecuted by his enemies like this? This is the right hand with which I chased the Gauls off from your shrines—is it now going to be in bonds and chains?'

There was no one who, on seeing and hearing this, could bear the indignity of it, but the citizens, very respectful as they were of legitimate authority, had made certain things inviolable for themselves, so neither the plebeian tribunes nor the plebs themselves dared raise their eyes or open their mouths in defiance of the dictator's might. It is well established, however, that after Manlius was thrown into prison large numbers of the plebs changed into mourning garb, that many men let their hair and beards grow long,* and that a dejected crowd milled about the prison forecourt.

The dictator celebrated a triumph over the Volsci, but the triumph earned him more resentment than glory; for there were mutterings to the effect that it had been won at home, not in the field, and celebrated over a fellow-citizen, not an enemy. The man's arrogance had stopped short of only one thing, they said—Marcus Manlius had not been taken along before his chariot.* By now open discord was not far off, and to assuage it, though nobody actually made the demand, the Senate suddenly became philanthropic and ordered the settlement of a colony of two thousand Roman citizens at Satricum. The settlers were each granted two and a half *iugera** of land, but as they saw this as being little and given only to a few, and also as payment for their betrayal of Marcus Manlius, the discord was only exacerbated by the 'remedy'. And now Manlius' followers were more in evidence because they wore clothes of mourning and looked like men facing accusation, and Cornelius' retirement from the dictatorship after his triumph had removed people's fears and freed both their minds and their tongues.

17. So it was that one would hear criticisms openly made of the common people for consistently raising their defenders to dangerous heights by their favour, and then deserting them in their very hour of danger. They had done it to Spurius Cassius* when he called on the plebs to take possession of the land; to Spurius Maelius when, at his own expense, he attempted to keep famine away from his fellow-citizens; and to Marcus Manlius, whom they betrayed to his enemies as he tried to bring back into freedom and the light some citizens drowning in a sea of debt. The plebs fattened up their favourites for the killing! Was this what an ex-consul had to suffer if he failed to respond to a dictator's command? Suppose that he had lied earlier and that that was why he had no reply. What slave was ever imprisoned for a lie? Did they not remember that famous night that was nearly the last for the name of Rome, nearly a night everlasting? Had they not pictured the band of Gauls scaling the Tarpeian rock? Had they not pictured Marcus Manlius himself just as they had seen him then, in his armour and dripping with sweat and blood, having virtually snatched Jupiter himself from the hands of the enemy? Did their thanks to the saviour of the country lie solely in the half-pound measures of grain?* They had almost made the man a god, and in his *cognomen* Capitolinus, at least, put him on a par with Jupiter. Were they to allow him to remain chained in prison, in the darkness, drawing his breath only at the whim of the executioner? Could it be that in one man there was aid enough for all of them, but in so many no help for one?

By now the crowds were not leaving the prison even at night, and were threatening to break into it when what they were about to seize was released and Manlius was freed from his bonds by decree of the Senate. That did not mean an end to the sedition; rather, the sedition was given a leader.

At about this time, too, the Latins and the Hernici, along with colonists from Circeii and Velitrae, sought to clear themselves of the charge of official involvement in the war with the Volsci, and to reclaim prisoners of war for punishment under their own laws. The replies they received were pitiless, those to the colonists the more so since they had, though Roman citizens, entered into unholy plans to attack their native land. Thus they were not only refused the prison-ers of war but were issued a directive, which the allies were spared: they were ordered by senatorial decree to quit the city promptly and remove themselves from the Roman people's presence and eyes in case they failed to receive protection from ambassadorial rights, which applied only to foreigners, not citizens.

18. Towards the year's end, as the sedition of Manlius was breaking out afresh, elections were held and the following were elected military tribunes with consular power: Servius Cornelius Maluginensis (second term), Publius Valerius Potitus (second term), Marcus Furius Camillus (fifth term), Servius Sulpicius Rufus (sec-ond term), Gaius Papirius Crassus, and Titus Quinctius Cincinnatus (second term).

At the beginning of the following year both patricians and plebs were granted a period of peace abroad that was very welcome to both. In the case of the plebs, they were not conscripted for military serv-ice, and they conceived the hope of winning the war on usury, as long as they had such a strong leader; for the patricians, it was a case of not wanting their attention diverted from healing domestic afflictions by any external threat. Thus both sides had opened hostilities with considerably greater energy, and the battle was now imminent. Manlius had actually been inviting plebeians home and was night and day discussing plans for a revolution with their leaders; he was far more resolute and wrathful than before. What had inflamed his anger was his recent humiliation, which stuck in a mind unfamiliar with insult. Moreover, his spirit was strengthened by the thought that the dictator had not dared to treat him as Quinctius Cincinnatus had treated Spurius Maelius, and that not only had the dictator resigned his dictatorship to avoid the resentment aroused by Manlius' imprisonment, but even the Senate had been unable to face it. Self-satisfied and at the same time embittered by such thoughts, he set to work on rousing the already inflamed passions of the plebs.

'So how long* are you going to remain ignorant of your strength?' he asked them. 'That is something that nature has decided even wild animals should not be unaware of. At least count how many you are yourselves and how many you have against you. The numbers that you had when you were clients around each of your various patrons—those are the numbers you will now have against a single adversary! If you were going to face them one-on-one, I would still think that you would fight for your freedom more fiercely than they would for their supremacy. Just show them a fight and you will have peace. Let them see you ready to use force and they will of their own accord concede you your rights. We must together bring off some daring coup, or individually submit to all kinds of mistreatment.

'How long are you going to look at me in expectation? Certainly, I shall not fail any of you; but you must see to it that fortune does not fail me. I was your defender but, suddenly, when your enemy decided it should be so, I was done for! And you all watched the man who had kept prison away from each one of you being hauled off to prison. What am I to hope for if my enemies' attacks on me become bolder? Am I to expect death, like Cassius and Maelius? You are right in averting the omen. 'The gods will prevent this,' you say. But they will never descend from heaven for my sake. They have to give *you* the will to prevent it, just as they gave *me*, in time of war and then of peace, the will to defend you from barbarous enemies and then high-handed citizens. Is this great people's spirit so small* that you are ever satisfied to have help against your personal enemies, yet your only struggle with the patricians is over how far you allow them to dominate you? This is not ingrained in you from birth—you are under their control from habit. Otherwise, why is it that you show such confidence in dealing with foreigners as to think you have the right to rule them? It is because you are used to struggling with them for *empire*, whereas with these men it is a case of attempting to achieve (rather than defend) *freedom*. Even so, such have been the leaders you have had, and such the qualities you have shown yourselves to possess, that you have so far achieved everything that you have sought, whether by force or good luck. Now it is time for an even greater effort. Just put your own good fortune to the test—and me, too, whom you have, I hope, already successfully tested. You will have less difficulty establishing a ruler over the patricians than you had in establishing the men to oppose them. Dictatorships and consulships must be razed to the ground to enable the common people of Rome to lift its head.

'So give me your assistance, and put a stop to legal decisions on debt. I openly declare myself patron of the plebs,* a title which my dedication and loyalty vests in me. If you want for your leader some designation that more clearly reflects his authority or position, you will find it more effective for achieving your ends.'

It was from this, it is said, that discussions of granting Manlius royal power began, but with regard to those sharing his plans, and the aim of those plans, there is no clear account.*

19. Now, on the other side, the Senate was discussing the withdrawal of the plebs to a private home (which also happened to lie in the citadel*) and the serious threat to liberty. There were cries from most of them that what was needed was another Servilius Ahala who would finish off the internal conflict by sacrificing one citizen rather than provoke a public enemy by dragging him off to prison. They eventually fell back on a proposal milder in tone but with the same force: the magistrates were to see that the state suffered no harm* from the pernicious designs of Marcus Manlius. At that point the military tribunes with consular power and the plebeian tribunes entered into discussions—for the tribunes could see that an end to everybody's freedom would also mean an end to their power, and they had deferred to the authority of the Senate.* These all then discussed what needed to be done.

No one could come up with anything short of violence and bloodshed, which would obviously mean a terrible conflict, but then the plebeian tribunes* Marcus Menenius and Quintus Publilius addressed the house as follows:

'Why are we making into a battle between patricians and plebeians what ought to be seen as the state pitted against one pernicious citizen? Why are we attacking the plebs along with Manlius, when it is safer to attack him *through* the plebs, with his own strength precipitating his downfall? We intend to prosecute him. Nothing is less popular than royal power. The masses will observe that our struggle is not with them; they will become Manlius' judges rather than his

supporters; they will see that the prosecutors derive from the plebs
and that the defendant is patrician, and that the charge before them is
one of having royal aspirations. As soon as that happens they will
have more concern for their own liberty than they will for any man.'

20. This met with unanimous approval and the Senate arraigned
Manlius. When this happened, the plebs were first of all in an uproar,
especially when they saw the defendant in mourning clothes and no
member of the patrician class at his side, not even family members
or marriage-relations, and finally not even his brothers Aulus and
Titus Manlius. This was something that had never happened before
that day, that a man's closest friends had not even put on mourning
garb when he faced such danger. When Appius Claudius was imprisoned,* they recalled, his personal enemy Gaius Claudius and the
whole Claudian family had put on mourning clothes. It was through
a conspiracy, they reasoned, that a supporter of the people was
being crushed for having been the first to defect from the patricians
to the plebs.

The day of the trial then arrived. However, apart from Manlius'
encounters with the masses, his seditious speeches, money-
distributions, and the false allegation he made, I find in no source
any evidence brought against the defendant by the prosecution that
was directly pertinent to the charge of seeking royal power.
Nevertheless, I have no doubt that the evidence was not trivial, since
the obstacle in finding him guilty, as far as the plebs were concerned,
was not the actual case but the trial's location. Attention should,
I think, be drawn to one feature of the case so people may be aware of
the sort of achievements, and the magnitude of the achievements,
that the foul lust for regal power rendered not only undervalued but
downright hated. Manlius is said to have produced almost four hundred men whom he had provided with interest-free loans, thus preventing their goods from being sold off and the men themselves from
being arrested as debtors. In addition, he not only listed, but also
produced for inspection, his awards for distinguished war service: the
spoils of some thirty enemies killed by him, and about forty decor-
ations from commanders, including two mural crowns and eight civic
crowns.* He is also said to have produced citizens whom he had saved
from the enemy, and he named as one of them the master of horse
Gaius Servilius, who was not in attendance. And after the discourse
on his war record, which he delivered in a speech that matched

the greatness of his achievements in its brilliance, making his words equal to the events, they say that he bared his chest, which was lined with battle-scars. Time and again, they say, he looked up to the Capitol and called on Jupiter and the other gods to descend and assist his troubled fortunes, and prayed that, in his hour of danger, they would give the Roman people the same will that they gave him when he was protecting the Capitoline hill for their safety. They say, too, that he begged the people one and all to look upon the Capitol and the citadel, turning towards the immortal gods, as they pronounced judgement on him.

The people were being summoned by centuries to vote in the Campus Martius,* and the defendant, raising his hands towards the Capitol, had turned his entreaties away from men to direct them to the gods. It was now clear to the tribunes that unless they could also free the eyes of men from that memorial of Manlius' glorious exploit, there could never be an opening for an accusation, valid though it be, in hearts preoccupied with the service he had rendered to them. Accordingly an adjournment was called, and a people's assembly* was scheduled for a meeting in the Peteline Wood outside the Porta Flumentana, from which there was no view of the Capitol.* In that location the charge stuck and, with the citizens' hearts firmly set, a harsh sentence came down that even those who passed it found odious. Some authors claim that he was condemned by duumvirs who had been appointed to bring an indictment of high treason. The tribunes threw him down from the Tarpeian rock, and the same place served, in the case of the one man, as a monument to his extraordinary distinction as well as to his final punishment.

On his death, two measures to mark disapproval were taken. The first was at the level of the state: Manlius' house had stood where the temple and mint of Moneta* stand today, and a motion was brought before the people that no patrician should live in the citadel or on the Capitol. The second was at the level of the family: a decree issued by the Manlian family forbade anyone thereafter to bear the name 'Marcus Manlius'.

Such was the end of a man who, but for his having been born in a free state, would have left a distinguished memory. Shortly afterwards, when there was no danger to be feared from him, the people regretted his loss, remembering only his virtues. A plague also followed soon afterwards and, there being no apparent causes for such an affliction, it began to be thought by many to be a result of Manlius' execution. The Capitol, it was believed, had been defiled with the blood of its saviour, and the gods had been displeased when the man by whom their temples had been wrested from enemy hands had been punished almost before their eyes.

21. The plague was followed by famine* and also, the following year when news of the two calamities had spread abroad, by war on several fronts. The military tribunes with consular power were at that time Lucius Valerius (his fourth term), Aulus Manlius, Servius Sulpicius, Lucius Lucretius, Lucius Aemilius (all serving a third term), and Marcus Trebonius. A fresh enemy now appeared in addition to the Volsci, who had been virtually fated to provide ongoing training for the Roman soldier, to the colonies of Circeii and Velitrae, who had long been engineering revolt, and to Latium, whose loyalty was suspect. Suddenly there was an uprising of the people of Lanuvium,* which had been a very loyal city.

The senators felt this had been motivated by disdain on the part of the Lanuvians because the defection of the people of Velitrae, who were Roman citizens, had so long gone unpunished, and so they decreed that a motion proposing a declaration of war on them be put to the people at the earliest possible moment. To have the plebs more amenable to the campaign, they appointed a board of five to section the Pomptine land and a board of three to found a colony at Nepete. Then the proposal for the declaration of war was put before the people, and the tribes voted unanimously for war,* the plebeian tribunes' efforts to dissuade them coming to nothing. Preparations for the war were made that year, but because of the plague the army did not take the field. This delay provided the colonists with an opportunity to intercede with the Senate, and most people inclined towards the idea of a deputation being sent to Rome to ask for pardon. However, as happens, the communal danger was entwined with that of private citizens, and the ringleaders of the defection from Rome, fearing they might be the only ones to face charges and become scapegoats for the anger of the Romans, deterred the colonies from peaceful measures. Not only did they block the proposal for the deputation in their Senate, but they also incited most of the plebs to go out on pillaging expeditions on Roman land. This fresh affront removed any hope of peace.

That year was also the first time that talk arose of defection by the Praenestines.* Accusations were made against them by the Tusculans, the Gabini, and the Labicani, into whose territory they had made incursions, but the response from the Senate was so subdued that it was clear that their refusal to believe the charges stemmed from a wish that they not be true.

22. The following year, the new military tribunes with consular power, Spurius and Lucius Papirius, led the legions out to Velitrae. Their four colleagues Servius Cornelius Maluginensis (his third term), Quintus Servilius, Gaius Sulpicius, and Lucius Aemilius (his fourth term) remained behind to see to the city's security and counter any fresh unrest that might be reported from Etruria, for everything from there was eyed with suspicion.

A successful engagement was fought near Velitrae, where the Romans faced auxiliary troops from Praeneste whose numbers almost exceeded those of the entire colony. It turned out that, for the enemy, the proximity of the city both prompted a premature flight and offered them their sole refuge in that flight. The tribunes held back from assaulting the town: it was a hazardous venture, and they also thought their campaign should not result in the colony's destruction.

The letter they sent to the Senate in Rome containing the report of the victory was more critical of the enemy from Praeneste than the one from Velitrae. And so, by senatorial decree and the order of the people, war was declared on the people of Praeneste. These joined forces with the Volsci the following year and took Satricum, a colony of the Roman people, by assault, despite stiff resistance from the colonists, but in victory they treated their prisoners of war disgracefully. The Romans were angry over this, and they appointed Marcus Furius Camillus to his sixth military tribunate. As his colleagues he was given Aulus and Lucius Postumius Regillensis and Lucius Furius, along with Lucius Lucretius and Marcus Fabius Ambustus. The war with the Volsci was given to Marcus Furius as an extraordinary commission, and from the other tribunes the one selected by sortition as his assistant was Lucius Furius.* This turned out to be not in the state's interest, but it proved for his colleague Camillus a means of winning all manner of plaudits, both officially in that he restored a situation that had degenerated through the other man's recklessness, and on a personal level inasmuch as he used the blunder to win gratitude from the man rather than prestige for himself.

Camillus was now at an advanced age, and at the election it was only the unanimous will of the people that held him back when he was ready to swear the customary oath for excusing oneself on grounds of poor health. But he had an alert mind alive in a vigorous body, his senses were unimpaired, and though he was not greatly involved in civic affairs he found warfare exciting. He conscripted four legions, each four thousand strong,* and instructed the army to assemble at the Esquiline gate the following day; he then set off for Satricum. There, waiting for him and by no means demoralized, were those who had taken the colony; for they had confidence in their numbers, in which they were considerably superior. When they saw the Romans approaching they immediately deployed in battle formation, since they had no intention of putting off what would be a decisive contest. This would mean that the inferior numbers of their enemy would not gain any advantage from the skills of their singular commander, the one thing that could give them confidence.

23. That same fervour was to be found in the Roman army and also in one of its commanders, and there was nothing to delay their risking an immediate engagement apart from the prudence and authority of one man who sought a chance to use strategy to augment his strength by prolonging the campaign. This made the enemy all the more insistent. Now they were not merely deploying their battle-line before their camp—they marched to the middle of the plain and proceeded to advertise their haughty confidence in their strength by bringing their standards almost to their enemy's rampart. The Roman soldiers were incensed at this, and one of the military tribunes was much more incensed than they—Lucius Furius, whose youth and nature made him impetuous, while he was also filled with hope by the mood of the rank-and-file whose confidence had very little justification. He was further stimulating his already-excited soldiers by undermining his colleague's authority on the only grounds he could, the man's age. Wars, he would say, were for the young, and courage flourished and declined along with the body. From being a spirited warrior, he said, Camillus had become a foot-dragger: he had usually seized camps and cities on his arrival and with his first assault, and now he was passive, whiling away the time within the fortifications. What did he expect was going to add strength to his own forces or decrease the enemy's? What opportunity was he hoping for, what time or place for setting up an ambush? The old man's ideas were feeble and spiritless. Camillus had had enough of life and enough glory, he would add, but

why should that mean letting the strength of the state, which should be immortal, languish along with one man's mortal body?

With such talk Furius brought the whole camp over to him, and everywhere the call for battle went up.

'Marcus Furius,' he then said, 'we cannot check the ardour of the men, and the enemy, whose morale we have boosted by our hesitation, is scoffing at us with an arrogance that is now absolutely intolerable. You, one man, must yield to the consensus and allow yourself to be defeated in policy so that you may the sooner conquer in war.'

In reply, Camillus observed that in the wars that up to that day had been fought under his auspices alone, neither he nor the Roman people had had any regrets about his strategy or his results. Now, however, he understood that he had a colleague who was his equal in rights and authority, he said, and one who surpassed him in the vigour of his years. And so, as far as the army was concerned, although he had been accustomed to give orders rather than take them, he could not stand in the way of his colleague's exercise of command. Let him act in what he thought were the republic's interests and may the gods graciously lend their help. He asked in consideration of his old age that he not be placed in the front line, but, he said, he would not be found wanting in respect of the duties an old man usually shoulders in warfare. He also had this prayer to the immortal gods, that there be no mishap to make his own strategy seem the one deserving praise.

But his salutary advice received no hearing from men nor his pious prayers from the gods. The man championing engagement deployed the front line and Camillus strengthened the reserve troops and set a powerful guard-emplacement before the camp. Camillus himself then took up a position on some high ground, where he kept a close eye on how another's strategy would turn out.

24. When weapons clashed at the first onset, the enemy immediately fell back, not from fear but as a trick. There was a gentle slope to the rear between their battle-line and their camp, and their large numbers had permitted them to leave behind in the camp some cohorts all armed and at the ready; these were to launch a counter-attack when the battle had been joined and their enemy had come close to the rampart. By giving disordered chase to the retreating enemy, the Roman troops were drawn into an unfavourable position and became a good target for this counter-attack. And so alarm fell on

the victors in their turn, and the combination of the new enemy forces and the sloping ground made the Roman line buckle. The fresh forces of the Volsci who had counter-attacked from the camp bore down on them, and those who had fallen back, pretending to flee, also renewed the fight.

By this point the Roman forces were not just withdrawing; with no thought for their hastiness a moment ago or their erstwhile glory, they were everywhere turning tail and heading for the camp in a headlong rush. At that juncture Camillus, hoisted onto his horse by those around him, swiftly set his reserve troops in the fugitives' way and said to them:

'Men, is this the battle you insisted upon? What man or what god could you blame for it? It was your recklessness that was to blame then, and your cowardice now! You followed another commander; now follow Camillus and carry the day, as you usually do under my leadership. Why are you gazing at the rampart and the camp? It will let none of you in unless you are victorious.'

It was shame that initially stayed their flight, but then they saw the standards turning around and the line veering to face the enemy. Then there was their commander who, in addition to the distinction of his many triumphs and his venerable age, was now engaged in the front ranks where the effort and danger were most intense. They all reproached themselves and each other, and their shouts of reciprocal encouragement ran through the whole battle formation with a rousing clamour. The other tribune was not absent from the action either, having been sent to the cavalry by his colleague, who was in the process of re-establishing the infantry line. Avoiding reprimand—his share of the blame had diminished his authority to do this—Furius switched entirely from giving orders to entreaty, begging them one and all to rescue him, responsible though he was for that day's result, from being reproached for it.

'My colleague objected and tried to check me,' he said, 'but I chose to go along with everyone's hastiness rather than the prudent advice of one man. Camillus can see glory for himself, whatever your fortunes, but in my case, if the battle is not restored, I shall have the truly wretched experience of sharing the result with everybody else but the disgrace of it alone.'

Since the line was wavering the best course seemed to be to hand over their horses and make an attack on the enemy on foot.*

They advanced wherever they saw the infantry in most trouble, their arms and courage giving them special prominence. There was no holding back either by officers or soldiers from this supreme test of valour. And the effect of their valiant efforts was seen in the outcome, with the Volsci scattering in genuine flight over terrain where they had a little earlier withdrawn in simulated fright. Large numbers were cut down, both in the actual battle and the ensuing flight, and others then in their camp, which was taken with the same charge. More, however, were taken prisoner than killed.

25. Some Tusculans were recognized among the prisoners when the count was made, and these were separated from the rest and brought before the tribunes. When the tribunes interrogated them, they admitted that they had taken part in the war with the authorization of their state. Fearful of a war so close at hand, Camillus said that he was going to take the prisoners to Rome forthwith so that the senators would not remain unaware that the Tusculans had abandoned their alliance. In the meantime, he said, his colleague should, if he agreed, assume command of the camp and the army.

One day had served as a warning to Furius not to set his own plans ahead of better ones, but neither Furius himself nor anyone else in the army thought that Camillus would quite calmly tolerate his guilt, through which the republic had been brought to the brink of disaster. Both in the army and in Rome everybody was saying the same thing, that amid the fluctuating fortunes of the war with the Volsci the blame for the unsuccessful battle and flight lay with Lucius Furius, while all the kudos for the successful engagement went to Marcus Furius.

The prisoners were brought into the Senate, where members voted for a campaign against Tusculum and put conduct of the war in Camillus' hands. For the operations Camillus asked for a single adjutant, and given freedom to choose anyone he liked from his colleagues he took everyone by surprise and chose Lucius Furius. By such forbearance Camillus alleviated his colleague's disgrace while at the same time winning great distinction for himself.

There was, however, no war with the people of Tusculum. By remaining constantly at peace they fended off a forceful response from Rome, something that they could not have achieved by taking up arms. When the Romans came into their lands they did not move away from the areas close to the road; there was no interruption of their work in the fields; the city gates lay open and people came out in droves and wearing the toga to meet the Roman officers; and supplies for the army were courteously brought to the camp from the city and the fields. Camillus pitched camp before the gates, and, wishing to see whether the same peaceful aspect obtained within the walls as in the fields, he went into the city. There he saw doors standing ajar and all manner of merchandise set out on display before open shops; workmen all intently plying their various trades; elementary schools humming with pupils' voices; and roads bustling with women and children going this way and that, amidst the general crowd, wherever their various needs took them. Nowhere was there anything to suggest not just fear but even surprise. Camillus looked all around him, his eyes searching for any indication of war preparations, but there was no trace of anything having been removed or put on view just for the moment. Everything was in such a state of uninterrupted and tranquil peace that it barely seemed possible that even a rumour of war had reached there.

26. And so, overwhelmed by his enemy's complaisance, Camillus ordered their senate to be convened. 'Men of Tusculum,' he said, 'to this point you alone have found the true weapons and strength with which to defend your property from the wrath of Rome. Go to the Senate in Rome. The senators will judge which you deserve more, punishment for your former conduct or pardon in the light of your conduct now. I shall not anticipate gratitude for indulgence that belongs to the state. An opportunity to ask for mercy is what you will receive from me, but the Senate will grant you an outcome to your entreaties that it judges correct.'

The Tusculans came to Rome, and the senate of a people who had shortly before been Rome's faithful allies were seen in the vestibule of the Senate house with misery written on their faces. The Roman senators were immediately moved by this and, in a tone that was already more hospitable than hostile, ordered them to be ushered in. The dictator of Tusculum* then addressed them as follows:

'Senators: we are those on whom you recently declared war and made war, but when we came forward to meet your commanders and legions we were armed and equipped exactly us you see us now standing in the vestibule of your Senate house. Such was our attire and that of our plebs, and such will it always be, unless at some point we are given arms by you to use on your behalf. We thank your commanders and armies both, because they believed their eyes rather than their ears, and because, where there existed no hostility, they themselves created none. That peace that *we* showed to you we now petition *from* you, and we beg you to turn war from us to any place that war exists. If we must discover by experience the strength of your arms against us, then we shall do so unarmed. Such are our sentiments, and may the gods make them as successful as they are loyal! As regards the charges that pushed you into the declaration of war, it may well be that there is no point in rebutting in words what has been disproved by the facts; nevertheless, even if they had validity, we believe that it is safe for us to plead guilty to them since our remorse is so patently obvious. Let people do you wrong as long as you are worthy of receiving such satisfaction.'

Such was the tenor of the Tusculans' words. They succeeded in gaining peace for the present, and Roman citizenship not long afterwards.* The legions were marched back from Tusculum.

27. Camillus won fame for his prudence and bravery in the war with the Volsci, for his success with the Tusculan expedition, and for his outstanding forbearance and self-restraint with regard to his colleague in both operations. He then left office after seeing to the election of the military tribunes for the following year.* The tribunes were: Lucius and Publius Valerius (Lucius' fifth term and Publius' third), Gaius Sergius (his third term), Licinus Menenius (his second term), Publius Papirius, and Servius Cornelius Maluginensis.

This year also required the appointment of censors, particularly in the light of some imprecise reports of indebtedness. The plebeian tribunes were trying to arouse bad feeling by inflating the total of the debt, and it was downplayed by people whose interests were served if the difficulty of the repayment of loans were seen as arising from the borrowers' unreliability rather than their unfortunate circumstances.

The censors appointed were Gaius Sulpicius Camerinus and Spurius Postumius Regillensis. The process had already got under way when it was interrupted by the death of Postumius, since there was a religious impediment to the appointment of a replacement for the colleague of a censor. Sulpicius therefore resigned his office, but there was a flaw in the election of the replacement censors and so they did not take up their positions. Then religious worries prevented the appointment of a third pair since the gods seemed to be opposed to a censorship for that year.*

The tribunes' reaction, however, was to say that playing such games with the plebs was unacceptable. The Senate, they said, was circumventing the witnesses—the public records of everyone's property—because they did not wish the extent of the debt to attract attention. For that would make it clear that one part of the community had been plunged into ruin by the other part, and in the meantime the debt-ridden plebs were being exposed to enemy after enemy. Pretexts for war were now being sought in every quarter, they declared: the legions had been marched from Antium to Satricum, from Satricum to Velitrae, and from there to Tusculum; and now it was the Latins, the Hernici, and the Praenestines who were threatened with offensive action, and this was from hatred of Roman citizens rather than of the enemy. The aim was to exhaust the plebs in military service, not allowing them any breathing-space in the city or any free time to remember their liberty or to take their place in an assembly, where they could at some point hear the voice of a tribune talking about reducing interest and urging an end to other injustices. But if the plebs had the spirit to recall the liberty gained by their forefathers, they would not permit any citizen of Rome to become a credit-prisoner* over an unpaid debt nor any troop-levy to be held until the debt situation had been examined, and a plan for diminishing it devised. Thus everyone would know what belonged to him and what to another, and whether his own person remained free or whether this, too, was to be kept in fetters.

The reward that was proffered for public disobedience quickly aroused that disobedience. Many were becoming credit-prisoners and, with rumours spreading of a war with Praeneste, the senators had voted for enrolling fresh legions. Both procedures simultaneously began to face obstruction from tribunician intervention and unified resistance of the plebs: the tribunes would not allow the credit-prisoners to be hauled away nor would the young men volunteer their names. For the moment the senators were less concerned with enforcing sentences for indebtedness than they were with the troop-levy, for reports were arriving that the enemy had already set off from Praeneste and had taken up a position in the territory of Gabii. For the plebeian tribunes, however, that news had meanwhile only served as a stimulant, rather than a deterrent, for the struggle they had undertaken, and nothing had the power to smother the sedition in the city short of the war being brought right up to the city walls.

28. This was because when the report was made to the people of Praeneste that no army had been raised in Rome, that there was no clear selection of a commander, and that patricians and plebs had turned on each other, their leaders thought that this was their opportunity. They hurriedly put their troops in marching order, and then, laying waste their enemies' fields en route, advanced to the Porta Collina.* There was sheer panic in the city. The call to arms went up, and people rushed to the walls and gates; and, finally turning from civil strife to warfare, they named Titus Quinctius Cincinnatus dictator, after which Cincinnatus proclaimed Aulus Sempronius Atratinus his master of horse. When this was heard, the enemy fell back from the walls, and at the same time the younger Roman men mustered in accordance with the edict, and without demur—such was the awe inspired by that particular office.

During the time that the army was being enrolled in Rome, the enemy camp was established not far from the River Allia. From there they ravaged the countryside far and wide, boasting amongst themselves that they had taken up a position in a spot that spelled doom for the city of Rome.* There would be another panic-stricken flight from there as in the Gallic war, they claimed; for if the Romans dreaded a day as being infected with religious pollution and actually named it after that place, how much more would they fear the Allia itself, which was a monument of that terrible defeat? There they would certainly have visions of the bloodthirsty Gauls before their eyes, and the sound of their voices would fill their ears.

Such were the futile notions and futile topics that they were mulling over, having pinned all their hopes on fortune being attached to a location. The Romans, by contrast, knew well that wherever their Latin enemy was to be found, he was the one they had defeated at Lake Regillus and had for a hundred years kept in peace and under control. They thought that the place being renowned for the defeat would inspire them to erase the record rather than make them afraid that some piece of ground was ill-omened for their victory. In fact, were the Gauls themselves to meet them in that place, they would fight them as they fought them in Rome to take back their homeland, and as they did the following day at Gabii,* when they saw to it that no enemy soldier who had entered the walls of Rome would carry home news of their fortunes, good or bad.

29. Such was the thinking on each side when they arrived at

the Allia. When the enemy, drawn up and ready for action, were in view, the Roman dictator said to his colleague: 'Do you see, Aulus Sempronius, how the enemy have taken up a position at the Allia because they are relying on the fortune of the place? It will transpire that the immortal gods have given them no stronger grounds for confidence than that, and nothing that would be of greater help. You, however, have arms and courage to rely on, and with those you must attack their centre at a gallop; I shall bear down on them with the legions when they are thrown into disorder and confusion. Attend us, you gods of the treaty,* and exact the punishment due for the injuries brought upon you and the duplicity inflicted on us in your name.

The Praenestines withstood neither the cavalry nor the infantry. Their ranks were broken with the first shout of the first attack. Then, as their formation was holding together at no point, they turned to run, and in the turmoil were carried even beyond their own camp, not halting their disordered retreat until they were within sight of Praeneste. At that point, after their scattered flight, they occupied a piece of ground on which to put up some makeshift defences, fearing that if they withdrew within their walls their land would immediately be put to the torch and, after everything there was destroyed, the city would be blockaded. But when the Roman victors arrived after sacking the camp at the Allia, this fortification was also abandoned; and, scarcely believing their walls provided safety, they shut themselves up in the town of Praeneste.

There were a further eight towns that were under the control of Praeneste. Hostilities were directed at each in turn, and when they were captured without much of a struggle the army was marched to Velitrae, which was also taken by storm. The Romans came next to the source of the war, Praeneste, which was taken not by force, but through capitulation. Titus Quinctius then returned to Rome. He had been victorious in battle once, had stormed two enemy camps and nine towns, and had accepted the surrender of Praeneste; and in his triumph he had a statue of Jupiter Imperator* that he had taken from Praeneste borne along to the Capitol. The statue was dedicated between the shrine of Jupiter and the shrine of Minerva,* with a tablet set below it as a record of his achievements and inscribed much as follows: 'Jupiter and all the gods granted that the dictator Titus Quinctius should capture nine towns.' Nineteen days after his appointment Cincinnatus resigned his dictatorship.

30. Elections were then held for military tribunes with consular power, and in these an equal number of patricians and plebeians was elected. From the patricians Publius and Gaius Manlius were elected, along with Lucius Julius, while the plebs secured the appointment of Gaius Sextilius, Marcus Albinius, and Lucius Antistius. Because the Manlii surpassed the plebeian appointees in terms of family background, and Julius in popularity, they were given the Volsci as their area of responsibility by special arrangement, without sortition or mutual agreement,* something the men themselves presently came to regret, as did the senators who had given it to them. Without any reconnoitring, the two sent out some cohorts on a foraging mission. Then, thinking, on the basis of a fallacious report, that the men had been cut off, they rushed off to give them support, without even keeping the author of the story under observation (the man was, in fact, an enemy, a Latin who had duped them posing as a Roman soldier), and they themselves fell into an ambush. There, in an unfavourable position, they held their ground thanks only to the courage of the rank-and-file, both suffering and inflicting losses, and meanwhile the enemy attacked their camp, which lay in the plain, from the other side. In both sectors the engagement was sabotaged by the generals through their recklessness and incompetence. Whatever remained of the Roman people's good fortune was saved by the courage of the ordinary soldiers, which remained unshakeable even without anyone to direct it.

When the news was brought to Rome, the initial decision was to appoint a dictator. Then, after reports started coming in that things were quiet with the Volsci, and it became clear that they did not know how to capitalize on their victory and their opportunity, even the forces and commanders in the region were recalled; and, following that, all remained calm as far as the Volsci were concerned. The only unrest came at the year's end when the Praenestines took up arms after inciting the Latin peoples to revolt.

That same year new colonists were recruited for Setia,* whose inhabitants were complaining of a shortage of manpower. Domestic peace, attained by the personal influence of the plebeian military tribunes and the awe in which they were held by their followers, was some consolation for lack of success in the military sphere.

31. The start of the following year immediately witnessed an explosion of civil discord,* when the military tribunes with consular authority were Spurius Furius, Quintus Servilius (his second term), Licinus Menenius (third term), Publius Cloelius, Marcus Horatius, and Lucius Geganius. Now the fuel and cause of the discord was debt, and to look into the problem Spurius Servilius Priscus and Quintus Cloelius Siculus were made censors, but were prevented by war from fulfilling their role. First there were alarmed messengers, then people fleeing the countryside, bringing reports that Volscian legions had crossed the border and were inflicting widespread devastation on Roman territory. However, even in the ensuing consternation, the threat from without was far from suppressing the internal struggles. On the contrary, the tribunes were all the more frenzied in the use of their power to prevent a troop-levy, until conditions were imposed on the senators stipulating that, for as long as the fighting went on, no one was to pay the property tax* and no one was to sit in judgement on debt cases. When the plebs were conceded this respite, the troop-levy suffered no further delay.

When the new legions had been enrolled, it was decided that two armies be led into Volscian territory, the legions being divided between the two. Spurius Furius and Marcus Horatius headed to the right, towards the coast and Antium, while Quintus Servilius and Lucius Geganius went left towards the mountains and Ecetra.* They were confronted by the enemy in neither direction, and so plundering the fields came next. This was not the sort of haphazard plundering that the Volsci had hurriedly and fearfully done, acting like bandits and relying on their enemy's quarrelling, but also fearing his courage. This was carried out by a regular army with good reason for anger, and it also caused greater destruction because time was spent on it. In fact, the Volscian raids had been confined to the borderlands from fear that an army might at any moment come out from Rome, whereas the Romans had a further reason for lingering in the enemy's territory, namely to try to lure him into combat. And so they everywhere burned buildings in the countryside as well as some villages and, leaving behind no fruit tree or sown fields with any hope of a harvest, they drove off as their booty all people and cattle to be found outside the town walls. Then the two armies were led back to Rome.

32. The people in debt had been given a brief breathing-space, but after peace was re-established with the enemy court cases once more came thick and fast. There was little prospect of lightening the old debt-load either—in fact, new debt was incurred by a tax for building

a wall of dressed stone* that the censors had put out for contract. The plebs were compelled to shoulder this burden: the tribunes of the plebs had no troop-levy to impede! They were even forced by the influence exerted by the nobles to elect military tribunes who were all patricians. Elected were Lucius Aemilius, Publius Valerius (his fourth term), Gaius Veturius, Servius Sulpicius, and Lucius and Gaius Quinctius Cincinnatus. Thanks to the same influence they also succeeded in having three armies raised to deal with the Latins and the Volsci, who had united their legions and were encamped near Satricum, and there were no objections raised when all men of fighting age were put under oath. One of the armies was for the defence of the city; the second was to be available to meet sudden crises, should unrest break out elsewhere; and the third, and by far the strongest, Publius Valerius and Lucius Aemilius led to Satricum.

At Satricum they found the enemy deployed on even ground, and immediately went on the attack; and though victory was not yet quite assured, a heavy rainfall attended by high winds broke off what was a promising engagement. The next day the battle was restarted, and for quite some time the enemy, and in particular the Latin legions (who, thanks to their long-standing alliance, had Roman military training), resisted with valour and good fortune that matched the Romans'. But a cavalry charge threw their ranks into disorder, and in this disorder they were attacked by the infantry. They were thrust back from their position as the Roman line pushed forward; and there was no withstanding the Roman pressure as soon as the fight turned in their favour. The enemy scattered, and since they headed not for their camp but for Satricum, which was two miles away,* they suffered heavy casualties, especially from the cavalry. Their camp was captured and pillaged. On the night following the battle they left Satricum and made for Antium, on a march that resembled flight, and when the Roman army dogged their footsteps fear was speedier than anger. The enemy thus got within the town walls before the Romans could bring pressure to bear on their rearguard, or even slow it down. After that, a number of days were spent plundering the fields: the Romans were insufficiently equipped with military hardware for attacking the walls, and the enemy were in no state to risk a battle.

33. There followed a rift between the people of Antium and the Latins, and the people of Antium, crushed by their misfortunes and broken by a war that had witnessed both their birth and their old age,

were considering surrender. In the case of the Latins, their defection was new and followed a long period of peace, and their spirit was still fresh, making them all the more fiercely determined to continue the war. The quarrel ended only when it became clear to both parties that there was no way that one could stop the other from carrying through with its designs. The Latins set out for war, ridding themselves of association with a peace treaty they considered dishonourable, while the people of Antium, with the removal of these offensive witnesses to policies that could ensure safety, surrendered their city and agricultural lands to the Romans.

The Latins had been able neither to inflict damage on the Romans in warfare nor to keep the Volsci in arms, and such was the frenzied rage that flared up in them that they burned down Satricum, the town which had first provided them with refuge after their defeat. They put the torch to buildings both sacred and profane, and no structure in that city survived apart from the temple of Mater Matuta. It is said that it was neither their own religious scruples nor respect for the gods that kept them away from this building, but a ghastly voice that emanated from the temple, threatening dire consequences if they did not keep the sacrilegious fires far away from the shrine. An impulse drove them in a paroxysm of rage to Tusculum: they were angry that the Tusculans had abandoned the general assembly of the Latins and accepted not just an alliance with Rome but even Roman citizenship. Since the attack was unexpected, they found the gates open, and the town was taken at the first shout, apart from the citadel.

The townspeople sought refuge in the citadel with their wives and children, and sent messengers to Rome to apprise the Senate of their situation. An army was brought to Tusculum with haste, in keeping with the fidelity of the Roman people, and led by the military tribunes Lucius Quinctius and Servius Sulpicius. These observed that the gates of Tusculum were closed and that the Latins felt they were simultaneously mounting a siege and facing a siege, defending the walls on one side, and attacking the citadel on the other, inspiring fear and also feeling it themselves. The arrival of the Romans altered the morale on both sides. It turned the Tusculans from abject fear to the greatest enthusiasm, and the Latins from almost total assurance of soon taking the citadel, since they held the town, to very little hope for their own lives. The battle-cry went up from the Tusculans in the citadel, to be answered by a considerably louder one from the

Roman army. On both sides the Latins were under pressure; they failed to withstand the onslaught of the Tusculans, who charged down from their higher position, and they were also unable to keep at bay the Romans who were mounting the walls and forcing the gates that blocked their way. First the walls were taken with scaling-ladders, and then the bars of the gates were broken. The enemy were attacking them on two sides, putting pressure on the front and back, and they no longer had either the strength to fight or any opening for flight. Caught in the middle, they were killed to the very last man. With Tusculum recovered from the enemy, the army was led back to Rome.

34. The overall peace abroad, after the successful military campaigns of that year, was balanced at home by patrician violence and the miserable plight of the plebs, both of which were increasing day by day because the ability to pay one's debts was hampered by the very fact that payment was compulsory. Thus, when there was no longer property from which to make payment, people would satisfy creditors by surrendering their reputation and their persons when adjudged guilty and handed over to them, and punishment had taken the place of credit. To such a level of submission had not only the humblest members of the plebs, but even their leaders, been reduced that there was amongst them not one vigorous and enterprising man with the nerve to assume, or stand for, even the plebeian magistracies, much less to compete with patricians* for a military tribunate, a right for which they had so forcefully striven. So it looked as if the patricians had recovered permanent title to an office of which the plebs had merely taken possession for a few years.

But so that the jubilation of one or other side would not be excessive, a trivial event intervened* which, as is often the case, had momentous consequences. Marcus Fabius Ambustus was a man who wielded great influence not only among members of his own class, but also with the plebs, since he was thought by that order not to look down on them. He had two married daughters, the elder married to Servius Sulpicius, and the younger to Gaius Licinius, a man of some distinction, but a plebeian (and the fact that he had not rejected such a marriage had itself won Fabius some favour with the common people).

It so happened that the two Fabian sisters were spending some time chatting together, as is normal, at the home of Servius Sulpicius, who was a military tribune. When Sulpicius was returning home from the Forum, his lictor followed the usual procedure of knocking on the door with his rod, and the younger Fabia, unacquainted with the convention,* became alarmed. This drew laughter from her sister, who expressed surprise at her ignorance of the practice, but that laugh had a sting for a female heart, which is easily affected by things of no consequence. In addition, the large number of people attending Sulpicius and bidding him farewell made her sister's marriage seem fortunate, I suppose, and caused her to feel regretful about her own, because of that unfortunate inclination that makes one want to be outdone least of all by one's nearest and dearest.

She was still upset from the recent blow to her pride when her father happened to see her and asked if all was well. She tried to keep the reason for her melancholy to herself, since it demonstrated little affection for her sister and not much regard at all for her husband, but his gentle probing elicited from her the admission that the melancholy came from her marriage to a man not of her class, and the fact that she was a wife in a house to which neither high honours nor influence would come. Then, consoling his daughter, Ambustus told her to cheer up, that any day now she would see in her home the same honours that she saw in her sister's. He then proceeded to form plans with his son-in-law,* also taking into his confidence Lucius Sextius, an enterprising young man whose future prospects lacked nothing but patrician birth.

35. There seemed to be an opportunity for radical change because of the enormous amount of debt, since the plebs could expect no alleviation of the problem except by setting their own people in the highest positions of power. They should arm themselves for this plan, these men decided. By their struggles and endeavours, they said, the plebeians had already climbed to a level from which a further effort would enable them to reach the top, and to become the equals of the patricians in honour as well as virtue. For the time being they decided they should become plebeian tribunes, and in this office they would be able to open up the way to the other top positions. So Gaius Licinius and Lucius Sextius were elected tribunes, and all the bills that they announced* opposed the power of the patricians and supported the plebs. One concerned debt, the proposal being that what had already been paid in interest should be deducted from the principal, with the remainder to be paid off in three equal instalments over a period of three years. A second concerned limitations on rural property, stipulating that no one should own more than 500 *iugera*.

The third prohibited the election of military tribunes and specified that one of the two consuls elected should, without fail, be from the plebs.* These were all very important demands, which could not succeed without a bitter fight.

Now what was being proposed put at risk simultaneously those things for which all human beings have an inordinate craving: land, money, and high office. The patricians were terrified. After feverish public and private consultation they found no other solution than the veto, already put to use in many earlier disputes, and they procured some of the men's own colleagues to oppose the tribunes' bills. When they saw the tribes being called to the vote by Licinius and Sextius, these men, closely attended by patrician bodyguards, would not permit the bills to be read out, or any other measure taken that was customary in the case of a plebiscite. When the assembly had already been called several times, without success, and the bills were virtually rejected, Sextius declared: 'All right, since it is your wish that your veto should be so powerful, that is the very weapon we shall use to safeguard the plebs. Come on, then, senators, give notice of an election for the appointment of military tribunes. I'll see to it that you get no pleasure from that word "veto" that you are so happy to hear our colleagues now chanting in unison.'

His threats proved not to be idle. No elections were held apart from those for the aediles and plebeian tribunes. Licinius and Sextius were reappointed as tribunes of the plebs, and they allowed the election of no curule magistrates. This lack of magistrates held back the city for five years,* with the plebs re-electing the two men as tribunes while they put a stop to the election of military tribunes.

36. It was as well that other wars remained dormant: the colonists at Velitrae became restless in peacetime and, because there was no Roman army, they made raids on Roman territory on a number of occasions and also proceeded to attack Tusculum. That filled not only the senators, but the plebs as well, with shame, since the Tusculans, old allies and now new citizens, were begging them for help. The tribunes of the plebs relented somewhat, and elections were held by an *interrex*,* the following being returned as military tribunes: Lucius Furius, Aulus Manlius, Servius Sulpicius, Servius Cornelius, and Publius and Gaius Valerius. These found the plebs nothing like as compliant in the matter of the troop-levy as they had been in the election, but they did enrol an army after a great effort, and then set off

and not only dislodged the enemy from Tusculum but penned him within his own walls. Velitrae was then subjected to a siege considerably more aggressive than that of Tusculum had been. However, it could not be taken by those by whom the siege had been initiated; before that new military tribunes were elected—Quintus Servilius, Gaius Veturius, Aulus and Marcus Cornelius, Quintus Quinctius, and Marcus Fabius. But there was nothing noteworthy accomplished at Velitrae* even by these tribunes.

Things were taking a more dangerous turn at home. Sextius and Licinius—the men who drafted the legislation—had by now been re-elected eight times* as plebeian tribunes, and there was also the military tribune Fabius, father-in-law of Stolo, who was making it quite clear that he was advocating the laws that he had earlier suggested. And whereas there had earlier been eight members of the college of plebeian tribunes ready to veto the legislation, there were now only five; and, as usually happens with those who break ranks with their own party, these were stunned and bewildered, giving as reasons for their veto, in words belonging to others, only what they had been privately rehearsed to say. Most of the plebs were away at Velitrae in the army, they said, and elections should be postponed until the soldiers returned so that the plebs as a whole could vote on what was in their own interests.

Sextius and Licinius, along with a number of their colleagues and one of the military tribunes, Fabius, were by now experts at manipulating the feelings of the plebs* after so many years of experience. They began to bring forward leading senators and badger them with questions about each of the proposals that were being brought before the people. In the division of land, the plebeians were allocated two *iugera* each, they said. How dare the senators demand that they be granted possession of more than 500 *iugera** themselves, which meant that they would individually own as much land as almost three hundred of their fellow-citizens, while a plebeian's land-holding was scarcely enough for a bare roof over his head and a plot for his burial! Or did they want to see the plebs trapped by interest-payments and surrendering their persons to detention and torture rather than paying off the principal of their loans? Did they want to have them dragged in droves from the Forum* every day and condemned to servitude for debt, and to see the houses of the nobles fill up with convicts, with anywhere a patrician lived becoming a private prison?

37. These scandalous and distressing allegations they loudly made before people who feared that same fate, and they generated more indignation in their hearers than they felt themselves. Even so, they kept asserting that there would never be a limit to the patricians' land-grab and their deadly extortion of interest from the plebs until they made one of the two consuls plebeian to safeguard their freedom. The plebeian tribunes, they said, were in disrepute in that their office was undermining its own authority because of their use of the veto. There was no question of equal rights, when the patricians held all the power and they themselves had only the ability to offer help by veto; without a division of power, the plebs would never have an equal share in the government. And no one should think it enough if plebeians are merely considered eligible for the consular elections. Without it being obligatory that one of the two consuls should come from the plebs, there would be no plebeian consul. Had it already slipped from their memory that it had been decided that military tribunes (rather than consuls) should be elected for the very purpose of having the highest office open to plebeians as well, and that in forty-four years there was nobody from the plebs elected military tribune? The patricians had been used to seizing eight places in the election of military tribunes. Who would believe that with only two places free in this case they were going to voluntarily confer one office on the plebs, and allow the road to the consulship to be open when they had kept the tribunate shut off for so long? They had to use the law to grasp what they could not achieve through personal influence in the elections; and one of the consulships had to be taken out of the competition to be filled exclusively by plebeian candidates, since, left in the competition, it would always be the prize of the stronger party.

The argument that the patricians always bandied about in the past, namely that there were amongst the plebeians no men suitable for curule magistracies, could no longer be used, they said. Had the running of the state been in any way more remiss or neglectful after the tribunate of Publius Licinius Calvus, the first man elected from the plebs,* than it had been during the years when no one but a patrician was a military tribune? In fact a number of patricians had been impeached following their tribunate, but no plebeian. A few years back quaestors, too,* had like military tribunes begun to be elected from the plebs, and the Roman people had not regretted the appointment of any of them. Only the consulship remained for the plebeians to gain—that was the citadel of freedom, that was its cornerstone. If they reached that point, then the Roman people would consider the kings truly to have been driven from the city, and their freedom to be assured, because from that day everything that now gave the patricians their superiority would come to the plebs: power and honour, glory in war, social standing and nobility—great things for them to enjoy personally, and even greater to leave to their children.

The tribunes saw that speeches of this kind were getting a warm reception, and they made public a new proposal, that the duumvirs for sacred rites be replaced by ten elected officials drawn half from the plebs and half from the patricians. The voting on all these proposals they deferred until the return of the army besieging Velitrae.

38. A year went by before the legions were marched back from Velitrae, and so the matter of the laws remained in abeyance, deferred until the installation of the new military tribunes. As for the plebeian tribunes, the plebs were still re-electing the same ones, these two at any rate because they were proposing the legislation. Elected as the military tribunes were: Titus Quinctius, Servius Cornelius, Servius Sulpicius, Spurius Servilius, Lucius Papirius, and Lucius Veturius.

Right at the start of the year came the final confrontation over the laws. When the tribes were called and those proposing the measures were not blocked by their colleagues' veto, the patricians panicked and turned to their two last resorts—their supreme office, and their supreme citizen. They decided on the appointment of a dictator, and the appointee was Marcus Furius Camillus,* who, in turn, chose Lucius Aemilius as his master of horse. To combat such impressive preparations by their opponents, the proposers of the bills for their part bolstered the cause of the plebs by rousing huge support for it. They then gave notice of a meeting of the council of the plebs, and called the tribes to vote.

The dictator, surrounded by a throng of patricians, took his seat, full of anger and menace; and the proceedings started off with the customary squabbling between the plebeian tribunes, who were either urging passage of the legislation or interposing their veto. The veto had greater power judicially, but it was failing in the face of the support for the bills themselves and for the proponents of them; and when the first tribes began voting to approve the legislation, Camillus spoke.

'Citizens,' he said, 'it is now tribunician capriciousness, not tribunician authority, that is guiding you, and you are undermining the veto that was once won by the secession of the plebs, undermining it by the same unruly behaviour through which you gained it. So for the sake of the republic, and just as much for your own sake, I shall as dictator support the veto and with my power protect that safeguard of yours that you are intent on destroying. Accordingly, if Gaius Licinius and Lucius Sextius acquiesce in the veto of their colleagues, I shall certainly not have a patrician magistracy intrude into the council of the plebs. If, however, contravening the veto, they try to impose their legislation on what can be called a captive city, I shall not permit the power of the tribunes to self-destruct.'

The tribunes reacted with disdain, and pressed ahead with their design no less vigorously. In a fit of anger, Camillus sent his lictors to remove the plebs, adding the threat that, if they persisted, he would put under oath all men of military age and immediately lead the army out of the city. With that he struck sheer terror into the plebs, but in the case of the plebeian tribunes he intensified their resolution instead of curbing it with the prospect of confrontation.

However, the issue had gone neither one way nor the other when Camillus resigned his office. Either there had been some flaw in his election,* as certain authors have maintained, or the plebs decreed, on a motion made by the tribunes, that any action taken by Marcus Furius in his capacity as dictator should be punished with a fine of 500,000 *asses*.* What inclines me to believe that what deterred him from continuing was the auspices rather than such an unprecedented piece of legislation is, first of all, the man's temperament, and then the fact that Publius Manlius* immediately replaced him as dictator—what was the point in Manlius being elected to face a struggle in which Marcus Furius had been bested? In addition, the following year saw Marcus Furius as dictator again, and he could not have reassumed that power without feeling ashamed had it been broken during his tenure the year before. Further, at the time at which the measure concerning his fine is reported to have been proposed, either he had the power to block this bill (by which he could see that he was being forced back into line) or else he did not have the power to oppose those measures on account of which the proposal to fine him was made. And also, right down to our times, there have been power-struggles between tribunes and consuls, but the position of dictator has always been at a higher level.

39. Between the abdication of the former dictator and the entry into office of Manlius, the new one, a council of the plebs was convened by the tribunes as if an *interregnum* were in place, and it there became clear which of the proposed measures were more appealing to the plebs, and which to the proposers of them. The tribes were on the point of passing the bills concerning debt and land, but rejecting that concerning a plebeian consul. Both issues would have been settled had not the tribunes declared that they were placing an omnibus bill before the plebs. Then Publius Manlius, now dictator, tipped the balance in favour of the plebs by naming as his master of horse Gaius Licinius,* who had been a military tribune and was of plebeian origin. I gather that the patricians were angry at this, but that, as his excuse to the patricians for making the appointment, the dictator repeatedly would plead his close relationship with Licinius, at the same time noting that a master of horse had no more authority than a consular tribune.

When elections had been scheduled for choosing the plebeian tribunes, Licinius' and Sextius' conduct was such that, by declaring a wish to continue in office, they made the plebs very eager to grant them what they wanted but pretended not to want. It was now the ninth year of their standing in the battle-line against the patricians, they declared, at great risk to themselves and with no benefit to the public. They had grown old, they said, and so had the bills they had put forward and the efficacy of their tribunician power. The first attack on their legislation had come from their colleagues' veto, the second when the young men had been sent off to the war at Velitrae; and finally there was the dictator's thunderbolt that had been aimed at them. But now what stood in their way was not their colleagues or a war or a dictator (in fact, the dictator had actually provided them with a forecast of a plebeian consul by naming one of the plebs as his master of horse); it was the plebs who were retarding their own progress and their own interests. They could, if they wished, immediately have a city and a forum freed of creditors, and lands freed of unjust occupants. When, the tribunes asked, would they finally appreciate what they had been given, and show enough gratitude for it, if they passed bills that were to their own advantage and at the same time cut off all hope of further office from the authors of the bills? It was not in keeping with the decency of the Roman people to demand relief from interest and settlement on lands unlawfully occupied by the powerful while leaving those through whose efforts they gained these benefits as ageing former tribunes who were not only devoid of honours but even devoid of all hope of honours. Thus they should decide what they wanted, and then make known their wishes at the tribunician elections. If they wanted the proposals put forward as a joint bill, then there was reason for re-electing the same men as plebeian tribunes, since they would see their proposals through to the end. If, however, all they wanted passed was what served individual interests, there was no need to prolong a term of office that exposed the two of them to hatred—they themselves would not have the tribunate and the people would not have the advantages that had been proposed.

40. Such a determined speech by the tribunes left all the senators— apart from Appius Claudius Crassus, grandson of the decemvir*— stunned and speechless at their outrageous remarks. Claudius, it is said, more from loathing and anger than any hope of deterring them, came forward to oppose them, and spoke much as follows:*

'Citizens: it would not be a new or unexpected experience for me to hear, on this occasion, too, the one rebuke that has always been levelled at our family by seditious tribunes, namely that nothing in our state has been more important to the Claudian family from the very start than the dignity of the Senate, and that members of the family have always opposed the interests of the plebs. One of these charges I do not deny or repudiate. Ever since we were at one and the same time admitted to citizenship and membership of the Senate, we have done our utmost to see that, through our efforts, the dignity of those families in the class to which you wanted us to belong should be enhanced rather than diminished. With regard to the other charge, I would presume to claim, citizens, on my behalf and on behalf of my ancestors, that unless someone thinks that what is done for the state as a whole is against the interests of the plebs (as though they lived in another city), then we have knowingly done nothing, either as private citizens or as magistrates, that is against the interests of the plebs. Nothing we have done or said can truly be claimed to be contrary to your advantage, though some things may have been contrary to your wishes. But suppose that I were not of the Claudian family and not born of patrician blood, but that I were just any one of the citizens and that I knew only that I came from two freeborn parents and lived in a free state. Could I even then keep from asking the following question? Have these men, this Lucius Sextius and Gaius

Licinius—our permanent tribunes, for God's sake!—become so brazen in the nine years of their "reign" as to claim that they will not let you use your right to vote freely, either in the elections or in enacting legislation?

'"Only on one condition will you elect us tribunes for the tenth time," he says. What else does that mean but "We are so sick of what others canvass for that we refuse to accept it without handsome remuneration"? But I ask you, what is that remuneration which allows us to have you as plebeian tribunes for ever? "That you accept all our proposals as an omnibus bill, whether you like them or not, whether they are practical or not." Please, you Tarquinian* tribunes of the plebs, imagine me just as one ordinary citizen shouting out from the heart of the assembly: "With your permission, allow us to choose from these bills the ones we think beneficial, and to reject the others." "No," says he. "You will not be allowed to vote to enact laws on interest and land, matters of concern to you all, without accepting this horrific phenomenon in the city of Rome, something you resent and hate, that is seeing Lucius Sextius and Gaius Licinius here as consuls. Accept the lot, or I propose nothing." It is like setting poison along with food before a man in the throes of starvation and telling him to refuse what would sustain his life or else mix in the deadly with what is nourishing. So, if this were a free community, wouldn't the crowded assembly have cried out to you "Get out of here with your tribunates and your bills!" Well, if you will not propose what it is in the public interest to accept, will there be no one to make the proposal? Suppose some patrician, or suppose some Claudius (a thing those men claim is more hateful still) were to say, "take the lot or else I propose nothing," who amongst you would accept it, citizens? Will you never heed the facts rather than those who set them before you? Will you always accept with willing ears what that "magistrate" tells you, but with unwilling ears whatever is said by any of us?

'His language for sure is not appropriate for a citizen; but what about the bill whose rejection by you makes the two of them angry? It's just like his language, citizens. "I propose that you not be allowed to choose the consuls you want," he says. Is he saying anything other than that when he gives orders for one consul to come from the plebs willy-nilly, and does not allow you the power to elect two patricians? Suppose we were to have wars today like the Etruscan war when Porsenna occupied the Janiculum,* or the Gallic war just recently, when all this was in enemy hands with the exception of the Capitol and the citadel; and suppose that man Lucius Sextius were a candidate for the consulship alongside Marcus Furius here and any other patrician whatsoever. Could you bear to see Sextius become consul without any question while Camillus was contending with defeat? Is this what bringing public offices to both parties means, that for two plebeians to become consuls is permitted, but not two patricians? That one consul has to be chosen from the plebs, but in the case of both positions patricians can be passed over? What sort of partnership, what sort of collaboration is this? Is getting part of something of which you previously had no part too little for you? Must you take the whole while asking just for a part? "I am afraid that if the election of two patricians is allowed," he says, "then you will elect no plebeian." What is he saying other than "Because you are not going to elect undeserving candidates, I am going to oblige you to choose men you do not want"? So, what follows from this? Clearly that a plebeian candidate would not even need to thank the people if he were a candidate alongside two patricians, and would say he was elected by the law and not their vote!

41. 'What they are seeking is a way to wring offices out of us, not petition for them; and they intend to gain the highest of them without incurring even the obligations attached to the lowest. And they prefer to aim at these offices by waiting for an opportune moment rather than by merit. Is there anyone who would disdain to be examined and evaluated, who would deem it fair that he alone should be assured of public offices while his competitors must fight for them? Anyone who would exempt himself from your judgement and make your votes predetermined instead of voluntary,* captive instead of free? I make an exception of Licinius and Sextius! Their years in perpetual power you can count like those of the kings on the Capitol. Who is there, in our state today, so humble that he does not have an easier path to the consulship, thanks to the opportunity provided by *that* legislation, than we and our children have? For you will on occasion not be able to elect us as consuls, even if you want to; and in their case, you would have to elect them even if you did not want to.

'Enough has been said about the indignity of this situation— dignity is something in the human sphere. But what shall I say about religion and the auspices? There lack of respect and observance directly affect the immortal gods. Who is ignorant of the fact that this city was founded with auspices, that all actions, in both peace and war, are taken with auspices? In whose hands, then, do the auspices lie, by ancestral tradition? In the patricians' hands, of course!* No plebeian magistrate's election is attended by the auspices. The auspices are ours exclusively, to the extent that not only must the election of patrician candidates chosen by the people be attended by the auspices, but it is our prerogative, too, to appoint an *interrex* using the auspices, without a vote of the people, and we may also take the auspices as private citizens, a right plebeians do not have even during tenure of office. So if someone, by creating plebeian consuls, takes the auspices away from the patricians, who have exclusive rights to them, what else is he doing but depriving the state of them? They can mock our rituals now: "So what if the chickens will not eat,* if they are quite slow emerging from the coop, or if the bird gives a cry of ill-omen?" These are little things; but it was by not disregarding those little things that your ancestors made this republic great, whereas we now, as though we no longer stood in need of heaven's blessing, are defiling all our religious rites.

'So let us have pontifs, augurs, and the kings of sacrifice chosen at random, and let us put the mitre of the Flamen Dialis on anyone's head as long as he's human! Let us hand over the shields,* the inner sanctums, the gods and the service of the gods to those barred from them by religious law! Let us have laws proposed, and magistrates voted on, without the auspices, and let us not have patricians sanction the centuriate or the curiate assemblies. Let us have Sextius and Licinius ruling in the city of Rome like Romulus and Tatius,* since they make gifts of other people's money and other people's lands. Is the pleasure of plundering the fortunes of others so great? Does it not occur to them that the effect of one of their laws will be the creation of vast deserts in the countryside, because it will drive owners from their property, and that, thanks to the other law, credit will be undermined, precipitating the breakdown of all human society?

'For all these reasons my opinion is that you should reject these bills. My wish is that the gods give their blessing to whatever you decide.'

42. Appius' words did no more than defer the passing of the bills. The same men, Sextius and Licinius, were reappointed for the tenth time, and they carried the bill prescribing that the decemvirs in charge of sacred rites be elected partly from the plebs. Five patricians

were elected, and five plebeians, and by this step it looked as if the way to the consulship had been opened up. Satisfied with this victory, the plebs, as a concession to the patricians, agreed to the election of military tribunes with no further mention of consuls. Those elected were Aulus and Marcus Cornelius (second terms), Marcus Geganius, Publius Manlius, Lucius Veturius, and Publius Valerius (sixth term).

Apart from the siege of Velitrae, the result of which was slow in coming rather than uncertain, all was quiet abroad for the Romans. Then a report suddenly arrived of a war in Gaul, which compelled the state to have Marcus Furius appointed dictator for the fifth time; and Furius named Titus Quinctius Poenus* as his master of horse. According to Claudius' account,* there was in that year fighting with the Gauls at the River Anio, and this included the famous battle, fought on a bridge, in which Titus Manlius grappled with a Gaul by whom he had been challenged, killed him, and stripped him of his torque before the eyes of both armies. I am inclined to agree with most of our sources that these events took place at least ten years after this,* and that in this particular year, when Marcus Furius was dictator, it was in Alban territory that a battle was fought with the Gauls. And the victory for the Romans was neither indecisive nor difficult, despite the great terror that the Gauls had inspired in them when they remembered their disastrous encounter of old. Many thousand barbarians were cut down in the battle, and also when their camp was taken. The others scattered, heading for Apulia for the most part, and saved themselves from their enemy first by the distance they covered in their flight and then because they lost their way in their panic and became widely dispersed. By the agreement of the patricians and the plebs the dictator was awarded a triumph.

Scarcely was Camillus finished with the war when he was faced with internal strife even more fierce.* After some great struggles, the dictator and Senate proved to be the losers, with the adoption of the bills of the tribunes, and over the opposition of the nobles consular elections were held, in which Lucius Sextius was the first member of the plebs to become consul. And not even that marked the end of the conflict. The senators declared they would not ratify the election, and the situation almost resulted in a secession of the plebs and other circumstances that posed fearful threats of civil discord. Eventually, thanks to the dictator, an agreement was reached for settling the strife: the nobles yielded to the plebs on the issue of the plebeian consul, and the plebs yielded to the nobility in the matter of electing from the patricians a sole praetor to oversee justice in the city. So it was that, after a long period of bad blood between them, the orders were restored to harmony. The Senate felt that this was an achievement worthy of the holding of the Great Games* and the addition of one day to the traditional three—and that this was something the immortal gods deserved now more than ever—and when the plebeian aediles refused to take on this responsibility, the young patricians loudly proclaimed* that they would be happy to accept it in honour of the gods. They were thanked by the whole community; and a senatorial decree followed which directed the dictator to propose to the people the election of two aediles from the patrician class, and enjoining the senators to ratify all that year's elections.

BOOK SEVEN

1. This year will remain noteworthy for the consulship being held by a 'new man',* and noteworthy, too, for two new offices, the praetorship and the curule aedileship. These were positions that the patricians sought in return for conceding one of the two consulships to the plebs. The plebs conferred that consulship on Lucius Sextius, whose legislation had secured it. Through their influence in the Campus, the patricians won the praetorship for Spurius Furius Camillus, son of Marcus, and the aedileship for Gnaeus Quinctius Capitolinus and Publius Cornelius Scipio, these men being from patrician families. Lucius Sextius was given Lucius Aemilius Mamercus as his colleague from amongst the patricians.*

At the start of the year there was some talk about the Gauls*—they had at first scattered throughout Apulia but word had it that they were now regrouping—and also about a revolt of the Hernici. Everything was deliberately left in abeyance so that no business should pass through the hands of the plebeian consul; silence fell over everything and there was a general inaction that resembled a formal cessation of business. The sole exception was the tribunes' refusal to leave unmentioned the fact that, in return for one plebeian consul, the nobles had acquired for themselves three patrician magistrates, and that these sat like consuls, wearing the *praetexta*, on curule chairs.* The praetor also dispensed justice, they noted, and was elected as a colleague of the consuls and under the same auspices. This caused the Senate embarrassment over their insistence that curule aediles be appointed from the patricians. It was decided at first that they should come from the plebs every other year; then it became generally open to all.

In the consulship of Lucius Genucius and Quintus Servilius that followed there was a respite both from factional strife and from warfare but, so that there should at no point be relief from fear and danger,* a virulent epidemic broke out. They say that a censor,* a curule aedile, and three tribunes of the plebs succumbed, and that there was a commensurate number of fatalities in the rest of the population; but the death that made it particularly noteworthy was that of Marcus Furius,* as distressing as it was late in coming. He was certainly a man without peer in all circumstances, pre-eminent in peace and war before his exile, and more illustrious yet during his exile. He was sorely missed by the state, which in his absence begged for his help when it was captured, and he brought it joy when, restored to his native land, he restored that land along with himself. Then, for twenty-five years (the number that he lived after that), he retained the glorious reputation he had won, being considered worthy of having people refer to him as the city of Rome's second founder after Romulus.

2. The plague continued throughout this year and the next (which was the consulship of Gaius Sulpicius Peticus and Gaius Licinius Stolo*). In that period there was no event worthy of record, apart from the holding of a *lectisternium*—the third since the city's foundation—in order to appease the gods. When the violence of the epidemic did not abate either through human remedies or divine intervention, people's minds were overwhelmed with religious fear. Then, they say, theatrical performances were introduced* as one of the means of appeasing the anger of heaven, a strange recourse for a bellicose people, for the only spectacle that had been known to them was circus games. But these, too, like almost everything, had small beginnings and, what is more, they also came from abroad.

With no singing and no action representing the content of songs, dancers imported from Etruria would dance to the measures of a flute-player, producing movements in Etruscan fashion that were not without charm. Then young people began to imitate the dancers, while at the same time they would throw out jokes amongst themselves in unpolished verse, and their movements were not out of keeping with their diction. The phenomenon became accepted, and repeated practice raised its quality. Home-produced practitioners were given the name 'histriones', 'ister' being the Etruscan for dancer, but these no longer threw out in alternation primitive impromptu compositions, similar to Fescennine verse,* as happened before. Instead they put on medleys filled with musical airs, and with lyrics now scripted for performance accompanied by the flute and appropriate choreography.

It was Livius* who, some years later, first took the initiative to move away from writing medleys and to add a plot to his performance. Naturally, like all at the time, he was the performer of his own compositions, and it is said that because he was repeatedly called upon for encores he strained his voice. He was then granted permission to place a boy in front of the flute-player to do the singing, and he himself acted out what was sung, with somewhat more vigorous movements because he was not now restricted by using his voice. After that actors began to have the singing done for them, and only the spoken parts were left to their voices. When such rules were applied to plays, and there was a movement away from laughter and boisterous jesting, the young men left comedic acting to the professional actors and began to go back to the ancient practice of hurling at each other banter fashioned into verse. It was from this that what were later called *exodia* came into being, and these were usually attached to Atellan farces.* This type of show, which was borrowed from the Oscans, the young men kept as their own and did not allow it to be sullied by professional actors. Hence the established custom that actors of Atellan farces are not removed from their tribes, and that they perform army service, just as if they had no connection with the stage.

It seemed to me that the origins of entertainments ought to be set on paper along with the humble beginnings of other institutions; then it might become apparent how sound the beginnings were of something that has reached this pitch of madness where it can barely be supported by wealthy kingdoms!

3. Nevertheless, the very first production of stage performances, the purpose of which was religious expiation, did nothing to alleviate religious fears in minds or the sickness in bodies. Quite the reverse, in fact, because it so happened that, in the middle of the games, the Tiber flooded the Circus* and halted them, and that occasioned panic on a large scale, looking as it did as if the gods were already against them and rejecting attempts at appeasement. So it was that in the second consulship of Gnaeus Genucius and Lucius Aemilius Mamercus, when the search for rites of expiation was bringing more mental anguish than the disease brought physical pain, older people are said to have remembered that an epidemic had once been alleviated when a nail was hammered in by a dictator. Prompted by this piece of religious lore, the Senate ordered the appointment of a dictator to hammer in a nail,* and the man appointed to the position was Lucius Manlius Imperiosus, who then appointed Lucius Pinarius master of horse.

There is an old law, written in archaic script and language, stipulating that the chief praetor* should hammer in a nail on September 13th; it was fixed on the right side of the temple of Jupiter Optimus Maximus, at the spot where the temple of Minerva stands. Because literacy was rare in those days, that nail, they say, served to enumerate the passage of years, and the reason for its consecration in the temple of Minerva was that enumeration was Minerva's invention. (Cincius, who is a meticulous scholar of such monuments, claims that nails as an annual numerical indicator are also to be seen at Volsinii, driven into the temple of the Etruscan goddess Nortia.*) The consul Marcus Horatius established that law and dedicated the temple of Jupiter Optimus Maximus in the year after the expulsion of the kings. Subsequently the ceremony of hammering in the nail passed from the consuls to dictators, because these had greater authority. Then, when there was a lapse in the tradition, it was thought to be important enough in itself to have a dictator appointed expressly for that purpose. This was the reason for Lucius Manlius' appointment, but he acted as if he had been appointed for military purposes* and not in order to correct a failure in religious observance. He harboured ambitions for war with the Hernici, and plagued the young men with an oppressive conscription, but finally all the plebeian tribunes rose up against him and he resigned his dictatorship, overcome by their force or his feelings of shame.

4. Even so, at the start of the following year, when the consuls were Quintus Servilius Ahala and Lucius Genucius, Manlius was arraigned by the plebeian tribune Marcus Pomponius. The severity he had shown in raising troops had aroused hatred, since it had caused the citizen body not only financial loss but physical trauma, too, with some being flogged for not answering to their names, and others being hauled off to prison. More than anything it was his ruthless nature that was hated, as well as his *cognomen* 'Imperiosus'. This name was hard for a free society to tolerate, and had been applied to him because of his display of vicious behaviour towards close friends and blood relatives as much as towards strangers.

One of the charges that the tribune made against Manlius centred on his treatment of his young son,* who had been found to have done nothing wrong. Manlius, it was claimed, had driven him out of the city, from his house and home, and had kept him away from the Forum, from public life, and interaction with his coevals, consigning him to servile labour, almost to a prison or workhouse. There the young son of a dictator, who came from a very privileged background, would learn from his daily misery that he really was the child of an 'imperious' father. And of what, it was asked, was he guilty? Of lacking speaking ability and not having a ready tongue! This was a defect of nature. If there was any spark of humanity in his father, should he not have tried to remedy it, instead of carping at it as he did and calling attention to it by harassing him as he did? Even wild beasts do not fail to nourish and care for any of their offspring who are less fortunate. But, for sure, Lucius Manlius only piled problem on problem in his son's case; he exacerbated his slow-wittedness and snuffed out what little natural vigour he had by making him live the rustic life of a peasant amongst the beasts.

5. Everybody was more enraged at these charges than was the young man himself. In fact, he was actually upset at being the cause of resentment and charges against his father. So that all the gods and humans should understand that he preferred to help his father rather than his father's enemies, he adopted a plan that did indeed reflect his uncouth and wild character, but which, though inappropriate for a citizen, was nevertheless commendable for its filial piety.

Without anyone knowing, he armed himself with a knife, came into the city one morning, and proceeded immediately from the city gate to the home of the tribune Marcus Pomponius. He told the doorkeeper that he needed to see his master right away, and that he should tell him that it was Titus Manlius, son of Lucius Manlius. He was soon shown in, as it was hoped that he had been roused to anger against his father and was bringing some fresh charge or plan for expediting the matter. Greetings were exchanged, and Manlius said he wanted to discuss something with the tribune in private. All present were instructed to leave. The young man then drew his dagger and, standing over the man's couch with the knife pointed at him, threatened to stab him right then and there if he did not swear, in terms that he himself dictated, that he would never hold a council of the plebs to bring a charge against his father. The tribune was terrified. He could see the weapon glinting before his eyes, and saw that he was alone, that this was a very strong young man and (something no less to be feared) that he had a blockheaded pride in his strength. He took the oath as it was dictated to him, and later on openly declared that it was under duress that he had abandoned his intended course of action. And for all that the plebs would have preferred to

have the opportunity to vote on such a heartless and arrogant defendant, they nevertheless were not annoyed at the son's daring to take
such action on his father's behalf—that the father's egregious severity had not deterred the boy from his loyalty to him made it all the
more commendable. Thus, not only was the hearing of the case
against the father dropped, but the affair also brought the young man
renown. In fact, it had been decided that in that year, for the first
time, military tribunes for the legions would be elected—hitherto
the generals themselves appointed them, as they do today in the case
of the so-called 'Rufuli'*—and the young Manlius took second place
out of six. And that happened despite the fact that he had no services
to his credit either in civil or military life to win electoral favour,
inasmuch as he had spent his youth in the country, far from human
society.

6. That same year, as the result of an earthquake or some other
cataclysmic event, an area roughly at the centre of the Forum is said
to have collapsed, forming a huge chasm of enormous depth, and the
gaping hole could not be filled by everyone bringing earth to throw
into it. Finally, advised by the gods, it is said, they began to ask where
the greatest strength of the Roman people lay; for the soothsayers
prophesied that this was what had to be sacrificed to the place if they
wanted the Roman republic to last for ever. At that Marcus Curtius,
who was a fine soldier, purportedly berated the people for wondering
if there was any greater good the Romans enjoyed than weapons and
courage. Silence fell. Curtius turned his gaze to the temples of the
immortal gods overlooking the Forum, and to the Capitol, and
stretching out his hands at one moment to the sky, and the next to the
gaping cavity in the earth and the gods of the underworld, he promised himself as a devotional sacrifice. Then, seated on a horse that was
fitted out as splendidly as can be, he hurled himself into the chasm,
fully armed, and gifts and fruits were showered down upon him by
the crowd of onlookers, both men and women. The Curtian Lake,* it
is claimed, was not named after Curtius Mettius, a soldier of Titus
Tatius in very early times, but after this man. I would have spared no
pains if the truth could be reached by historical investigation, but as
things are we must accept tradition where the antiquity of events
does not allow certainty. And the lake's name is more famous because
of this more recent story.

Following the expiatory sacrifice for this dreadful portent, the

Senate that same year considered the matter of the Hernici. They sent fetial priests to demand redress but, meeting with no success, they resolved to propose to the people, on the earliest possible date, a declaration of war on the Hernici, and in a crowded assembly the people voted for the war. The consul Lucius Genucius was, by sortition, given responsibility for its conduct. The whole state was in suspense, for he would be the first consul from the plebs to fight a war under his own auspices, and it was on how the matter turned out that they would decide whether sharing the office had been a good idea or not.

As chance would have it, Genucius fell into an ambush after setting off on a great expedition against the enemy; the legions suddenly panicked and were routed; and the consul was surrounded and killed by soldiers unaware of the identity of the man they had caught. When word of this was brought to Rome, the patricians, so far from being saddened by the communal disaster, arrogantly gloated over the unfortunate leadership of the plebeian consul, filling all parts of the city with their outcry. Let men go and choose consuls from the plebs, they cried, and let them pass auspices on to those who had not the right to take them! They had by a plebiscite managed to remove the patricians from honours rightfully theirs; but their law, not sanctioned by auspices, had not had validity with the gods, had it? The gods themselves had defended their own divine power and their own auspices! For as soon as these were touched by one who had neither the legal nor the religious authority to touch them, an army and its commander had been wiped out, and that was a warning for the future against holding elections that violated the rights of families.

The Curia and Forum rang with such cries. Because Appius Claudius had spoken against the law, it was now with greater authority that he inveighed against the results of a decision that he had denounced, and the consul Servilius, with the approval of the patricians, appointed him dictator. A proclamation for a troop-levy and a suspension of business followed.

7. Before the dictator and the new legions reached the Hernici, a successful operation was brought off under the leadership of the legate Gaius Sulpicius, who capitalized on a favourable opportunity. After the death of the consul, the Hernici disdainfully moved up close to the Roman camp, fully expecting to storm it, but the legate encouraged the men, whose hearts were full of wrathful indignation,

and they made a counter-attack. The action left the Hernici far from realizing their hope of reaching the Roman rampart, and in fact they fell back, their ranks in disorder.

Then, with the arrival of the dictator, a new army was added to the old one, doubling the troop numbers. At an assembly the dictator sang the praises of the legate and the men by whose valour the camp had been defended, and by this he both raised the spirits of those receiving the well-earned commendation and also stimulated the others to emulate their feats of courage. Preparations for combat were no less spirited on the enemy side: remembering the distinction they had earned earlier and not unaware that their enemy's forces had been enlarged, they proceeded to augment their own. All of fighting age in the nation of the Hernici were called up, and eight cohorts of four hundred men, the elite of their soldiers, were duly enrolled.* They also filled this select group of outstanding warriors with hope and fervour by means of a decree that allowed them to draw double pay. They were, in addition, excused military chores so that by being kept in reserve for one task only—fighting—they would know that they were to put in a greater effort than the ordinary soldier. They were also positioned outside the regular battle formation so that their courage would be more visible.

A plain two miles in extent separated the Roman camp from that of the Hernici, and it was at its centre, at a point roughly equidistant from the two camps, that the battle took place. At first the issue was uncertain, and the Roman cavalry's efforts to disrupt the enemy line with its charges came to nothing. When, for all their exertion, their strikes proved ineffective, the cavalrymen consulted the dictator and, with his permission, left their horses behind, rushed before the lines with a noisy shout, and began the battle anew.* Stemming their attack would have been impossible, had not the enemy's elite cohorts stood in their way with a strength and spirit that was a match for theirs.

8. It then became a fight between the champions of the two peoples, and whatever damage was inflicted on either side by the common fortunes of war, it was many times greater than could be expected from their numbers. The others, the mass of ordinary soldiers, all regarded it as a fight entrusted to the champions, and placed their fate in the courage of others.

Many fell on both sides, and more were wounded. Finally, the cavalrymen fell to reprimanding each other. What was now left for them to do, they asked if on horseback they had failed to drive back the enemy and were now achieving no decisive result on foot, either? Was there some third sort of engagement for which they were waiting? Why had they boldly sprung forward before the lines and why were they fighting in a position belonging to someone else? Galvanized by these exchanges, they raised the battle-cry again and, launching their attack, first of all made the enemy falter, then pushed him back, and, eventually, quite clearly put him to flight. It is not easy to say what the critical factor was that brought victory when the sides were equally strong, unless the fortune constantly attending the two was able to raise the spirits in the one case and diminish them in the other.

The Romans followed the fleeing Hernici all the way to their camp, but because it was late in the day they refrained from attacking it. (The dictator's long failure to obtain favourable omens had held him back from giving the signal before noon, so that the fighting had gone on till nightfall.) The next day it was discovered that the Hernici had fled, leaving the camp deserted, and that a number of wounded had been left behind. As the enemy retreated, their standards, with only a few in attendance, were seen passing the town of Signia* by its inhabitants, and these scattered their column and sent them off in aimless, panic-stricken flight through the countryside. Nor was it a bloodless victory for the Romans. A quarter of their infantry fell and—no less grave a loss—a number of cavalrymen were killed.

9. The following year the consuls Gaius Sulpicius and Gaius Licinius Calvus led an army against the Hernici. When they did not find the enemy in the countryside, they took the Hernican city of Ferentinum by assault; but as they were returning the people of Tibur* closed their gates on them. There had already been many complaints hurled back and forth between the two peoples, but this was what ultimately caused the Romans to demand reparations by means of the fetial priests and then to declare war on the people of Tibur.

It is well documented that Titus Quinctius Poenus was dictator that year and that his master of horse was Servius Cornelius Maluginensis. Licinius Macer* states that Poenus was declared dictator by the consul Licinius, and that the purpose for it was the holding of elections. Macer claims that Licinius' colleague was trying to speed up the elections in order to have them fall before the military campaign (so that he could continue in office for a further year), and that his unconscionable wishes had to be checked. However, such efforts to glorify his own family make Licinius (Macer) somewhat suspect as an authority. Since I find no mention of the affair in earlier annals, I am inclined to think the reason for his appointment as dictator was the Gallic war. At any rate, it was in that year that the Gauls pitched their camp at the third milestone on the Via Salaria,* on the far side of the bridge over the Anio.

The dictator then proclaimed a suspension of business* because of the Gallic uprising. He had all the younger men take the military oath and, setting forth from the city with a huge army, he encamped on the nearer bank of the Anio. There was a bridge between the two sides, but neither tried to destroy it in case that were seen as a sign of fear. There were numerous battles for possession of the bridge but, the relative strength of each side being uncertain, it could not be ascertained who could hold it. Then a Gaul of huge build stepped forward* onto the empty bridge and, raising his voice as loudly as he could, said: 'Come on, then! Let the man that Rome now considers her bravest come forward to fight so that the outcome of our duel may show which people is the better in war!'

10. There followed a long silence amongst the finest of the young Romans: they shrank from refusing the fight, but they were also disinclined to run this particularly dangerous risk. Then Titus Manlius son of Lucius—the man who had championed his father against the tribune's harassment—left his post and marched up to the dictator.

'I would not dream of fighting outside the ranks without your order, general,' he said, 'not even if I saw the prospect of certain victory. But since that animal is prancing around so cockily before the standards of the enemy, I want to show him, if you let me, that I am born of a family that threw the army of the Gauls down from the Tarpeian rock.'*

'God bless your courage and your devotion to your father and fatherland, Titus Manlius,' the dictator replied. 'Go, and with heaven's help demonstrate the invincibility of the Roman name!'

The young man's companions then helped him on with his armour. He took an infantryman's shield, and strapped on a Spanish sword* that was suitable for close combat. His friends then took him forward, armed and outfitted, to face the Gaul, who was foolishly elated and (a detail that the ancient authors also thought worthy of mention*) was even sticking out his tongue to mock him. Manlius' friends withdrew to their posts, and the two armed men were left between the armies—more like participants in a gladiatorial show than in regular warfare, and (to any spectators judging them by their external appearance) by no means evenly matched. The one had a build of extraordinary proportions and was replendent in his multicoloured garb and his painted armour embossed with gold.* The other's stature was average for a military man and there was little that was impressive about his weapons, which were serviceable rather than decorative. There was no singing, no jumping around, and no pointless brandishing of weapons, but his heart was full of courage and silent anger, and all his fighting spirit he had kept back for the decisive moment of the duel.

When they took up their position between the two armies, and hope and fear had all those human hearts on tenterhooks, the Gaul, his boulder-like frame towering over his opponent, thrust forward his shield with his left hand to counter the weapons of his advancing foe; and with a slashing stroke he brought down his sword to deliver a harmless but loudly resounding blow. The Roman raised the point of his sword and, striking the bottom of the Gaul's shield with his own, slipped between the man's body and his weapons, his whole frame being too close to him to be exposed to any risk of a wound. He thereupon delivered one thrust and then another, piercing the man's belly and groin, bringing him crashing down and laying him out over a large area.

As the Gaul lay there, Manlius spared his corpse all other forms of abuse* but did take from it a single torque, which was spattered with blood, and put it around his own neck. A mixture of fear and admiration had left the Gauls rooted to the spot. The Romans, however, left their posts, went forward in high spirits to meet their comrade, and, showering him with felicitations and praise, brought him to the dictator. Amidst the coarse and jocular quasi-poetical banter* that soldiers indulge in, the name Torquatus was heard, a name celebrated even in later generations and one redounding to the honour of the family. The dictator also made Manlius a gift of a golden crown, and before a gathering of the troops paid tribute to that duel with a magnificent laudation.

11. That encounter was actually of great importance for the outcome of the entire war; indeed, the Gallic army abandoned their camp in a panic during the night that followed and moved into Tiburtine territory.

There the Gauls struck a military alliance with the Tiburtines, and after receiving a generous supply of provisions from them soon moved on into Campania. This was why, the following year, the consul Gaius Poetelius Balbus led an army against the Tiburtines on the orders of the people after his colleague Fabius Ambustus had been allotted the Hernici as his sphere of duty. With that the Gauls returned from Campania to lend assistance to the Tiburtines, and there were terrible depredations conducted in the area of Labici, Tusculum, and Alba that were certainly instigated by the Tiburtines. To combat the Tiburtine enemy the state was content to have a consular commander, but the Gallic incursion made the appointment of a dictator imperative. The man appointed was Quintus Servilius Ahala, who named Titus Quinctius as his master of horse, and with the authority of the Senate made a vow of Great Games should that war prove successful. To keep the Tiburtines pinned down in their own theatre of operations, the dictator ordered the consul's army to remain in place and he made all the younger men take the oath of loyalty (and none tried to avoid service).

The battle, fought not far from the Colline gate,* saw the Romans fight with the entire strength of the city before the eyes of their parents, their wives, and their children, which are strong stimuli to bravery in men even when they are away from them, and which on that occasion, set before their eyes, fired the soldiers with feelings of pride and pity. There was great carnage on both sides, but finally the army of the Gauls was repulsed. They headed towards Tibur, regarding it as the headquarters of the Gallic campaign, and as they straggled along they were intercepted by the consul Poetelius not far from the town. When the Tiburtines came out to help, the Gauls were driven within the gates along with them. The operation was admirably conducted by dictator and consul alike. Fabius, the other consul, also won a decisive victory over the Hernici, at first in minor skirmishes, and then finally in an outstanding engagement in which the enemy launched an all-out attack.

The dictator praised the consuls to the skies in the Senate and before the people, even conceding to them the glory of his own successful exploits, and after that he resigned the dictatorship. Poetelius held a double triumph, over the Gauls and the Tiburtines; entering Rome with an ovation was thought sufficient for Fabius.

The Tiburtines scoffed at Poetelius' triumph, asking where it was that he had clashed in battle with them. A few had ventured out of the gates to observe the panic-stricken flight of the Gauls, they said, and when they found that they too came under attack and that any that the Romans met were indiscriminately cut down by them, these men withdrew into the city. And this was the feat that the Romans thought worthy of a triumph! Just in case they considered provoking panic at the gates of their enemy to be some wonderful and great achievement, they added, the panic they were going to see before their own walls would be greater!

12. And so, the following year, in the consulship of Marcus Popilius Laenas and Gnaeus Manlius, the enemy set out from Tibur in battle formation at the dead of night, and came to Rome. Suddenly awoken from their sleep, people were terrified by the surprise attack and the alarm it precipitated in the dark, as well as by the fact that many were ignorant of who the enemy were and whence they had come. Nevertheless there was a speedy call to arms, and the gates were manned with sentries and the walls with military units. When dawn revealed that the numbers before the walls were relatively small, and that the enemy consisted only of Tiburtines, the consuls came out through two of the gates and attacked their forces on both sides as they approached the walls. It then became clear that they had come relying more on opportunism than courage—they barely held out against the initial onset of the Romans. In fact, their attack was generally recognized as having been beneficial for Rome: the antagonism between patricians and plebeians that was already developing had been quelled by fear of a war so close at hand.

A quite different invasion by an enemy posed a greater threat to the agricultural lands. A Tarquinian raiding force* overran Roman territory, particularly where it is adjacent to Etruria and, when demands for redress met with no success, the new consuls, Gaius Fabius and Gaius Plautius, on the orders of the people declared war on the people of Tarquinii. Responsibility for that war fell to Fabius, and that with the Hernici to Plautius.

Talk of a war with the Gauls also became more widespread. Faced with these numerous crises, however, the Romans received some consolation from granting the Latins the peace they sought, and from the large numbers of troops received from them under the terms of the old treaty that they had for many years allowed to lapse.* With the Roman cause bolstered by such support, they were less concerned on hearing that the Gauls had recently reached Praeneste and then encamped near Pedum. They decided that Gaius Sulpicius* should be appointed dictator and the consul Gaius Plautius, who was expressly summoned for the purpose, made that appointment; and Marcus Valerius was named the dictator's master of horse. These men led against the Gauls the cream of the two consular armies.

The war proceeded at a somewhat slower pace than was to the liking of either side. At first only the Gauls were hungry for battle, but then the Roman soldiers far surpassed the Gauls' furious desire to rush to arms and into the fight. Being under no pressure, however, the dictator was not at all inclined to trust to the vagaries of fortune when facing an enemy whom the passage of time was weakening every day, and who was on hostile soil without supply-lines and solid defence works. Furthermore, physically and mentally, the enemy's make-up was such that all his force was concentrated in the initial attack, but this would flag after a short interval.

Bearing that in mind, the dictator proceeded to drag out the war, and he had given notice of severe punishment for anyone engaging the enemy without his order. The men were annoyed, and at first they fell to criticizing the dictator amongst themselves at their posts and on guard-duty, occasionally vituperating the senators collectively for not having put direction of the war in the consuls' hands. A fine commander they had chosen, they would say, a unique leader who thought victory would come wafting down from heaven into his arms while he himself did nothing. Then they proceeded to bandy about such comments quite openly in public, and with greater animosity, threatening either to fight without the general's order or else make for Rome in a body. The centurions also began to mingle with the men, and it was no longer merely a case of murmuring amongst groups of individuals. Now there was one chaotic uproar at the camp headquarters and before the commander's tent, with the crowd swelling to the size of a general assembly and noisy demands arising everywhere that they should immediately go to the dictator and that, as befitted his courage, Sextus Tullius should make the case on behalf of the army.*

13. This was now the seventh time that Tullius had been serving as chief centurion, and no one in the army, at least among the infantrymen, had a more distinguished military record. He now went ahead of the men and came to the commander's dais, where Sulpicius'

surprise at seeing the crowd was less than it was at seeing it led by Tullius, a soldier who scrupulously followed orders.

'If I may speak, Dictator,' said Tullius, 'the whole army feels that it stands guilty of cowardice in your eyes, and that it has been left virtually stripped of its arms as a mark of disgrace; and it has asked me to put its case before you. Even if we could be charged with giving ground in any quarter, with turning our backs to the enemy, or with disgracefully losing our standards—even then I would think it only fair for you to grant our request that we be allowed to make amends for our shortcomings by our courage, and to erase the memory of our disgrace by winning fresh glory. Even the legions put to flight at the Allia later marched out from Veii and won back by their courage the homeland they had lost through their fear. In our case, thanks to heaven's blessing, and to your good fortune and that of the Roman people, our military situation and our honour remain intact. And yet I scarcely dare talk about honour when the enemy have us hiding within our defences like women, and subject us to all manner of degrading taunts! And when, too—something we find more painful—you, our commander, judge your army to be without courage, without weapons and without hands! When, before you have put us to the test, you have so lost confidence in us that you think you are the leader of a bunch of handicapped weaklings!

'What other explanation can we accept for you, a veteran commander with a superb record in battle, to be sitting "with arms folded", as the saying goes. Whatever the facts of the matter, you certainly seem to have greater doubts about our worth than we do about yours. But perhaps this policy is not yours but that of the state, and it is some conspiracy of the senators, and not the Gallic war, that keeps us away from Rome and our homes. If so, then please accept what I have to say as being addressed not by soldiers to their commander but by plebeians to the patricians; and if the plebeians say that they are going to have their own policies, just as you have yours, who could be angry with them? So, I say that we are your soldiers, not your slaves, and that we were sent off to war, not to exile! If someone gives the signal and leads us out to battle, we shall put up a fight worthy of true men and Romans; if military action is not needed, we shall spend our free time in Rome rather than the camp. Let the patricians be told this. But you, commander—we beg you to give us the opportunity to fight. We want victory, but we also want victory under *your* command. It is on *you* we want to confer the glorious laurel; it is with *you* we want to enter the city in triumph; it is following *your* chariot that we want to approach the temple of Jupiter Optimus Maximus with cries of joy and exultation!' Tullius' words were followed by entreaties from the crowd, and on every side the men clamoured for the commander's signal and his order to take up arms.

14. Thinking that what had happened was a good thing, but that it set a bad precedent, the dictator nevertheless decided to carry out the soldiers' wishes. He withdrew from the gathering and privately asked Tullius what was actually going on and how it had happened. Tullius implored the dictator not to think that he had forgotten his military discipline or his own position or the respect due to the commander's office. An agitated crowd normally had the characteristics of its leaders, he said, and his reason for not refusing his leadership was fear that someone else would appear who was of the type that an excited crowd usually picked. He personally would not act contrary to the commander's wishes. But, he added, the dictator, too, should make every effort to see that he had the army under his control: spirits so roused could not be kept waiting, and the men would of their own initiative choose the place and time to do battle if these were not provided by their commander.

As they were conversing, a Gaul attempted to drive off some pack-animals that happened to be grazing outside the palisade, and two Roman soldiers took them from him. Stones were hurled at the soldiers by the Gauls, and then a shout went up from the Roman guard-post, and men charged forward on both sides. It was on the point of developing into a regular battle, but the mêlée was swiftly broken up by the centurions. Tullius' credibility was confirmed for the dictator by this episode, and since the situation allowed for no delay the order was given for pitched battle the following day.

The dictator, however, realized that he was entering the fray relying more on his men's morale than their actual strength, and he therefore proceeded to look around and search for a way to strike fear into the enemy by some trick. By his ingenuity he came up with a novel stratagem that many commanders, both Roman and of other nations, have since employed, a number even in our time. He ordered the mules to be relieved of their packs and, leaving on them only two blankets, had their grooms mount them equipped with weapons that had been either captured or belonged to the sick. Having prepared about a thousand men like this, he interspersed amongst them a hundred mounted troops. He then ordered them to climb the mountains above the camp at night, to hide out in the woods, and not to move from there before receiving the signal from him. At first light, the dictator began to extend his line of battle along the lower slopes of the mountains, doing so carefully in order to have the enemy take a stand facing the mountains. On these the preparation for filling the foe with groundless terror—but a terror more effective than real strength might produce—was already in place. Initially, the Gallic chieftains thought that the Romans would not come down to the level ground. Then, on seeing them suddenly descending, they too, being eager for battle themselves, threw themselves into the fray, and the fighting began before the signal could be given by the commanders.

15. The brunt of the Gallic attack fell on the Roman right wing. Stemming it would have been impossible had not the dictator happened to be on the spot, personally reproaching Sextus Tullius and asking him if that was how he had promised him his men would fight.

Where now were those shouts they uttered when they demanded their weapons, he asked, where the threats they made to go into battle without their commander's order? Look, he said, here was their commander in person, loudly calling them to battle and going in arms ahead of the front line. Just recently they were men ready to lead, but would any now follow—any of these men who were all bluster in camp, and weak-kneed in the field?

They were being told the truth, and shame provided such a stimulus that they charged into the enemy's weapons, all thought of danger gone from their minds. The almost crazed onset at first threw the enemy into confusion, and then, in that confusion, a cavalry charge routed them. Seeing their battle-line wavering at one point, the dictator himself focused his thrust on the left wing, where he could see a large number of the foe coming together, and he also gave those on the mountain the prearranged signal. When a fresh battle-cry went up from that quarter, too, and the Romans could be seen heading downhill at an angle towards the camp of the Gauls, the enemy, scared of being cut off, gave up the fight and made for the camp in a wild rush. There they were met by the master of horse Marcus Valerius who, after overwhelming their right wing, was riding up to the enemy's fortifications. They redirected their flight towards the woods on the hills, but most were intercepted by the grooms who were posing as horsemen; and those whose panic had actually taken them into the woods faced merciless slaughter when the fighting subsided. No one after Marcus Furius celebrated a triumph over the Gauls more richly deserved than did Gaius Sulpicius. A large quantity of gold also accrued from the Gallic spoils, and this Sulpicius consecrated on the Capitol, enclosing it with a barrier of dressed stone.

That same year there were also campaigns conducted by the consuls, with mixed results. The Hernici were defeated and brought to their knees by Gaius Plautius, but his colleague Fabius' battle against the Tarquinienses was marked by lack of caution and circumspection on Fabius' part. Nor was the disastrous outcome for the Romans confined to the battlefield; 307 Roman soldiers were taken prisoner and offered in sacrifice by the Tarquinienses,* and the humiliation of the Roman people was considerably heightened by this unspeakable form of punishment. The calamity was compounded by the devastation of Roman territory in lightning raids made by the Privernates, and by the Veliterni after them.

The same year saw the addition of two tribes, the Pomptine and the Publilian;* votive games that Marcus Furius had promised while dictator were celebrated; and for the first time a law dealing with electoral corruption* was brought before the people, by the plebeian tribune Gaius Poetelius, with the senators' authorization. (By this bill they thought that corruption had been arrested, particularly in the case of 'new men', who had made a practice of doing the rounds of country markets and administrative centres.)

16. Not so welcome to the senators was the bill successfully presented the following year (in the consulship of Gaius Marcius and Gnaeus Manlius*) by the plebeian tribunes Marcus Duillius and Lucius Menenius, which set the rate of interest at 8⅓ per cent.* The plebs were considerably more enthusiastic about ratifying this particular bill.

To add to the new wars scheduled the previous year, the Falisci* also emerged as enemies, over two misdeeds: their young soldiers had fought alongside the Tarquinienses; and they had not returned, when the fetials demanded them, the men who had fled to Falerii after the battle went badly. Responsibility for this war fell to Gnaeus Manlius.

Marcius led an army into the territory of Privernum,* which a long peace had left intact, and gave his men their fill of plunder. In addition to the plentiful supply available, he added an act of munificence: by leaving nothing aside for the state treasury, he aided the ordinary soldiers' efforts to increase their private means. When the Privernates took up a position before their walls with a well-fortified encampment, Marcius called his men to an assembly and said to them: 'I now make you a gift of the enemy's camp and city to plunder, if you promise me that in the battle you will make a brave and determined effort, and that you are not more ready to plunder than to fight.'

The men called for the signal with a resounding shout, and went into battle elated and buoyed with unwavering confidence. There, before the standards, the Sextus Tullius who was mentioned earlier loudly exclaimed: 'Look at how your army is keeping the promises it made to you, commander,' and with that he laid aside his javelin, drew his sword, and charged into the enemy. Tullius was followed by all the front-rank men, who threw back the enemy with their first charge. They then chased the foe in disordered rout to the town, and while they were in the process of moving up the scaling-ladders they received the city's surrender. A triumph was awarded for victory over the Privernates.

Nothing worth mentioning was achieved by the other consul apart from his setting a precedent in having a law proposed in his camp at Sutrium,* through a tribal assembly, which levied a 5 per cent tax on manumitted slaves.* Since no insignificant revenue accrued to the depleted treasury from this law, the senators ratified it. The plebeian tribunes, however, less concerned about the law than they were about the precedent, made it a capital offence for anyone in future to hold an assembly of the people outside Rome. For, they claimed, when soldiers were sworn to obey a consul, there was nothing that could not be brought into law by them, no matter how detrimental to the people it might be.

That same year Gaius Licinius Stolo was prosecuted under his own law by Marcus Popilius Laenas, and fined 10,000 *asses*. The charge was one of possessing, along with his son, a thousand *iugera* of land, and of having fraudulently circumvented the law by releasing the son from his authority.*

17. The two incoming consuls, Marcus Fabius Ambustus and Marcus Popilius Laenas (both in office for the second time), faced

two wars. The first, against the people of Tibur, was an easy one and Laenas, who fought it, simply drove the enemy into their city and devastated their lands. The Falisci and Tarquinienses, however, routed the other consul in the first engagement. Great panic was there generated by the enemy's priests who advanced like Furies, bearing blazing torches and snakes* before them, and throwing the Roman soldiers into disarray with the bizarre sight. And these, like men stupefied and out of their minds, ran back to their own fortifications in a panic-stricken crowd. But then, when the consul, the legates,* and the tribunes ridiculed them and reproached them for their childish fear of fatuous 'wonders', shame suddenly brought a change of heart and they began a blind charge at the very things from which they had run away. Sweeping away the useless paraphernalia of the enemy, they threw themselves onto genuine combatants and drove back their entire battle formation. They also captured the enemy camp that day, and returned as victors after taking huge amounts of plunder, all the while making scornful comments in their soldiers' banter about both the enemy's paraphernalia and their own panic.

There followed an insurrection of the entire Etruscan race,* whose forces, led by the Tarquinienses and Falisci, reached the salt deposits.* To meet this threat Gaius Marcius Rutulus was named dictator—the first member of the plebs to be so—and he declared Gaius Plautius, also from the plebs, as his master of horse. To the patricians, however, it seemed unconscionable that the dictatorship should also be generally accessible, and they made every effort to see that nothing be decreed or made ready for the dictator for prosecuting the war. The upshot was that the people were all the more prompt in authorizing everything that the dictator proposed.

Leaving the city, Rutulus had his troops cross the Tiber on rafts to wherever reports of an enemy presence drew him; and he caught large numbers of marauders off-guard as they wandered out of formation along both banks. He also captured their camp with a surprise attack and took eight thousand enemy prisoners, the rest being killed or driven from Roman territory. For this he celebrated a triumph on the orders of the people, but without senatorial authorization.

As the patricians were reluctant to see consular elections presided over by a plebeian dictator or a plebeian consul, and as the other consul, Fabius, was held back by the war, an *interregnum* followed. The *interreges*, serving in succession, were: Quintus Servilius Ahala,

Marcus Fabius, Gnaeus Manlius, Gaius Fabius, Gaius Sulpicius, Lucius Aemilius, Quintus Servilius, and Marcus Fabius Ambustus.

In the second *interregnum* a dispute arose over the fact that both consuls being appointed to office were patricians. When the tribunes tried to veto the procedure the *interrex* Fabius stated that there was a rule laid down in the Twelve Tables that the people's most recent decree should be binding and have the force of law, and that their votes constituted a decree.* When, by interposing their veto, the tribunes succeeded only in delaying the elections, the two patricians—Gaius Sulpicius Peticus (for his third term) and Marcus Valerius Publicola—were elected as the consuls, and they took office that same day.

18. And so, in the four hundredth year* after Rome's foundation, and the thirty-fifth after it was taken back from the Gauls, this marked the removal of the consulship from the plebs after they had held it for a period of ten years.

Empulum* was captured from the Tiburtines that year, but without any battle worthy of note. The war in this sector was fought either under the auspices of both consuls, as some have recorded, or else the lands of Tarquinii were pillaged by the consul Sulpicius while Valerius simultaneously led his legions against the Tiburtines.

The consuls faced a harder struggle at home with the plebs and their tribunes. Since two patricians had been appointed to the consulship, they believed that it was a matter of honour as well as a moral obligation for them to pass the position on to two men who were also both patricians. Either they should entirely abandon the consulship, if it were now a magistracy open to plebeians, they thought, or they should keep intact what they had received undivided from their fathers. The plebs, on their side, were indignant. What were they living for, they asked, and why be counted as part of the citizen body if, all together, they could not maintain what had been gained by the courage of two men, Lucius Sextius and Gaius Licinius. Better to put up with kings or decemvirs or any other more repressive regime than to accept two patricians as the consuls, they said. Better that than to have no alternation in giving and receiving orders but to see instead the one side perpetually in power and believing the plebs to be by nature fit for nothing other than servitude.

Tribunes to foment disorder were not lacking, either, but with everybody infuriated of their own accord the leaders barely stood out.

The people made a number of fruitless descents to the Campus, and many election days were taken up with factional discord, until finally the determination of the consuls prevailed. Such was the anguish that erupted amongst the plebs that they sadly joined the tribunes, who were now crying out that their freedom was done for and they should leave not just the Campus but the city, too, since it had been taken over and trodden down by the despotism of the patricians. The consuls were then abandoned by a section of the populace, but despite the diminished attendance they were no less energetic in completing the electoral process. The consuls elected—Marcus Fabius Ambustus (for a third term) and Titus Quinctius—were both patricians. In some histories I find Marcus Popilius* named as consul rather than Titus Quinctius.

19. That year saw two wars successfully fought, the Tarquinienses and Tiburtines* being brought to submission by force of arms. The city of Sassula was captured from the Tiburtines, and the rest of their cities would have met the same fate had not the entire people laid down their arms and entrusted themselves to the protection of the consul. A triumph was celebrated for the defeat of the Tiburtines, but otherwise it was a victory marked by leniency. In the case of the Tarquinienses there were brutal reprisals. Many men were killed on the field of battle, and from the hordes of captives 358 were selected to be sent to Rome, all of very high birth. The others were massacred. But the people showed no more mercy to those prisoners sent to Rome: all were flogged and beheaded in the centre of the Forum. Such was the punishment inflicted on the enemy for their sacrifice of the Romans in the forum of Tarquinii. The military success of the Romans also led the Samnites* to seek friendly relations with them. Their delegates were given a warm reply, and the Samnites were accepted as allies with a treaty.

The Roman plebs did not enjoy the same success at home as in war. Despite having their interest payments alleviated through the rate being fixed at one-twelfth, the poor were overwhelmed by the principal itself and were being reduced to bondage. Thus the plebs, faced with their personal difficulties, could not turn their thoughts to the question of the two patrician consuls, to concerns about the elections, or to public affairs in general. Both consulships remained with the patricians, the consuls elected being Gaius Sulpicius Peticus (for the fourth time) and Marcus Valerius Publicola (for the second).

The state was now focused on war with Etruria as the rumour was rife that the people of Caere* had joined up with the Tarquinienses because of their kinship. However, a delegation from the Latins then turned attention to the Volsci since it brought news that the Volsci had raised an army and equipped it with weapons, and that this was now closing in on Latin territory. From there, they said, it would enter and plunder Roman farmlands. The Senate decided that neither emergency should be ignored, and gave orders for legions to be enrolled for both operations, and for the consuls to proceed to sortition for their areas of responsibility. Subsequently, however, the balance tilted towards the Etruscan war as a greater concern after a letter arrived from the consul Sulpicius, to whom Tarquinii had fallen as his responsibility. It was learned from this that raids had been conducted on lands in the neighbourhood of the Roman salt deposits, that some of the spoils had been carried off into the territory of Caere, and that there was no doubt that young men of Caere had been amongst the raiders.

The Senate therefore recalled the consul Valerius, who had been sent against the Volsci and was encamped close to the border of Tusculum, and ordered him to name a dictator. Valerius named Titus Manlius,* son of Lucius. After naming Aulus Cornelius Cossus as his master of horse, Manlius, satisfied with the consular army for the task, declared war on Caere with the authority of the Senate and on the orders of the people.

20. It was only then that the people of Caere were truly overcome with dread of war. It was as if the words of their enemy had greater power to show them war was coming than had their own actions in provoking the Romans by their depredations; and they could see how insufficient their strength was for that conflict. They now regretted the depredations, and they cursed the people of Tarquinii for inciting them to insurrection. Nobody prepared weapons or made ready for war; instead they clamoured one and all for representatives to be dispatched to seek pardon for their mistake.

When the representatives came to the Senate they were redirected to the people. There they called upon the gods whose sacred objects they had piously taken in and looked after during the Gallic war, and asked that the now-prosperous Romans have as much pity for *them* as the people of Caere had earlier had for the Roman people in *their* adversity. Turning to the shrine of Vesta, they appealed to the pure and pious hospitality they had accorded the Roman flamens and Vestals, and asked whether one could really believe that those with such a claim on their gratitude could suddenly and without reason become their enemies. Could one believe that any hostile act of theirs was premeditated and not occasioned by a sudden onset of madness? That they would undermine by recent misdeeds the benefits they had conferred in the past, and especially benefits that had been received with such gratitude? That they would make an enemy of the Roman people when these were now enjoying prosperity and great military success—and after cultivating friendship with them when they were in difficulties? They should not use the word 'premeditation' of what should be termed 'constraint' and 'necessity'.

The people of Tarquinii, they continued, in traversing their territory with an army ready for war had asked them for nothing more than a passage through, but had drawn along with them from there a number of their peasants who joined them in the pillaging forays with which the people of Caere were now being charged. If the Romans wanted those men turned over to them, they were ready to turn them over; if they wanted them punished, they would be dealt with. But Caere had been a sanctuary of the Roman people, a refuge for their priests and a shelter for their sacred objects; in recognition of its hospitality accorded the Vestals, and the respect paid to their gods, the Romans should leave it intact and unhurt by the charge of making war.

What impressed the people was not so much the present circumstances as the past services, and they preferred to forget the bad rather than the good that had been done. The people of Caere were accordingly granted peace, and it was decided that a hundred-year truce should be concluded and recorded on bronze.* The main thrust of the war was then directed against the Falisci, who were guilty of the same crime, but the enemy was nowhere to be found. After widespread devastation of Faliscan territory, the Romans stopped short of attacking their cities. The legions were led back to Rome and the remainder of the year was spent repairing walls and towers; and a temple was also dedicated to Apollo.

21. At the end of the year the consular elections were disrupted by a struggle between the patricians and the plebs. The tribunes said they would not allow the elections to be held unless they were held in accordance with the Licinian law, and the dictator was determined to

remove the consulship entirely from the constitution rather than have it open to patricians and plebeians alike. This led to regular adjournments of the assembly, and when the dictator left office the state reverted to an *interregnum*. The *interreges* found the plebeians pitted against the patricians, and the factional wrangling went on until the appointment of the eleventh *interrex*. The tribunes kept making much of their defence of the Licinian law, but for the plebs the growing burden of interest was a worry closer to home, and their private anxieties burst forth in the public disputes.

Weary of the confrontations, the senators ordered the *interrex* Lucius Cornelius Scipio, in the interests of national unity, to respect the Licinian law in the consular elections, and Valerius Publicola was given a colleague from the plebs, Gaius Marcius Rutulus. With hearts now inclined towards unity, the new consuls also attempted to alleviate the problem of interest, which seemed to be the sole cause of dissension. They made the repayment of debt a matter of public policy, and in that connection appointed a board of five whom they called 'bankers' (from their supervision of finances). Because of their even-handed and painstaking work, these men—Gaius Duillius, Publius Decius Mus, Marcus Papirius, Quintus Publilius, and Titus Aemilius*—deserved the fame that attends their names in all historical records. It was a business that was very difficult to handle, very often painful for both parties and always for one or other of them, and these men managed it with restraint in general, and by an outlay of public moneys that involved no waste. For there were loans long outstanding that were made more difficult by the indolence of the debtors rather than inability to pay, and these they managed to settle. Either they had the treasury pay them off (there were tables with cash set up in the Forum), with a guarantee first taken in the interests of the people, or they had an evaluation settle the matter, with fair prices settled on for the debtors' property. The result was that a huge amount of debt was wiped off not only without harm done to either party but even without objections from either.

Unjustified fear of a war with Etruria then arose when a report arrived of the twelve peoples having banded together, and this made the appointment of a dictator necessary. Gaius Julius* was appointed, and appointed in his camp, since the decree of the Senate was sent to the consuls on campaign. He was assigned Lucius Aemilius as his master of horse. Otherwise all remained quiet abroad.

22. At home an attempt was made by the dictator to have two patricians elected as the consuls, and this led to an *interregnum*. There were two *interreges* in succession, Gaius Sulpicius and Marcus Fabius, and they managed to do what the dictator had unsuccessfully attempted, that is to have two patrician consuls elected (the plebs being now more flexible after recently benefiting from alleviation of their debts). Elected were Gaius Sulpicius Peticus himself, the earlier of the two *interreges* to leave office, and Titus Quinctius Poenus (some give Kaeso as Quinctius' *praenomen*, others Gaius). Both set off for war, Quinctius against the Falisci and Sulpicius against the Tarquinienses, but they nowhere met the enemy on the battlefield, and by burning and pillaging they waged their wars against the countryside rather than against men. The obstinacy of both peoples was eventually overcome by this, as by a long, lingering disease, and they sought a truce, first from the consuls and then, with their permission, from the Senate. They succeeded in gaining a forty-year truce.

And so, with the worry of two wars that threatened now removed, it was decided that a census should be conducted while there was a respite from fighting; for the clearing of debts had entailed a change of ownership of many properties. However, when notice was given of an assembly for the election of censors, Gaius Marcius Rutulus, who had been the first dictator to come from the plebs, upset the harmony between the classes when he announced that he would stand for the office. It did indeed appear that his action was poorly timed, because both consuls then serving happened to be patricians, and they declared that they would not accept his candidacy. But Rutulus doggedly held to his purpose and, in addition, the tribunes did everything within their power to help him (in order to regain the right they had lost in the consular elections). Moreover, there was no high office to which the man's own merit was unequal, and the plebs were wishing to be summoned to their share of the censorship as well, through the agency of the same man who had blazed the trail to the dictatorship. Nor was there any disagreement with this in the election: Marcius was elected †censor along with Manlius Naevius†.*

This year also saw a dictator in office, Marcus Fabius, not because there was any serious threat of war, but simply to prevent the application of the Licinian law at the consular elections. The dictator was assigned Quintus Servilius as his master of horse. But the dictatorship made the consensus of the patricians no more effective at the consular elections than it had been at the elections for the censors. (23.) Marcus Popilius Laenas was returned from the plebs, Lucius Cornelius Scipio from the patricians.

Moreover, fortune gave greater glory to the plebeian consul. News arrived that a huge army of the Gauls had encamped in Latin territory and, since Scipio was incapacitated with a serious illness, Popilius was given the Gallic war as an extraordinary command. Popilius energetically enrolled an army, ordering all the military-age recruits to come together under arms at the temple of Mars outside the Porta Capena*, while the quaestors were told to bring the standards from the treasury to the same spot. After providing a full complement for four legions, Popilius entrusted the surplus soldiers to the praetor Publius Valerius Publicola, and recommended to the senators that they enrol another army that the state could hold in reserve to meet the unforeseen emergencies of war.

When all was ready and prepared to his satisfaction, Popilius proceeded towards the enemy; and so that he could ascertain their strength before experiencing it in a final dangerous confrontation he seized a hill as close to the Gallic camp as he possibly could and began to construct a palisade. The Gauls are a ferocious race, with an innate appetite for fighting, and when they saw the Roman standards in the distance they immediately deployed their battle-line in order to engage at once. But then they saw that the Roman troops were not being marched down to level ground and that they were trying to protect themselves both with the high ground and with a palisade. They therefore assumed that they were panic-stricken and at the same time thought them an easier target because they were at that moment intent on their work, and so they attacked with a furious yell. There was no interruption of the work on the Roman side—it was the *triarii* who were doing the building—and the fighting started with the *hastati* and *principes*,* who had been standing alert and under arms in front of the building crew.

In addition to their courage, the elevated location also helped the Romans: so far from falling ineffectually, as happens on level ground, all their javelins and spears unfailingly pierced their target because they were kept accurate by their weight. The Gauls were overwhelmed by these projectiles, which either pierced their bodies or stuck in their shields, making them very heavy to wield. After having almost scaled the slope with their charge, they first stopped, unsure what to do, but then, when their very hesitation diminished their fervour and increased that of their enemy, they were pushed back and in their haste trampled over each other, producing a more horrendous bloodbath amongst themselves than the carnage of the battle. In the chaotic mêlée more were trodden under foot than were killed by the sword.

24. Victory for the Romans was not yet assured, however—another ordeal was awaiting them on the descent to the plain. The huge numbers of the Gauls made them totally insensitive to such losses and, as if a new army were arising again, they were urging on fresh troops against their victorious enemy. The Roman impetus faltered and they came to a halt. Exhausted though they were, they had to face another battle and, in addition, the consul had had his left shoulder run almost completely through by a Gallic spear as he was manoeuvring with too little care in the front line, and had momentarily left the battle. The victory was all but lost through the delay, when the consul, his wound bandaged, rode back to the front line and said: 'Why are you just standing there, soldier? Your fight is not with a Latin or a Sabine foe, whom you can defeat with your weapons and turn from an enemy into an ally. We have drawn our swords against wild animals, and we must either shed their blood or give them ours. You have pushed them out of your camp; you have driven them headlong down the valley; and you are standing on the prostrate corpses of your enemy. Cover the plains with the same slaughter with which you covered the hills! Do not wait for them to run away from you as you just stand around! You must advance and attack the enemy!'

Roused to action again by these exhortations, the Romans dislodged the front maniples of the Gauls* and then, in wedge-formation, burst through to their centre. With that, the barbarian formation came apart and, having no clear orders or chain of command, they turned their attack on their own comrades. Scattered throughout the countryside, and carried in their flight even beyond their own camp, they made for the highest point that met their eyes in the generally uniform range of hills before them, namely the citadel of Alba.*

The consul did not continue the pursuit beyond the camp: his wound was causing him distress and he was also reluctant to march his army below hills occupied by the enemy. He gave the men all the plunder from the camp and led back to Rome a triumphant army rich with Gallic spoils.* The consul's wound delayed the triumph and also made the Senate eager for a dictator (so someone could hold the elections while the consuls were out of action). The man appointed dictator, Lucius Furius Camillus* (who was assigned Publius Cornelius Scipio as his master of horse), restored to the patricians their ancient monopoly of the consulship. Because of this favour Camillus won massive support amongst the patricians; he was himself elected consul and then announced the election of Appius Claudius Crassus as his colleague.

25. Before the new consuls entered office, Popilius celebrated his triumph over the Gauls. This was welcomed with great enthusiasm by the plebs who, muttering among themselves, asked whether anyone now regretted having a plebeian as consul. At the same time they had harsh words for the dictator. He had, they said, in having himself declared consul while he was dictator, received his payment for flouting the Licinian law—a payment that was more dishonourable for his personal greed than the wrong he had done to the state.

The year was noteworthy for its many different turbulent events. The Gauls came down from the Alban Hills because they had been unable to tolerate the severity of the winter, and they roamed through the plains and coastal areas pillaging the land. The sea was prey to Greek fleets,* as were the shoreline of Antium, the region of Laurentum, and the mouth of the Tiber. This resulted in seaborne bandits on one occasion running across those on land and fighting an indecisive battle, with the Gauls leaving for their camp and the Greeks retiring to their ships, neither of them sure whether they had lost or won. But, of all the threats, by far the greatest came from the meetings of the Latin peoples at the grove of Ferentina,* and the unequivocal reply they gave to the Roman request for troops. The Romans should stop giving orders to those whose help they needed, they said; the Latins would bear arms for their own freedom, not for another's imperial aspirations.

Caught between two concurrent foreign wars, and with the added anxiety of a defection of their allies, the Senate saw that men whom loyalty to an oath had not held in check had to be checked by fear. They therefore instructed the consuls to apply the full powers of their office in raising troops since the desertion of their allies meant relying on a citizen army. It is said that ten legions were conscripted,* each comprising 4,200 infantry and 300 cavalry, made up of men of military age from the countryside as well as the city. If today, in the face of foreign aggression, one were to muster the existing forces of the Roman people—and the world can barely contain them—raising such an army would still not be easy. Such are the problems caused by the only things deriving from the growth of our power—riches and luxury.*

Among the distressing events of that year was the death of one of the consuls, Appius Claudius, amidst the actual preparations for war. Command thus returned to Camillus, who remained sole consul, since the senators decided that it was inappropriate to appoint a dictator over him. (Either they thought a man of his distinction should not be subjected to a dictatorship, or perhaps they were influenced by the happy omen of his *cognomen* in the context of a Gallic emergency.) The consul assigned two legions to the defence of the city, and divided the remaining eight between himself and Lucius Pinarius. Remembering his father's military prowess, Camillus himself assumed the direction of the Gallic war without sortition, and he instructed the praetor to see to the defence of the maritime areas and keep the Greeks away from the shores. Then, marching down into Pomptine territory, he picked out a suitable location for a permanent camp. He did not wish to engage on open ground unless he were forced into it, and he believed that keeping them from pillaging would be enough to bring low an enemy who were obliged to live on plunder.

26. While the Romans remained quietly at their guard-posts, a Gaul came forward* who stood out because of his size and armour. He obtained silence by beating his shield with his spear and then, by means of an interpreter, issued a challenge for one of the Romans to decide the issue with him in a duel. There was a young military tribune, Marcus Valerius,* who thought himself no less deserving of that honour than Titus Manlius, and after ascertaining that he had the consul's approval, he advanced in arms to a point between the armies. The human aspect of the contest, however, was overshadowed by divine intervention; for, as the Roman closed with the Gaul, a raven suddenly landed on his helmet,* facing his adversary. The tribune first welcomed this as a heaven-sent omen, and then made a prayer that whichever god or goddess had sent him the favourable augury would stand by him with grace and favour. Incredibly, the bird not

only kept the position it had taken, but whenever the men clashed it raised itself with its wings and attacked the face and eyes of the Roman's opponent with its beak and talons. Finally, terrified by such a portentous manifestation, and dazed and half-blinded, the Gaul was cut down by Valerius, and the raven took off and vanished as it headed east.

Up to this point the guard-posts on both sides had remained calm, but when the tribune started stripping the spoils from the body of his dead adversary, the Gauls no longer held back at their posts, and there was an even swifter rush towards the victor by the Romans. A scuffle broke out there, around the body of the prostrate Gaul, and that turned into a ferocious brawl; and soon the action was not confined to the units of the closest guard-posts but included the legions, which came pouring out from both sides. Camillus ordered his men to advance into the fray, elated as they were by the tribune's victory, and elated, too, at having the gods with them and giving them support; and pointing to the tribune, adorned with his spoils, he said repeatedly: 'This is the man to emulate, soldiers! Bring the Gallic hordes down to the ground about their leader!'

Gods and men were present in that battle, and the struggle with the Gauls reached a conclusion that was never in doubt—to such an extent had both armies foreseen a result mirroring that of the soldiers' duel. The battle against the Gauls who initiated the fight, and whose clash had brought others into it, was fierce; but the rest of the Gallic horde turned to flight before coming within javelin range. Initially they scattered amongst the Volsci and in the territory of Falernum, and from there they made for Apulia and the Adriatic Sea.*

The consul convened an assembly at which he showered praise on the tribune and presented him with ten oxen and a golden crown. He himself was instructed by the Senate to assume responsibility for the war along the coast, and for this he joined forces with the praetor. As things seemed to be moving slowly in that theatre because of the inertia of the Greeks, who would not commit themselves to pitched battle, Camillus, with senatorial authority, appointed Titus Manlius Torquatus as dictator for the holding of elections. After appointing Cornelius Cossus as his master of horse, the dictator then held the consular elections, and proclaimed as consul, in his absence, Marcus Valerius Corvus (for that was the man's *cognomen* from that point on). Valerius, who was then only twenty-three, was Camillus' rival in glory, and his election was very warmly welcomed by the people. He was given as his colleague from the plebs Marcus Popilius, who would become consul for the fourth time.

As for the Greeks, no noteworthy action was taken against them by Camillus; they were not fighters on land, nor were the Romans on the sea. Finally, since they kept away from the shoreline, their water supply, as well as all the other necessities, ran out and they left Italy. There is no certainty about the people or race to which the fleet belonged. I incline most to the belief that it was to tyrants of Sicily, Greece proper being at that time exhausted by civil wars and already trembling before the power of Macedon.

27. The armies were demobilized, and there was both peace abroad and, thanks to the harmony between the orders, tranquillity at home; but so things should not be going too well,* a plague then struck the city. That forced the Senate to order the decemvirs to consult the Sibylline Books, and at these men's urging a *lectisternium* was held. In that same year a colony was founded at Satricum* by the people of Antium, and the city that the Latins had destroyed was rebuilt. In addition, a treaty was struck in Rome with ambassadors from Carthage* after they came with a request for friendship and an alliance.

The same peaceful state obtained at home and abroad during the consulship of Titus Manlius Torquatus and Gaius Plautius. The rate of interest dropped from 8⅓ per cent to 4⅙ per cent,* and repayment of debt was so arranged that there were three equal instalments over the three-year period, with a fourth payable immediately. Even with such provisions some of the plebs were hard pressed, but the Senate felt more concern about the public credit than individual hardship. The problem was alleviated most by the suppression of the property tax and the levy.

Two years after Satricum was rebuilt by the Volsci, Marcus Valerius Corvus had become consul (his second term) with Gaius Poetelius when word arrived from Latium that spokesmen from the Volsci were doing the rounds of the Latin peoples in order to incite them to war. Valerius was therefore instructed to open hostilities with the Volsci before more enemies came on the scene, and he marched to Satricum with his army on a war footing. There the people of Antium and other Volsci confronted him, having mobilized their troops in advance in the event of action being taken in Rome, and there was no putting off the clash between peoples with a long-standing hatred of each other.

The Volsci, a race with more energy for restarting than conducting a war, were defeated in battle and headed for the defences of Satricum in headlong flight. And having insufficient confidence even in the walls, they surrendered when the town was ringed by troops and was in the process of being captured by means of scaling-ladders. They numbered about four thousand fighting men in addition to the civilian population. The town was demolished and burned, and only the temple of Mater Matuta was spared the torch. The spoils were all turned over to the troops. The four thousand men who surrendered were not considered part of the spoils; the consul had them marched in chains before his chariot during his triumph, after which they were put on sale, and brought a large sum of money to the treasury. There are some who have it on record that this large horde of prisoners consisted of slaves, and this is more plausible than that men who surrendered would have been put on sale.

28. These consuls were followed by Marcus Fabius Dorsuo and Servius Sulpicius Camerinus. War with the Aurunci* then broke out following a surprise plundering expedition by them and, as there was fear that this action taken by one people might have been the joint plan of all of Latin nationality, Lucius Furius was made dictator (as if to face a Latium already under arms). Furius appointed Gnaeus Manlius Capitolinus as his master of horse. Then (the normal practice in major crises) he proclaimed a suspension of legal business, and a troop-levy without exemptions was held, after which the legions were led out with all possible dispatch to face the Aurunci. These were found to have the mentality of marauders rather than a true enemy and the war was over with the first battle. Nevertheless, as it was they who had initiated hostilities and committed themselves unhesitatingly to battle, the dictator felt he should call upon the help of the gods and in the midst of the fighting he made a vow of a temple to Juno Moneta.* Returning victorious to Rome, he was now duty-bound to fulfil the vow and he resigned the dictatorship. The Senate gave the order for duumvirs to be appointed for the construction of a temple consistent with the greatness of the Roman people, and a spot was earmarked for it on the citadel which had been the site of Marcus Manlius Capitolinus' house. The consuls then availed themselves of the dictator's army for the war with the Volsci, and they took Sora* from the enemy with a surprise attack.

The temple of Moneta was consecrated the year after it had been promised in the vow, in the consulship of Gaius Marcius Rutulus (his third term) and Titus Manlius Torquatus (his second). A prodigy immediately followed the consecration, one similar to the prodigy of old on the Alban mount:* stones fell as rain, and in the daytime darkness appeared to spread across the sky. When the Books were consulted and the city was full of religious foreboding, the Senate decided that a dictator should be appointed to establish days of religious observance.* The appointee was Publius Valerius Publicola, who was given Quintus Fabius Ambustus as his master of horse. It was further decided that, in addition to the Roman tribes, the neighbouring peoples should also make supplicatory offerings, and a calendar was arranged of the days on which each was to make its offerings.

Tradition has it that there were severe judgements brought against usurers by the people that year after they were indicted by the aediles. The state now returned to an *interregnum*, though no clear reason for it has been transmitted in the sources, and following the *interregnum* two patrician consuls were elected (making it look as if this was the reason): Marcus Valerius Corvus (his third term) and Aulus Cornelius Cossus.

29. From this point* my account will deal with wars that were more important in terms of the strength of the enemies, the distance of the regions involved, and the length of time the fighting took. That year military operations were launched against the Samnites,* a wealthy and powerful people; and after the Samnite war, which was fought with varying fortunes, Pyrrhus became the enemy, and after Pyrrhus the Carthaginians. What massive undertakings these were! How often did we face situations of extreme danger so that the empire could be raised up to its present greatness, which is now barely sustainable!

The cause of the Romans' war with the Samnites, with whom they had earlier had a treaty and friendly relations, came from without and did not originate with the two peoples themselves. Relying on their greater strength, the Samnites had launched an unprovoked attack on the Sidicini* who, forced by their weakness to have recourse to a richer people for help, joined forces with the Campanians.* The Campanians, however, brought to their allies' defence a reputation rather than real strength, enervated as they were by luxurious living, and they were defeated in the lands of the Sidicini by a side hardened in armed combat. They then drew upon themselves the whole brunt of the war. For the Samnites now ignored the Sidicini and proceeded to attack the citadel of their neighbours—victory over the Campanians would be just as easy, and there would be more plunder and glory. They occupied Tifata,* a range of hills overlooking Capua, with a powerful garrison, and then went down in battle formation into the plain lying between Capua and Tifata. Here a second engagement took place, and the Campanians, who came off badly, were driven behind their fortifications. The strongest of their troops had been slaughtered, there was no hope of help from close by, and so they were compelled to seek aid from the Romans.*

30. The Campanian representatives were ushered into the Senate, where they spoke very much as follows:*

'Senators: the people of Capua have sent us to you as their representatives to request of you a permanent friendship and immediate assistance. Had we made this request when things were going well for us, that friendship would have been formed earlier, but on a less firm footing. That is because we would have remembered that we began our friendship with you as equals, and would perhaps have been just as much your friends as now, but less subordinate and less indebted to you. As things are, should we now be brought into a friendship with you through your compassion, and should we be defended by you in our time of adversity, we must perforce also feel an obligation for the favour you have done us, so as not to be found ungrateful and unworthy of any help, divine or human.

'And (heaven knows!) the fact that the Samnites were your friends and allies before us is not, I think, good reason for us, too, not to be welcomed into your friendship; that is reason only for their having precedence in terms of seniority and status within it. There is no clause in your treaty with the Samnites to prevent you from concluding new treaties.

'In your view a valid enough reason for friendship has always been simply the fact that anyone appealing to you wanted to be your friend. We are Campanians and, even if our present circumstances prevent us from boasting, we take second place to no people apart from you in the eminence of our city and the productivity of our lands. And in coming to seek your friendship we bring no insignificant addition to your prosperity. As for the Aequi and the Volsci, constant enemies of this city, they will have us on their backs with every move they make; and such action as you will have taken first for our protection, that action we shall always take to promote your empire and your glory. Crush the races that stand between you and us—something that both your good fortune and your valour promise will very soon happen— and you will have sovereignty without interruption all the way to us.

'It is a bitter and sad confession that our unfortunate situation forces us to make, Senators, but we have reached the point where, Campanians though we are, we are to be in the power either of our friends or our enemies. If you defend us, we shall be in your power; if you abandon us, in the Samnites'. So think about whether you want Capua and the whole of Campania added to *your* strength or to Samnium's.

'It is only fair, Men of Rome, that your sympathy and aid should be accessible to all, but it should especially be so to those who have overstretched themselves responding to others' cries for help, and then, like us, found they were in dire need of it themselves. Actually, our fight for the Sidicini was in name only; it was really for ourselves. We saw a neighbouring people as the target of villainous marauding by the Samnites and we saw, too, that once the Sidicini had gone up in flames, that conflagration would pass over to us. In fact, it is not from resentment over an injury they have suffered that the Samnites are coming to attack us; they are happy that they have been offered a pretext to do so. If this were simply satisfying a longing for revenge rather than taking an opportunity to indulge their greed, would it not have been enough to have cut down our legions once in the territory of the Sidicini and again in Campania itself? What sort of anger is this, anger so furious that the blood shed in two battles could not sate it? Add to that the destruction of our fields, plunder driven off (both men and farm animals), farmhouses burned and wrecked— everything laid waste by fire and the sword. Could their anger not have been satisfied by this? No, it is their greed that has to be satis- fied. This is what brings them rushing to attack Capua; they want to destroy a magnificent city or have it for their own. But, Men of Rome, *you* should take it over by doing us a kindness rather than let them have it through doing us wrong.

'I am not addressing a people that refuses just wars; however, merely let them see your support for us and I do not think you will have to go to war. The disdain of the Samnites reaches only as far as us; it goes no further. Thus we can be protected by the mere shadow of your assistance, Men of Rome, and we shall consider whatever we have after that, and whatever we shall be, as being all yours. It will be for you that Campania's farmland will be cultivated, for you that the city of Capua's population will grow. For us you will be founders, parents, and immortal gods, and there will be no colony of yours that will outdo us in deference and loyalty to you.

'Give the Campanians the sign of your divine and invincible support, Men of Rome, and tell them to keep alive the hope that Capua will remain intact. When we were setting off from there, can you imagine the great crowd—one made up of all sorts of people—that was milling around to see us off? Can you imagine how the whole scene was full of prayers and tears? How great do you suppose the suspense is now amongst the senate and people of Capua, and our wives and children, too? I know for sure that they are all in a crowd at the gates, their eyes trained on the road from Rome. What reply would you have us take back to these people full of worry and anxiety? One answer will bring salvation, victory, light, and freedom; the other—no, I shudder to predict what that might bring! So consider now our fate, whether we are to be your future allies and friends, or whether we are to have no future at all.'

31. The representatives were then ushered out while the Senate conducted its deliberations. It struck a large number of the members that Capua was Italy's largest and wealthiest city, and that its fertile lands, which were also close to the sea, would represent a granary for the Roman people as a cushion against the vagaries of their corn-supply. Nevertheless, their word of honour counted for more than so great a benefit, and the consul, on the authorization of the Senate, gave the following reply:*

'Men of Campania: the Senate deems you worthy of our aid, but friendly relations with you should be established only on condition that no older friendship and alliance is thereby violated. The Samnites are bound to us by a treaty, and so we refuse to take up arms against them, an act that would harm the sanctity of the gods before harming men. But, as is only right and just, we shall send a deputation to our allies and friends to ask them to ensure that no violence is done to you.'

The leader of the delegation, following the instructions they had brought with them, replied as follows:

'Since you are unwilling to resort to justifiable force to protect what is ours against unjustified force, then you will at least defend what is yours. Accordingly, Senators, we surrender to your and the Roman people's authority the Campanian people and the city of Capua, its lands, the temples of the gods, and everything else, both divine and secular, ready now to suffer whatever we shall suffer as subjects who have surrendered to you.'*

With these words the representatives all fell to their knees in the vestibule of the Senate house, stretching forth their hands to the consuls and weeping copiously. The senators were deeply touched by the changeability of human fortunes. Here was an exceedingly wealthy people, famed for its high living and its pride, a people from whom its neighbours had sought assistance a short while ago; and now its spirit was so broken that that it was of its own accord placing itself and all its possessions under another's authority. They felt now that honour demanded that they not betray those who had surrendered,* and they thought that the Samnite people would not be acting justly if they attacked lands and a city that had come into the hands of the Roman people through surrender. And so it was decided that emissaries be sent immediately to the Samnites. The emissaries were instructed to inform the Samnites of the entreaties of the Campanians and the Senate's reply that took cognizance of its friendship with Samnium; and finally they were to point out that this was a case of surrender. The emissaries were to ask the Samnites, in consideration of their alliance and friendly relations, to show mercy on those who had surrendered to them and not take up arms against lands that had become the property of the Roman people. If the gentle approach was making little headway, they were to issue a warning to the Samnites, on behalf of the people and Senate of Rome, to keep their hands off the city of Capua and the lands of Campania.

The emissaries met with a hostile response as they raised these points in the assembly of the Samnites. Not only did the Samnites defiantly reply that they would fight this war, but their magistrates filed out of the Senate house while the emissaries were still standing there. They summoned the prefects of their cohorts, and loudly ordered them to leave immediately on a marauding expedition into Campanian territory.

32. When news of this embassy was brought back to Rome the senators set aside consideration of all other matters. They sent the fetial priests to demand satisfaction and, because this was not forthcoming, they then made a formal declaration of war,* passing a

resolution that the matter be put to the people for ratification at the earliest possible moment. On the order of the people, the two consuls set off from the city with two armies, Valerius heading for Campania and Cornelius for Samnium. Valerius then encamped near Mount Gaurus, and Cornelius near Saticula.*

It was Valerius that the Samnite legions met first, since this was the area where they thought the whole brunt of the war would be concentrated, and in addition they had anger inciting them against the Campanians, who had been so ready at one moment to supply aid against them, and at another to ask others to supply it. On seeing the Roman camp, they to a man aggressively demanded the battle-signal, declaring that the Romans would have as much luck in assisting the Campanians as the Campanians had had in assisting the Sidicini.

When he had spent not many days on light skirmishes to test his enemy, Valerius put up the battle-signal and addressed a few words of encouragement to his men. They were not to let a new war and a new enemy cause them fear, he said—the further from the city they advanced with their arms, the weaker were the peoples they came up against. They were not to gauge the mettle of the Samnites on the basis of defeats these had inflicted on the Sidicini and the Campanians. Whatever the quality of the two sides in a struggle, one had to come off the loser. In the case of the Campanians, their defeat quite clearly resulted from their environment of excessive luxury and its enervating effects more than from their enemy's strength. Besides, what were two successful wars fought by the Samnites in all those centuries compared with so many glorious exploits of the Roman people who, since the city's foundation, could count to their credit almost more triumphs than years? They were a people who had conquered in war, and now had under their control, everything surrounding them—the Sabines, Etruria, the Latins, the Hernici, the Aequi, the Volsci, the Aurunci—and who had cut down the Gauls in so many encounters and eventually compelled them to run off to the sea and their ships.*

They should go into battle, said Valerius, all of them confident in their glorious military records and courage, and they should also consider under whose leadership and auspices it was that they must enter combat. They should consider whether he was to be listened to only as a man giving pompous encouragement, dynamic in words alone but lacking hard military experience, or as one who was himself skilled in handling weapons, in marching before the standards, in taking his place right in the thick of the fighting.

'Men,' he said, 'it is my actions, not my words, that I want you to bear in mind, and it is not only discipline but an example that I want you to look for in me! I won for myself three consulships and the greatest plaudits not through politicking and the cliques that are common among the nobles, but by this right hand of mine. There was a time when one could have said: "Yes, but you were a patrician and one descended from the country's liberators, and that family of yours held the consulship in the very year that this city first had a consul." Nowadays, however, the consulship is open to all without distinction, to us patricians and to you members of the plebs, and it is a prize not awarded for birth, as before, but for individual merit. And so, my soldiers, keep your eyes on all the highest honours. If you men have, with the approval of the gods, given me this new *cognomen* Corvinus,* the old *cognomen* of our family—Publicola—has not vanished from my memory. I have always respected (and respect still) the Roman plebs, and I have done so in war, and at home; as private civilian, and in magistracies small and great; and with the same steadfastness throughout all my subsequent consulships. Now, with regard to what is in hand, join me in seeking, with heaven's help, a new experience for us—a triumph over the Samnites.'

33. No other leader* had ever been on better terms with his men through sharing the soldiers' tasks, without demur, with the lowest in rank. Furthermore, in military games, when men of similar age would engage in contests of speed or strength, he was affable and easy-going; win or lose, he had the same expression on his face, and he was not above accepting a challenge from anyone who offered it. In his actions he was as accommodating as the situation allowed, and in his speech he was as concerned for another's freedom of expression as he was for his own dignity; and—a feature than which nothing is more appealing to the people—his conduct during his magistracies was the same as when he had been a candidate. So it was that the whole army marched from the camp with unbelievable fervour after listening to their commander's words of encouragement.

The battle began, to an extent hitherto unparalleled in any encounter, with equally high hopes on both sides, with strength equally matched, and with a self-confidence that nevertheless lacked disdain for the enemy. The Samnites' fighting spirit was enhanced by their recent exploits and their twin victories a few days earlier, the Romans' by four hundred years of glorious achievements and victories going back to the city's foundation. Even so, facing a new enemy caused both sides heightened anxiety.

The engagement served to demonstrate the resolve of both, for they clashed with such determination that for some time neither battle-line would give ground. Then, since the enemy could not be driven back by force, the consul thought panic should be instilled into them and he sent in his cavalry in an attempt to create confusion in their front ranks. But when he saw that the cavalry units, which were operating in a confined space, were failing to create disorder, and that they could not penetrate the enemy, he rode back to the front-rank troops, jumped down from his horse, and addressed them.

'Men,' he said, 'that is a job for us, the infantry. Come on! When you see me making a path with the sword wherever I advance into the enemy line, all of you must do the same and cut down those you find before you. That area where now the enemy's raised spears are flashing—all that you will see opened up with devastating carnage!'

Scarcely had he uttered these words when the cavalry, following the consul's instructions, galloped off to the wings, opening a path for the legions to the centre of the enemy line. It was the consul who was the very first to charge the enemy, cutting down anyone he happened to encounter. Fired by the sight of this, every single Roman, on left and right, charged forward and put up a memorable fight. The Samnites took a firm stand against them, but received more wounds than they inflicted.

The battle had already gone on for quite some time, and there was terrible loss of life around the Samnite standards, but as yet no falling back by the enemy at any point—so firmly had they made up their minds to be overcome by death and nothing else. The Romans felt their strength now draining away from fatigue, and saw that not much of the day remained, and so they burned with anger and rushed at the enemy. That was when the enemy first seemed to give ground and the encounter to turn into a rout; that was when Samnites were taken prisoner or killed, and not many of them would have survived had not night broken off what was a victory rather than a battle. For their part the Romans admitted that they had never engaged a more determined enemy, while the Samnites, when asked about the initial cause of their flight after such a determined stand, claimed that for them it was the eyes of the Romans, which seemed to be ablaze, and their wild looks and furious expressions. That more than anything, they said, was the source of their terror. And their admission of that terror was borne out not only by the outcome of the battle, but also by the fact that they left during the night. The next day the Romans took over a camp abandoned by the enemy, and the entire Campanian population came streaming out to it to offer congratulations.

34. However, the joy of this victory was almost spoiled by a serious defeat in Samnium. Setting out from Saticula, the consul Cornelius recklessly led his army into some woods through which ran a deep ravine, on the sides of which the enemy lay in ambush; and he did not see the enemy above his head until he could no longer withdraw in safety. The Samnites were waiting only for Cornelius to bring down his whole army to the lowest part of the ravine, but meanwhile the tribune Publius Decius* spotted one lofty hill in the woods that rose above the enemy camp. To reach it was a formidable undertaking for a column with baggage, but not difficult for light-armed troops.

'Do you see that peak rising above the enemy, Aulus Cornelius?' said Decius to the consul, who was in a state of shock. 'That is the citadel of our hope and safety, if we take it promptly—the Samnites have foolishly ignored it! Give me only the *hastati* and *principes* of a single legion.* When I have reached the top with them, go forward fearlessly from here and save yourself and your army! The enemy will not be able to move without suffering disastrous losses, exposed as he will be to all our projectiles. As for us, the good fortune of the Roman people or our own courage will get us out later.'

Decius was showered with praise by the consul and received the detachment. He then moved unobserved through the woods, and was not spotted by the enemy until he was close to his objective. The surprise struck terror into them all, and by having everybody's attention turned on him Decius gave the consul time to lead the army away to a more favourable location, while he himself established a position at the top of the hill. As the Samnites moved their troops this way and that, they lost their chance on both counts. They could not follow the consul except along the same ravine in which they had shortly before had him exposed to their projectiles; but no more could they march their troops up the hill that Decius had seized above them. However, their blazing anger goaded them more against those who had snatched away a good opportunity of success, as also did consideration of the proximity of their location and their small numbers. At one moment they wanted to surround the hill entirely with an armed cordon so as to cut Decius off from the consul, at the next to leave a path open for him so they could attack him and his men as they came down to the ravine. They were still unsure of their choice when night came upon them.

Decius at first hoped to engage the enemy from his higher position as they climbed the hill. Then, to his surprise, he realized that they were not starting to attack him, and that, if they were put off such a plan by the difficult terrain, they were not fencing him in with siege-works and a palisade, either. He called his centurions to him and said: 'What is this—this military incompetence, this lack of action? How did those people gain a victory over the Sidicini and the Campanians? You can see them moving their troops this way and that, at one moment concentrating them, at the next drawing them out. Nobody is getting down to work, although we could, by now, have been surrounded by a palisade. We'd be just like them if we stayed here longer than is good for us. Come on, come with me while some light remains, so we can find out where they are placing their sentry-posts and where there is a way out of here.' He then carefully examined the whole situation, wearing an ordinary soldier's cloak, and taking along his centurions likewise dressed as common soldiers, so the enemy would not recognize the leader on his reconnaissance expedition.

35. After that Decius posted sentries and ordered the word passed around for all to take up their weapons when the trumpet-call was given for the second watch,* and to gather before him. When they had quietly gathered in accordance with his instructions, he said:

'Men: you must maintain this silence while you listen to me, and forget the usual cheering of the soldier. When I have explained my idea to you, those of you who are in favour quietly cross over to the right, and whichever side has the majority, it is their decision that will stand. Now listen to what I have in mind. The enemy has you surrounded here not because you fled or were left behind because of your lethargy. It was by your courage that you took the position, and by your courage you should get out of it. By coming here, you have preserved a superb army for the people of Rome. Save yourselves now by breaking out of here! Few though you are, you have brought help to greater numbers of men, and you yourselves should need help from no one else. Your fight is with an enemy whose lethargy yesterday made him fail to capitalize on an opportunity to wipe out our entire army, and who did not see above his own head, until it was taken by us, this hill so favourably situated. We are so few, and yet he with all his thousands of men could not prevent us from climbing up, and while we occupied the position he failed to surround it with a palisade when so much daylight still remained. You eluded this enemy while his eyes were open and he was on his guard. You should therefore take him by surprise—no, you *must* take him by surprise— while he sleeps. Our situation is such that, rather than propose some plan of campaign, I can only point out to you what *has* to be done. Nor can there be any discussion of whether you stay or leave; fortune has left you nothing but your weapons and the courage to use them, and you must die of hunger and thirst if we fear the sword more than men should, and Roman men at that.

'The only way to safety, then, is to break out of here and get away, and we have to do that in the daytime or at night. But, look, here is something about which there is even less doubt. If we wait for daylight, what hope is there that the enemy will not fence us in with a palisade and a continuous ditch? Below us, as you can see, they have now completely surrounded the hill with their own persons! And if the night is the most favourable time for a break-out, as indeed it is, then this is certainly the most opportune hour of the night. You have assembled at the signal for the second watch, the time that sees men sunk in the deepest sleep. You will advance through sleeping bodies, and you will either escape their notice by your silence while they are off-guard, or you will strike panic into them with a sudden shout if they become aware of you. Just follow me, as you have before, and I shall follow the same fortune that brought us here. All who think this a plan that can save us, come on, move to the right.'

36. They all moved over and then followed Decius as he proceeded through the spaces left unguarded by the sentries. They had already made it halfway through the camp when one soldier, in stepping over the bodies of sentries lying asleep, made a noise when he bumped into a shield. A sentry was awakened by this and nudged the man next to him. Standing up, the two proceeded to wake the others, not knowing whether the intruders were fellow-citizens or the enemy, whether it was the detachment breaking out or whether the consul had taken the camp. Since they could no longer escape notice, Decius ordered his men to raise a shout and paralysed with fear men who were also

drowsy from sleep. This moreover prevented them from taking up their arms promptly, and from blocking the enemy's passage or giving chase. In the alarm and confusion amongst the Samnites, the Roman unit cut down any sentries they met and went on through towards the consul's camp.

A period of darkness still remained, and it looked as though they were now safe when Decius said: 'God bless your courage, soldiers of Rome. All ages to come will sing the praises of your march and your return. But for such gallantry to be brought to attention we need the light of day, and you do not deserve to have silence and darkness obscuring such a glorious return to camp. Let us quietly wait here for dawn.'* His suggestion was accepted, and as soon as dawn broke Decius sent a messenger ahead to the consul. The camp came to life with exuberant joy, and after word was passed around that the men were returning unharmed—men who, for the salvation of all, had exposed their persons to undeniable danger—they each and every one came pouring out to meet them with words of praise and congratulations. They called them all their saviours, they offered praise and thanks to the gods, and they lauded Decius to the skies. This was a triumph in the camp for Decius;* he made his way through the centre with his detachment under arms, and all eyes were on him, as the men put the tribune on a level with the consul in according him every honour.

When he reached the commander's tent, the consul had the men summoned to an assembly by trumpet-call, and there started on a well-deserved speech of praise for Decius, but deferred it when interrupted by Decius himself. Decius proposed that everything be suspended while they had an opportunity in hand, and he convinced the consul to attack the enemy while they were still dazed after their shock during the night and were scattered around the hill in small camps. He added that he also believed that men had been sent out in pursuit of him and that they were wandering about in the woods.

The legions were ordered to take up arms. They marched out of camp, and were led towards the enemy by a more open path, the woods now being better known to them because of the scouts' work. They caught the enemy off-guard with a surprise attack: the Samnite troops were scattered all over, most them without weapons, and were unable to unite, take up arms, or pull back within their stockade.* At first the Romans pushed them back into their camp in fear, and then after creating havoc in the guard-posts they took the camp itself. The shouting carried around the hill and sent everyone running from their positions. So it was that most gave ground to an enemy who was not there! Those whom fear had driven into the stockade (there were about thirty thousand of them*) were all butchered and the camp was sacked.

37. Things having taken this turn, the consul called an assembly at which he accorded Decius not only the praises that he had commenced earlier but also heaped more on him for his fresh exploit. Moreover, apart from the various military presentations, Cornelius made him a further gift* of a golden crown and a hundred oxen, plus an exceptional one that was fat and white, with gilded horns. The soldiers who had been in Decius' squadron were awarded double grain rations on a permanent basis, and on the spot were each given an ox and two tunics. After the consul's presentations, the legions placed a 'siege-crown' of grass* on Decius, with a cheer to express their approval of the award, and a second crown, marking the same honour, was set upon him by his detachment. Wearing these emblems of honour, Decius sacrificed the exceptional ox to Mars, and made a gift of the hundred others to the men who had accompanied him on the mission. To these same soldiers the legions made a contribution of a pound of wholemeal and a half-litre of wine per man; and all of this was done in an atmosphere of great gaiety, with the soldiers' cheers demonstrating their unanimous approval.

There was a third battle fought near Suessula.* After their army was put to flight by Marcus Valerius, the Samnites had summoned from home the cream of their fighting men and decided to put fortune to the test with a final engagement. Messengers came in panic from Suessula to Capua, and from Capua horsemen came post-haste to the consul Valerius to request assistance. The troops were immediately mobilized and, with the baggage left in camp along with a strong garrison, the column was marched along at the double. Not far from the enemy they occupied a very small piece of ground for their encampment—they had no large numbers of animals or camp-followers with them, only their horses.

Anticipating no delay in the engagement, the Samnite army deployed its battle formation, but then, seeing no one coming forward to meet them, they advanced battle-ready to the enemy camp. They saw soldiers on the defence-works, and when the men sent out to reconnoitre reported from all sides on the very restricted size of the camp, they inferred that their enemy were few in number. The whole army now began to demand noisily that they fill in the ditches, break through the defence-works, and burst into the camp, and by such a reckless action the war might have been finished off, but the commanders restrained their men's impetuosity.

The Samnites' large numbers, however, were proving to be a heavy burden on their supplies, and because of the time they had spent earlier at Suessula and the current delay in fighting they were not far away from a dearth of all commodities. They therefore decided that men should be led out to forage in the countryside while the enemy was penned in and fearful. Meanwhile, having come lightly armed and bringing with them only whatever grain they could carry on their backs among their weapons, the Romans would run out of everything if they remained inactive.

When he saw the enemy scattered about the countryside and their armed posts undermanned, the consul addressed a few words of encouragement to his men and led them out for an attack on the enemy camp. This they took with their first shout and their first charge, killing more of the enemy in their tents than in the gateways or on the defence-works. Valerius ordered standards that were captured to be brought together in one place, and left there two legions as a garrison to protect the camp, strictly warning them to refrain from looting it until he himself returned. He then set out, his men formed into a column, after first sending ahead his cavalry which, acting like a ring of huntsmen, drove the scattered Samnites together, and he wreaked slaughter on a massive scale. The terrified Samnites could not agree under which standard they should unite or whether they should head for the camp or run even further. And so widespread was the flight and panic that the consul was brought some forty thousand shields* (though the dead were nowhere near that number) and about 170 military standards, including those that had been captured in the camp. The Romans then returned to the enemy's camp, and there the booty was turned over entirely to the men.

38. The success of this engagement prompted the Falisci, then under a truce, to petition the Senate for a treaty, and the Latins, who had now raised armies, to direct hostilities away from the Romans and towards the Paeligni.* The fame of the operation was not confined to the bounds of Italy, either: the Carthaginians also sent

spokesmen to Rome to offer their congratulations and the gift of a golden crown, weighing twenty-five pounds, which was to be lodged in the sanctuary of Jupiter on the Capitol. The two consuls held a triumph over the Samnites, and following them was Decius, a celebrity after the praise and awards he had received (and in the uncouth jokes of the soldiers* the tribune's name arose no less frequently than the names of the consuls).

After that embassies from Campania and Suessula were granted an audience, and they received a positive response to their request for a garrison to be sent to winter with them to ward off any offensive operations by the Samnites.

Capua was even at that time a very unhealthy place for military discipline.* Able to provide all sorts of pleasures, it had a seductive effect on the minds of the men, and turned their thoughts away from their native land. They began to form plans in winter quarters to take Capua away from the Campanians by the same nefarious means by which the Campanians had taken the city from its former inhabitants. It would not be an injustice, they reasoned, to turn their own example against them. And why should the Campanians have the richest land in Italy, anyway, they asked, and a city matching that land, when they were people unable to defend themselves or their possessions? Why they, rather than the victorious army that had driven out the Samnites with its sweat and blood? Was it fair that men who had capitulated should bask in the fertility and charms of that land while they, exhausted with fighting wars, struggled with noxious and arid soil around Rome, or endured the oppressive burden of interest that increased in the city every day?

Such plans had been discussed in secret meetings but not yet generally made public. However, the new consul Gaius Marcius Rutulus, who had received Campania as his province by sortition, and had left his colleague Quintus Servilius at Rome, found out about them. Rutulus had the wisdom of both age and experience (he was now consul for the fourth time, and had also been a dictator and a censor), and when, through his tribunes, he had precise information on the matter, he believed it best to counteract the soldiers' impetuosity by spreading about the hope that they could implement their plan any time they chose. He therefore had the rumour put around that the garrisons would again be wintering in the same towns the following year—for they had been distributed amongst the Campanian cities, and the plans had trickled out from Capua to reach the entire army. Their designs were thus given a respite, and for the moment the sedition died down.

39. When he had led the men out to their summer camp, the consul proceeded to take advantage of the calm that reigned amongst the Samnites* to purge his army by discharging the disaffected. Some, he claimed, had served their time, and others were now advanced in age or were physically too weak. A number were sent on leave, individuals at first, and then even certain cohorts, on the grounds that they had spent the winter far from their homes and their own private concerns. A large number, too, were disposed of by being sent off in various directions on specious military operations. This whole crowd of men the other consul and the praetor detained in Rome, giving various pretexts for delaying them. And at first, in fact, the men, being unaware of the ruse, were not at all reluctant to return to their homes. But then they saw that the earliest leavers did not return to service, and that hardly anyone was sent off other than those who had wintered in Campania, and especially those amongst them who had been ringleaders in the sedition. They were struck initially by surprise, and then by outright fear that their plans had been discovered. They would soon be facing enquiries, they mused, denunciations, secret executions of individuals, and the violent and cruel despotism that the consuls and senators wielded over them. Such were the subjects of discussion in the furtive conversations of those in camp, who now realized that their conspiracy had been gutted by the consul's manoeuvre.

One cohort, located not far from Anxur,* ensconced itself near Lautulae in a narrow defile between the sea and the mountains to intercept the men whom the consul was dismissing, as noted above, on various pretexts. They were by now a body quite large in number, and the only thing they lacked to form a regular army was a leader. In no formation they made their way into Alban territory, pillaging as they went, and proceeded to establish a camp that they surrounded with fortifications beneath the mountain ridge of Alba Longa. The work completed, they argued for the rest of the day over the choice of a commander, since they had little confidence in any of their present number. But what man could they call to them from Rome? What member of the patricians or plebs would knowingly put himself at such risk, or to whom could the cause of an army out of its mind with the injustices it had suffered be appropriately entrusted?

When the same discussion continued the next day, one man amongst the roaming bands of marauders reported that he had been told that Titus Quinctius* was on a farm in the area of Tusculum, giving no thought to the city and its offices. Quinctius was a man of patrician family whose glorious military career had been ended by a limp in one of his feet, the result of a wound, and he had decided to spend his life in the country, far from the political rivalry of the Forum. When they heard the name, those present immediately called the man to mind and, with a prayer that all might turn out well, ordered him to be sent for. There was, however, little hope that he would do anything willingly, and so they decided to employ coercion and intimidation.

Those sent on the mission therefore entered his farmhouse in the dead of night, and found Quinctius in a deep sleep. They offered him no compromise: it was to be either leadership and honour or, in the case of resistance, death, which they threatened if he refused to accompany them. They then forcefully took him to the camp. On his arrival, Quinctius was immediately hailed as 'imperator'.* He was terrified by the astounding suddenness of it all, but they placed the insignia of office on him, and told him to lead them to Rome. They then pulled up their standards, more on their own initiative than their leader's instructions, and marched ready for battle to the eighth milestone of the road that is now the Appian Way.* They would have gone straight to the city had they not heard that an army was coming to meet them under Marcus Valerius Corvus—he had been appointed dictator specifically for that purpose—and his master of horse, Lucius Aemilius Mamercus.*

40. As soon as they came within sight of each other and recognized their respective arms and standards, the memory of their fatherland calmed the anger in all of them. Not yet were Romans so hardened as to spill citizen blood,* nor did they know of wars other than those against foreigners, and seceding from one's own people was then deemed to be the height of madness. The result was that leaders and men on both sides were looking for a way to come together to parley. There was Quinctius, who was tired of fighting even for his country—and much less would he fight against it—and Corvus, who felt affection for all citizens of Rome, especially the soldiers and his own army above all. Corvus now came forward to parley, and when he was recognized he was immediately granted silence and shown as much respect by his adversaries as by his own men.

'Men, in setting out from the city,' he said, 'I offered prayers to the immortal gods—your gods and mine—and as a suppliant I begged their indulgence to grant me not victory but the glory of coming to terms with you. There have been, and will be, occasions enough to win renown in war; this time peace must be sought. You yourselves are able to grant me what I asked of the immortal gods in my vows, if you are prepared to recognize that you have your camp not in Samnium or in Volscian territory, but on Roman soil. Just be prepared to remember that the hills that you see are the hills of your homeland,* that this army is composed of your fellow-citizens, and that I am your consul, under whose leadership and auspices you last year twice put to flight the Samnite legions and twice captured their camp. I am Marcus Valerius Corvus, men, whose noble background you have found to be a source of benefit to you, not injustice; I have not proposed any high-handed legislation against you, or any oppressive senatorial decree, and in all my positions of command I have been harder on myself than on you. And if family or personal merit, or even high standing or honours, could have inspired vanity in any man, then such was my background, such the proof that I have given of my worth, such the age at which I reached the consulship that I could, a consul at twenty-three, have looked down my nose not just on the plebs but even on patricians. But what have you heard of me saying or doing as consul that was harsher than when I was a tribune? I followed the same line with my two following consulships, and that same line will be followed in this dictatorship with its extensive powers. Thus, I shall be no more lenient on these soldiers of mine who are also soldiers of my homeland than I shall be on you who are—I shudder at the word—enemies.

'So you will draw the sword on me before I shall on you. If we must fight, it is on your side that the battle-signal will ring out, on yours that the battle-cry will be given first and the charge commence. Be resolved to do what your fathers and grandfathers did not do, neither those who withdrew to the Sacred Mountain nor those who later occupied the Aventine.* Wait for your mothers and wives to come from the city to meet each of you with dishevelled hair, as once happened to Coriolanus! On that occasion the legions of the Volsci did not act, because they had a Roman leader. Will you, a Roman army, not step back from an unholy war?

'Titus Quinctius, whatever the position you have taken over there, whether it be willingly or unwillingly, go back to the rearmost ranks if fight we must—more honourable it will prove for you to flee and turn your back on your fellow-citizens than to fight against your native land. But in the case of making peace you can rightly and honourably stand in the front lines, and be a sound mediator in the discussions. Make fair requests and accept fair offers, although one should settle even for what is unfair rather than see us lay impious hands on each other.'

His eyes brimming with tears, Titus Quinctius turned to his troops and said: 'If I am to be of any use to you, soldiers, you have in me, too, one better in leading you to peace than to war. It was not a Volscian or a Samnite who made that address, but a Roman—your consul and your commander, soldiers! You have experienced his auspices working for you; do not now experience them working against you! The Senate had other leaders who could put up a more ruthless fight against you, but they chose one who would be most forgiving with you, his own soldiers, and one in whom you would have most trust, your own commander. Even those with the power to win want peace—so what should we want? Why do we not, rather, set aside anger and hope, those treacherous advisers, and entrust ourselves and all our concerns to the man's well-proven integrity?'

41. A shout of approval went up from all, and Titus Quinctius, advancing to a point before the standards, declared that his soldiers would accept the dictator's authority. He begged Valerius to take on the cause of his unfortunate fellow-citizens and, if he took it on, to devote to it the same commitment that he accorded to affairs of state. For himself personally, he said, he needed no guarantees—he wanted his hopes based on nothing other than his innocence. However, there had to be guarantees for his soldiers, just as, in the time of their forefathers, guarantees had once been given first to the plebs, and on a second occasion to the legions,* that their defection would not be liable to punishment.

The dictator commended Quinctius and told the others to keep their spirits up, and then he speedily rode back to the city. There, after securing the approval of the Senate, he brought a proposal before the people in the Peteline Wood to the effect that none of the men should be liable to punishment for their defection. He further made the request (while begging pardon for the implication) that none should reproach any of the men with the incident, either joking or in earnest. A military sacred law* was also passed prohibiting the name of any registered soldier to be struck off without his consent, and a clause was attached to the law that prohibited anyone who had been a military tribune from subsequently serving as a chief centurion. The clause was insisted upon by the conspirators because of Publius Salonius,* who had been serving as a military tribune and first centurion (now known as *primipilus*) almost in alternate years. The ordinary soldiers had been angry with Salonius for his unfailing opposition to their rebellious schemes, and he had run away from Lautulae so as not to be party to them. The result was that, out of consideration for Salonius, this was the only demand that was turned down by the Senate; but then Salonius appealed to the senators not to put his dignity ahead of harmony in the state and convinced them to let this pass as well. There was an equally unconscionable demand for a reduction in the cavalrymen's pay (they were then earning triple that of the infantry*) for having opposed the conspiracy.

42. I also find in some sources that a plebeian tribune, Lucius Genucius,* brought to the plebs a proposal to ban the lending of money at interest. In addition, I find that provision was made against anyone holding the same magistracy twice in a ten-year period or holding two magistracies in one year, and that the election of plebeian candidates to both consulships be allowed. If all these concessions were made to the plebs, then clearly the revolt had no small impact.

In other annalistic works* it is recorded that Valerius was not named dictator but that the matter was taken care of entirely by the consuls, and that it was not before coming to Rome, but actually in Rome, that this large band of conspirators was driven to take up arms; that it was not on Titus Quinctius' farmhouse that the break-in was made in the night, but on the city home of Gaius Manlius; and that Manlius was the man abducted by the conspirators to be their leader. They set off from there to the fourth milestone, according to this version, and there took up a position in a fortified spot. Nor was it with the leaders that talk of reconciliation began; rather, the two armies, under arms, had proceeded to battle stations when suddenly they greeted each other, and the soldiers began to mingle together, clasping hands and exchanging tearful embraces. When they saw that the men were set against fighting, the consuls were then obliged to put before the Senate a proposal for re-establishing accord. So great is the lack of agreement among the ancient authorities on all but the fact that there was discord and that it was resolved.

Word of this discord, along with the seriousness of the war conducted against the Samnites, led to a number of peoples abandoning their alliance with Rome. Apart from the Latins, long unreliable with regard to their treaty, the Privernates, too, pillaged the neighbouring Roman colonies of Norba and Setia with a lightning attack.*

BOOK EIGHT

1. It was when Gaius Plautius and Lucius Aemilius Mamercus were already consuls (Plautius for the second time) that the people of Setia and Norba came to Rome to report the revolt of the Privernates and complain about the destruction suffered at their hands. News was also brought that an army of the Volsci, with the people of Antium at the forefront, had established a camp at Satricum. Both wars fell by lot to Plautius,* who marched first on Privernum where he immediately took the field. The enemy were decisively beaten without much of a fight; their town was captured but returned to the Privernates strongly garrisoned, and two-thirds of their agricultural land was confiscated.

The victorious troops were then led against the Antiates at Satricum,* and there a fierce battle took place with much blood spilled on both sides, but a storm broke off the fight before hopes of success inclined to either side. The Romans, however, in no way demoralized by such an indecisive engagement, prepared for battle on the following day. The Volsci, though, counting the men they had lost in the engagement, had no such enthusiasm for facing the danger once again, and they left fearfully for Antium during the night like beaten men, abandoning their wounded and part of their baggage. A large quantity of weapons came to light, both amongst the corpses of the enemy and in their camp. The consul declared that he was making a gift of these to Lua Mater,* and he pillaged the lands of the enemy all the way to the coast.

The other consul, Aemilius, entered Sabellian territory* but nowhere encountered resistance from any Samnite camp or legions. He was in the process of destroying the fields with fire and sword when representatives of the Samnites came to him with a request for peace. They were referred to the Senate by Aemilius, and there, given leave to speak, they dropped their defiant attitude and asked the Romans for peace and the right to make war on the Sidicini. These requests were the more reasonable, they said, for their having entered into friendship with the Roman people when things were going well for themselves, not badly, as was the case with the Campanians, and also because they were taking up arms against the Sidicini who had always been their enemies, and had never been friends of the Roman people. These people, they added, had never, like the Samnites, asked for their friendship in peacetime, nor, like the Campanians, had they asked for help in time of war; and they were neither under the protection of the Roman people, nor under their sway.

2. The praetor Titus Aemilius submitted the requests of the Samnites to the Senate, and the senators decided on a renewal of their treaty. The praetor then gave the Samnites the following reply. It had been through no fault of the Roman people that their friendship with the Samnites had not continued, he said, and since the Samnites had now become weary of a war for which they were themselves responsible, there was no objection from them to the resumption of that friendship. As far as the Sidicini were concerned, there was nothing to stop the Samnite people from independently making a decision about war or peace with them.

A treaty was concluded and the Samnites returned home. The Roman army was then immediately withdrawn, after first being given a year's pay and three months' grain supply, a stipulation that the consul had made to cover the time of the truce until the return of the representatives.

With the same troops that they had used for the war against Rome, the Samnites set off against the Sidicini, with no uncertain hopes of soon capturing their enemies' city. At that point the Sidicini tried to steal a march on them by declaring their surrender to the Romans. The senators, however, rejected their overtures on the grounds that they came too late and were wrung out of them only because of their desperate situation; and they then made their offer to the Latins, who had already taken up arms of their own accord. Even the Campanians did not hold back from the conflict—so much clearer in their memory was the offence of the Samnites than the generosity of the Romans.

From all these peoples came one huge army which, under a Latin commander, burst into Samnite territory where it caused more damage in predatory raids than pitched battles; and then, although the Latins had the upper hand in the confrontations, they not reluctantly quit the enemy's countryside in order to avoid the all-too-frequent encounters. That gave the Samnites a respite to send spokesmen to Rome. These came before the Senate and protested that they were suffering as much when they were allies of Rome as they had as her enemies, and with abject entreaties they begged the Romans to be satisfied with having snatched from the Samnites victory over the Campanians and Sidicini, and not allow them also to endure defeat at the hands of the most cowardly of peoples.* If the Latins and Campanians were actually under the sway of the Roman people, they said, then they should by virtue of their authority keep them away from Samnite land; if they rejected that authority they should restrain them by force of arms.

The Romans' response was equivocal because they were averse to admitting that the Latins were no longer under their authority, but also afraid of alienating them through censure. The Campanians, they said, were in a different category: they had come under Rome's protection not by a treaty but through surrender, and so they would remain at peace whether they wished to or not. In the case of their treaty with the Latins, however, there was nothing preventing them from going to war with whomsoever they liked.

3. The reply left the Samnites wondering what the Romans were going to do. It also frightened and alienated the Campanians, and made the Latins more arrogant, since they assumed that there was now no concession the Romans would not make. And so, feigning to prepare for war against the Samnites, their leading men called frequent assemblies and in all their discussions began secretly to cook up schemes for war with Rome. The Campanians also supported this putative war against their deliverers. Everything was deliberately kept secret—they wanted the Samnite enemy off their back before the Romans could mobilize—but even so information about the conspiracy leaked out to Rome through a number of people with social or family connections. The consuls were instructed to leave office before their time to accelerate the election of new consuls for a war of such great proportions, but this led to religious concerns over elections held by men whose authority had been curtailed. Thus an *interregnum* followed.* There were two *interreges*, Marcus Valerius and Marcus Fabius, and the second of these declared Titus Manlius Torquatus (for his third term) and Publius Decius Mus elected as consuls.

It is generally accepted that it was in this year* that King Alexander of Epirus came to Italy with a fleet, a war that would undoubtedly have reached Rome had it met with enough success at the start. This was the same period as the exploits of Alexander the Great, who was the son of this Alexander's sister, a man invincible in war whom

Fortune snuffed out with a sickness, while he was still a young man, in another part of the world.

As for the Romans, they were in no doubt about the disaffection of their allies and the Latins. That notwithstanding, they behaved as though their uneasiness was not for themselves but for the Samnites, and they summoned to Rome ten leaders of the Latins to receive the orders they had for them. At that time Latium had two praetors, Lucius Annius of Setia, and Lucius Numisius of Circei. Both were from Roman colonies,* and it was through them that, in addition to Signia and Velitrae (which were themselves also Roman colonies), even the Volsci had been roused to military action. It was decided that these men would be named in the summons. No one was in doubt about the reason for their being called. Accordingly, before setting off for Rome, the praetors convened an assembly, announced that they had been summoned by the Roman Senate, and then laid before the meeting the matters they thought would be discussed with them, asking what responses the council wanted them to give.

4. The members made various suggestions, and then Annius said:

'I have myself brought before you the question of what responses you would want to be made. However, I believe that what we should do is more pertinent to our situation than what we should say. Once our plans are settled it will be easy to make our words fit the circumstances. For if we can now endure slavery, with a pretence of enjoying a treaty on equal terms, how far short are we, after abandoning the Sidicini, from bending the knee not just to the Romans but to the Samnites, as well, and from replying to the Romans that we shall lay down our arms whenever they give the sign?

'But what if desire for freedom at last gnaws away at our hearts? What if our treaty and our alliance really do mean equality of rights? If we really do pride ourselves on being blood-relatives of the Romans, something we felt ashamed about before? If "allied army" simply means their forces being doubled when it is added to their own, and if it is an army that their consuls would not wish to see terminating and starting its own wars independently of them? In that case why isn't everything made equal between us? Why is one of the consuls not provided by the Latins? Where strength is shared let the power be shared as well.

'In fact, this is not in itself too generous a concession to us given that we acknowledge Rome as the capital of Latium; but by our long-suffering patience we have allowed it to look generous. But if you have ever longed for a time to share power and reclaim your liberty, that time has come, brought to you by your own courage and the generosity of heaven! You tried their patience by refusing them fighting men. Who can doubt that they burned with anger when we broke with a tradition of more than two hundred years? And yet they put up with the pain of it! We fought a war independently against the Paeligni and, though they would not earlier grant us the right to protect our own territory ourselves, they did nothing to intervene. They have heard that the Sidicini were taken under our protection, that the Campanians left them for us, and that we are making ready armies to march on their treaty-allies, the Samnites, and yet they have not budged from their city. Why such forbearance on their part if not because of their awareness both of our strength and their own? I have it on good authority that when the Samnites complained about us the response they received from the Senate made it readily apparent that the Romans themselves were no longer demanding that Latium remain under Roman control. With your demands simply take possession now of what they are tacitly ceding to you. If fear prevents anyone saying this, well, here I am, and I promise to say it not only in the hearing of the Roman people and Senate but in the hearing of Jupiter himself, whose home is the Capitol, namely that, if they want us in a treaty of alliance, they must agree to one of the consuls and part of the Senate coming from our ranks.'

Annius was offering not only brash advice but promises, too, all received with noisy applause, and they unanimously gave him leave to do and say everything that seemed in the interest of the Latin community and in keeping with his own conscience.

5. On reaching Rome, the Latin envoys were granted an audience with the Senate on the Capitol. There the consul Titus Manlius, with the authorization of the senators, requested of them in the discussion that they not make war on the Samnites, who were their treaty-allies. Annius then proceeded to speak like a victor who had stormed the Capitol, not an envoy whose security depended on international convention.

'Titus Manlius and you, Senators,' he said, 'it is high time that you finally stopped dealing with us as our masters. At this time, thanks to heaven's blessing, you can see that Latium is rich in arms and men, with the Samnites defeated militarily, the Sidicini and Campanians as her allies, and now the Volsci, too; and you further see that your own colonies have preferred Latin rule over Roman. But you cannot bring yourselves to put an end to your tyrannical reign. We have the power to champion Latium's independence by force of arms, but we shall, nevertheless, in recognition of our blood-relationship, venture to propose conditions of peace equally fair for both sides, since the immortal gods have decided that we should be equal in strength, as well. One of the consuls should be elected from Rome, the other from Latium; the Senate should be drawn equally from the two nations, with us becoming one people and one state; and so that our seat of empire may be the same and we all have the same name, then—since one of the two parties must give way (and may that turn out well for us both!)—let this city rather be ours in common and let us all be called Romans.'

It so happened that the Romans also had as consul a man, Titus Manlius, who was Annius' equal in impetuosity. He did not hold back his anger, actually going so far as to openly declare that if such insanity overtook the senators as to accept terms from a man of Setia he would enter the Senate wearing his sword and with his own hand kill any Latin he saw in the house. Then, turning to the statue of Jupiter, he said: 'Listen to this wickedness, Jupiter! Listen to it, Law and Justice! Will you too be overcome and taken captive, Jupiter? Will you set eyes on foreign consuls and a foreign Senate in your temple, a temple sanctified with auguries? Latins: are these the treaties that Tullus, the Roman king, made with your Alban ancestors, and the ones Lucius Tarquinius later made with you? Do you not remember the battle at Lake Regillus? Have you forgotten your defeats of old and our kindnesses towards you?'

6. The consul's words were immediately followed by an outburst of indignation from the senators; and it is on record that many supplications went up to the gods from the consuls, who repeatedly called them as witnesses to their treaties, while scornful comments on the power of Roman Jupiter were heard from Annius. At all events, as he rushed precipitately from the temple vestibule, fired with anger, he slipped on the stairs and bumped his head so badly on the lowest step that he passed out. The sources are not unanimous in saying that he was killed, and so let me, too, leave that matter open, along with the story that, while the gods were being invoked to witness the broken treaties, there was a huge thunderclap and a violent storm.

These things could be true, but they could also be fictions* intended to give an appropriate picture of the anger of the gods.

Torquatus had been sent by the Senate to see the embassy off, and when he saw Annius on the ground he said, at such a pitch that his voice was audible to the people and the senators alike: 'That's good! The gods have set in motion a righteous war. Divine power does exist! The power of the gods exists! You exist, great Jupiter! Not for nothing did we enshrine you in this seat as father of gods and men. Citizens, and you, Senators, why hesitate to take up arms if the gods are leading you? I shall have the Latin legions laid out as flat as you see their ambassador lying here.' The consul's words found approval with the people and put such fire in their souls that the departing envoys were protected from an angry assault by the men present less by international law than by the vigilance of the magistrates who were escorting them on the Senate's orders. The Senate, too, was in agreement on the war. The consuls then raised two armies and set off through Marsian and Paelignian territory,* and after uniting a Samnite army with their own they encamped near Capua, where the Latins and their allies had already come together.

It was there, in the dead of night, that both consuls are said to have had the same spectre appear to them, a figure larger than a human and more imposing. It told them that the gods of the netherworld and Mother Earth* had to be given the commander of one side and the army of the other, and that victory would come to the people and side of whichever army's commander devoted to the gods the enemy legions and, in addition, his own life. After comparing what they had seen in the night, the consuls agreed that sacrificial animals should be slaughtered to avert the gods' anger, and also that one or the other of them should fulfill his destiny if the same portents were revealed by the entrails as had been seen in their dream.

When the responses of the soothsayers proved in accord with the religious presentiment already lurking in the consuls' hearts, they then brought in their legates and tribunes. They told them plainly about the gods' instructions, so that the voluntary death of a consul should not alarm the troops in battle, and they agreed between them that the consul positioned on whichever flank it was that started to give ground should surrender his life for the Roman state and its citizens. There was also discussion in council of how, if ever any war had been prosecuted with a firm hand, then this was the time for military discipline to be restored to its ancient character. The fact that it was against the Latins that they had to fight intensified anxiety: these were people like themselves in language, culture, type of weaponry, and especially in military practices. One side's soldiers were like soldiers of the other, centurions were like centurions, tribunes like tribunes, and they had mingled as colleagues in the same garrisons and often in the same maniples.* To prevent any error on the men's part because of this, the consuls issued a proclamation forbidding anyone to engage the enemy outside the ranks.

7. Among the squadron-leaders sent off on reconnaissance in every direction happened to be Titus Manlius, the consul's son, who with his fellow-cavalrymen had gone beyond the enemy's encampment to a point where he was barely a javelin-throw from their closest outpost. In that post there were some Tusculan cavalry commanded by Geminus Maecius, a man distinguished amongst his people both for his family background and his military record. He recognized the Roman horsemen and the consul's son, who cut a fine figure at the head of the group (for they all knew each other, the men of rank in particular).

'Is it with one squadron that you are going to make war on the Latins and their allies?' he said to Manlius. 'What will the consuls and the two armies do in the meantime?'

'They'll be here at the right moment,' replied Manlius, 'and with them, as witness to the treaties you have broken, will be Jupiter himself, who is greater and more powerful than they are! If we fought you at Lake Regillus till you had had your fill, here too we are going to see to it that meeting our army in pitched battle will not be to your liking!' In response, Geminus rode out a short distance from his men, and asked: 'So, in the meantime, until that day comes when you make that great effort and move your armies against us, do you want a personal fight with me so that the superiority of a Latin horseman over a Roman can be seen from the outcome of our duel?'

The young man's fiery spirit was roused, by anger or by the shame that refusing the challenge would bring or by the inexorable power of fate. With no thought for his father's command and the consuls' edict he was swept headlong into a contest in which winning or losing was to make little difference. The other cavalrymen were moved back as though to watch a show, and the pair spurred on their horses against each other across the empty space between them. They clashed, their lances levelled, but Manlius' lance passed over his adversary's helmet, while Maecius' went over the neck of the other's horse. They wheeled their horses round, but it was Manlius who was first to gather himself for a second thrust, and he directed the point of his javelin between the ears of his enemy's horse. The horse's reaction to the pain of the wound was to rear up and shake its head violently, unseating the rider, and as Geminus was getting up after his heavy fall, using his spear and shield to support himself, Manlius pinned him to the ground with a thrust to the throat that brought the lance out through his ribs. Gathering together his spoils, Manlius rode back to his men and made his way to the camp, his squadron with him joyfully celebrating his victory, and then went to his father at his headquarters. He had no idea of the fate awaiting him, or whether he had earned praise or punishment.

'Father,' said Manlius, 'so all may say that I am truly of your bloodline, I bring these equestrian spoils taken from the enemy I killed when challenged by him.' On hearing this, the consul immediately turned from his son and ordered an assembly summoned with a trumpet-call. When a large number had come together, the consul said:

'You, Titus Manlius, have not shown respect either for a consul's authority or a father's dignity. Defying my edict, you left your post in the line to fight an enemy. You have, as far as was in your power, undermined military discipline, which has been the basis of Roman power down to this day, and you have forced me to disregard either the interests of the state or my personal feelings. We shall therefore choose to be punished for our own mistake rather than see the state pay so heavily for our misdeeds. We shall provide a grim example, but one salutary for the youth of tomorrow. Personally, I am touched both by the natural affection one has for one's children and by that act of exemplary courage on your part, perverted though it was by a misguided conception of glory. But the orders given by consuls must be confirmed by your death or else be forever undermined by the failure to punish you. I do not expect that even you—if you do have any of my blood in you—would refuse to restore by your punishment the military discipline that you subverted by the wrong you did. Go, lictor—tie him to the stake!'

All were stunned by such an inhumane order, each man looking on the axe as if it had been taken out for use on himself, and they remained silent more from fear than respect. And so they stood there, rooted to the spot in deep shock and silence, and then suddenly, when the blood flowed from the severed neck, cries of open disapproval went up, with endless lamentation and cursing. The young man's body, covered over with his spoils, was burned on a pyre erected outside the rampart, and he was granted all the honours a funeral can receive from soldiers. And 'the orders of Manlius' not only made people shudder at the time but were also to be a grim example for posterity.*

8. The heartlessness of the punishment, however, did increase the men's obedience to their commander; guard-duty by day and night, and the succession of the watches, were all tightened up and, in addition, the severity proved beneficial when the troops took the field. The fighting, however, resembled that of a civil war more than anything—so little did the Latins differ from the Romans in everything but fighting spirit.

In earlier days* the Romans used the *clipeus* but then, after pay was introduced for military duties, they manufactured the *scutum* instead,* and what had previously been a phalanx, like that of the Macedonians,* became instead a battle-line formation structured with maniples, and with the troops at the rear formed up in several companies. The first line comprised the *hastati*, in fifteen maniples that were slightly separated from each other. A maniple* contained twenty light-armed soldiers, the remaining crowd made up of troops in full armour (and the term 'light-armed' meant men carrying only a spear and Gallic javelins). This front row in the battle-line was made up of young men in the prime of youth just reaching military age. The *hastati* were then followed by the men of sturdier age in the same number of maniples; they bore the name *principes*, and were all fully armed troops equipped with the most distinctive armour.

This whole corps of thirty maniples they called *antepilani*, because immediately behind the standards were located another fifteen companies, all of them individually made up of three detachments, the first of which, in each case, they named a *pilus*. A company was constituted of three *vexilla*,* and one *vexillum* had sixty men, two centurions, and a *vexillarius*, making a total of 186 men. The first *vexillum* preceded the *triarii*, who were veteran soldiers of conspicuous valour; the second *vexillum* preceded the *rorarii*, who were younger men with less experience; and the third preceded the *accensi*, the least reliable unit* (which was, for that reason, sent back to the rear of the line).

When the army had been deployed in this formation, the *hastati* were the very first to enter the battle. If the *hastati* could not put the enemy to flight, they would fall back at a measured pace* and the *principes* would receive them through the gaps between their maniples. Then the *principes* would take up the fight, and the *hastati* would follow them. The *triarii* remained in position near the standards, kneeling with the left leg stretched in front of them, keeping their shields resting against their shoulders and their spears fixed in the ground, with the points partially in the air—it was like an army behind a bristling palisade.

If the fight did not go successfully for the *principes*, either, they made a gradual retreat from the front line to the *triarii* (whence the common proverbial expression for when one is hard pressed: 'the action has reached the *triarii*').* The *triarii* would then get to their feet, and after taking back the *principes* and *hastati* through the gaps between their maniples, would immediately close ranks and, as it were, shut off the access routes. Then, aware that there was no hope beyond them, they would charge the enemy in one solid mass. That was particularly unnerving for the enemy since, after pursuing supposedly beaten men, they could see a new battle-line suddenly rise before them, and in numbers greater than their own. As a rule, four legions were raised, each numbering five thousand infantrymen* and with three hundred cavalrymen per legion.

A like number also used to be added from the Latin recruitment, but the Latins were at this time enemies of the Romans, and they had marshalled their battle-line in the same formation. And they were aware that, unless the ranks were thrown into disorder, it was not only a matter of their *vexilla* having to fight against *vexilla*, all the *hastati* against *hastati*, and all the *principes* against *principes*, but that it would be centurion against centurion, too. There were two *primi pili*,* one in each army, amongst the *triarii*, the Roman not very strong physically but an enterprising man possessed of superior military expertise, while the Latin was a very strong individual who was also a first-rate fighter. The two knew each other very well because they had always been leaders of units of similar standing. Lacking confidence in his strength, the Roman had already been granted permission by the consuls to have a man of his own choosing as his deputy to give him protection from the one man earmarked as his opponent. This young man triumphed over the Latin centurion when he met him in battle.

The battle was fought not far from the foot of Mount Vesuvius,†
at the point where the road led off to the Veseris.*

9. Before they led out their troops to battle, the Roman consuls
made sacrificial offerings. It is said that the augur pointed out to
Decius that there was a gash in the 'head' of the liver in the section
relating to him,* but that his animal was otherwise acceptable to the
gods, and Manlius' sacrifice had been extremely auspicious. 'Well,
that's all right,' commented Decius, 'if my colleague's sacrifice has
been favourable.'

They proceeded to the battlefield in the formation described above,
with Manlius in command on the right wing, Decius on the left. The
battle started with strength equally matched on the two sides, and
with the same fiery spirit evident in both; but then, on the left wing,
the Roman *hastati* failed to withstand the onslaught of the Latins
and withdrew to their *principes*. At this moment of panic the consul
Decius loudly called upon Marcus Valerius,* saying: 'Marcus
Valerius, we need the help of the gods. Come on! You are an official
pontiff of the people of Rome; dictate for me the words to use to
devote myself for my legions.'*

The pontiff told him to put on the *toga praetexta*, to veil his head,
to stretch out one hand under his toga to touch his chin, and, standing on a spear set under his feet, to say the following: 'Janus,* Jupiter,
Father Mars, Quirinus, Bellona, Lares, Divi Novensiles, Di Indigetes,
all gods who have power over us and the enemy, and you, too, Gods
of the Underworld: I entreat and supplicate you, I beg and pray for
your indulgence. I pray that you aid the might and the victory of the
Roman people, the Quirites,* and that you afflict with terror, fear and
death the enemies of the Roman people, the Quirites. Just as I have
made this formal declaration, so do I devote the legions and auxiliary
troops of the enemy, along with myself, to the gods of the netherworld and to earth, and do so on behalf of the republic of the Roman
people, the Quirites, and on behalf of the army, the legions, and the
auxiliary troops of the Roman people, the Quirites.'

Such was Decius' prayer, and he then ordered the lictors to go to
Titus Manlius and promptly inform his colleague that he had
devoted himself on the army's behalf. He then arranged his toga in
the Gabine manner,* leaped onto his horse fully armed, and charged
into the midst of the enemy. He was visible to both sides, cutting a
figure more august than an ordinary man's; it was as if he had been

sent from heaven as expiation for all the anger of the gods, and to turn aside disaster from his own people onto their enemy. All the fear and terror that he brought with him at first sowed confusion around the standards of the Latins, and then it spread deep into their entire force. The clearest sign of this was the fact that wherever he rode men became frightened, as though they had been struck by some deadly star. When he collapsed under a mass of projectiles the panic in the Latin cohorts was palpable, and they took to flight and deserted the field. At the same time the Romans, their minds now freed of any religious fear, sprang to the attack as though the battle-signal had then been given for the first time. The *rorarii* had run forward between the *antepilani* and added their strength to the *hastati* and the *principes*, while the *triarii* were kneeling on their right knees and waiting for the consul's signal for them to get to their feet.

10. The struggle then continued, and in other sectors the superior numbers of the Latins were giving them the upper hand. When the consul Manlius heard of his colleague's fate, he paid his respects to such a noteworthy death, as human and divine law required, with the tears as well as the praise it was owed, and momentarily pondered whether it was not time for the *triarii* to get to their feet. Then, deciding that it was better for them to be kept fresh for the final struggle, he ordered the *accensi* to move from the rear* to the front of the standards. When they came up, the Latins brought out their *triarii* on the assumption that this was just what their adversaries had done. Engaged in a fierce battle for some time, these men exhausted themselves and shattered or blunted their spears, but they still kept pushing back their enemy, believing that the battle was over and that they had reached their last line. It was then that the consul addressed his *triarii*, saying: 'Get up now. You are fresh and face a weary foe. Remember your country, your parents, your wives and children, and remember the consul who lies dead to give you victory.'

The *triarii* then stood up, their strength unimpaired, their armour shimmering—a new line of battle suddenly appearing on the scene. They received the *antepilani* in the gaps between their maniples, and raising the battle-cry threw the front ranks of the Latins into disorder. They stabbed at the faces of the enemy with their spears and, after cutting down the cream of their fighters, passed almost without loss through the rest of their maniples, as if these were unarmed. Such was the slaughter they precipitated in bursting through the wedge-shaped companies that they left barely a quarter of them alive. In addition, the Samnites deployed at the foot of the mountain filled the Latins with terror.

But, of all the citizens and allies, it was to the consuls that kudos for that war especially went. One had brought on himself, and himself alone, all the menaces and threats from the gods above and below. The other had displayed such courage and strategic acumen in the engagement that, amongst the Romans and Latins who have transmitted an account* of the battle to posterity, there is ready agreement that victory would certainly have gone to whichever side Titus Manlius had commanded. Following their flight, the Latins made their way to Minturnae. Their camp was captured after the battle, and many men were overpowered and taken alive, mostly Campanians. Night overtook those looking for Decius' body and prevented it from being found that day. It was found the next day amidst a huge pile of enemy dead and covered with spear-wounds. Decius received a funeral befitting his death, which his colleague conducted.

I think the following information should be added.* When a consul, dictator, or praetor devotes the enemy's legions to death, he does not necessarily have to devote himself but may devote any citizen he chooses from a Roman legion that has been duly enrolled. If the man who has been devoted dies, then all is deemed correct. If he does not die, then a statue of him that is seven feet tall or more is buried in the ground and an expiatory sacrifice is made; and no Roman magistrate may tread where that statue has been buried. If he wishes to devote his own person, as Decius did, and does not die, he shall not be able to conduct any religious ceremony, on his own behalf or that of the state, with clean hands, whether it be with a sacrificial animal or anything else he chooses. Whoever devotes himself is permitted to dedicate his weapons to Vulcan or any other god of his choosing. Religion forbids the enemy to take possession of the spear on which the consul has stood to offer his prayer; should the enemy take possession of it, an expiatory sacrifice of a boar, ram, and bull must be made to Mars.

11. Although all memory of religious and secular convention has now been erased by a preference for the new and foreign* over what is historic and our own, I have still considered it pertinent to give an account of this ritual with the exact terminology with which it was formulated and transmitted to us.

In some sources I find it stated that it was only when the battle was finally over that the Samnites came to assist the Romans, and that they had been waiting to see how the fight would turn out. In the case of the Latins, too, it was after their defeat that help finally began to be sent to them from Lavinium,* where people had been wasting time in discussion. They say that when the foremost standards and part of the army had come out of the gates, news of the Latin defeat arrived, at which point they turned around and went back into the city. Their praetor, a man named Milionius, is said to have commented that they would have to pay the Romans a heavy price for a very short march!

The Latins who had survived the battle scattered along many different roads, but then came together and found refuge in the town of Vescia.* There, in meetings, their commander Numisius claimed that the mishaps of the war had actually been evenly shared and had brought both armies low with comparable losses—the Romans were only nominal victors, and apart from that were in the same position as the defeated. The headquarters of both consuls were in mourning, he said, the one over the execution of a son, and the other over the killing of the consul who had devoted himself. Their entire army had been cut to shreds, the *hastati* and *principes* had been slaughtered, and there had been carnage before and behind the standards, with only the *triarii* finally restoring their fortunes. The troops of the Latins had suffered losses equal to the Romans, he said, but to make them good Latium or the Volsci were closer than Rome. So, if they approved, he would quickly send for troops from the Latin and Volscian peoples and return to Capua with an army ready for action. The last thing the Romans would be expecting was a battle, and he would strike terror into them with his unexpected arrival. False information was circulated in letters around Latium and the Volscian people and, because those not present at the battle were quite disposed to take this on trust, a scratch army was assembled, hurriedly conscripted from all quarters.

The consul Torquatus met this army near Trifanum, which is located between Sinuessa and Minturnae. Before sites for their encampments were chosen, both armies threw down their baggage in piles, fought, and ended the war. For so shattered was the strength of the enemy that when the consul led out his victorious army to plunder their farmlands all the Latins surrendered and the Campanians followed their lead.

Latium and Capua suffered land-confiscation. The Latin lands, together with those of Privernum, were distributed amongst the Roman plebs, as was the Falernian territory,* which had belonged to the Campanian people, as far as the River Volturnus. The recipients were each given two *iugera* in Latium, with the addition of two-thirds of a *iugerum* from the territory of Privernum, or else three *iugera* in Falernian lands with a further quarter added because of the distance involved.

Spared the punishment, because they had not been part of the defection, were the Laurentes, amongst the Latins, and the Campanian knights.* An order was given for the renewal of the treaty with the Laurentes, and it has been renewed annually, on the tenth day following the Latin Festival, since that time. The Campanian knights were granted Roman citizenship, and the Romans fastened up a bronze tablet in the temple of Castor at Rome to mark the award. The people of Campania were also ordered to make an annual payment of 450 *denarii** to each of them, and they numbered sixteen hundred.

12. With the war thus finished and rewards and punishment paid out as individuals deserved, Titus Manlius returned to Rome. It is on record that, as he arrived, it was only the older men who came out to meet him, but that the young people shunned him with abhorrence, both then and for the rest of his life.

The people of Antium conducted raids on the farmlands of Ostia, Ardea, and Solonium. Since he was unable to prosecute the war himself because of illness, the consul Manlius appointed as dictator Lucius Papirius Crassus (who happened to be praetor at the time), and Lucius Papirius Cursor* was in turn appointed master of horse by Crassus. No significant results were achieved against the people of Antium by the dictator, despite his maintaining a permanent camp in Antiate territory for several months.

That was a year renowned for victories over so many and such powerful peoples, and in addition for the noble death of one of the consuls and for the order given by the other that was brutal but also famous in the historical record. It was followed by the consulship of Tiberius Aemilius Mamercinus and Quintus Publilius Philo,* who did not succeed to such opportunities for action, and who were also themselves more preoccupied with their own affairs and party politics than they were with their country.

When the Latins rose up again in anger* over the confiscation of their land, the consuls defeated them on the Fenectan Fields and took their camp from them. Then Publilius, under whose leadership and auspices the battle had been fought, remained in place accepting the surrender of the Latin peoples whose troops had been killed there, and meanwhile Aemilius led the army to Pedum. Pedum had the support of the peoples of Tibur, Praeneste, and Velitrae, and reinforcements had also arrived from Lanuvium and Antium. Though the Romans came off better in the pitched battles, the work of dealing with the town of Pedum itself, and with the camp of its allied peoples next to it, had not even been started. But at that point the consul suddenly abandoned the war when it was still unfinished: he had heard that his colleague had been decreed a triumph, and he returned to Rome to ask for a triumph himself—before the victory was won! The senators were appalled at such opportunism and refused him the triumph unless Pedum were captured or itself surrendered. Now at odds with the Senate, Aemilius made the rest of his consulship resemble an undisciplined tribunate. As long as he remained consul he never stopped criticizing the senators before the people, meeting no opposition from his colleague (because he himself also came from the plebs), and what formed the basis of his criticisms was the miserly distribution of land to the plebs in the areas of Latium and Falernum. Then, when the Senate, wishing to see an end to the consuls' authority, ordered that a dictator be appointed to face the insurgent Latins, Aemilius, who held the *fasces*, named his colleague as the dictator (and by the dictator Junius Brutus* was named master of horse).

Publilius' dictatorship was well liked because of the vitriolic speeches he made against the Senate and also for the three laws that he sponsored that were very favourable to the plebs but contrary to the nobles' interests.* One of these ordained that decrees of the plebs be binding on all citizens;* a second that the senators should approve before voting began* any bills put before the assembly of the centuries; and the third that, since they had reached the stage of allowing both censors to be plebeian, then at least one should come from the plebs. The senators believed that the damage done at home by the consuls and the dictator outweighed any benefit in terms of imperial expansion arising from their victory and military campaigns abroad.

13. The consuls for the following year were Lucius Furius Camillus and Gaius Maenius.* To emphasize their censure of Aemilius for dropping the matter when he was consul the previous year, the

Senate clamoured for arms, men, and unlimited force to be used to take and destroy Pedum; and the new consuls, forced to give the operation top priority, set out for the town.

The situation in Latium was now such that its people could countenance neither war nor peace. For war they lacked the means; peace they rejected from indignation over the appropriation of their lands. It seemed that an intermediate stance was called for: keeping to their towns (so that the Romans would not be provoked and have reason to open hostilities) and, if there were news of any town under siege, getting help sent from all their communities to the beleaguered population. In fact, however, the number of communities from which the people of Pedum received help was very small. Troops from Tibur and Praeneste, their territory being relatively close, did reach Pedum; but those from Aricia, Lanuvium, and Velitrae were joining up with the Volsci of Antium at the River Astura when they were suddenly attacked by Maenius and put to flight. Camillus fought the Tiburtines' extremely powerful army at Pedum; it required greater effort, but the result was equally successful. Townspeople suddenly bursting out during the battle caused great confusion, but Camillus directed a section of his army against them, and not only drove them back within their walls but on that very same day took the town with scaling-ladders after striking terror into them and their helpers. The consuls, redoubling their effort and determination, then decided to lead their victorious troops from the conquest of a single town to the complete subjugation of Latium; nor did they rest until, by storming individual cities or accepting their surrender, they had brought under their control the whole of Latium. Then, after establishing garrisons amongst the captured cities, they left for Rome where they had, by unanimous consensus, been assigned a triumph. A further distinction was added to the triumph: the erection in the Forum of equestrian statues in their honour, a rare occurrence in those days.

Before elections were held for the following year's consuls, Camillus raised the question of the Latin peoples before the Senate, and spoke as follows: 'Conscript Fathers:* the military action needing to be undertaken in Latium has now, thanks to the favour of the gods and the courage of our soldiers, reached its end. The armies of our enemies were cut to pieces at Pedum and the Astura. All the Latin towns as well as Antium in Volscian territory have either been taken by force or their surrender has been accepted, and they are now occupied by your garrisons. What remains, since they cause us so much concern with their insurgencies, is discussion of how we can keep them pacified with a lasting peace. The immortal gods have granted you such discretionary power in this brief that they have left it to you to decide whether Latium should continue to exist or not; and so, as far as the Latins are concerned, you can provide yourselves with eternal peace by being either ruthless with them, or forgiving.

'Do you want to adopt a cruel approach towards people who have surrendered and been defeated? You can destroy the whole of Latium, making desolate wastelands where you have often raised a fine allied army for use in many important wars. Do you want rather to follow the example of our forefathers and expand Roman power by welcoming the defeated to share our citizenship? The potential for expanding the state with the greatest glory lies with you. Certainly the authority that is by far the strongest is that which subjects are happy to accept. But whatever you decide to do, speed is of the essence. You have so many peoples anxiously wavering between hope and fear; you should therefore rid yourselves as soon as possible of your own concerns about them, and also take the initiative by either punishing them or showing them kindness while they are paralysed with anticipation. Our duty was to see that you had the power to deliberate the whole question; yours is to decide what is best for you and for the state.'

14. The leading members of the Senate praised the consul's presentation of the matter as a whole. They noted, however, that since the cases of the various peoples varied, their own decision could be expedited if the consuls, in their proposals about the individual states, actually named them, so that a determination could be made of the merits of each. The proposals were therefore made and a decision reached on them individually.*

The people of Lanuvium were awarded citizenship and given back their cults, with the proviso that the temple and grove of Juno Sospita be held in common by the citizens of Lanuvium and the Roman people. The peoples of Aricia,* Nomentum, and Pedum were accepted as citizens on the same conditions as the people of Lanuvium. The people of Tusculum retained the citizenship which they had already, and the charge of rebellion was limited to the few ringleaders, with no liability attaching to the community. The people of Velitrae, long-time citizens of Rome, were severely treated for having revolted so often. Their walls were demolished, and their senate removed from the town and its members ordered to live on the other side of the Tiber. Anyone caught on the near side of the Tiber would need to be ransomed for a sum as high as a thousand *asses*,* and the man who had captured him was not to release him from confinement before the money was paid. Colonists were dispatched to the farm-lands of the senators, and when these were enrolled Velitrae appeared again to have the dense population of its earlier days. A new colony was also sent to Antium, with the inhabitants of the town granted leave to be enrolled as colonists themselves if they so wished. Their warships* were taken from them and the population of Antium was barred from any maritime activity, but they were granted citizenship. The people of Tibur and Praeneste were subjected to land-confiscations. This was not only because of the recent revolt, with which they stood charged along with the other Latins, but also because they had once, weary of Roman domination, formed a military pact with the Gauls, a barbaric race.

The Romans deprived all the other Latin peoples* of the rights of intermarriage, cooperative trade, and communal assemblies. Citizenship without the right to vote* was conferred on the Campanians, in recognition of their cavalry's refusal to join the Latins in their revolt, and on the Fundani and Formiani* for always providing a secure and peaceful passage through their lands. It was decided that the people of Cumae and Suessula should have the same rights and status as Capua. Some of the Antiate vessels were dry-docked in the shipyards in Rome; others were burned, and it was decided that their prows be used to embellish a dais erected in the Forum. That sacred spot was given the name 'the Rostra'.*

15. In the consulship of Gaius Sulpicius Longus and Publius Aelius Paetus, at a time when, thanks as much to the gratitude Rome had won by her generosity as to her power, a secure peace reigned everywhere, war broke out between the Sidicini and the Aurunci. After their surrender was accepted, when Titus Manlius was consul, the Aurunci had caused no further trouble, and so they had more right to seek help from the Romans. But before the consuls could lead their army out of Rome—the Senate having issued instructions that the Aurunci be given protection*—news came that the Aurunci had, out of fear, abandoned their town and, taking flight with their wives and children, had strengthened the defences of Suessa, today called

Suessa Aurunca. Their ancient walls and city had, it was reported, been destroyed by the Sidicini.

Angry with the consuls whose dawdling had let down their allies, the Senate called for the appointment of a dictator. Gaius Claudius Inregillensis* was appointed, and he in turn appointed Gaius Claudius Hortator as his master of horse. Then religious concern was raised over the choice of dictator, and when the augurs declared that there was some irregularity in his appointment the dictator and his master of horse both abdicated.*

That year the Vestal Minucia* first of all raised suspicions because of her dress, which was more stylish than was appropriate, and then was arraigned before the pontiffs on the evidence of a slave. She was ordered by pontifical decree to quit her religious functions and to maintain her slaves under her authority.* Judgement was then passed on her and she was buried alive near the Colline gate, to the right of the paved road, in the Sinful Field,* a place named, I believe, from her sexual impropriety.

In that same year Quintus Publilius Philo was elected praetor,* the first time for a plebeian. The consul Sulpicius opposed this, saying that he would not recognize Philo's candidacy, but the Senate, having had no success in the case of the highest offices, would not exert itself in the case of the praetorship.

16. The following year—the consulship of Lucius Papirius Crassus and Kaeso Duillius—was noted for a war with the Ausones that was new rather than important. The Ausones, a people inhabiting the city of Cales,* had joined forces with the Sidicini, their neighbours. When they were defeated in one battle of little significance, the closeness of their towns made the army of the two peoples more inclined to flight, and also offered greater safety in the flight.

The senators, however, did not disregard that war: the Sidicini had so often in the past either initiated hostilities themselves, or brought assistance to others doing so, or been the cause of armed conflict. They therefore did all they could to make the greatest commander of the day, Marcus Valerius Corvus, consul for the fourth time, and as his colleague Corvus was given Marcus Atilius Regulus. To avoid any error through the vagaries of fortune, the consuls were asked to let Corvus assume this responsibility without sortition.

Corvus took over from the former consuls their victorious army and set off for Cales, where the war had started. There he routed with the first shout and first charge an enemy still terror-stricken from the memory of the previous encounter, and he proceeded with an assault on the town itself. Such, too, was the enthusiasm of the men that they wanted right then to move up to the walls with ladders, and they assured him that they would scale them. This was a difficult operation, however, and Corvus wanted to accomplish it by his men's labour rather than by risking their lives. He therefore raised an earthwork, brought forward siege-shelters, and moved towers up to the wall, but a chance opportunity made their employment unnecessary. A Roman prisoner of war, Marcus Fabius, thanks to the negligence of his guards on a day of festivities, was able to break his shackles and with his hands lower himself down the side of the wall, suspended on a rope tied to a battlement, between the Roman siege-works. He convinced the commander to make an attack on the enemy while they were drowsy from wine and feasting, and the Ausones along with their city were captured with no more effort than their defeat in battle had required. The plunder taken was enormous, and after a garrison had been installed in Cales the legions were led back to Rome. The consul celebrated a triumph by decree of the Senate and, so that Atilius should not miss his share of the glory, the two consuls were ordered to lead the army against the Sidicini. Before that, following a senatorial decree, they appointed a dictator for the purpose of holding elections, and this was Lucius Aemilius Mamercinus. He in turn appointed Quintus Publilius Philo as his master of horse.*

With the dictator presiding over the elections, Titus Veturius and Spurius Postumius were elected consuls. Half of the war with the Sidicini still remained. The consuls, however, wanted to pre-empt the wishes of the plebs by a kind service, and they made a proposal for sending out a colony to Cales. This was followed by a senatorial decree authorizing two thousand five hundred men to be enrolled for the colony, and the senators then appointed Kaeso Duillius, Titus Quinctius, and Marcus Fabius as a board of three to lead the colonists and apportion the land.

17. The new consuls then took over the army from their predecessors.* They entered the territory of the enemy and came as far as the walls of the city, plundering as they went. The Sidicini had also raised a huge army there, and it looked as if they would fight hard for what would be their last hope; and there was also a rumour that Samnium was preparing for war. A dictator, Publius Cornelius Rufinus, was

therefore appointed by the consuls, on the authorization of the Senate, and Marcus Antonius became his master of horse. There was then religious concern over an irregularity in their appointment, and they resigned their offices; and since a plague followed, making it appear that all the auspices were flawed by that irregularity, there was another *interregnum*.

It was only with the fifth *interrex* from the start of the *interregnum*, Marcus Valerius Corvus, that consuls were elected, and they were Aulus Cornelius (his second term) and Gnaeus Domitius. There was now peace, but a rumour of a Gallic war had the force of an insurrection,* making the Senate decide that a dictator should be appointed. Marcus Papirius Crassus was appointed, and Publius Valerius Publicola became his master of horse. While a troop-levy was being conducted by these men (more rigorously than they would have been for local wars), scouts that had been sent out brought news that peace reigned everywhere amongst the Gauls.

For more than a year now it had been suspected that revolutionary schemes were being hatched in Samnium, and for that reason the Roman army had not been removed from the territory of the Sidicini. However, a war with Alexander of Epirus drew the Samnites into Lucania, and the two peoples fought a pitched battle with the king as he marched inland from Paestum. Alexander came off better in that engagement, and he concluded a peace treaty with the Romans,* though it is unclear how faithfully he would have respected it if everything else had gone as well for him.

During that same year a census was held and new citizens were registered. Because of these, the tribes Maecia and Scaptia* were added, and the censors who added them were Quintus Publilius Philo and Spurius Postumius. The people of Acerrae* became Romans by a law proposed by the praetor Lucius Papirius under which they were granted citizenship without voting rights. Such were that year's events at home and abroad.

18. The year that followed, when Marcus Claudius Marcellus* and Gaius Valerius held the consulship, proved disastrous, be it for the terrible climatic conditions* or for human misconduct. I find the consul Valerius' *cognomen* given in the annalistic sources variously as Flaccus and Potitus, but in this case accuracy is of little importance. I would wish that one thing had been recorded incorrectly (and the sources are not unanimous about it), namely that those whose death

made that year infamous for the plague were carried off by poison. However, for me not to impugn any author's credibility, the affair must be presented here exactly as it has been transmitted. When the civic leaders were afflicted with similar maladies, almost all facing the same fatal outcome, a female slave approached the curule aedile Quintus Fabius Maximus* with a promise to disclose the cause of the communal disease if assured by him that her information would do her no harm. Fabius immediately brought the matter to the consuls, who brought it to the Senate, and the informant was given her assurance with the unanimous agreement of that body.

It was then revealed that the state was the victim of a heinous crime perpetrated by women,* that some married ladies were concocting poisons and that, if men immediately accompanied her, these women could be caught red-handed. Going with the informant, they found a number of women actually concocting poisons and other poisons already stored away. The potions were brought into the Forum and up to twenty married women, at whose homes they had been seized, were issued a summons by a bailiff. Two of them, Cornelia and Sergia, both from patrician families, claimed that the concoctions were in fact wholesome medicines. The informant denied this, and told them to drink them to prove that she had been lying. The two then took some time to discuss the matter, and when the crowd had been moved back put it to the other women. These women, like them, did not refuse to drink, and after imbibing the potions before the eyes of everybody they all perished, victims of their own vile scheme. Their attendants were immediately arrested, and these informed on a large number of married women, of whom some 170 were found guilty; and before that day there had never been a trial for poisoning in Rome.

The episode was regarded as a portent, and it seemed more like a case of insanity than criminal intent. And people now recalled from the chronicles how, during the secessions of the plebs in former days, a nail had been hammered in by a dictator* and how men's minds, driven to distraction by civil discord, had been restored to sanity by that act of atonement. They therefore decided that a dictator should be appointed to hammer in a nail. Gnaeus Quinctilius* was appointed and he declared Lucius Valerius his master of horse. Both resigned their offices after the hammering in of the nail.

19. The men elected as consuls were Lucius Papirius Crassus (his

second term) and Lucius Plautius Venox. At the start of that year Volscian envoys arrived in Rome from Fabrateria and Luca* with a plea for Roman protection; if they were defended against the weapons of the Samnites, they said, they would faithfully and loyally accept the authority of the Roman people. With that, envoys were in turn sent out by the Senate and the Samnites were warned to refrain from any aggressive action against the territory of those peoples. The embassy proved successful, not so much because the Samnites wanted peace as because they were not yet prepared for war.

That same year the war with Privernum began. The people of Fundi were allies of Privernum, and even the commander of the Privernates, Vitruvius Vaccus, was a Fundanian citizen. He was a man well known not only in his own land but in Rome as well; he had a house on the Palatine and, after the building was torn down, and the site made public property, the place was called Vaccus' Meadows. Vitruvius was conducting widespread plundering expeditions in the lands of Setia, Norba, and Cora when Lucius Papirius set off to face him and dug in not far from his camp. Vitruvius did not have the common sense to defend himself with a rampart against a stronger opponent, but no more did he have the courage to engage at a distance from his camp. He had scarcely taken the time to deploy the whole of his battle-line outside the gate when he went into battle without a master plan and without commitment, his soldiers looking behind for the possibility of flight rather than of engaging the enemy. He was defeated with little effort and quite decisively, but had no difficulty in protecting his men from heavy losses, thanks to the confined space and the easy retreat to a camp that was so close. In fact, hardly anyone was killed in the actual engagement, and only few at the rear in the disordered flight, when they were rushing into the camp. As darkness began to fall they left there for Privernum in a fearful column so as to have the protection of walls rather than a palisade.

The other consul, Plautius,* marched his army from Privernum into the territory of Fundi, laying waste the fields en route and driving off farm-animals as plunder. When he entered their territory, the members of Fundi's senate met him. They told him they had come to plead not for Vitruvius and those supporting his cause, but for the people of Fundi. These, they said, even Vitruvius had judged to be free of blame for the war: he had chosen Privernum as a refuge in his flight, not his own land. It was therefore in Privernum that the enemies of the Roman people were to be sought and punished—they had defected from both the people of Fundi and from the Romans, with no thought for either of their native towns. In Fundi there was peace, pro-Roman sentiments, and gratitude for the citizenship they had received, and they were begging the consul to abstain from war with an innocent people—their lands, their city, their own persons and those of their wives and children were, and would be, in the power of the Romans.

The consul commended the people of Fundi and sent a dispatch to Rome saying that Fundi remained loyal. He then veered towards Privernum. Claudius, however, relates that he first punished those who had been at the head of the conspiracy. According to him, as many as 350 of the conspirators were dispatched to Rome in irons, but their surrender was not accepted by the Senate, who believed that the people of Fundi wished to get off merely with the punishment of some poor and unimportant individuals.

20. While Privernum was under siege from the two consular armies, one of the consuls was recalled to Rome to hold elections. That year starting-barriers* were set up for the first time in the Circus.

The Romans were not yet free of anxiety over the war with Privernum when the grim news came of a Gallic uprising, news that was hardly ever disregarded by the Senate. The new consuls, Lucius Aemilius Mamercinus and Gaius Plautius,* were immediately ordered—on the very day of their entry into office, July 1st—to come to an arrangement on their respective duties. The Gallic war fell to Mamercinus, who was ordered to enroll an army with no exemption permitted; in fact, it is said that even a gang of tradesmen and some sedentary labourers, the sort of people least suited to military service, were called up. The huge army was brought together at Veii, from where it was to march against the Gauls; but it was decided that it should proceed no further for fear of the enemy taking another road and advancing on Rome unobserved. It was then discovered, a few days later, that all was peaceful with the Gauls at that time, and the whole force turned on Privernum.

After that there are two versions of events. Some have it that the city was taken by storm and that Vitruvius fell into the hands of the Romans alive; others that, before the final push was made, the citizens, carrying the caduceus before them,* surrendered to the consul and that Vitruvius was handed over by his own men. Consulted about the fate of Vitruvius and the Privernian people, the Senate gave orders for the consul Plautius to tear down the walls of Privernum and install there a strong garrison, after which he was to come to Rome for a triumph. Vitruvius was to be kept in prison until the consul's return, and then flogged and executed; and his house on the Palatine was to be demolished and his assets offered to Semo Sancus.* (The money realized from the sale of these was actually used for making bronze dishes that were placed in the shrine of Sancus opposite the temple of Quirinus.) The decision reached with regard to the senate of Privernum was that any senator who had remained in Privernum after its defection from Rome should reside across the Tiber under the same conditions as the senators of Velitrae.

After these decrees were passed, there was silence about the people of Privernum up to the time of Plautius' triumph. Following the triumph, the consul executed Vitruvius and his accomplices, and then thought he could safely bring up the matter of the Privernates before people who had by now had enough of punishing the guilty.

'Senators,' he said, 'the ringleaders of the rebellion have received, both from the gods and from you, the punishment they deserved. What do you want done about the innocent population? It is my role to solicit opinions rather than express them, but when I observe that the Privernates are neighbours of the Samnites, with whom we now have a very shaky peace, I should like to see animosity between us left at a minimum.'

21. It was an intrinsically difficult question, with views expressed for harsh or lenient treatment depending on the speaker's character. Then everything was made even more unclear by one spokesman from Privernum who was more aware of the position into which he had been born than the plight he was in. Asked by a senator who supported the more severe position what punishment he thought the Privernates deserved, the man replied: 'One that those deserve who believe themselves worthy of freedom.'*

The consul saw that the hostility of those men earlier opposing the Privernate cause was heightened by the defiant reply, and he himself tried to elicit a more judicious response by framing the question in friendly terms.

'What if we spare you punishment?' he asked. 'What sort of peace could we expect to have with you then?'

'Grant us a good one, and it will be loyally and eternally kept,' the man replied. 'A bad one, and it will be short-lived.'

At this point some declared that the Privernate was making threats, and not vague threats, either, and that it was by such comments that pacified peoples were incited to rebellion. The better members of the Senate were advocating a milder response, saying that what they heard was the opinion of a man, a free man. Could it be believed, they asked, that any nation or any person would remain longer than necessary in circumstances that they found objectionable? A lasting peace was to be found only where the settlement was accepted willingly, and they should not expect loyalty anywhere that they wanted servitude.

It was the consul himself who was most responsible for bringing opinions around to this view. Time and again he would turn to the ex-consuls, who expressed their opinions first,* and declare at a level that could be heard by most present that the only people who deserved to become Romans were those whose thoughts were focused on liberty alone. So it was that they won their case in the Senate, and on the authority of the senators a bill to award citizenship to the Privernates was brought before the people.

That same year three hundred people were sent out to colonize Anxur,* each being given two *iugera* of land.

22. There followed a year, the consulship of Publius Plautius Proculus and Publius Cornelius Scapula, that was marked by nothing of significance in the field or at home. The exceptions were a colony sent out to Fregellae* (the land there had belonged to the Signini* and later to the Volsci) and a meat-distribution to the people made by Marcus Flavius on the occasion of his mother's funeral. There were some who construed this as a recompense that Flavius owed to the people—for acquitting him when arraigned by the aediles on a charge of sexual relations with a married woman—being made under the guise of respects paid to a parent. The distribution may have been made in gratitude for a verdict in the past, but it was also the reason for his elevation to office, and in the next elections for the plebeian tribunate he was *in absentia* preferred over the candidates canvassing for it.

Palaepolis* was not far from where Neapolis now stands, and the two cities were inhabited by the same people. Their place of origin was Cumae, and the people of Cumae trace their roots back to Chalcis in Euboea. Thanks to the fleet with which they sailed from their home, they gained great power over the sea-coast on which they are settled (after landing initially on the islands of Aenaria and Pithecusae, they later ventured to move their home to the mainland). This city-state committed numerous acts of hostility against Romans living in Campanian and Falernian territory, relying on their own strength as well as the fact that the alliance that the Samnites had with the Romans was unreliable, or else encouraged by the plague that was reported to have struck the city of Rome. Thus, in the consulship of Lucius Cornelius Lentulus and Quintus Publilius Philo (serving his second term), fetial priests were sent to Palaepolis to demand satis-faction. They received an insolent response from the Greeks, a race stronger in speech than action,* and with the authorization of the Senate the people ordered war declared on Palaepolis. In the settle-ment of responsibilities between the consuls conduct of the war with the Greeks came to Publilius. With the other army Cornelius pos-itioned himself to counteract the Samnites if they made a move—there was a rumour that they would move up their forces as soon as the Campanians revolted. That, then, seemed to Cornelius the best place to have his base camp.*

23. The Senate was informed by both consuls that there was faint hope of peace with the Samnites. Publilius added that two thousand soldiers from Nola and four thousand from Samnium had been admitted to Palaepolis, but that this was due to Nolan pressure rather than the Greeks' own wishes. Cornelius reported that notice had been given by the Samnite magistrates for troop-recruitment, that the whole of Samnium was up in arms, and that the neighbouring peoples in Privernum, Fundi, and Formiae were quite openly being urged to join them. In the light of this, it was decided that spokesmen should be sent to the Samnites before the outbreak of any hostilities, but they received an insolent response. The Samnites went so far as to attribute the wrongdoing to the Romans, and they just as vigor-ously tried to exonerate themselves of the charges made against them. There had been no official advice or aid given to the Greeks, they said, nor had Fundi or Formiae been encouraged to join them—if they wanted war, they declared, they were not at all dissatisfied with their own forces. On the other hand, they could not hide the displeasure of the Samnite nation over the fact that the Roman people had rebuilt Fregellae, which the Samnites had taken from the

Volsci and destroyed, and that they had established a colony in
Samnite territory which the Roman colonists actually called
'Fregellae'. This was an insult and an injustice, they said, and if those
responsible did not make amends for it, they themselves would
employ all the force they could to remove it.

One Roman envoy then called on them to discuss the issue with
the friends and allies they had in common, to which the Samnite
chief magistrate responded: 'Why are we quibbling? Our quarrels,
Romans, will be resolved not by the words of spokesmen or some
mediator, but by the Campanian field on which we must fight, and by
our weapons and the fortunes of war common to both of us. So let us
encamp close to each other between Capua and Suessula, and let us
sort out whether Samnite or Roman is to have power over Italy.' The
Roman spokesmen replied that they would not go where their enemy
invited them but where their commanders led them [...]*

Publilius had taken up a position favourably located between
Palaepolis and Neapolis, thus cutting the enemy off from the mutual
assistance that they employed when one or the other was under pressure. Election day was at hand, however, and it was not in the republic's interest for Publilius, who was now threatening the enemy's
walls, to be called away from the prospect of taking the city in the
coming days. An arrangement was therefore made with the tribunes,
who would propose to the people that, when Quintus Publilius Philo
left his consulship, he should continue the campaign as 'proconsul'*
until the war with the Greeks was finished.

Lucius Cornelius had already entered Samnium, and there was no
wish for his recall, either, from a war that he was vigorously prosecuting, and so a dispatch was sent directing him to appoint a dictator to
hold the elections. Cornelius appointed Marcus Claudius Marcellus,
and by him Spurius Postumius was appointed master of horse. Even
so elections were not held by the dictator, because the question arose
of whether there had been some flaw in his appointment. When the
augurs were consulted, they announced that the dictator's appointment appeared to be flawed. This matter was rendered suspect and of
dubious validity by charges levelled by the tribunes. Detecting the
flaw could not have been easy, they observed, since the consul arose
during the night and appointed the dictator in silence,* and there had
been no written communication on the subject, official or private,
from the consul to any person. Nor, they said, was there any mortal

alive who could say he had seen or heard anything that could interrupt the auspices, and the augurs, sitting in Rome, could not have
divined what flaw might have turned up for the consul in his camp.
To whom was it not obvious, they asked, that what the augurs deemed
a flaw was the fact that the dictator was a plebeian?* These and other
objections raised by the tribunes had no effect. The state had recourse
to an *interregnum*, and the elections were deferred for one reason or
another until the fourteenth *interrex*, Lucius Aemilius, finally had
Gaius Poetelius and Lucius Papirius Mugillanus* (I find the name
Cursor in other annals) elected consuls.

24. It is recorded that Alexandrea in Egypt* was also founded in
that year, and further that Alexander, king of Epirus, was killed by a
Lucanian exile, fulfilling by his fate an oracle of Jupiter at Dodona.*
Invited to Italy by the people of Tarentum, Alexander had been
warned by an oracle 'to beware of the Acherusian water and the city
of Pandosia': it was there that his end was fated to come. He therefore
crossed to Italy with all the more speed in order to distance himself as
much as he could from the city of Pandosia in Epirus and from the
River Acheron, which flows from Molossis into the Pools of Hell
before debouching into the Thesprotian Gulf. However, it usually
happens that in avoiding one's fate one runs straight into it. Alexander
had on many occasions defeated the legions of Bruttium and Lucania.
He had taken the Tarentine colony of Heraclea from the Lucanians,
and captured Sipontum,* the Bruttian towns of Consentia and
Terina, and then other cities belonging to the Messapii and the
Lucanians; and he had sent to Epirus three hundred distinguished
families so he could hold them as hostages. He then dug in not far
from the city of Pandosia (which is close to the regions of Lucania
and Bruttium) on three hills some distance from each other, intending to launch raids from those vantage-points into all parts of the
territory of the enemy. He had around him about two hundred exiles
from Lucania whom he considered reliable but whose loyalty altered
with the circumstances (a general feature of that race).

Continuous rains had flooded all the flat country and prevented
the three divisions of the army from assisting each other, and two
of the bodies (the ones without the king) were crushed by a surprise attack from the enemy. With these wiped out, the enemy
focused entirely on a blockade of the king himself. Messages were
then transmitted from the Lucanian exiles to their countrymen with

an undertaking to hand over the king, dead or alive, in return for their reinstatement. Alexander, however, took some hand-picked men and with a bold stroke broke through the midst of the enemy, killing the Lucanian leader in hand-to-hand fighting. He then brought together his men who had become separated in the break-out, and came to a river where the fresh remnants of a bridge, which the violent waters had swept away, indicated a fording place. As the column made the crossing by the precarious ford, a soldier, weary from fear and the struggle, scornfully commented on the river's abominable name, saying: 'You are rightly named Acheros.'*

When this reached the king's ears, he at once reflected on the prophecy and came to a halt, in two minds about crossing. Then Sotimus, one of the royal pages in attendance on him, asked why he was hesitating at such a critical moment and pointed out that the Lucanians were looking for an opportunity to trap him. Glancing back, the king saw them in the distance, advancing in a body, whereupon he drew his sword and pushed his horse on through the middle of the river. He was just coming into shallow water when a Lucanian exile transfixed him with a spear at long range. He fell, and the stream washed his lifeless body, the spear still stuck in it, down to the enemy posts. There the body was subjected to hideous mutilation. Severing it in the middle, they sent half of it to Consentia, keeping back the other half for their own amusement. It was serving as a target for their javelins and stones, hurled from a distance, when one lone woman joined this crowd whose wanton cruelty went beyond what one might think human anger could produce. She begged them to hold off for a moment and explained tearfully that her husband and children were captives in the enemy's hands, and that she hoped to ransom them with the king's body, no matter how mangled it was. That ended the mutilation. What remained of the limbs was buried at Consentia, thanks to the solicitude of the one woman, and Alexander's bones were sent to the enemy in Metapontum,* from where they were taken to Epirus to his wife Cleopatra and his sister Olympias (the latter being the mother of Alexander the Great, and the other his sister). This brief account of the sad fate of Alexander of Epirus must suffice; it has been included because, although fortune kept him from a war with Rome, he did fight wars in Italy.

25. A *lectisternium*—the fifth since the city's foundation—was also held this year, and for the propitiation of the same gods as before.

Then the new consuls, on the people's orders, sent a deputation to declare war on the Samnites, and themselves began all the preparations for war, with more energy than for that against the Greeks. They also received fresh assistance that was at the time totally contrary to their expectations. The Lucanians and Apulians had had no dealings with the Roman people up to that time, but they now put themselves under their protection, promising weapons and fighting men for the war. They were accordingly granted a treaty of friendship. At the same time things went well in Samnium. Three towns—Allifae, Callifae, and Rufrium*—came into their hands, and other Samnite territory was laid waste far and wide on the consuls' first arrival.

While this war had started so successfully, the other, which involved the blockade of the Greeks, was also now nearing its end. Not only were some of the Greeks isolated from the others through being cut off by enemy siege-works, but what they were suffering inside the walls was considerably more frightful than any threat they were facing from the enemy. They were virtually captives of their very own garrisons, and enduring indignities being visited even on their children and their wives, and all the outrages experienced by captured cities. Thus when news came that fresh reinforcements would be coming from Tarentum and from the Samnites, the Greeks thought there were already more Samnites within their walls than they wanted. In the case of the young soldiers from Tarentum, however, they, as Greeks themselves, were looking forward to seeing other Greeks, so as to have their help against the Samnites and the Nolans as much as against the enemy, the Romans. They finally decided that surrender to the Romans was the least painful of the evils facing them. The leading citizens of the town, Charilaus and Nymphius, conferred with each other and arranged between them their roles for achieving their end: one would desert to the Roman commander, and the other remain behind to prime the city for their project.

It was Charilaus who came to Publilius Philo, saying that he had decided to hand over the city walls, and that he prayed that this prove to be auspicious, fortunate, and advantageous* for the Palaepolitans and for the Roman people. Whether by that action he would be thought to have betrayed or to have saved his native city, he added, depended on the honour of the Romans. For himself he set down no conditions and asked for nothing; but for his people he had a request, though it was not a condition. If the undertaking were a success, the Roman people should reflect on the enthusiasm with which the Palaepolitani had returned to their friendship,* and the risks they had run, rather than on their stupidity and rashness in abandoning their obligations.

Charilaus was commended by the general and given three thousand fighting men to seize the part of the city that the Samnites were occupying. The tribune Lucius Quinctius was put in command of that detachment.

26. At the same time Nymphius had also set about manipulating the Samnite general. He had called his attention to the fact that the entire Roman army was either in the area of Palaepolis or in Samnium, and had induced him to let him sail around with a fleet to Roman territory so he could lay waste not only the coastline but the region close to the city itself. But to do that unobserved, he said, he had to set off at night and the ships had to be launched immediately. To speed up the process, all the Samnite soldiers, apart from those needed to guard the city, were sent to the shore.

In the darkness, where the large numbers were causing confusion anyway, Nymphius stalled for time by deliberately issuing contradictory commands to increase the disorder, and meanwhile Charilaus was, according to plan, let into the city by his co-conspirators. When he had occupied the heights of the town with his Roman force, he told the men to raise a shout, at which the Greeks, who had been given a signal by their leaders, made no move, but the Nolans ran off through the other side of the city, taking the road that led to Nola. The Samnites were now shut out of the town, and while their flight was easier for the moment, it appeared all the more disgraceful after they were out of danger. They were unarmed and there was nothing of theirs that they had not left in the enemy's possession, so they returned home, stripped and impoverished,* an object of derision not only to foreigners but even to their own people.

I am not ignorant of the alternative version according to which the town was betrayed by the Samnites. I have, in the first place, given precedence to sources that are more reliable* and, secondly, the treaty with Neapolis (which subsequently became the hub of Greek affairs) makes it more likely that it was Greeks who of their own volition renewed the friendship. Publilius was decreed a triumph as it was generally believed that the enemy had come to terms because they had been broken by the siege. This man received two exceptional and hitherto unprecedented honours: an extension of his command, never before granted to anyone, and a triumph when his term of office was over.

27. Another war* then immediately broke out with the Greeks on the other coast. The Tarentines had for some time kept alive the Palaepolitan cause by giving false hopes of support, and on hearing that the Romans were in possession of the city they indignantly reproached the Palaepolitans, as though they themselves had been betrayed and were not in fact the betrayers. They were in paroxysms of rage and jealousy, and the more so because they were brought news that the Lucanians and Apulians had put themselves under the protection of the Roman people (both alliances commenced that year). The Romans had almost reached the Tarentines themselves, they said, and it would soon come to the point where they would have to have the Romans either as their enemy or as their masters. A critical turning-point for their own affairs was sure to be the outcome of their war with the Samnites. The Samnites were the only people still resisting Rome, and they were not as strong since the Lucanians abandoned them, though it was possible that these could still be brought back on side and induced to annul their alliance with Rome, if some artistry were applied to sowing dissension.

This idea found favour with an audience eager for radical change. Some young Lucanians, whose notoriety amongst their compatriots was greater than their integrity, were then bribed to inflict injuries on each other with sticks and present their naked bodies before a gathering of their fellow-citizens. There they loudly proclaimed that orders had come from the consuls for them to be beaten with sticks for having dared to enter the Roman camp,* and that they had almost been put to death. It was in its very nature a shameful scene, one that gave the impression of outrageous treatment rather than duplicity, and the shocked onlookers by their outcry forced the magistrates to convene the senate. Some then stood around the members of that body and demanded war against Rome, while others rushed off in various directions to rouse crowds of peasants to arms. As the uproar unsettled even the level-headed, it was decided that the alliance with the Samnites should be renewed, and spokesmen were sent off on that mission. This precipitate action, having no rational grounding, did not carry conviction, either, and led to their being forced by the Samnites to give hostages, and to accept garrisons in their fortified places; but blinded as they were by the deception and their anger, they refused nothing. In a little while, after those who had made the false charges moved to Tarentum, it began to dawn on them that they had been deceived; but now that they had lost all their autonomy, they were left with nothing more than futile regrets.

28. That year the Roman plebs saw what was virtually a new era of liberty with the ending of slavery for debt.* The change in the law came about as a result of the egregious combination of lechery and ruthlessness in a single moneylender.* This was Lucius Papirius, under whose power Gaius Publilius had placed himself because of a debt owed by his father, and Publilius' age and good looks, which might have induced pity on the lender's part, instead sparked off his lecherous and abusive behaviour. Regarding the boy's youthful charms as some windfall profit on the loan, he first attempted to seduce the young man with salacious conversation, but then, finding his ears deaf to any degrading proposition, he resorted to threats and time after time reminded him of his situation. Eventually, when he could see that the boy was more concerned with his freeborn status than his present circumstances, he ordered him to be stripped and given the lash.*

Bearing the stripes of the lash, the boy burst into the street, loudly protesting against the moneylender's lechery and ruthlessness. A huge crowd of people gathered, fired with compassion for his young age and the humiliating mistreatment he had suffered, and thinking, too, of their own situation and that of their children, and they rushed to the Forum, and from there, in a body, to the Senate house. Faced with this sudden outcry, the consuls were forced to convene the Senate,* and as the senators came into the house people fell at the feet of each of them and pointed to the young man's bloodied back. On that day the mighty bond of credit was broken by one man's violent and outrageous act. The consuls were ordered to bring before the people legislation forbidding anyone—unless he had deserved punishment for a crime—to be fettered or held in custody while awaiting punishment, and stipulating that, in the case of money loaned, it was the debtor's possessions, not his person, that was liable to seizure. Thus, those imprisoned for debt were freed, and imprisonment for debt was banned thereafter.

29. Although the war with the Samnites, the sudden uprising of

the Lucanians, and the Tarentine responsibility for that uprising were sufficient in themselves to keep the senators worried, there was also in this same year additional concern over the Vestini* joining the Samnites. This was a matter that during that year came up frequently in conversation all over, but not in any official forum. However, the consuls for the following year were Lucius Furius Camillus (his second term) and Junius Brutus Scaeva, and nothing appeared to them more important and pressing for referral to the Senate than this. And though it was not a new item, such anxiety pervaded the senators* that they felt equal apprehension about raising it and ignoring it. Their fear was that leaving the Vestini unpunished might rouse neighbouring peoples to arms through insolence and arrogance, while punishing them with war would do the same by raising fears of immediate danger and exasperation. Furthermore, their race was, as a whole, quite the equal of the Samnites militarily, comprising as it did the Marsi, the Paeligni, and the Marrucini,* all of whom must be regarded as enemies if the Vestini came under attack.

The side that prevailed, however, was the one that for the moment might have been thought to have more spirit than sense, but the outcome demonstrated that fortune helps the brave. On the Senate's authorization, the people passed a decree for war on the Vestini. That responsibility fell to Brutus in the sortition, and Samnium to Camillus. Armies were marched to both places, and the enemy were prevented from joining forces by concern for protecting their respective territories. However, one of the consuls, Lucius Furius, who had been given the greater responsibility, fortune took out of the war when he was struck by a serious illness. Instructed to appoint a dictator for the operations, Furius appointed Lucius Papirius Cursor, the man with by far the best military record of the time, and Quintus Fabius Maximus Rullianus was appointed by Papirius as his master of horse. The two were renowned for their military exploits in that magistracy, but more renowned for their differences, which almost ended in violent conflict.

The war prosecuted by the other consul was multifaceted, but the results were uniformly successful. Scaeva devastated farmland, and by looting and burning the enemy's buildings and crops drew them reluctantly into a pitched battle. Then in that one encounter he delivered such a blow to the strength of the Vestini (though his own men were certainly not free of casualties) that the enemy not only ran back to their encampment but, with no confidence now even in their rampart and ditches, slipped away to their towns to defend themselves by their position and fortifications. Eventually the consul also started storming the towns. First, using scaling-ladders, he took Cutina—this thanks to the fierce ardour of his soldiers who were angered by their wounds, hardly any having left the battle unscathed—and then Cingilia.* He turned the booty from both towns over to the men, because neither the gates nor the walls of the enemy had kept them out.

30. The march into Samnium was made under dubious auspices.* Their irregularity, however, did not affect the outcome of the war, which was successful, but did affect the insane animosity between the commanders. When the dictator Papirius, on advice from the keeper of the chickens, was setting off for Rome to retake the auspices, he warned his master of horse to remain where he was and not engage the enemy during his absence.

After the dictator set out, Quintus Fabius learned from his scouts that there was complete lack of discipline on the enemy side, as if there were no Roman present in Samnium. The headstrong young man may have been stung by the indignity of seeing all initiative resting with the dictator, or he may have been led on by the chance of bringing off a successful enterprise; at all events, he set off with his army formed up and ready for action to a place called Imbrinium, and there fought a set battle with the Samnites. Such was the success of the battle that there was no aspect of it that could have been improved by the dictator's presence. The commander did not let down his men, nor the men their commander.

After making a number of charges, the cavalry were unable to break through the enemy's ranks but then, on the advice of the military tribune Lucius Cominius, they removed the bridles from their horses* and, putting the spurs to them, had them gallop ahead at such a pace that no force could withstand them. Passing through the midst of weapons and men, they created carnage far and wide. The infantry followed the cavalry charge, advancing on an enemy in disarray. Twenty thousand of the enemy* were reportedly killed that day. I find it in some sources* that there were two battles fought with the enemy during the dictator's absence, and two fine victories, but in the earliest authors only this one battle is found. In some annals the whole episode is passed over.

After such a bloodbath the master of horse took possession of spoils in large quantities; and he swept into a huge pile the weapons of the enemy, set them alight, and burned them. This was possibly a vow he had made to one of the gods, or possibly, if one chooses to accept Fabius' version, he did it to prevent the dictator profiting from his glorious achievement by setting on the weapons an inscription with his name or carrying the spoils in a triumph. In addition, a letter about the successful engagement was sent to the Senate, not the dictator, which suggests that Fabius had no wish to share with him the credit for it. At all events, the dictator's acceptance of the news was marked by anger and surliness, while everybody else was delighted with the victory. Thus, after suddenly adjourning the Senate, Papirius charged from the Senate house, repeatedly commenting that the defeat and overthrow of the Samnite legion by the master of horse was certainly no greater than his defeat and overthrow of the prestige of the dictator's office and military discipline, if he went unpunished for disobeying an order. He set off for the camp full of menace and anger, but despite long daily marches, he could not outrun the word of his coming. Men had quickly left the city before him to report that the dictator was coming bent on revenge, and that with every other word he was praising the act of Titus Manlius.

31. Fabius immediately called an assembly* and appealed to the men to summon up the same courage with which they had defended the republic from the most implacable enemy to protect him—the man under whose leadership and auspices* they had won their victory—from the manic cruelty of the dictator. Papirius was coming, he said, crazed with jealousy, and angry over another's courage and good fortune. He was furious that the state's affairs had been well handled in his absence, and he would prefer—if he had the power to change fortune—to see the Samnites victorious rather than the Romans. He kept saying that his authority had been flouted, Fabius noted, as if his order not to engage did not reveal the same attitude as his resentment now over the engagement itself. In the former case, so there would be no action in his absence, he had, from jealousy, wanted to impede the valour of others, and would have taken weapons away from soldiers who were itching to fight. Now he was furious and resentful that, without Lucius Papirius, the troops had not lacked weapons and strength, and that Quintus Fabius had conducted himself as master of horse, not the dictator's attendant.

What would he have done if the battle had gone against them, Fabius asked, such being the chances of war and the dangers of combat that are equal to both sides? Now the enemy had been defeated, and Fabius' public responsibility had been so successfully discharged that it could not have been better discharged by that peerless leader—and Papirius was threatening his master of horse despite the victory! And that man's antipathy to the master of horse was no greater than it was to the military tribunes, to the centurions, and to the men! Had he been able, he would have directed his fury against them all! Since he could not, he was directing it against one man. Now the fact is that jealousy, like lightning, goes for the heights, and Papirius was attacking the head of their strategy, their commander. If he managed to eliminate him, and with him the glory of their exploit, he would, a man lording it over a captive army, have the nerve to inflict on the men whatever he had been allowed to inflict on his master of horse. So they should champion the liberty of all by rallying to his cause. If Papirius saw the same solidarity in the army in defending its victory as was present in the battle, and if he saw that one man's security was a concern to all, he would incline to more lenient sentiments. In short, Fabius concluded, he was entrusting his life and his fortunes to their loyalty and courage.*

32. A cry went up from the entire assembly, telling him to take heart—no one would do him harm while the Roman legions remained intact.

Not much later the dictator arrived, and he immediately had an assembly convened with a trumpet-call. Then, when silence was obtained, the herald summoned Quintus Fabius, the master of horse. From his place below Fabius mounted the dais, and the dictator immediately said: 'Quintus Fabius, I have a question for you. Since a dictator has supreme authority, and is obeyed by the consuls who have regal prerogative,* and by the praetors who have been elected under the same auspices as the consuls, do you or do you not think that a master of horse should follow his orders? I have this to ask you as well. Since I knew that I had left home when there was uncertainty surrounding the auspices, should I have exposed the republic to danger through overturning religious scruples, or should I have retaken the auspices to avoid doing anything when the gods' will was uncertain? There is also the question of whether the master of horse could be unrestricted and free to do what religious scruple has prevented the dictator from doing.

'But why do I bother with these questions? Had *I* said nothing on leaving, *your* decision should have been made on the basis of your understanding of what my wishes would be. So come, answer me. Did I order you not to initiate any action in my absence, and did I order you not to engage the enemy? You disobeyed my command and, when there was uncertainty about the auspices and there were religious complications, you contravened military practice, our fore-fathers' discipline, and the will of the gods by engaging the enemy in battle. Answer the questions that you have been asked, but see that you do not utter a word more! Lictor, come here!'

To answer the individual charges was not easy. Fabius protested at one moment that he had the same man as both accuser and judge in a case of life or death, and at the next he cried out that he would sooner see life taken from him than the glory of his exploits, in turn justify-ing his action and accusing the dictator. Then Papirius, his anger risen anew, ordered the master of horse stripped, and the rods and axes brought out.* Appealing to the loyalty of the men, and while the lictors were tearing the clothes from him, Fabius escaped to the *tri-arii*, who were stirring up a commotion at the back of the assembly.

From there the clamour spread throughout the assembly, with entreaties heard in one quarter and threats in another. Those who happened to be standing next to the dais were under the eyes of the dictator and thus able to be recognized; these were begging him to spare the master of horse and not condemn the whole army along with him. Those on the fringes of the assembly, however, and those clustered around Fabius, were excoriating the dictator's heartless-ness and were close to mutiny. There was no calm even on the com-mander's dais; legates standing around his seat kept imploring him to defer the issue to the following day so his anger could have some respite, and he had some time to judge the matter. Fabius had been chastised enough for his youthful impetuosity, they told him, and his victory had been sufficiently tarnished. They urged him not to take his punishment to the final extremity or inflict such disgrace on an outstanding young man, or on his father, a man of great distinction, or on the Fabian family. Making little progress with entreaty or argu-ment, however, they told him to look at the seething assembly. When the feelings of soldiers were so ruffled, they said, one did not expect a man of his age and good sense to add fire and fuel to a mutiny. If Papirius, blind with anger, turned the hostile crowd against himself with a wrong-headed altercation, no one was going to hold Quintus Fabius responsible for that—he was merely begging to be spared punishment—they would blame the dictator. Finally, they said, in case he thought they were saying this out of partiality for Quintus Fabius, they were prepared to take an oath swearing that, in their view, it was not in the interests of the state that Quintus Fabius be punished at that time.

33. With these remarks the legates did more to stir up the dictator against themselves than soothe his anger against his master of horse, and they were ordered off the dais. The dictator tried vainly to obtain silence through a herald, but as neither his words nor those of his attendants could be heard over the uproar and commotion, it was night that brought an end to the wrangling as though to a battle.

The master of horse had been commanded to appear the following day but, as everybody assured him that Papirius, now vexed and exasperated over the altercation, would be even more furious, he furtively left the camp for Rome. On the advice of his father Marcus Fabius, three times consul and also a former dictator, Fabius immediately called a meeting of the Senate. Just when he was deploring the dictator's violent and iniquitous behaviour before the senators, the noise was suddenly heard of lictors pushing people aside outside the Senate house, and there, full of anger, was the man himself. On learning that Fabius had left the camp, he had followed with a troop of light-armed horsemen.

The wrangling then began again, and Papirius ordered Fabius' arrest. The leading senators and the Senate as a whole tried to intercede, but his pitiless heart was set on its design. Then the father, Marcus Fabius, said:* 'You are swayed neither by the authority of the Senate, nor by my age, on which you prepare to inflict the loss of a child, nor by the valour and noble birth of the master of horse, who was appointed by your very self, nor by prayers, which have often mollified an enemy and which appease the anger of the gods. That being so, I call upon the tribunes of the plebs for help and I appeal to the people.* You shy away from the judgement of your army and shy away from that of the Senate, so I make the people your judge, the only one to have more power and strength than your dictatorship. I shall see whether you will give way to the appeal to which the Roman king Tullus Hostilius gave way.'*

They left the Senate house for the assembly, where the dictator went up with a few of his people, and the master of horse with the entire body of principal senators. Papirius then gave orders for Fabius to be removed from the Rostra to the area below. Fabius' father followed him, saying: 'Well done! You have ordered us to be taken to where we can speak out even as private citizens!'

There, at first, rather than continuous speeches, it was only wrangling that could be heard. Then the aged Fabius' angry words quelled the uproar as he berated Papirius' pride and heartlessness. He, too, had been a dictator in Rome, said Fabius, and nobody, not a plebeian, not a centurion, not a soldier, had been mistreated by him, but Papirius was trying to win a victory and a triumph over a Roman general as though over enemy leaders! What a difference there was between the restraint of the ancients and today's pride and heartlessness! After the dictator Quinctius Cincinnatus had extricated the consul Lucius Minucius* from a blockade, his anger with the man went no further than leaving him as a legate, instead of consul, in his army. Lucius Furius, showing no respect for Marcus Furius Camillus' advanced age and his authority, had fought a battle with the most disastrous result, but Camillus not only restrained his anger on the spot and made no negative report on his colleague in his dispatches to the people and Senate, but on his return, when given the right by the Senate to choose anyone he wanted as his partner in command, it was Furius that he selected out of all the consular tribunes.

In fact, Fabius continued, even the people, who hold supreme power in everything, had never been so angry with those who had lost armies through recklessness and incompetence as to do more than levy a fine; a capital charge had never, until this day, been brought against any general for military failure. But now generals of the Roman people who were victorious and thoroughly deserving of triumphs—these faced the threat of rods and axes, something formerly not thought right even for those *defeated* in war! What on earth would his son have suffered, he asked, if he had lost his army, been defeated, routed, had his camp taken from him? How much further could Papirius' wrath and aggression have gone beyond flogging and executing him? It was thanks to Quintus Fabius that the state was joyfully celebrating a victory with prayers and thanksgiving. How appropriate it now was for this man, thanks to whom the gods' temples were open, the altars smoking with sacrifices and loaded with offerings and gifts—how appropriate for him to be stripped and flayed with rods before the eyes of the Roman people, as he gazed at the Capitol and the citadel and the gods on whom he called for help (and not without result) in two battles! With what feelings would the army, victorious under his leadership and auspices, accept this? What grief there was going to be in the Roman camp, what joy amongst the enemy!

Such were Fabius' words, which were accompanied by a flood of tears, as he mingled reproaches and lamentation, and called on the protection of gods and men, all the time embracing his son.

34. In Fabius' favour there was the prestige of the Senate, the support of the people, the help of the tribunes, and the memory of the absent army. On the other side the arguments put forward hinged on the invincible authority of the Roman people, military discipline, the dictator's edict (ever thought to have quasi-divine status), and the 'Manlian orders', with love for a son subordinated to the interests of the state. There was also Lucius Brutus, creator of Roman liberty, who had dealt the same way with his two children. These days, said Papirius, fathers were indulgent and old men too ready to accept lack of respect for another person's authority, and they overlooked breaches of military discipline by the young as trivial offences. He, however, was going to abide by his resolution, and would not mitigate in any way the just penalty for a man who had, against his orders, fought when there were religious complications and uncertainty surrounding the auspices.

It was not in his power to see that the prestige of dictatorial authority would last for ever, he continued, but he, Lucius Papirius, was not going to diminish it in any way! He prayed that the power held by the tribunes (itself inviolate) would not violate the power of the Roman government by the use of the veto, and that the people would not snuff out the power and rights of the dictatorship just when he was dictator. If they did so, it would not be Lucius Papirius that their descendants would blame (and to no purpose then), but the tribunes and the misguided judgement of the people. Once military discipline was debased, he argued, the common soldier would not obey the order of the centurion, or the centurion the order of the tribune, the tribune that of the legate, the legate that of the consul, or the master of horse that of the dictator. Nobody would have respect for men, or for the gods, and the edicts of commanders would not be heeded, nor the auspices, either. Soldiers would wander aimlessly in lands both pacified and hostile without furlough and, with no thought for their oath, would capriciously release themselves from service whenever they chose. The standards would be left undermanned; there would be no assembling when the edict was given; the men would fight indiscriminately—by night or day, on favourable or unfavourable ground, with or without the command of the general. They would not follow the standards or keep their ranks, and a blind, hit-or-miss, marauder-style soldiering would replace the established and venerable style we have now.

'For all ages to come, tribunes of the plebs, expose yourselves to accusation on such charges!' Papirius concluded. 'Bring the responsibility for Quintus Fabius' insubordination upon your own heads!'

35. The tribunes were stunned, more worried now for themselves than for the man for whom their assistance was being sought, but then they were extricated from their dilemma by the united will of the Roman people, who turned to prayers and appeals, begging the dictator to lighten the punishment of his master of horse for their sake. The tribunes also followed this retreat into appeals and fervently proceeded to beg the dictator to pardon a human error and Quintus Fabius' immaturity—he had been punished enough, they said. And now the young man himself, and now his father, too, dropping their animosity, threw themselves at the dictator's feet and endeavoured to appease his anger with entreaties.*

Then, when he had obtained silence, the dictator said: 'That's good, citizens of Rome. Military discipline has prevailed, and so has the authority of command—they were in danger of not surviving beyond this day. Quintus Fabius, who went into battle against his commander's order, has not been absolved of guilt. He has been found guilty of wrongdoing, but is spared as a gift to the Roman people and as a gift to the power of the tribunes, who bring him help with their moral support rather than legal authority. Live on, Quintus Fabius, happier through this united wish of the citizen body to protect you than through the victory which you were gloating over a short time ago. Live on, though you ventured to commit a crime that even your father, had he been in Lucius Papirius' place, would not have forgiven. With me you can be reconciled when you wish; to the Roman people, to whom you owe your life, you can best demonstrate your gratitude if this day will have truly shown you how to accept legitimate orders in war and peace.'

Declaring that he would not further detain the master of horse,* Papirius then came down from the Rostra. The senators were happy, and the people happier; and they escorted him away, milling about and congratulating both the master of horse and the dictator. Military authority had apparently been reinforced no less by Quintus Fabius' perilous situation as by the sad punishment of the young Manlius.

It so happened that year that, whenever the dictator left the army, the enemy in Samnium became restive. However, the legate Marcus Valerius, the camp commander, had before his eyes the example of Quintus Fabius, which made his fear of an enemy attack not as great as his fear of the dictator's fierce anger. Thus, when some foragers were caught in an ambush and cut to pieces on unfavourable ground, it was commonly thought that help could have been brought by the legate had he not shuddered at the thought of those grim commands. That anger further alienated the soldiers from the dictator, with whom they were already annoyed for having shown himself implacable with Quintus Fabius but then pardoning him to please the Roman people, when he had rejected their own entreaties on his behalf.

36. After giving Lucius Papirius Crassus authority over the city,* and forbidding the master of horse, Quintus Fabius, to exercise his magistracy in any way, the dictator returned to his camp. His arrival there brought little joy to his fellow-citizens and no fear to the enemy—the next day, the Samnites formed up their battle-line and marched towards the dictator's camp, either unaware of his coming or caring little whether or not he was there. But so important was the presence of one man, Lucius Papirius, that if the commander's plans had then had the support of his men, it was thought certain that the war with the Samnites could have been ended that day, so adroitly did he form up the battle-line and strengthen it with all the resources of his military skill. But there was lack of action on the men's part, and the victory was deliberately lost in order to sully the commander's reputation. More Samnites were killed, more Romans wounded. From experience the commander realized what was obstructing victory: he needed to restrain his natural tendencies and temper his austerity with some cordiality. Summoning his legates, he went around the wounded in person, sticking his head into their tents and asking each man how he was feeling; then, supplying their

names, he issued instructions for their care to the legates, tribunes, and prefects. This exercise was itself popular, but Papirius brought it off so adroitly that treating their bodies won the men's minds over to the commander long before their recovery, and there was nothing more effective in restoring them to health than the gratitude felt for such attention.

When the army was back on its feet, he engaged the enemy, both he and the men confident of victory, and so complete was his defeat and rout of the Samnites that that was the last day they fought a pitched battle with the dictator. The triumphant army then advanced where hopes of plunder led them, and they ranged far and wide over enemy territory, meeting no military force and no opposition, either in the open or from ambush. The fact that the dictator had proclaimed that the plunder would all go to the men intensified their fervour, and in stimulating them against the foe their communal anger with him was no more effective than individual gain. Cowed by the reverses, the Samnites asked the dictator for a peace, and negotiated with him to provide one garment and a year's pay for each soldier. They were instructed to appear before the Senate, but replied that they would go there with the dictator, relying entirely on his integrity and sense of honour to champion their cause. With that the army was withdrawn from Samnium.

37. The dictator entered the city in triumph. He wanted to resign the dictatorship, but before his resignation he presided over the election of the consuls, on the order of the Senate. Elected were Gaius Sulpicius Longus (his second term) and Quintus Aemilius Cerretanus.* Because of a dispute over terms, the peace treaty was not concluded and the Samnites instead left Rome with a year's truce. Even that they did not observe faithfully, so excited were they about opening hostilities on the news of Papirius' resignation from office.

In the consulship of Gaius Sulpicius and Quintus Aemilius (though some annals give Aulius), there was, in addition to the insurgency of the Samnites, a new war with the Apulians.* Armies were sent to both places, and the Samnites fell by sortition to Sulpicius, and the Apulians to Aemilius. There are some sources that claim that the war was not launched against the Apulians themselves, but that peoples allied to the Apulians were being defended against Samnite aggression and injustice. However, the plight of the Samnites, who were at that time barely able to repel an attack on them, makes it more likely that there was no Samnite aggression against the Apulians, but that the Romans were simultaneously at war with the two peoples. But there was no action worthy of record. Apulian territory and Samnium suffered complete devastation, and the enemy was encountered in neither the one nor the other.

In Rome there was an alarm at night that woke the sleeping populace, suddenly filling them with such fright that the Capitol and citadel, and the walls and gates, were filled with armed men. People ran to and fro, and there was a call to arms, but at dawn no one responsible for the panic was to be found, and no reason for it.

In that same year, under the Flavian bill, the inhabitants of Tusculum faced judgement before the people.* Marcus Flavius, a tribune of the plebs, proposed to the people that the Tusculans should face punishment for having given assistance and advice to the Veliterni and Privernates in the war they had fought against the Roman people. The men of Tusculum then came to Rome with their wives and children. The large crowd changed into mourning dress and, looking like defendants in court, made the rounds of the tribes, throwing themselves before everyone's knees. So it was that pity did more to gain them pardon than the merits of their case did to clear them of the charges. The tribes all rejected the bill, apart from the Pollian, which voted that the men of fighting age be flogged and executed, and their wives and children auctioned off under the rules of war. Resentment towards those who advocated such a ferocious penalty lingered in the Tusculan population, and its memory remained alive down to the time of our fathers, with a candidate from the Pollian tribe hardly ever carrying the vote of the Papirian.*

38. The next year, which was the consulship of Quintus Fabius* and Lucius Fulvius, there were fears of a more serious war in Samnium (it was said that mercenaries had been hired from amongst their neighbours). The dictator Aulus Cornelius Arvina* and his master of horse Marcus Fabius Ambustus accordingly held a particularly strict troop-levy and led out an excellent army to face the Samnites. However, they were careless in establishing their camp in hostile territory, as though the enemy were far off. The Samnite legions suddenly arrived and had such overwhelming confidence as to move their rampart forward all the way to the Roman outposts.

Night was now approaching, and that prevented the Samnites from attacking the Roman fortifications, but they did not hide their intention of doing so at daybreak the next day. The dictator could see a battle was coming sooner than he had expected and, so their position would not damage his men's morale, he left numerous fires burning so the sight would mislead the enemy and silently led away his legions. He could not, however, slip away unseen, the camps being so close. The enemy cavalry immediately gave chase and put pressure on his column, but avoided engaging until daybreak, while their infantry did not even leave camp before dawn. It was at dawn that the cavalry finally dared to attack, and it held back the Roman column by harrying the rear and putting pressure on the soldiers in areas that were difficult to cross. Meanwhile their infantry had now caught up with their cavalry, and the Samnites launched an attack in full force. At that point, unable to forge ahead without great difficulty, the dictator gave the order to measure out a camp on the spot where he had stopped. But with cavalry completely encircling them, it was impossible to search for stakes and start work on the palisade.

Aware that he could not advance but that he could not remain there, either, Cornelius deployed his line of battle, after removing the baggage from the column. The enemy also deployed theirs opposite his, a match for the Romans in both courage and strength. What had especially increased their confidence was their failure to realize that the Romans' retreat had been prompted by their unfavourable position, not their enemy; and their belief that they had inspired panic and had been pursuing an enemy in terrified flight.

This for a time kept the fight even, though the Samnites had long been unaccustomed to enduring the battle-cry of the Roman army. On that day, amazingly, from the third hour to the eighth, the contest is said to have remained so much in doubt that the battle-cry was raised once at the initial clash and was not raised again, the standards were neither moved forward nor pulled back, and there was no giving ground at any point. They fought standing firm in their positions, pushing with their shields, and without pausing for breath or looking behind. There was the same roar of battle as it proceeded uniformly on both sides, and it promised to end only in total exhaustion or with the onset of night.

Men were now losing strength, weapons their edge, and the commanders their battle plans. Then suddenly the Samnite cavalry heard from a squadron that had advanced some distance that the baggage of the Romans was lying unguarded, far removed from their soldiers, and they charged forward, hungry for plunder. A fearful messenger brought the dictator the news, and he retorted: 'Just let them load themselves down with plunder!' Then others came up, followed by more again, all shouting out that the soldiers' fortunes were being pillaged and carried off everywhere.

Cornelius sent for the master of horse. 'Marcus Fabius,' he said, 'do you see how the battle has been abandoned by the enemy cavalry? They are stuck, caught up in our baggage. Attack them while they are dispersed like any crowd engaged in looting. You will find few on their horses, few with a sword in their hands. While they burden themselves and their horses with plunder, cut them down unarmed and turn it into bloody plunder for them! I shall look after the legions and the infantry battle; you take the glory for the cavalry!

39. The cavalry line, drawn up in the best possible order, charged an enemy that was scattered and encumbered, and filled the whole field with carnage. Amidst the packs that they had swiftly abandoned, and which obstructed the hooves of the horses as they fled in panic, the Samnites found that neither fight nor flight was possible, and they were butchered. After almost wiping out the enemy cavalry, Marcus Fabius then wheeled his squadrons around slightly and attacked their infantry line from the rear. The fresh clamour reaching their ears from that quarter terrified the Samnites, and the dictator could see their front-rank troops looking back, their standards in disorder and the battle-line wavering. He then shouted to his men; he encouraged them; and he called on the tribunes and company commanders by name to join him in reviving the attack. There was a renewed battle-cry, the troops advanced, and with every forward move they could see the enemy more and more in disarray. Their horsemen were now visible to the front ranks, and Cornelius, looking back at the infantry units, did all he could with hand gestures and voice to show them that he could see the banners and small shields of the cavalry. Hearing this and, at one and the same time, spotting the cavalry, the men suddenly forgot their wounds and the hardships they had suffered almost the whole day through. Indeed, they hurled themselves on the enemy just like men coming fresh from the camp after receiving the signal for battle. No longer could the Samnites withstand the terror inspired by the cavalry and the violent charge of

the infantry; some were finished off in the action, others scattered in flight. The infantry surrounded and cut down those who held their ground; those who fled faced slaughter at the hands of the cavalry, and their commander himself died amongst them.*

This battle finally broke the Samnites' strength, to such an extent that in all their councils they angrily commented that it was not at all surprising if they were meeting with no success—it was an unholy war that broke a treaty, and the gods had more reason than men to be angry with them. That war would have to be expiated and atoned for at heavy cost. The only real issue, they said, was whether they should make reparation with the guilty blood of a few or the innocent blood of all—and by now a number of people were daring to name those responsible for the war. There was one name in particular being heard: amid the clamour there was agreement on Papius Brutulus. A powerful aristocrat, he was undoubtedly the man to blame for the breaking of the last truce. The praetors were obliged to put the matter up for debate, and the decision was that Papius Brutulus should be surrendered to Romans; that all the Roman plunder and prisoners of war should be sent with him to Rome: and that restitution should be made, as law and religion demanded, of whatever property the fetial priests had reclaimed under the treaty.

The fetial priests were dispatched to Rome in accordance with the people's resolution, as was the lifeless body of Brutulus; he had himself escaped ignominy and punishment by suicide. It was decided that his possessions should also be surrendered along with his corpse. However, none of these items were accepted, apart from the prisoners of war and articles amongst the plunder that were identified by their owners. The surrender of everything else served no purpose. By a decision of the Senate the dictator celebrated a triumph.

40. According to some authors,* this war was fought by the consuls, and they held the triumph over the Samnites. These also relate that Fabius advanced into Apulia and took a great deal of plunder from there. There is no disagreement over whether Aulus Cornelius was dictator that year. What *is* disputed, however, is whether the purpose of his appointment was fighting the war or giving the starting signal to the four-horse chariots at the Roman Games (because the praetor Lucius Plautius happened to have been struck by a serious illness) and whether he resigned the dictatorship after discharging this not particularly noteworthy function of his office. It is not easy either to give preference either to one version over another or to one author over another. I believe the historical record has been marred by funerary eulogies and false inscriptions on ancestral busts, with the various families all illegitimately appropriating to themselves military campaigns and public offices.* This, at least, is the source of uncertainty with respect to the achievements of individuals and public records of events. And there is no writer contemporaneous with those events* whose account can be regarded as authoritative.

BOOK NINE

1. The following year, the consulship of Titus Veturius Calvinus and Spurius Postumius, saw the celebrated Caudine peace as the aftermath of a Roman debacle.* The Samnites that year had as their commander Gaius Pontius, son of Herennius;* he was the Samnites' foremost warrior and general, while his father was by far the most prudent of them. When the ambassadors who had been sent to make the surrender returned without a peace treaty, Pontius declared: 'Do not think nothing has been achieved by this embassy—atonement has now been made for whatever anger the gods harboured towards us as a result of the broken treaty. Whoever the gods were that wanted us forced into surrendering what had been reclaimed from us under the treaty, I am convinced that they did not want our reparations for the treaty to be so high-handedly dismissed by the Romans. What could have been done beyond what we did to placate the gods and soften the hearts of men? We returned enemy property that had been taken as plunder, although it was regarded as ours under the conventions of warfare. Unable to surrender alive the fomenters of war, we surrendered them dead; and their possessions we transported to Rome so that no taint of guilt could remain with us from contact with them. Roman, what more must I do for you, for the treaty and for the gods who witnessed the treaty? What judge can I propose to decide how great your wrath and my punishment should be? I reject no state for that office, and no individual.

'If, however, the weak are left no basic rights in dealing with a stronger power, I shall appeal to the gods who punish insufferable arrogance. I shall beg them to turn their wrath on those for whom the return of their own possessions as well as accumulating those of others is not enough; on those whose bloodthirsty nature is not sated with the death of the guilty, with the surrender of dead bodies, or with the goods of the dead owners surrendered with them; and on those who cannot be placated unless we offer them our blood to drink dry and our flesh to rip apart!

'Men of Samnium: a war is justified for those who have to fight, and arms are rightly borne by those left no hope except in arms. In short, since the most important consideration in human affairs is whether actions have either the blessing or the disapproval of the gods, rest assured of this: you fought the earlier wars against the gods rather than men, but the one at hand you will fight under the leadership of the gods themselves.'

2. With this prediction, accurate as well as favourable, Pontius led out his force and, with as much stealth as he could, established camp in the area of Caudium.* From there he sent off to Calatia—where, he was told, the Roman consuls were already encamped—ten soldiers dressed as shepherds, under orders to put their animals out to pasture at various points not far from the Roman outposts. When they came upon raiding parties, they were all to say the same thing, that the Samnite legions were in Apulia, and that they were blockading Luceria* with all their troops and were close to capturing it. Such a rumour had been intentionally spread abroad even before this, and had reached the Romans, but these prisoners increased its credibility, all the more so given the consistency of their accounts. There was no doubt that the Romans would bring aid to the Lucerians, who were good, loyal allies, and there was the further incentive of preventing the defection of all Apulia in the face of the present threat. The only question was the route they would take.

Two roads led to Luceria, one skirting the coast of the Upper Sea* (it was open and clear but, while it was safer, it was correspondingly longer), and the other, which was shorter, by way of the Caudine Forks.* This one, however, has the following characteristics. There are two deep gorges, both of them narrow and wooded, which are interconnected, with an unbroken line of hills on both sides, and enclosed between them is a rather wide plain, verdant and well watered, through the middle of which runs the road. Before reaching the plain, however, one must enter the first narrow defile, and afterwards either make the return journey by the same route by which you entered or, if you go ahead, exit by the other defile which is narrower and more difficult to negotiate.

The Romans sent their column down into this plain by one of the paths, which went through a rocky gorge. They then went forward immediately to the second ravine, which they found blocked by felled trees and a pile of huge rocks that stood in their way. This was evidently an enemy trap, and a detachment of them was now also spotted on the heights above the pass. The Romans beat a hasty retreat and tried to take again the path by which they had come, only to find that this also had its barricade and armed men cutting them off. They halted, with no order given. A daze came over the minds of all and an odd sort of paralysis seized their limbs.* They looked at each other, each thinking the next man more capable of thought and making a decision than he was himself, and for a long time they were silent and motionless. Then they saw the consuls' tents being pitched and some men preparing the tools for that operation and, although they could see that constructing fortifications would be absurd when the situation was desperate and all hope lost, they were unwilling to add the charge of negligence to their misfortunes. Accordingly, though no one was encouraging them or ordering them to do so, they all individually took the initiative and turned to building defences, surrounding a camp close to water with an entrenchment. And all the while, to add to the scornful taunts of the enemy, they themselves joked about their effort and their work, pitifully acknowledging its futility. The legates and tribunes* of their own accord gathered before the dispirited consuls, who did not even summon them to a council meeting since the situation offered no chance of salutary advice or help; and the men turned to the generals' tent and demanded of their leaders help that not even the immortal gods could provide.

3. When night came upon them they were lamenting rather than deliberating, each of them muttering remarks reflecting his temperament. One would say: 'Let us break through the roadblocks, climb the mountains before us, go through the forests—let us go wherever arms can be carried, as long as we can get to the enemy that we've been defeating for almost thirty years now! A Roman fighting against a treacherous Samnite will find it all smooth and easy going!' Another would ask: 'Where are we to go, and how? Do we really intend to shift mountains from their base? How will you get at the enemy while these heights tower above us? Armed or unarmed, hero or coward, we are all in the same situation, all prisoners and defeated men. The enemy is not even going to offer us the chance of dying well by the sword—he will end the war sitting down!' It was with such conversations that the night was drawn out, with no thought given to food or sleep.

In such happy circumstances the Samnites had no plan of action either,* and so they all agreed to consult their general's father, Herennius Pontius, by letter. Age was by now weighing heavily on Pontius, and he had retired not only from military duties but from civil duties, too. Nevertheless, although he was physically weakened his intelligence and judgement still remained strong. When he received the news that the Roman armies were pinned down between two passes at the Caudine Forks, and was asked for his advice by the messenger from his son, he expressed the opinion that they all should be released unharmed as soon as possible. That view was rejected, and when the same messenger came back, and Pontius was again asked for his advice, his opinion now was that the Romans should be killed to the last man. The replies given by the man were so contradictory as to resemble an ambiguous response from an oracle, and his own son was among the first to think that his father's wits had given way to senility within his enfeebled body. He was, however, won over by the general consensus to send for the man to appear in person before their council.

The old man, it is said, did not refuse, and he was brought to the camp in a wagon and summoned to the council meeting. There, it is said, his address revealed no change in his opinion; he merely added his reasons for it. He explained that his first proposal (which he thought was the best) established lasting peace and friendship with a very powerful people by doing them a very great service. The second deferred war for many generations to come, during which time Rome would find it not easy to regain its strength after losing two armies. There was, he said, no third option.

Herennius' son and the other leaders then kept asking how it would be if they took his proposal half-way, the soldiers being released unharmed but also with conditions imposed on them, under the rules of war, as the defeated party. 'That', said Herennius, 'is an idea that neither wins friends nor removes enemies. Just try leaving alive men you have provoked with humiliation! The Romans are a people unable to remain at peace when defeated, and whatever their current plight will have branded in their hearts will always remain there and will not permit them to rest before they have punished you many times over.' Neither of Herennius' suggestions was accepted, and he was transported home from the camp.

4. In the Roman camp, meanwhile, numerous attempts to break free had failed,* and there was now a shortage of all supplies. Overwhelmed by the dire situation, the Romans sent out spokesmen who were first to sue for a fair peace treaty and, failing to obtain peace, to challenge the enemy to fight. Pontius' reply was that the war was

over, and that since the Romans could not acknowledge their situation even when they were defeated and taken prisoner, he was going to send them under the yoke* stripped of their weapons and with just one garment apiece. The other peace conditions, he said, would be fair for the vanquished and victors alike. If the Romans quit Samnite territory and their colonies were withdrawn, Roman and Samnite would from then on live under their own laws, their treaty based on equality. Such were the terms on which he was ready to conclude a treaty with the consuls, he said, and he ordered the spokesmen not to return to him if any of them was found unacceptable. When this reply was brought back, so great was the lamentation that suddenly arose throughout the Roman troops, and so overwhelming the distress that beset them, that it was apparent that they would not be more pained to receive the news that they were all to perish on the spot.

There was a long silence, the consuls being unable to open their mouths in favour of a treaty so humiliating or against a treaty so urgently needed. Then Lucius Lentulus spoke,* a man who was the foremost of the spokesmen in courage and the offices he had held.

'Consuls,' he said, 'I often heard my father tell of how he alone on the Capitol would not support the Senate on the payment of gold to ransom the city from the Gauls. This, he said, was because the blockade was conducted without a ditch and a rampart by an enemy who was particularly indolent when it came to siege-works and building, and because breaking out of there did not entail inevitable destruction even if it involved great danger. They had the opportunity to charge down at the enemy, with their weapons, from the Capitol, as those under siege have often made a sortie against their besiegers; and if we likewise had the opportunity to engage our enemy, on ground favourable or unfavourable, I would not be lacking my father's temperament in the advice I proffered. Indeed, I admit that death for one's country is glorious, and I am ready to face devoting myself on behalf of the Roman people and its legions by throwing myself into the midst of the enemy. But it is here that I see my country, it is here that I see what remains of the Roman legions, and, unless these want to rush to their deaths for their own satisfaction, what do they have that they can save by dying?

'Someone may answer "The buildings of the city, its walls, and its horde of inhabitants." Not so, for heaven's sake! All these are abandoned, not saved, if this army is destroyed. Who is going to protect them? A crowd with no military skills or weapons, I suppose! Yes, of course, just as effectively as it defended them against the Gallic invasion! Or will they cry out for an army to come from Veii with a Camillus leading it? Here is where all our hopes and resources lie. Saving them we save our country; committing them to destruction we desert and betray our country.

'"But surrender is shameful and ignominious!" But such is love of one's country that we should save it by our ignomy, if needs be, as readily as by our death. So let us accept that shame, no matter how great it is, and bend before necessity, which not even the gods can rise above. Go, consuls, and surrender your arms to redeem the city that your ancestors redeemed with gold.'

5. The consuls set off to parley with Pontius, but when the victor kept bringing up the matter of a treaty they declared that no treaty could be made without the order of the people or without the fetial priests and the other formalities. Thus the peace of Caudium came about not through a treaty, as is commonly believed and as Claudius even records, but by a solemn pledge.* Why would one have needed guarantors or hostages in the case of a treaty, in which the process is settled with a prayer asking Jupiter to strike the people responsible for any infraction of the stated terms as a pig is struck by the fetials? Those making the pledge were the consuls, the legates, the quaestors, and the military tribunes, and the names of all who made it are on record, whereas if the procedure had been the formulation of a treaty no names would be on record apart from those of the fetials. Moreover, because of the delay inevitably involved in concluding a treaty, a demand was made for six hundred *equites* who were to pay with their lives for failure to stand by the pledge. A timetable was then laid down for the surrender of the hostages and for sending the army under the yoke unarmed.

The consuls' return renewed the sorrow in the camp, to the point where the men had difficulty keeping their hands off those whose recklessness had brought them to that spot and thanks to whose cowardice they were going to leave in greater disgrace than they had come. They had had no guide to the area, no scout, they said. They had been driven blindly, like animals, into a pit. They looked at each other, and ran their eyes over their arms that were soon to be surrendered, over their right hands that would lose their weapons and over their bodies that were to be in the enemy's power. Before their eyes they had the enemy's yoke, the jibes of the victors and their arrogant expressions, their own advance as unarmed men past soldiers in arms. And after that they pictured the miserable trek of their disgraced column through the cities of the allies, and the return to their homeland and parents—where they themselves had often come in triumph, and their ancestors before them. They alone had been defeated with no wound, no weapon, no battle; they had not been permitted to draw their swords or to come to grips with the enemy; and it was for nothing that they had been granted arms, strength, and courage.

They were still uttering these complaints when the hour fate had appointed for their disgrace came upon them, an hour in which experience would make everything more agonizing than they had imagined. Right at the start they were instructed to leave their fortifications unarmed and wearing one garment, and first the hostages were handed over and led off into confinement. Then the lictors were instructed to step aside from the consuls, and the consuls were relieved of their military cloaks.* This instilled such pity in those very men who, moments before, had been bringing curses down on their heads and claiming they should be surrendered and tortured, that they all forgot their own plight and turned their gaze aside from the desecration of such an exalted office as from some horrific spectacle.

6. The consuls, almost semi-nude, were the first sent under the yoke; then each officer was exposed to the humiliation in order of seniority; and after that came the legions, one by one. The enemy stood around them in arms, jeering and ridiculing them. A number even had swords pointed at them, and some were wounded or killed if their expressions offended the victors by showing too much resentment at the indignity.

And so they were passed under the yoke and (what was almost more painful) it was under the gaze of the enemy. Coming out of the gorge they looked like men raised from hell who were seeing the light for the first time, but that light itself was for them, as they surveyed such a dismal column, more dismal than any form of death. Thus, though reaching Capua before nightfall was within their capability, they were unsure about the loyalty of the allies and feelings of shame also held them back, and so, deprived of everything though they were, they flung themselves down on the ground at the roadside not far from Capua. News of this was brought to Capua, and a natural feeling of compassion for their allies overwhelmed the inbred haughtiness of the Campanians. In an immediate display of kindness, they sent the appropriate insignia for the consuls,* and weapons, clothing, and provisions for the enlisted men. When the Romans were approaching Capua the entire senate and people of the town came forth to meet them and duly discharged all the regular duties of hospitality on both the private and official level. And yet the generosity of their allies, their kind faces and encouraging words, were not merely unable to elicit any conversation from the Romans but could not even bring them to raise their eyes or look the friends who were consoling them in the face. To such an extent did their shame, in addition to their dejection, force them to avoid conversing or interacting with people.

The next day some young noblemen, who had been sent from Capua to escort the Romans to the Campanian frontier, were summoned to the Senate house and questioned by the senior members. They reported that the Romans had seemed to them far more disheartened and dejected than earlier—in such silence had their column trudged on, almost as though they were mute. The renowned Roman character was crushed, and their spirit had been taken from them along with their weapons. They did not offer greetings, and did not respond when greeted; none had been able to open his mouth from anxiety, as if they still had on their necks the yoke under which they had been sent. The Samnites, they said, had to their credit a victory that was not only glorious but permanent: they had captured not just Rome, as the Gauls before them had done, but—a much greater feat in war—the Romans' courage and defiant spirit.

7. Such were the comments being made and heard, and in the council of the loyal allies hope for the Roman name was all but abandoned. At that point, it is said, Aulus Calavius, son of Ovius, took the floor, a man distinguished for his family background and his career, and who at the time commanded respect for his age. He said that the facts were very different. That stubborn silence, the eyes fixed on the ground, the ears deaf to all forms of solace, the shame they felt at seeing the daylight—these were all symptoms of a soul arousing massive anger deep within. Either he did not know the Roman character, he continued, or else that silence was soon going to draw piteous wailing and groans from the Samnites, and the memory of the Caudine peace

would be more distressing for them than for the Romans. Each people would maintain its courage wherever the two met in battle, but there would not everywhere be a Caudine Pass for the Samnites.

By now Rome also knew of her humiliating defeat. People first heard of the army being trapped; then came the report of the shameful peace, more distressing than that of the danger. With the news of the blockade a troop-levy had begun, but, after they heard of the surrender on such ignominious terms, relief measures were abandoned and instantly, without any official announcement, they as one took up every form of lamentation. The shops around the Forum were closed and there was a spontaneous suspension of business before any formal declaration was made. The broad purple bands and golden rings were set aside,* and the citizen body was almost more despondent than the army itself: they were not only incensed with the leaders who had negotiated and supported the peace but they also harboured resentment towards the guiltless soldiers, saying they should not be allowed back in the city and their homes. This fiery reaction, however, was cut short by the army's arrival, which roused pity even in their angry hearts. Entering the city at a late hour, the soldiers did not look like men returning to their native soil unharmed when all hope for them had been lost. Their comportment and expressions were those of prisoners of war, and they all hid themselves away in their homes,* none of them wishing to set eyes on the Forum or streets the next day or on those that followed. The consuls remained incommunicado and saw to none of the business of their office, apart from appointing a dictator to hold elections, a duty that was imposed on them by senatorial decree. Their appointee was Quintus Fabius Ambustus, with Publius Aelius Paetus as his master of horse, but there was an irregularity in their appointment which led to their replacement by Marcus Aemilius Papus as dictator, and Lucius Valerius Flaccus as master of horse. However, elections were not held by these men, either, and because the people were displeased with all the magistrates of that year there was a return to an *interregnum*. The *interreges* were Quintus Fabius Maximus and Marcus Valerius Corvus. Corvus then presided over the election to the consulship of Quintus Publilius Philo (his third term) and Lucius Papirius Cursor (his second term), and there was no doubt about the citizens' agreement with this, since there were no generals more renowned than these at the time.

8. In accordance with a decree of the Senate, the two entered office on the day of their election. After first performing the sacred rituals prescribed by the Senate, they brought up the matter of the Caudine peace, and Publilius, who then held the *fasces*, said: 'You have the floor, Spurius Postumius.'

Spurius rose to his feet and, wearing the same expression as when he was sent under the yoke, he said: 'Consuls: I am not unaware that the reason for my being called upon and told to speak first is not to honour me but to humiliate me,* and that I am called on not as a senator but as a man charged with a disastrous campaign and an igno-minious peace. That notwithstanding, you have not brought up the matter either of our guilt or our punishment, and so I shall not bother to defend myself (though that would not be very difficult before men not unaware of the fortunes and pressures in the human condition), but I shall briefly state my opinion on the subject you have put up for discussion. This opinion will demonstrate whether it was I myself or your legions that I saved when I made a pledge that was either dis-graceful or essential.* And I add that, since the pledge was made without the people's sanction, the Roman people are not bound by it, nor are the Samnites owed anything by it except our persons. Let us be surrendered to them, naked and shackled, by the fetials. Let us free the people from any religious obligation we incurred so that there may be no divine or human impediment to hostilities being renewed with justice and right on our side. Meanwhile, the consuls should enlist, equip, and lead forth an army, but not enter enemy territory until all the measures pertaining to our surrender have been completed. To you, immortal gods, I make this prayer and this plea. If it was not your wish that the consuls Spurius Postumius and Titus Veturius should conduct a successful campaign against the Samnites, then at least be satisfied with having seen us sent under the yoke, with having seen us bound by a disgraceful accord, and with seeing us delivered to the enemy naked and fettered, bringing down on our own heads all the wrath of the foe. And may it please you to have the new consuls and the Roman legions fight a war with the Samnites with such success as has attended all the wars of Rome before our consulship.'

After these words, such admiration and compassion for the man came over his hearers that they could hardly believe that this was the same Spurius Postumius who had negotiated such a dreadful peace.

They could only feel pity over a man of such character facing a singular kind of punishment at the hands of an enemy furious over his
breaking their peace agreement. When they all showered no end of
praise on the man and began to show support for his motion, an
attempt to veto it was briefly made by the plebeian tribunes Lucius
Livius and Quintus Maelius. The religious obligations could not be
met by the people through surrendering him, they said, unless the
situation that obtained for the Samnites at Caudium were completely
restored. Moreover, they added, they had deserved no punishment
for having saved an army of the Roman people by making a pledge of
peace, and finally, because of their sacrosanct status,* they could not
be handed over to the enemy or subjected to violence.

9. 'Well, in the meantime hand over those of us who are not sacrosanct,' retorted Postumius, 'those that you can hand over without
breaking any religious taboo. Later on hand over those sacrosanct
people as well, once they leave office; but if you listen to me you will
first have them flogged here in the Comitium as interest on the suspended penalty. They claim that the people cannot be freed of their
religious obligations by surrendering us, but who is so ignorant of
fetial law as not to realize that those fellows are saying this to prevent
their being surrendered rather than because this is actually the case?
Now I do not deny, Senators, that pledges given are thought to be as
sacred as treaties by those for whom loyalty between men stands next
in importance to our obligations to heaven. What I do dispute,
though, is that any agreement can be binding on the people if made
without the authorization of the people.

'Just suppose the Samnites had, with all the arrogance they demonstrated in squeezing that pledge out of us, forced us to enunciate
the standard formulae for the surrender of cities.* Would you tribunes then declare that the Roman people had been surrendered, and
that this city now belonged to the Samnites, along with its temples,
shrines, land, and waters? But I drop 'surrender', since what is in
question is a pledge. So what if we had made a pledge that the Roman
people would abandon this city? That they would burn it down? That
they would not have magistrates, a senate, laws? That they would live
under kings?

'"God forbid!" you say. And yet the shabbiness of its terms does
not weaken the bond of the pledge. If there is any one thing for which
the people can be bound by oath, they can for everything. Nor is it

important—something that perhaps influences certain people—whether it was a consul, a dictator, or a praetor who made the pledge. And this was the thinking even of the Samnites themselves. For them it was not enough for the consuls to make the pledge; they forced the legates, quaestors, and military tribunes to do so, as well.

'And let no one now ask me why I made such a pledge when a consul had no right to do that, and when I could not anyway guarantee them a peace on your behalf, that not being in my power since you had given me no such orders. Conscript Fathers, no action taken at Caudium was of human devising; the immortal gods stripped your commanders and those of the enemy of rational thought. In our case, our precautions in the operation were insufficient, and in their case foolishness lost them a victory that foolishness had given them—they had scarcely any trust in the location that had given them victory and they were in a hurry to take weapons, on any terms whatsoever, from men born to use them. Had they been in their right mind, would it have been difficult for them to send ambassadors to Rome—meanwhile summoning elder citizens from home for discussions—and to enter negotiations on a peace treaty and settlement with the Senate and people? If they travelled light, that was a three-day journey,* and in the meantime a truce would have been in effect until the ambassadors came bringing them either confirmation of their victory or peace. That alone would have resulted in a pledge that we might have made with the authorization of the people.

'In fact, though, you would not have accepted giving such a pledge, nor would we have made one. It was not Heaven's will for there to be any other outcome than that the enemy should be taken in by a dream too happy for them to absorb mentally; that the same fortune that had trapped us should also extricate us; that an illusory victory should be cancelled out by even more illusory peace; and that a pledge should be brought into play binding no one apart from its maker. What discussions were there with you, members of the Senate, or with the Roman people? Who can make a legitimate appeal to you, who claim he was duped by you? Can an enemy or a citizen do so? You made no pledge to the enemy and ordered no citizen to make one on your behalf. So you have nothing to discuss with us, since you gave us no instructions, and nothing with the Samnites, either, since you had no dealings with them. For the Samnites it is we who are the guarantors, and we are quite able to deliver what belongs to us and what we are able to hand over, namely our persons and our lives. On these let them vent their anger; on these let them whet their swords and their wrath. In the case of the tribunes, consider whether their surrender can be effected immediately or is to be postponed till later. Meanwhile, Titus Veturius and the rest of you, let us take to the enemy these worthless lives of ours to discharge our pledge, and by our suffering let us set Roman arms free.'

10. The Senate members were impressed both by the case put forward and by the speaker, and that included the plebeian tribunes, who said they would follow the Senate's ruling in the matter. The tribunes then immediately resigned their office and were handed over to the fetials to be taken to Caudium with the others. With the passing of this decree of the Senate, it seemed as though a light had shone upon the city. Postumius was the talk of the town; people praised him to the skies and put his gesture on a par with the devotion of the consul Publius Decius and other glorious acts. Thanks to his advice and his efforts, they said, the state had extricated itself from a degrading peace, while Postumius was resigning himself to torture and the enemy's wrath, sacrificing himself on behalf of the Roman people. All now had their gaze fixed on arms and war—when, oh when, they wondered, would the chance of meeting the Samnites in battle ever come.

In a city burning with anger and hatred the troop-levy consisted almost entirely of volunteers. Nine legions* were reconstituted from already-enlisted men, and the army was marched to Caudium. The fetials led the way, and on reaching the gate they gave orders for the men responsible for the pledge of peace to be stripped of their clothing and have their hands tied behind their backs. From respect for the man's standing, the attendant was tying the bonds loosely when Postumius said: 'No, tighten the strap so the surrender is properly made.'

When they reached the Samnite assembly and Pontius' dais, the fetial Aulus Cornelius Arvina made the following statement: 'Seeing that these men, with no instructions from the Quirites, the Roman people, made a commitment that a treaty would be struck and therefore were at fault, I surrender these men to you so that the Roman people may be freed of a sacrilegious crime.' As the fetial was uttering these words Postumius jabbed the man's thigh with his knee as hard as he could, and in a loud voice declared that he was a Samnite citizen* and that the fetial ambassador had been violated by him in contravention of international law. So now, he said, the Romans would have greater justification for waging war.

11. 'I personally shall not accept that surrender,' Pontius then replied,* 'nor will the Samnites recognize its validity. Spurius Postumius, if you believe the gods exist, why do you not cancel everything or else stand by your agreement? The Samnite people are owed all those men they had in their power or, in their place, peace. But why am I calling upon *you*, you who are displaying as much integrity as you can by surrendering yourself as a prisoner to your conqueror? I call upon the Roman people: if they have second thoughts about the commitment made at the Caudine Forks then let them put their legions back in the pass where they were surrounded. Let there be no double-dealing! Let everything return to the status quo. Let them take up the weapons they relinquished by the pact. Let them return to their camp. Let them have whatever they had on the day before they came to parley. That is the point at which they should be opting for war and stout-hearted decisions; that is when a pledge of peace should be rejected. Let us resume hostilities under the same conditions and in the same position that we were in before there was mention of peace. Let there be no complaint from the Roman people about the pledge made by the consuls, nor from us about Roman integrity.

'Will you never be without a pretext for reneging on your commitments in defeat? You gave Porsenna hostages; then you took them back by subterfuge. You ransomed your city from the Gauls with gold; they were massacred while accepting the gold. You made a pledge of a peace treaty with us on condition that we return to you the captured legions; you are revoking that peace treaty. And you invariably have some specious justification for your chicanery. The Roman people do not approve of their legions being saved by a degrading peace? So let them keep their peace and give back to the victor the captured legions! That would be a gesture in keeping with their integrity, their treaties, their fetial rituals! For you to have what you wanted after making your pledge, namely all those fellow-citizens unharmed, and for me not to have the peace I agreed to with you for releasing them to you—Aulus Cornelius, and you, the fetials, is this the kind of justice you dictate to the world?

'You make a pretence of surrendering these people. I do not accept them and I do not consider them surrendered. Nor do I stand in the way of their returning—wrathful though all the gods may be with the mockery that is being made of their divinity—to the city that is honour-bound by the commitment it made. Go to war—Spurius Postumius has just jabbed a fetial legate with his knee! The gods are then going to believe that Postumius is a citizen of Samnium not Rome, and that a Roman fetial ambassador has been violated by a Samnite; and so you are justified in making war on us! And to think you feel no shame at openly making a laughing-stock of religion, and searching out specious arguments that are hardly to be expected of children for breaking your oath, old men and ex-consuls though you are! Go, lictor, and untie* the Romans. And let no one hinder them from leaving when they want.' With that the men returned unharmed from Caudium to the Roman camp, with their personal pledge discharged, at least, and perhaps also that of the state.

12. The Samnites could see that the peace that they had arrogantly imposed had been replaced with the renewal of pitiless hostilities, and all that subsequently took place they not only pictured in their imagination but almost saw before their eyes. All too late—and to no purpose now, they realized—was their appreciation of the alternative policies proposed by the aged Pontius. They saw that in falling between the two they had exchanged a victory in their hands for a fragile peace, and that discarding the opportunity of doing a favour or doing harm meant they would fight men whom they could have permanently removed as enemies or else made their everlasting friends. There had been no battle to mark a shift in power since the peace of Caudium, but even so feelings had so changed that Postumius' surrender gave him greater distinction amongst the Romans than a bloodless victory did Pontius among the Samnites. In addition, the Romans now felt that the possibility of continuing the war guaranteed them victory, whereas the Samnites believed the Romans had, on reopening the war, simultaneously won it.

In the meantime the people of Satricum* defected to the Samnites, and the colony at Fregellae was occupied at night when the Samnites suddenly arrived (and it is well enough established that the Satricans were also with them). Mutual fear then kept both sides immobile until dawn, when daylight marked the start of the fighting. This the people of Fregellae managed to keep on even terms because the fight was for their altars and homes, and also because the unarmed population gave them support from the rooftops. It was trickery that tipped the balance: the defenders allowed an enemy herald to be heard delivering the message that anyone laying down his arms would leave unharmed. This prospect diminished enthusiasm for the fight, and weapons began to be thrown down on all sides. The more resolute retained their weapons and broke out through the gate on the other side, and their daring provided greater protection than did the others' fear-induced gullibility. These the Samnites surrounded with a ring of fire and burned to death as they vainly appealed to the gods' and their enemies' honour.

The consuls then divided their responsibilities.* Papirius made for Luceria in Apulia, where the Roman knights surrendered as hostages at Caudium were being kept under guard, and Publilius remained in Samnium to counter the enemy legions from Caudium. The manoeuvre was disconcerting for the Samnites: they did not dare march on Luceria for fear of having the enemy attacking their rear, nor did they dare remain where they were in case Luceria were lost in the meantime. The best plan seemed to trust to fortune and to decide the issue in battle with Publilius. They therefore deployed their troops for battle.

13. When the consul Publilius was about to take the field against them, he thought he should first address his men, and he had an assembly called. There was indeed a very spirited rush to the general's tent, but no words of encouragement from the commander could be heard over the shouting of the men demanding battle; for every one of them the recollection of his humiliation provided the incentive. They accordingly proceeded to the fight, pushing ahead the standard-bearers; and, so no time should be lost in engaging by hurling their javelins and only then unsheathing their swords, they threw aside the javelins, as if a signal had been given, and rushed at the enemy with swords drawn. The talent of the leader played no part in marshalling the ranks or the auxiliaries; the fury of the ordinary soldiers drove everything forward in an almost demented attack. Thus the enemy were not just repelled; not even daring to interrupt their retreat at their camp, they headed for Apulia in scattered flight (although they later regrouped and reached Luceria in a single body). The same fury that had driven the Romans through the middle of the enemy army also carried them into their camp, where there was more bloodshed and carnage than in the battle, and most of the plunder was damaged by them in their anger.

The other army, under the consul Papirius, had reached Arpi by way of the coastal area, finding everything en route to be peaceful, more because of the wrongs of the Samnites than because of any benefit conferred by the Roman people. This was because the Samnites, in those days living in scattered villages in the hills, would conduct raids on the plains and coastal regions; being wild mountain men, they felt only disdain for the milder temperament of the inhabitants which was, as often, in keeping with their environment. Had this area remained loyal to the Samnites, either the Roman army would have been unable to reach Arpi or, cut off from their supply-lines as they were, the shortage of all commodities in the spaces in between would have destroyed it. Even as things were, the besiegers as well as the besieged suffered from food shortages after the Romans set off from Arpi to Luceria. The Romans were supplied with everything from Arpi, but on a very restricted scale. In fact, the cavalry transported grain to the camp from Arpi while the infantry were busy manning the guard-posts, conducting patrols, and digging in; and they brought it in bags which, under attack from the enemy, they were sometimes obliged to jettison in order to fight. As for those under siege, they were receiving supplies from the mountains of the Samnites, and reinforcements were getting through as well, before the arrival of the other consul with his victorious army. Publilius' arrival, however, tightened up the whole situation. Leaving the siege under his colleague's authority, Publilius was given freedom to move through the countryside, where he rendered the whole area precarious for the enemy's supplies. The Samnites encamped at Luceria now therefore had no hope of enduring the shortages if the siege continued, and so they were obliged to concentrate their forces and engage with Papirius.

14. It was at this point, when the two sides were preparing for battle, that a delegation arrived from Tarentum* warning both Samnites and Romans to avoid military action. The Tarentines would, they said, join the other side in fighting against whichever stood in the way of an armistice. After hearing out the delegates, Papirius made a show of being impressed by what they said and replied that he would discuss it with his colleague. He sent for him, but meanwhile spent all his time in preparations for battle; and after discussing the matter, on which there could be no doubt, he put up the battle-signal. The consuls were attending to the matters, both religious and secular, customarily performed just before combat when the Tarentines came to them looking for their reply.

'The auspices are favourable, Tarentines, so the keeper of the chickens* says,' Papirius told them, 'and in addition the results of the sacrifice are excellent. As you see, we are going into action with the gods' support.' He then gave the order to advance the standards and led out his troops, meanwhile excoriating this fatuous nation which, incapable of conducting its own affairs because of its domestic squabbles and discord, felt it had the right to dictate the limits of peace and war for others.

On the other side the Samnites had dropped all their anxiety with regard to war. Either they really wanted peace or else it was in their interests to pretend that was so in order to win over the Tarentines and, when they caught sight of the Romans suddenly deployed for combat, they shouted out that they remained at the Tarentines' command and would not take the field or bear arms beyond their palisade. They had been duped, they said, but would accept whatever fortune might bring rather than appear to have slighted the Tarentines who were advocating peace.

The consuls declared that they took this as an omen and that they prayed that the enemy's inclinations meant that they would not even defend their stockade. They divided their troops between them, advanced to the enemy's defence-works and launched a simultaneous assault from all sides. Some of the men filled in the ditches while others demolished the stockade, hurling it into the ditches, as their innate courage, but anger, too, fired hearts deeply wounded by humiliation. They all reminded each other that here there were no Forks, no Caudium, no impassable defiles where trickery had arrogantly triumphed over misjudgement; here there was Roman courage that neither palisade nor ditches could hold back. And they cut down indiscriminately those who resisted and those who fled, the unarmed and armed, slave and free, boys and adults, men and animals; nor would anything living have survived had not the consuls given the signal to retreat and, with that order and with threats, driven their soldiers, thirsting for blood, back from the enemy camp. A speech was therefore hurriedly delivered before the men, who were in high dudgeon over the sweet venting of their anger being interrupted. This was so that the men should be assured that the consuls certainly had not been, and would not be, second to any of the soldiers in hatred for the enemy. In fact, they told them, insatiable as leaders in the battle, they would have been equally so in inflicting punishment, had not consideration for the six hundred *equites* held as hostages in Luceria checked their impulse—they feared that loss of all hope of clemency would drive the enemy to execute them in blind rage, wishing to kill before they were killed themselves. The soldiers approved of this reasoning and were happy that their wrath had been stemmed—better to endure anything, they said, than see the lives of so many of the foremost young men of Rome forfeited.

15. When the assembly was adjourned, a council of war was convened to decide whether to prosecute the siege of Luceria with all their forces or whether one of the armies and one of the commanders should be used to sound the feelings of the neighbouring Apulians, whose sympathies were to that point unclear. The consul Publilius set off to conduct a tour of Apulia, and in a single expedition he brought a number of its tribes into subjection by force, or else accepted them as allies by granting terms. Papirius had remained behind to conduct the siege of Luceria, and for him, too, the results soon matched his expectations. He blocked all roads by which supplies were being carted in from Samnium, and the Samnites garrisoning Luceria, overcome by hunger, sent a deputation to the Roman consul asking that he raise the siege if the *equites*, who provided the grounds for the war, were returned.

Papirius' reply was as follows. They should have consulted Pontius, son of Herennius, the man responsible for sending Romans under the yoke, on how the defeated side ought to be dealt with, he said. Since, however, their preference was to have a fair penalty dictated by their enemies rather than bring proposals forward for themselves, he told them to report back to Luceria that their men should leave there their weapons, baggage, pack-animals, and the entire civilian population. The soldiers, he said, he would send under a yoke wearing only one article of clothing, taking retribution for the humiliation inflicted earlier, not inflicting a new one.

There was no refusal. Seven thousand soldiers were sent under the yoke, and a huge quantity of plunder was taken in Luceria. All the standards and weapons lost at Caudium were retrieved and (their crowning joy!) the *equites*, whom the Samnites had consigned to Luceria to be kept under guard as security for the peace, were recovered. There is hardly any victory of the Roman people more famous than this because of the sudden reversal of fortunes involved, if indeed it is the case, as I find in certain annals, that Pontius, son of

Herennius, the Samnite commander, was sent under the yoke* with the others to pay for the humiliation of the consuls.

However, I am not very surprised that there is uncertainty about the enemy leader being surrendered and sent under the yoke; more startling is the doubt about who was responsible for this glorious achievement.* Was it the dictator Lucius Cornelius, together with his master of horse Lucius Papirius Cursor, who conducted those operations at Caudium and then at Luceria, to become an unprecedented avenger of Roman humiliation and to celebrate what I am inclined to believe was, down to that time, the most highly deserved triumph after that of Furius Camillus? Or does the glory belong to the consuls, and to Papirius in particular? This uncertainty is accompanied by another uncertainty. In the following elections was Papirius Cursor kept in office on account of his success at Luceria, being elected consul for the third time, along with Quintus Aulius Cerretanus (serving his second term)? Or was it Lucius Papirius Mugillanus,* the mistake lying in the *cognomen*?

16. There is general agreement that after this the rest of the war was finished off by the consuls. Aulius brought operations with the Frentani* to an end in one successful battle, and after demanding hostages he accepted the surrender of the actual town to which their defeated army had retreated. The other consul had similar success in his operations against the Satricans.* These were Roman citizens, but after the Caudine disaster they had defected to the Samnites and had accepted a Samnite garrison in their city. When the Roman army had moved up to the walls of Satricum, the inhabitants sent spokesmen to sue for peace with prayers of entreaty, only to receive a grim reply from the consul. Unless they executed or surrendered the Samnite garrison, they were told, they were not to return to him, and the colonists were filled with greater dread by these words than by the attack they were facing. The spokesmen therefore kept asking the consul how he could believe that they, few in number and weak, could make an attack on a garrison that was so strong and well armed. They were told to seek advice on that from the same men on whose recommendation they had admitted the garrison into the city. They then left and returned to their people after they had, with difficulty, gained permission to consult their senate on the matter and bring back their reply to him.

There were two interest-groups causing a rift in the senate of

Satricum, one with leaders who had promoted the defection from the Roman people, and the other made up of loyal citizens. Even so, they were falling over each other to oblige the consul so peace could be re-established. The Samnite garrison was going to leave the following night because no adequate preparations had been made for facing a siege, and one of the groups thought it enough to inform the consul of the hour of the night at which the enemy would be leaving, the gate they would use, and the road they would take. The other, which had opposed defection to the Samnites, went further, opening the gate to the consul that very night and admitting his armed men into the city without the enemy's knowledge. The result of the twofold betrayal was that the Samnite garrison, taken unawares, fell victim to an ambush set in the wooded area bordering the road and, in addition, a shout went up from the city, now full of their enemies. In the space of a single hour the Samnites were killed, the Satricans taken prisoner, and all was under the consul's control. The consul held an enquiry into who was responsible for the defection, and those whom he found guilty he had flogged and beheaded. He then installed a powerful garrison over the Satricans, whom he also disarmed.

After that, Papirius Cursor left for his triumph in Rome, according to those writers who claim that it was under his leadership that Luceria was recovered and the Samnites sent under the yoke. And he was, without doubt, a man worthy of all manner of praise for his military career, a man outstanding not only for his quick intelligence but for his physical strength as well. He was a particularly fast runner, which is what also gave him his *cognomen*,* and they say he bested all his contemporaries in the foot-race, thanks either to his naturally strong legs or to intense training. He had at the same time, it is said, an excellent capacity for food and wine,* and yet military service was, for foot- and horseman alike, more rigorous under him than under anyone else because the man himself was, when it came to hard work, indefatigable. The story goes that his cavalrymen once presumed to ask him for relief from some of their fatigues as a reward for a successful operation. His answer to them was: 'So you cannot say you have not been excused from anything, I excuse you from the obligation to pat your horses when you dismount.'*

In the man's command there was an authority equally powerful in the case of allies or citizens. A praetor from Praeneste* had, from apprehension, been rather slow in bringing up his men from the reserve ranks to the front line. Papirius, pacing up and down outside his tent, had him called out and ordered a lictor to take out his axe. At these words the man of Praeneste just stood there, petrified. 'Come, lictor,' said Papirius, 'chop out this root. It's a problem for people walking.' Then, after fining the man, Papirius let him go, sweating with fear of the death penalty. In that generation—and no other generation was more productive of examples of courage—there was without doubt no individual in whom the Roman state found greater support. In fact, people have it in their minds that he would have been a match for Alexander, had Alexander turned his arms on Europe after conquering Asia.

17. Clearly, nothing can appear more at odds with the principles of this work than for me to veer away, more than is reasonable, from a chronological progression, in order to provide diversion for my readers, and mental relaxation for myself, by embellishing it with sundry material. That said, the mention of a king and leader of such eminence gives rise to reflections* which have often been the subject of my silent musing, making me now disposed to inquire what might have been the outcome for the Roman state had there been a war with Alexander.

It is apparent that in warfare the most essential elements are the numbers and courage of the troops, the capability of their commanders, and fortune, a dominant force in all human activity,* and especially in the military sphere. Examining these things both individually and as a whole, one sees that they clearly demonstrate that Roman power would not have been overcome by this king, either, just as it has not been by other kings and peoples.

Let me begin with a comparison of the commanders, and at the outset I do not deny that Alexander was an outstanding leader. His reputation, however, was boosted by the fact that he was acting alone, and also that he died in his youth as his career was taking flight and when he had experienced no reversal of fortune. I say nothing of the other famous rulers and generals and turn to Cyrus,* for whom the Greeks reserve the highest praise. What was it that exposed him to changing fortunes if not the fact that he lived so long—as in the recent case of Pompey the Great?

Let me review the Roman generals—not all of them throughout history, but just the ones that Alexander would have had to contend with as consuls or dictators. I refer to Marcus Valerius Corvus,

Gaius Marcius Rutulus, Gaius Sulpicius, Titus Manlius Torquatus, Quintus Publilius Philo, Lucius Papirius Cursor, Quintus Fabius Maximus, the two Decii, Lucius Volumnius, and Manius Curius.* (These were succeeded by some very great men, as Alexander would have discovered had he turned his attention to war with Carthage before war with Rome, and then crossed to Italy as an older man.) The same innate qualities of courage and inventiveness were to be found in these as in Alexander, and by then the military discipline that had been a tradition since the city's inception had developed into a science organized on established principles. It was with these principles that the kings had fought their wars, and with them too the men who drove out the kings, the Junii and Valerii. The same applied, after them, to the Fabii, the Quinctii, and the Cornelii, and to Furius Camillus, whose later years had been witnessed by the young men* with whom Alexander would have had to fight.

As far as taking on a soldier's duties in the field is concerned (for that enhanced Alexander's reputation as much as anything else), we certainly cannot believe that Manlius Torquatus or Valerius Corvus would have been inferior to him had they faced him in battle. Not when these men had gained fame as soldiers before they did as generals! Nor would the Decii have been inferior—the men who rushed at the foe after pledging their lives to the underworld! Nor Papirius Cursor, a man of such physical strength and such strength of spirit!

The Senate would surely not have been outwitted by the strategies of this one man—the Senate which, not to name individuals, was said to be made up of kings by the one man who had an accurate picture* of the Roman governing body! Nor, of course, was there any danger of his selecting a spot for his encampment with greater skill than any of the men I have named! Or of more skilfully arranging his lines of supply, taking precautions against ambush, selecting the time for battle, deploying his battle-line, supporting it with his reserves! He was not now dealing with a Darius, Alexander would have said. The Persian dragged along with him a troop of women and eunuchs, and amid all the purple and gold was encumbered with the trappings of his status. He was plunder rather than foe, and all it took for a bloodless victory was having the enterprise to pay no attention to what did not matter. Italy would have seemed to Alexander very different in nature from India, through which he made his way partying with his drunken army.* He would have looked on the passes of

Apulia and the mountains of Lucania, seeing the traces of the disaster
that recently struck his own family when his uncle, King Alexander
of Epirus, fell in battle.

18. And we are talking about the Alexander who was not yet up to
his neck in success, to which nobody had less resistance than he. But
consider how matters were after the change in his fortunes and, one
might say, after the change of personality* to the one that he took on
after victory. He would then have come to Italy more of a Darius than
an Alexander, and brought an army that had forgotten Macedon and
was already lapsing into Persian ways. In the case of so great a king,
I am reluctant to mention* the conceited style of dress that he
adopted, and his wish to receive grovelling obeisance, which would
have been unacceptable even had the Macedonians been defeated,
and was much more so when they were victorious. I hesitate, too,
to mention the appalling punishments he inflicted, his killing of
friends over drinking and the dinner table, and his fatuous lies about
his parentage.

What if his fondness for drink had become progressively more
acute? Or his vicious and violent temper? And I am not talking of
anything that is a matter of dispute amongst historians. Do we consider none of these things detrimental to his standing as a general?
And, I am sure, there is no danger of there being any truth in that
idea always being brought up by those most simple-minded of the
Greeks who set the reputation of even the Parthians* above that of
Rome! These men claim that the Roman people would not have been
able to withstand just the eminence of Alexander's name—though
I do not think Alexander was known to them even from hearsay!*
Of all the leading men of Rome none would have dared utter a true
word against him, these men say—when, as we know from the
speeches on record, people dared openly to produce public orations
against him in Athens, a state shattered by Macedonian arms! And
they did this at the very moment when they were looking upon the
smoking ruins of Thebes close by.*

Whatever the man's greatness is conceived as being it is still the
greatness of a single individual, and derived from successes accumulated over little more than ten years. Some people extol Alexander on
the grounds that the Romans, while never defeated in a war, were in
fact defeated in numerous battles, whereas he never experienced a
reverse in combat. But they do not realize that they are comparing the

exploits of a man, and a young man at that, with those of a people that had already been engaged in warfare for four hundred years. When there are more generations to be counted on the one side than there are years on the other, should we be surprised that there were more fluctuating fortunes in such a long period of time than there were in a space of thirteen years? Should one not compare one man's fortunes with another's, and one leader's with another's? How many are the Roman commanders I could cite who never had an unsuccessful battle! In the annals and magistrate lists one can run one's eye over pages and pages of consuls and dictators, none of whom gave the Roman people cause to be dissatisfied with their courage and fortunes on any day at all.

And there is reason to consider these men more worthy of admiration than Alexander, or any other monarch. Some held a dictatorship for ten or twenty days, and none held a consulship for more than a year. Their troop-levies were hampered by plebeian tribunes. They came to military campaigns late, and were recalled early to preside over elections. The year would expire when they were in the very process of conducting an operation, and a colleague's foolhardiness, or perhaps his perversity, could stand in their way or cause them failure. They took over situations that another had handled badly, or assumed leadership of an army of untried recruits or one that was poorly disciplined. But monarchs are in a very different situation. They are not only free of all restraints but are the masters of situations and their timing; rather than following circumstances, they make circumstances conform to their strategy.*

And so an undefeated Alexander would have been in combat with undefeated commanders, giving the same pledges to fortune as they. In fact, he would have faced even greater danger than these would have because the Macedonians had only Alexander, a man who was not only exposed to numerous hazards but actually threw himself in their way. There would have been many Romans who were Alexander's equals in military renown and greatness of achievement, however, and each of these could have survived or died as his own fate dictated, without putting the state in jeopardy.

19. There remains the comparison of the two sets of troops in terms of numbers, quality, and the strength of their auxiliary forces. In the census of that period the population was found to be 250,000.* This meant that in the case of a total uprising of the Latin allies

ten legions were enlisted in what was virtually a troop-levy within the city. In those years four or five armies were often simultaneously engaged in operations in Etruria, in Umbria (where the Gauls were also our enemies), in Samnium, and in Lucania. Then Alexander would have found, as strong allies of Rome—or as enemies she had defeated in war—all of Latium, together with the Sabines, the Volsci, the Aequi, and all Campania. He would also have found parts of Umbria and Etruria to be in the same category, as well as the Picentes, the Marsi and the Paeligni, the Vestini and the Apulians, plus the Greeks of the entire coast of the Tyrrhenian Sea from Thurii to Neapolis and Cumae, and from there all the way to Antium and Ostia.*

Alexander would have crossed the sea with his Macedonian veterans who would have numbered no more than thirty thousand infantry and four thousand cavalry (mostly Thessalian, these constituting his army's main strength). Had he brought in alongside them Persians, Indians, and other races, he would have been trailing around with him something that was more a hindrance than a help.

Another point: for the Romans there were reinforcements available at home, whereas Alexander (as later happened to Hannibal) would have seen his army grow old as he campaigned on foreign soil. The Macedonian arms would have been the round shield and the *sarisa*; for the Roman they would have been the oblong shield, which gives the body greater protection, and the javelin, which has a considerably greater impact than the spear in both thrusting and throwing. Both sides would have been composed of stationary fighters who maintained ranks;* but the phalanx lacked mobility and comprised soldiers of only one kind, whereas the Roman battle-formation was more open and made up of numerous units, easy to divide wherever the need arose and easy to reunite. Further, what soldier can equal the Roman in building operations, or who is better at withstanding hard work? Had Alexander been defeated in one battle, he would have been defeated in the war; and what army could have broken Roman strength, which Caudium and Cannae failed to break? Even if he met with initial success, he would certainly have often wished to be facing Persians, Indians, and unwarlike Asia, and would have admitted that war for him in the past had been with women. This is exactly what they say King Alexander of Epirus admitted when he had been dealt his mortal wound and was comparing the fortunes of the wars fought by this same young man in Asia with what he had experienced himself.

In fact, when I reflect on our twenty-four years of naval fighting against the Carthaginians in the First Punic War, I think Alexander's life would hardly have been long enough for a single war. Furthermore, the Carthaginian and Roman states had been linked by age-old treaties. Fear of a common enemy might possibly have put under arms together two cities that were very powerful in armaments and manpower, and Alexander might have been brought to his knees in a war with both Carthage and Rome. The Romans have actually experienced facing Macedon as an enemy. This was not, admittedly, when Alexander was their leader or when Macedonian power was unimpaired, but they faced Antiochus, Philip, and Perses* without sustaining any defeat, and in fact without being in any danger. Let me be forgiven for saying so and may the civil wars remain at rest, but never have we been hard pressed* by an enemy's cavalry or infantry, never in open combat, never on neutral ground, and for sure never on favourable ground. The things our soldiers with their heavy armour have to fear are arrows, gorges difficult to surmount, and terrain that supplies cannot reach. But they have repelled and will repel a thousand armies more formidable than that of the Macedonians and Alexander, just as long as our love for this peace in which we live remains constant, and along with it our concern for harmony between our citizens.

20. Marcus Folius Flaccina and Lucius Plautius Venox followed as consuls, and in that year ambassadors from numerous Samnite tribes sought a renewal of their treaty.* They moved the Senate to pity by prostrating themselves on the ground, but when their request was referred to the people their entreaties were not nearly so effective. They were therefore denied a treaty, but they did gain a two-year armistice by intense lobbying of citizens individually over a number of days. Furthermore, the populations of Teanum and Canusium in Apulia* were worn down by raids on their lands and so submitted to the consul Lucius Plautius, to whom they surrendered hostages. That same year saw the start of the practice of appointed prefects being sent to Capua,* after legislation had been drafted by the praetor Lucius Furius. The people of Capua had themselves asked for both things as a remedy for a political situation sick with internal discord. Two tribes were added at Rome, the Ufentina and the Falerna.*

Such a movement having started in Apulia, the Apulian Teates* also came to the new consuls, Gaius Junius Bubulcus and Quintus

Aemilius Barbula, with a request for a treaty, and they committed themselves to providing peace throughout Apulia for the Roman people. This was a rash promise that did result in the request for a treaty being granted; it was not, however, a treaty made on equal terms, but one that made them subject to the Roman people. With Apulia totally under control (Junius had also taken Forentum,* a powerful stronghold) operations were extended into Lucania, where Nerulum was taken by assault after the sudden arrival of the consul Aemilius. Then the stability given to Capua by Roman discipline became common talk amongst the allies, and the people of Antium also complained that they were without fixed laws and magistrates. They were granted by the Senate the right to have the patrons of the actual colony* establish their laws. Roman law, and not just Roman military power, was now also beginning to have a widespread influence.

21. At the end of the year the consuls Gaius Junius Bubulcus and Quintus Aemilius Barbula passed on their legions not to the consuls over whose election they had presided (Spurius Nautius and Marcus Popilius), but to a dictator,* Lucius Aemilius. Together with his master of horse, Lucius Furius, Aemilius proceeded with an attack on Saticula,* thereby giving the Samnites a pretext for renewing hostilities. Thus the Romans were exposed to a twofold threat. On one side were the Samnites, who had levied a large army in order to raise the siege of their allies and who now pitched camp not far from the Roman camp. On the other were the Saticulani who, suddenly throwing open their gates, unleashed a tumultuous attack on the Roman outposts. Then both armies, each relying more on help from the other than on its own strength, soon engaged the Romans in pitched battle and put them under pressure. Nevertheless, despite fighting on two fronts, the dictator kept his line protected on both sides: he had taken up a position that was not easy to surround, and he also had his troops facing in different directions. However, his attack on those making the sortie was more aggressive. Without much of a struggle, Aemilius drove them back within their walls, and then turned his entire fighting-line towards the Samnites. Here there was more of a fight, but the victory, though late in coming, was indisputable and complete. Driven back to their camp in disorder, the Samnites extinguished their fires that night and retreated in silence. Abandoning hope of defending Saticula, they themselves invested

Plistica, an ally of the Romans, to pay their enemy back with similar pain.

22. At the turn of the year direction of the war was, without interruption, assumed by the dictator Quintus Fabius.* The new consuls,* like their predecessors, remained in Rome, and Fabius marched to Saticula with some reinforcements to take over the army from Aemilius. This was because the Samnites had not remained at Plistica but, having sent for fresh troops from home, and relying on their numbers, had encamped in the same location as before and were harassing the Romans with attacks in an attempt to distract them from the siege. That focused the dictator's attention all the more on the enemy's walls; he thought that the war really rested on the attack he was mounting on the city, and he paid little attention to the Samnites, going only so far as to station guard-posts to prevent any attack on the camp. The Samnites' cavalry charges* on the rampart then became all the more ferocious, allowing the Romans no rest. When the enemy were almost at the camp gates, the master of horse Quintus Aulius Cerretanus* rode out with all his squadrons in a violent charge, without any conferring with the dictator, and drove back the enemy. Then, in a battle characterized by very little determination, fortune so exercised her power as to produce significant losses on both sides and glorious deaths for the commanders themselves. First the Samnite general was angry at being dislodged and routed from a position he had gained with such a spirited cavalry charge, and he managed to renew the fight by pleading with and encouraging his riders. He stood out amongst his men as he spurred on the fight, and the Roman master of horse, without consulting the dictator, and with his lance poised, galloped at him with such speed that with a single thrust he hurled him lifeless from his horse.

The reaction of the rank-and-file to their leader's fate was not so much dismay, as is usually the case, as anger. While Aulius rode impetuously through the squadrons of the enemy, all those around him hurled their spears at him, but it was to the man's brother that the gods gave the special distinction of avenging the Samnite general. He pulled the victorious master of horse from his mount and, filled with grief and wrath, dealt him the death-blow; and the Samnites were also within a hair's breadth of taking possession of the body, because Aulius had fallen amidst the squadrons of the enemy. However, the Romans dismounted and got their feet on the ground, the Samnites were obliged to follow suit, and, hurriedly forming lines of battle, they proceeded with an infantry engagement around their leaders' bodies. In this the Romans clearly had the upper hand, Aulius' body was recovered, and the victors carried it back to camp with a mixture of joy and sorrow.

Their leader gone, and having put their strength to the test in a cavalry engagement, the Samnites abandoned Saticula, thinking their defence of it to be futile, and returned to the siege of Plistica. In a matter of days, the Romans took Saticula through surrender, and the Samnites took Plistica by storm.

23. The theatre of operations now changed and the legions were marched from Samnium and Apulia over to Sora,* which had defected to the Samnites, killing its Roman colonists. The Roman army reached the town first, coming by forced marches to avenge the murder of its fellow-citizens and recover the colony. Then scouts scattered along the roads kept bringing news, one after the other, that the Samnite legions were following behind and were already not far distant; and so the Romans marched out to meet the enemy and a battle, which proved inconclusive,* was fought near Lautulae. It was not a bloody defeat or rout on either side that broke off the engagement but the onset of night, which left both sides uncertain as to whether they were the victors or the vanquished. In some sources I find that the encounter went against the Romans, and that it was in this that the master of horse Quintus Aulius was killed. Gaius Fabius, who was appointed master of horse in Aulius' place, now proceeded to Sora from Rome with a fresh army. Sending messengers ahead, he consulted the dictator on where to halt, and when and from what direction he should attack the enemy. Then, having been thoroughly briefed, he took up a concealed position, ready for any move.

The dictator had kept his troops within their fortifications for a number of days following the battle—he was more like a man under siege than conducting one—but now he suddenly put up the signal for battle. He thought that to put fire in the hearts of brave men it was more effective that they have no hope in anything other than themselves, and so he kept the arrival of the master of horse and the new army hidden from the troops. Then, addressing them as if there was no hope except by breaking out of their impasse, he said:

'We are caught in a tight spot, men. We have no way out unless we open one up by victory. Our base camp is well enough protected by its fortifications, but lack of provisions still makes it a dangerous place. The area all around us from which supplies could be brought has defected, and even if there were people willing to help us we have the terrain against us. So I for my part will not give you false hopes by leaving the camp here for you to fall back on, as you did the other day, if you fail to win a victory. Defence-works should be secured by arms, not arms by defence-works. A camp to retreat to is for those with the time to drag out a war; *we*, however, must put aside thoughts of anything but victory. Advance on the enemy! Once the column gets beyond the rampart, those so ordered are to set fire to the camp. Your losses, men, will be made good by plunder taken from all the neighbouring peoples who defected from us.'

Fired by the dictator's address, which underlined their dire situation, the men marched out against the enemy, and simply looking back at their camp aflame—though it was only the parts closest to them that had, on the dictator's orders, been put to the torch—was no small incentive. And so they charged like maniacs, creating havoc in the enemy lines with their initial attack; and at the appropriate moment, on seeing the camp ablaze in the distance (which was the signal agreed upon), the master of horse attacked the enemy rear. The Samnites were thus surrounded, and they tried to flee in various directions, as best they could. A huge crowd of them, massed together in fear and getting in each other's way in the confusion, were massacred between the two armies. The enemy camp was taken and sacked, and the dictator led his men back to the Roman camp laden with spoils.* They were overjoyed, not so much with their victory as with finding that, contrary to their expectations, everything there was safe and sound, apart from a small section damaged by the fire.

24. They then returned to Sora,* where the new consuls, Marcus Poetelius and Gaius Sulpicius, assumed command of the army from the dictator Fabius; most of the veterans were demobilized and new cohorts were brought in to bring up its strength. But the lie of the city posed a problem, and no sure plan for an assault was forthcoming; victory would either take a long time or involve severe risk. A Soran deserter, however, left the town in secret, came as far as the Roman sentries, and insisted that he be taken immediately to the consuls. Brought to them, the man undertook to betray the city. When, in answer to their questions, he explained how he would make good his

commitment, his proposition did not seem unreasonable, and he induced them to withdraw the Roman camp, which was almost touching the walls, to a point six miles from the city. The sentinels and night watch, he explained, would then be less vigilant in safeguarding the city. The following night, after instructing some cohorts to position themselves in a wooded area below the town, the man himself took ten hand-picked men to the citadel, by a steep route that was almost impossible to negotiate. There he had stockpiled a quantity of projectiles greater than was needed for the group involved, and there were also stones, some just lying around, as one finds on broken ground, and others accumulated there on purpose by the townsmen, to increase the place's security.

After putting the Romans in position, he pointed out to them a narrow, steep path that led from the town up to the citadel, and said:

'Just three armed men could keep a crowd of any size from getting up here. You are ten in number and, what is more, you are Romans and you are the bravest of the Romans. You will have the terrain to help you, and night, whose obscurity magnifies everything when men are frightened. I myself shall now spread fear everywhere; you concentrate on holding the citadel.'

With that he ran down, creating as much commotion as he could and shouting: 'To arms!' and 'Please help me, citizens! The citadel has been taken by the enemy. Defend it!' He shouted these words when he came upon the doors of the town's leading men, and he shouted them to all the people that he met and to those who came fearfully rushing out into the streets. The panic, started by one man, overtook more people, who spread it through the city. In alarm, the magistrates sent scouts to the citadel, but when they were told that it was occupied by armed men—and the numbers given were highly inflated—they abandoned all hope of recovering it. People were rushing everywhere, and the gates were broken down by men half-asleep and mostly unarmed. Through one of these the Roman detachment burst in, roused to action by the uproar, and then proceeded to cut down townspeople who were running panic-stricken through the streets.

Sora had already been taken when the consuls arrived at dawn and proceeded to accept the surrender of those whom chance had left as survivors after a night of slaughter and tumult. Of these, there were 225 identified by general consensus as being the instigators of both the heinous murder of the colonists and the defection, and these they took to Rome in fetters. The rest of the population were left unharmed, with a garrison installed at Sora. All those taken to Rome were flogged in the Forum and beheaded, which occasioned very great rejoicing among the plebs, who were deeply concerned with guaranteeing the safety of people sent to colonies everywhere.

25. After leaving Sora, the consuls launched an attack on the territory and cities of the Ausones. This was because of the total upheaval occasioned by the arrival of the Samnites after the battle of Lautulae, and the growth of conspiracies throughout Campania. Capua itself was not above reproach, and indeed investigations even reached Rome, and a number of its prominent citizens. The nation of the Ausones, however, fell under the power of Rome through the betrayal of its cities, just as happened to Sora. The cities were Ausona, Minturnae, and Vescia. Some young noblemen, twelve in number, conspired to betray these towns, and came to the consuls. They informed them that their fellow-citizens had long been looking forward to the arrival of the Samnites, and the moment they heard of the battle of Lautulae they had assumed the Romans had been defeated and had assisted the Samnites with fighting men and weaponry. Since the rout of the Samnites, they continued, they had been living in an uneasy peace: they would not close their gates on the Romans for fear of bringing war on themselves, and yet they were set on closing them if an army approached. In such a hesitant frame of mind, they said, they could easily be taken by surprise.

On the young men's advice, the camp was moved closer and troops were sent at one and the same time around the three towns. Some of the men were armed, and these were to occupy concealed positions close to the walls of the cities; and the others, in civilian dress with swords hidden beneath their clothing, were to enter the cities before dawn when the gates were opened. These proceeded to kill the sentries, and at the same time they gave the signal to their armed colleagues to charge out from their hiding-place in a body. So it was that the gates were seized, and the three towns taken at the same time and with the same plan. The assault, however, was made in the absence of the leaders. As a result, there was no limit set to the massacre, and the Ausonian race was wiped out* just as if it had been a war to the death, when, in fact, their defection had not been clearly established.

26. That same year Luceria betrayed its Roman garrison to the

enemy and fell into Samnite hands. The traitors did not long remain unpunished for what they did, however: there was a Roman army not far away, and the city, situated on a plain,* was taken with the first assault. Lucerians and Samnites were butchered to the last man, and anger was such that in Rome, too, when the Senate debated sending colonists to Luceria, there were many who voted for razing the city. Apart from the venomous hatred that was felt for a people twice conquered, there was also the great distance involved, which made them recoil from banishing citizens to a place so far from home amongst such hostile peoples. Even so the motion for sending colonists prevailed, and two thousand five hundred were sent.

That same year, when disloyalty to the Romans was in evidence everywhere, there were conspiracies secretly hatched by leading citizens even in Capua. When information on them was brought to the Senate, the matter was certainly not ignored: a decree authorizing investigations was passed, and it was resolved that a dictator be appointed to conduct them. Gaius Maenius was appointed, and he appointed Marcus Folius his master of horse. The dread inspired by that office was terrible. Thus, before they could be denounced before the dictator, the ringleaders of the conspiracy, Ovius and Novius Calavius,* were removed from judgement by deaths which were quite clearly suicide, whether it was fear or a guilty conscience that forced them into it.

When the investigation ran out of material in Campania, it turned to Rome, with matters being given a particular interpretation, which was as follows. The Senate, it was claimed, had not expressly authorized an investigation to be held in Capua, but had ordered a general investigation into any who had, in any place, formed associations and conspired against the state—and cliques that had been formed for gaining magistracies* were against the interests of the state. The investigation was now opened up both in terms of charges and people, and the dictator did not object to having no limit set on the extent of his jurisdiction within it. Thus noblemen were indicted and, when these men appealed to the tribunes, no one would help them avoid judicial proceedings. With that, all members of the nobility en masse (not just those threatened with prosecution) declared that it was not nobles who were liable to this charge—the way to public office lay open to them—but the 'new men'. The dictator and his master of horse, they added, were going to find themselves in a more appropriate position as defendants on that charge rather than as investigators as soon as they left office!

It was at that point that Maenius, thinking more now of his reputation than his office, came into the assembly and spoke as follows:

'In all of you, citizens, I have witnesses to my past life, and in addition this office that has been conferred on me bears testimony to my innocence. On many other occasions, because of the demands of the situation in which the state would find itself, it has been necessary to appoint a man with an excellent military record as dictator for conducting enquiries; but not so now, when what is needed is a man whose life has been far removed from these cliques. However, certain noblemen have, in the first place, made every effort to crush these investigations—and it is better that you should consider for yourselves the reason for that rather than have me use my office to pronounce on something on which I have no reliable information. Then, finding they were not powerful enough to do that, they—patricians!—sought refuge in the defences provided by their adversaries, namely the right of appeal to, and assistance afforded by, the tribunes, in order to avoid appearing in court. Finally, driven back from that position, they have made an attack on us—such is the extent to which they thought anything safer than trying to establish their innocence—and were not ashamed as private citizens to demand that a dictator stand trial. So that all gods and men may know that those men are trying every avenue, even those not allowed, in order to avoid accounting for themselves, while I go forward to meet their accusation and offer myself to my enemies for trial, I now resign from the dictatorship. Consuls: should the responsibility be given to you by the Senate, I request that you begin your enquiries with me and Marcus Folius here so that it may be obvious that we are safeguarded against such accusations by virtue of our innocence rather than the dignity of our office.'

Maenius then resigned the dictatorship and immediately after him Folius resigned his position as master of horse. They were the first men to appear for trial before the consuls (who were indeed assigned responsibility for the affair by the Senate) and, facing the testimony of the nobles, were triumphantly acquitted. There was also Publilius Philo, who had on numerous occasions held the highest offices after many successes in his civil and military career, but was hated by the nobility. He, too, appeared in court and was acquitted. But, as is often the case, the investigation remained vigorous only while it was fresh, thanks to the famous names of the defendants. After that it descended to lesser individuals, until it was finally suppressed by the cliques and factions against which it had been set up.

27. The Samnites' attention had been turned to Apulia, but news of these events, and more so the hope of a Campanian revolt (the object of the conspiracy) brought them back again to Caudium. Their hope was that, from a position close by, they might divest the Romans of Capua, should any turmoil there open up such an opportunity. The consuls then came there with a powerful army. Initially, they hesitated near the pass since the route towards their enemy was difficult for both armies. The Samnites then made a short detour through the open spaces and marched their army down to level terrain;* and there for the first time the two enemies encamped in sight of each other. Some skirmishes then took place, both sides putting their cavalry to the test more often than their infantry, and the Romans felt no regret about the outcome of these brushes or about the delay with which they were dragging out the campaign. For the Samnite leaders it was different: their forces seemed to be eroding with slight losses every day and to be weakening as the war dragged on.

They therefore advanced to battle-stations, splitting their cavalry between the wings with instructions to focus more on the camp, and preventing any attack there, than on the battle, where the safety of the line would be assured by the infantry. Of the consuls, Sulpicius took up a position on the right wing, and Poetelius on the left. The Roman right was extended over a considerable distance because the Samnites were drawn up in that sector with ranks spread out, either with the purpose of outflanking their enemy or to prevent being outflanked themselves. On the left, in addition to a more compact formation, there was also strength added by an impromptu decision taken by the consul Poetelius. He immediately sent into the front line the reserve cohorts* to meet the vicissitudes of a prolonged battle, and with this combined strength he drove back the enemy with his initial charge.

The Samnites' infantry line was dislodged, and their cavalry joined the battle to give support. However, as they advanced at an angle between the two battle-lines, the Roman cavalry spurred their horses to a charge and caused havoc in the enemy ranks, amongst both their infantry and their cavalry, until they finally drove back their entire fighting line from that quarter. Poetelius was not alone on that wing encouraging the men—Sulpicius was there, too. He had left his own troops, who were not yet engaged, and ridden over towards the war-cry that had gone up first on the left. Seeing that the victory there was not in doubt, he then headed back for his own wing with twelve hundred men, to find fortunes here to be quite different: the Romans had been dislodged, and a triumphant enemy was charging demoralized men. The consul's arrival, however, changed everything in an instant. The men's morale was restored by the sight of their leader; the brave men who had arrived with him provided help beyond their numbers; and hearing of, and then seeing, the victory in the other sector revived the battle. The Romans were, from that moment, victorious all along the line and the Samnites, abandoning the fight, were cut down or taken prisoner, with the exception of those who made good their escape to Maleventum, a city now named Beneventum.* About thirty thousand Samnites were reportedly killed or taken prisoner.

28. The consuls had won a splendid victory,* and they immediately marched their legions off for an assault on Bovianum. They wintered at Bovianum, until Gaius Poetelius was appointed dictator by the new consuls Lucius Papirius Cursor (his fifth term) and Gaius Junius Bubulcus (his second), and Poetelius, along with his master of horse Marcus Folius, assumed command of their army.* When he heard that the citadel of Fregellae had been captured by the Samnites, the dictator left Bovianum and made for Fregellae. He took Fregellae without a fight, the Samnites having made off during the night, and after strongly garrisoning the town he headed back into Campania, mainly in order to recover Nola by force.*

On the dictator's approach, all the Samnite forces and the Nolan peasants had taken refuge within the walls. The dictator closely inspected the lie of the city and then, to open up the approach to the walls, had all the buildings burned that lay next to them (and the area was thickly populated). Not long afterwards, Nola was taken, either by the dictator Poetelius, or by the consul Gaius Junius—both versions are on record. Those who assign the glory of capturing Nola to the consul add that Atina and Calatia* were also captured by him, and claim that the reason for Poetelius' appointment as dictator was to hammer in a nail when a plague broke out.

In that same year colonies were sent to Suessa and Pontiae.* Suessa had belonged to the Aurunci, and the Volsci had inhabited Pontiae, an island within view of their own coastline. A senatorial decree was also passed for the establishment of a colony at Interamna Sucasina,* but it was the next consuls, Marcus Valerius and Publius Decius,* who appointed its triumvirs and sent out four thousand colonists.

29. The war with the Samnites was about at an end but, before it ceased to be a concern to the Roman Senate, the rumour arose of a war with the Etruscans.* In that period there was—after the Gauls and their incursions—no other race whose military power was more to be feared, both because of their geographical proximity and the size of their population. Thus, while the other consul was prosecuting what remained of the war in Samnium,* Publius Decius, who had remained behind in Rome seriously ill, was authorized by the Senate to name Gaius Sulpicius Longus dictator,* and Longus then named Gaius Junius Bubulcus as his master of horse. The dictator, as the gravity of the situation demanded, made all men of military age take the oath and took great pains to prepare weaponry and everything else required in the circumstances. He was not, however, so carried away by these momentous preparations as to consider mounting offensive operations; he was clearly going to make no move unless the Etruscans actually went on the attack. But on the Etruscan side, too, the same policy obtained—war-preparations without opening hostilities—and neither side went beyond its own frontiers.

The censorship held by Appius Claudius* and Gaius Plautius that year was also of significance, though Appius' name was more appreciatively remembered in posterity for the road that he built and the water he brought into the city. (For these works he alone was responsible.) This was because his revision of the Senate list was so notorious and excited such indignation that his colleague resigned his office from embarrassment.* Appius then, with that obstinacy ingrained in his family from its early days, held on to the censorship on his own. In the case of the Potitii clan,* too, who had held the priesthood of Hercules at the Ara Maxima as a family privilege, it was Appius who authorized them to teach public slaves the rites of that cult in order to pass the office on to them. An amazing story has come down in connection with that, one that might give rise to religious fears when it comes to altering the formalities of sacred observances. There were at the time twelve families in the clan Potitii, including some thirty adults, and within a year all were dead, and their posterity eliminated. Nor was it only a matter of the name of the Potitii dying out. The censor, too, some years later, was afflicted with blindness through the ever-mindful anger of the gods.

30. The upshot was that the consuls of the following year, Gaius Junius Bubulcus (his third term) and Quintus Aemilius Barbula (his second), brought a complaint before the people when the year began. The senatorial order, they declared, had been discredited by a wrongheaded revision of its members, through which some candidates had been passed over who were better than some who were appointed. They were therefore not going to recognize that list, they said, which did not discriminate between right and wrong and which had been biased and capricious; and they immediately proceeded with a roll-call of the Senate in the order that had obtained before the censorship of Appius Claudius and Gaius Plautius.

That year also witnessed the start of two commands being assigned by the people, both in the military sphere. First, it was decided that sixteen military tribunes should be elected by vote of the people for the four legions; earlier these posts had normally been conferred as gifts by dictators and consuls, with very few being left to the popular vote. That proposal was made by the tribunes of the plebs Lucius Atilius and Gaius Marcius. Secondly, it was decided that the people should also elect naval duumvirs responsible for equipping and servicing a fleet,* and the mover of this plebiscite was the plebeian tribune Marcus Decius.

I would pass over a rather insignificant event of this same year but for its apparent connection with religion. The flute-players* had been forbidden by the last censors to take their meal in the temple of Jupiter, a long-standing tradition, and in a fit of pique they decamped en masse to Tibur, leaving no one in the city to play the music at sacrifices. The religious implications of this affair held the Senate's attention, and they sent spokesmen to Tibur with a request that all efforts be made to have the men returned to Rome. The Tiburtines generously undertook to do so. They first of all had the flute-players summoned to the Senate house, where they encouraged them to return to Rome; but when they were unable to persuade them, they had recourse to a plan well suited to the men's character. On a feast day, various Tiburtine citizens invited groups of them home, ostensibly to provide the feast with music. They plied them with wine (for which that profession has an inordinate thirst) until they passed out; then they threw them, fast asleep, into wagons and carted them off to Rome. The pipers had no awareness of this until the light hit them the next morning, severely hungover, in the carts, which had been left in the Forum. People then gathered and persuaded them to stay; and they were granted a three-day period each year to wander through the city in ceremonial dress,* with music and the wild abandon that is the norm today. Furthermore, the right was restored to those who played at sacrifices to have their meal in the temple. This was going on while the city was preoccupied with two very serious wars.

31. The consuls divided their assignments between them, and the Samnites fell by lot to Junius, and the new war in Etruria to Aemilius. In Samnium the Roman garrison at Cluviae* could not be taken by storm but was starved into surrender. After accepting the surrender the Samnites still took the heinous step of flogging them and putting them to death. Junius was outraged by such barbarity and, feeling that nothing took precedence over an attack on Cluviae, he captured the place by force of arms the day of his assault on the walls, and put all male adults to death. The victorious army was then marched to Bovianum.* This was the capital of the Pentrian Samnites, and by far their wealthiest city and the best-equipped with men and arms. There was not the anger to motivate the men here, but they took the town because they were fired up with hope of plunder. As a result, the treatment of the enemy was less brutal, but there was almost more plunder taken than had accrued from the whole of Samnium up to that point, and this was all generously passed on to the soldiers.

The superior might of Roman arms could now be withstood by no armies, no camps, and no cities, and so in Samnium the attention of all its leaders was focused on finding a location for an ambush. Their hope was that the Roman army could somehow be caught and surrounded if it were spread out when given an opportunity to plunder. A number of deserters from the countryside and some prisoners who appeared in the consul's path—some by accident, others by design—brought him consistent accounts (which were also true) of livestock in enormous numbers having been herded together into an out-of-the-way glade. These convinced him to take his legions there, lightly equipped, on a raiding expedition.*

A huge army of the enemy had secretly occupied the roads at that spot, and on seeing that the Romans had entered the glade they suddenly rose up and, with shouting and uproar, took them by surprise. At first the unexpectedness of it all brought alarm as the men took up their weapons and stacked their baggage in the middle. Then, when they had all freed themselves of their loads and fitted on their armour, they began to rally to the standards from all sides; and since they knew their places in the ranks from their long experience of military discipline, they automatically formed up the line with no one giving an order. The consul rode to the point where the fighting was most dangerous, and there he leaped from his horse and called on Jupiter, Mars, and the other gods to bear witness that he had come to this place not seeking any glory for himself but only plunder for his men. All that he could be reprimanded for, he said, was being too anxious to enrich his men at the enemy's expense, and from the disgrace of that nothing could save him other than the courage of the men. They should, he told the men, just make a united effort to attack an enemy whom they had defeated in the battlefield, whose camp they had taken, whom they had deprived of their cities, and who was now resorting to his last hope with a treacherous ambush, relying on position, not arms. But what position was there, he asked, that Roman courage could not now take? And he reminded them of the citadels of Fregellae and Sora, and of all the places where they had succeeded in an unfavourable situation.

Fired by these words and with no thought for the difficulties, the soldiers advanced on the enemy line that stood above them. There was some difficulty while the column made its way up the slope of the hill. However, when the first units reached the plateau at the top and the troops felt that they were standing on level ground, the panic suddenly shifted to the ambushers who, scattering and now without weapons, began in flight to look for the very hiding-places in which they had earlier concealed themselves. But the difficult terrain that they had sought out was now causing problems for the enemy themselves, catching them in their own trap. Thus escape was possible only for very few. As many as twenty thousand men were killed,* and the triumphant Romans ran off in different directions for the plunder that had been presented to them by the enemy, the livestock.

32. In the course of these events in Samnium, all the peoples of Etruria, with the exception of the Arretini,* had taken up arms, and begun a huge war by besieging Sutrium, a city allied to the Romans and also virtually the gateway to Etruria. To Sutrium also came the other consul, Aemilius, with an army, for the purpose of raising the siege of the allies. As the Romans arrived, the people of Sutrium

generously brought supplies to their camp, which had been established before the city.

The Etruscans spent the first day discussing whether to speed up the war or prolong it. The next day their leaders opted for swiftness rather than caution in their planning; at sunrise the signal for battle was displayed, and the troops marched out to battle-stations. When this was reported to the consul, he immediately had the tablet sent around* with orders for the men to take their meal and then arm themselves after they had bolstered their strength with nourishment. The order was obeyed and, when he saw his men armed and ready, the consul ordered the standards to be advanced beyond the rampart and deployed his battle-line not far from the enemy. For a while both armies stood there, alert and waiting for the shouting and fighting to be started by their adversaries; and the midday sun had begun its descent before a weapon was thrown from one side or the other. At that point, so they would not be leaving with nothing achieved, a shout went up from the Etruscans, the trumpets sounded, and their standards went forward.

There was no reluctance to enter battle on the Roman side, either. They clashed with furious enmity, the enemy superior in numbers, the Roman in courage. The evenly matched engagement carried off many on both sides, and all the bravest; and there was no shift in fortunes until the Roman second line came up to the front, fresh fighters relieving the weary, while the Etruscans, whose front line lacked the support of new reserves, all fell before and around their standards. Never in any battle would there have been fewer fugitives and more bloodshed, had not nightfall given its protection to those Etruscans bent on dying, so that the conquerors stopped fighting before the conquered. After sunset the signal for retiring was given, and the two sides withdrew in the dark.*

There was that year no further action at Sutrium worthy of record. The entire front line of the enemy army had been destroyed in a single battle, leaving them only with their reserve troops—a force barely capable of protecting their camp—and also, on the Roman side, there were so many wounds sustained that more of the wounded died after the battle than had fallen in action.

33. Quintus Fabius,* as consul of the following year, took over the war at Sutrium, and was given Gaius Marcius Rutulus as his colleague. Fabius brought in reinforcements from Rome, and for the

Etruscans a fresh army arrived that had been summoned from their homeland.

For very many years there had been no feuding between the patrician magistrates and tribunes, but now a feud arose through the family †that was almost fated to quarrel with the tribunes and the plebs.† With the elapse of the eighteen months prescribed under the Aemilian law* as the time-limit for the censorship, the censor Appius Claudius could not be brought to resign by any pressure whatsoever,* despite his colleague Gaius Plautius having resigned *his* office. The plebeian tribune Publius Sempronius was a man who had already taken legal action to keep the censorship confined to the lawful time-limit, a process that was as popular as it was just, and as welcome to the common people as to all the aristocracy. Sempronius would time and again read out the Aemilian law and praise its sponsor Mamercus Aemilius for restricting the censorship to a year and six months—it had previously had a five-year term and had become oppressive because its power was so long-lasting.

'Come now, Appius Claudius,' said Sempronius, 'tell us what you would have done if you had been censor at the time that Gaius Furius and Marcus Geganius were censors.' Appius replied that the tribune's question was not particularly relevant to his own situation. The Aemilian law may have been binding on those censors, he argued, since it was passed in their term of office. But the people had voted the law into force after they had become censors, and because whatever the people had last voted into law was legal and valid, neither he nor any of those whose election as censors followed that legislation could have been bound by that law.

34. Such were Appius' quibbles, though he found no one in agreement. Then Sempronius continued:

'Citizens of Rome, here you have the descendant of the Appius who, elected member of the college of decemvirs for a year, declared himself appointed for a second year and then, in the third year, when he was now a private citizen and had been declared appointed neither by himself nor by anyone else, still held on to the *fasces* and *imperium*! In fact, he stopped retaining the office only when he was brought down by those powers criminally gained, criminally used, and criminally retained. This is the same family, Citizens of Rome, by whose violent outrages you were forced into self-inflicted exile when you occupied the Sacred Mount. This is the family against which you gained for yourselves the aid of the tribunate. This is the family that prompted you to take over the Aventine with two armies. This is the family that has always opposed the usury laws and the agrarian laws. This family broke up intermarriage between patrician and plebeian, and this family barred the way to curule magistracies for the plebs. This is a name far more dangerous for your freedom than that of the Tarquins. So, come on, Appius Claudius! It is now a hundred years since Mamercus Aemilius was dictator, and there have been so many dictators since then, men of the noblest birth and greatest courage. Has none of them read the Twelve Tables? Didn't any of them know that the decision most recently taken by the people constituted the law? Of course they all knew it! And that is why they complied with the Aemilian law rather than that ancient one under which censors were originally elected, and also because when two laws are at odds with each other the new one always takes precedence over the old.

'Or is this what you are saying, Appius, that the people are not subject to the Aemilian law? Or is it that the people are subject to it, but you alone are above the law? The Aemilian law was binding in the case of those violent censors, Gaius Furius and Marcus Geganius. (And these were men who made clear what damage that office could do in the state! Angry at their power being curtailed, they reduced Mamercus Aemilius to the status of poll-tax payer,* though he was the leading man of his generation in war and peace.) It was binding on all censors after that for a hundred years. It was binding in the case of your colleague Gaius Plautius, elected under the same auspices as you and with the same rights. Or did the people, in electing him censor, not grant him the full rights of his elected office? Are you the one special person in whose case this exceptional, singular exemption obtains? What man are you going to elect King of Sacrifices? He will fasten on the title 'king' and say his elections mean he has been elected king of Rome with all the position's prerogatives! Who do you think is going to be satisfied with a six-month dictatorship or five-day *interregnum*? Whom will you have the nerve to elect as dictator for hammering a nail or supervising games?

'Citizens, how stupid and lacking in initiative do you think that man finds those people who, after achieving great things, have resigned the dictatorship within the space of twenty days or resigned an office over a flaw in the electoral process? But why should I go back to antiquity? We have the recent example, within the last ten years, of the dictator Gaius Maenius. Conducting his investigations too rigorously for certain powerful men to feel secure, he was accused by his enemies of being himself tainted with the very criminality that he was investigating and, in order to answer the charge as a private citizen, he actually resigned his dictatorship. I have no wish to see that level of judiciousness in you Appius! Do not lower the standards of your arrogant, high-and-mighty family! Do not leave office a day or an hour before you have to; just do not go beyond the time-limit. Is it enough for you to add a day, or month, even, to your censorship? No. "I shall hold my censorship", he says, "three years and six months beyond the time allowed by the Licinian law, and I shall hold it on my own." This, in fact, now looks like monarchy.

'Or will you take a substitute colleague, when there is a religious ban on substitution even in the case of death? You are not satisfied with having been so punctilious in your censorship as to remove celebration of the most ancient rite—indeed, the only rite founded by the god for whom it is performed—from priests of the highest nobility, and to put it in the hands of slaves! You are not satisfied with seeing a family whose history pre-dates the foundation of this city being entirely eliminated within the space of a year because of you and your censorship, a family held sacred because it once offered hospitality to the gods! No, you have to implicate the entire state in this sacrilege, and my heart shudders at the thought of the outcome. The city was captured in that five-year period* during which, on the death of his colleague Gaius Julius, Lucius Papirius Cursor took Marcus Cornelius Maluginensis as his colleague so that he would not need to leave office. And how much more restrained his ambition was than yours, Appius! Lucius Papirius was not alone in his censorship, nor did he exceed the legal time-limit. Even so he found no one to follow his lead thereafter; all subsequent censors resigned their office after their colleague died. You cannot be obliged to do that—not by the expiry of the term of your censorship, not by your colleague's leaving office, not by the law, not by decency. For you virtue lies in pride, effrontery, and contempt for gods and men.

'Because of the dignity and respect attaching to that office you have held, Appius Claudius, I personally would not want you to receive any violence at my hands or even hear any harsh language from me. However, your inflexibility and arrogance have obliged me to speak as I have, and unless you follow the Aemilian law I shall have you taken into custody. Furthermore, it was established by our fore-fathers that unless, in the election of censors, two candidates gathered the legally required number of votes, the elections would be adjourned with neither position declared filled. And so, since you cannot be elected as a lone censor, I shall not now allow you to function in office alone.'

After these and other such comments, Sempronius ordered the censor to be arrested and taken into custody. Six tribunes approved of the colleague's action but, when Appius appealed, three came to his aid and to the great disgust of all the orders he remained alone in the censorship.*

35. While this was taking place in Rome, Sutrium was already under siege from the Etruscans.* There the consul Fabius was leading his force along the foothills to assist his allies and, wherever possible, attack the siege-works, when he was confronted by an army of the enemy in battle formation. The plains stretching far and wide below him clearly revealed the strength of their numbers and, to have his position compensate for his numerical disadvantage, he veered his march slightly towards the higher ground, where the broken surface was strewn with stones, before turning to face the enemy. The Etruscans were thinking of nothing but their numbers, the only thing on which they were relying, and they went into battle so swiftly and impulsively that, in order to come the more quickly to hand-to-hand fighting, they threw aside their projectiles and drew their swords as they advanced on their enemy. The Romans instead began to shower them with javelins at one moment, and at another with stones, the location itself providing them with a plentiful supply of such weapons. Thus, their shields and helmets struck by these brought consternation to the Etruscans, even those whom they had not wounded. It was no easy matter getting up to close quarters, and they had no projectiles with which to conduct the fighting at long range. They stood there exposed to enemy projectiles without any real protection and, as some also gave ground and their line began to waver and lose its stability, the Roman *hastati* and *principes* renewed the battle-cry, drew their swords, and charged.* The Etruscans could not resist the onslaught; they turned and headed for their camp in headlong flight. But the Roman cavalry galloped forward at an angle across the plain and confronted the fugitives, who then left the road to the camp and

made for the hills. From there, in a column, almost unarmed and tormented by their wounds, they went into the Ciminian Wood.* The Romans, who had killed many thousands of the Etruscans and captured thirty-eight military standards, also took possession of the enemy's camp, with plunder on a massive scale. Then they began discussing pursuit of the enemy.

36. The Ciminian Wood was in those days more impenetrable and more fearsome than the German forests were in recent times, and up to that point no one had ventured there, not even a merchant. Hardly anyone apart from the commander himself had confidence enough to set foot there; for all the rest the memory of the Caudine disaster had not yet faded. Then one of those present, Marcus Fabius, brother of the consul, volunteered to reconnoitre and in a short time bring back reliable information on everything. (Others claim the man involved was Caeso Fabius, and others again that it was Gaius Claudius, born of the same mother as the consul.*) Fabius had been brought up in Caere with some guest-friends,* and because of that he had some grounding in Etruscan literature and a good knowledge of the Etruscan language. I have it on good authority that in those times it was common for Roman boys to receive instruction in Etruscan literature, as now they do in Greek; but a more likely factor is that there was in Fabius some special quality that enabled him to mingle with the enemy in such a daring masquerade.

It is said that a single slave accompanied him, a man who had been brought up with him and so was also familiar with the language. On setting out they were given only a cursory briefing on the topography of the region they had to enter, and the names of the chieftains amongst the peoples there, to avoid the possibility of their being caught out by some tell-tale indication if they hesitated in conversation. They went off in shepherds' clothing and armed with rustic weapons, each carrying a pair of sickles and javelins. But neither command of the language nor style of dress and arms gave them as much protection as did the general unwillingness to accept that any stranger would venture into the Ciminian Wood.

It is said that the two men made their way to the Umbrian Camertes,* and that here the Roman ventured to reveal their identity. He was then reportedly taken into the senate of the Camertes, where on the consul's behalf he discussed the possibility of a treaty of alliance and friendship. He was then accorded warm hospitality and told to report to the Romans that thirty days' supplies would be ready for the army if it entered that region, and that the young warriors of the Umbrian Camertes would be ready, under arms, to follow their orders.

When this report was brought back to him, the consul sent the baggage on ahead at first watch and ordered the legions to follow it. He himself remained behind with the cavalry, and at dawn on the following day he rode up to the enemy outposts, which had been stationed at intervals around the wood. When he held the enemy's attention for a long enough time, he returned to his camp, left it by the other gate, and caught up with the column before nightfall.

At dawn the next day he was reaching the crest of Mount Ciminius, and after surveying the rich fields of Etruria he let the men loose on them. These had already taken away enormous quantities of plunder when some makeshift units of Etruscan peasants, hastily raised by the leaders of the region, came to confront the Romans, but they were so unorganized that the defenders of the spoils almost became spoils themselves. The Romans cut them down or chased them off, raided the agricultural land far and wide, and returned to camp victorious and well supplied with all manner of commodities. It so happened that five envoys had arrived in the camp with two plebeian tribunes to order Fabius in the name of the Senate not to pass through the Ciminian Wood. The envoys were pleased that they had arrived too late to hamper the conduct of the war, and they returned to Rome to report the victory.

37. This operation of the consul had the effect of escalating rather than finishing the war. The area lying at the foot of Mount Ciminius had been subject to the depredations, and the anger this caused had prompted an uprising not only of the peoples of Etruria but of the neighbouring parts of Umbria* as well. The upshot was that an army of hitherto unprecedented size came to Sutrium, and not only did they advance their camp from the woods but, eager to engage, came down into the plain at the first opportunity already formed up for battle. Then, in formation, they at first kept to their position, leaving space for their enemy to deploy opposite them. Then, aware that the enemy was declining battle, they moved up to his palisade. When they also became aware that his outposts had been withdrawn within the fortifications, the cry went up around the officers that they should give the order for their food-allowance to be brought down to them

in that spot from the camp—they would spend the night under arms and attack the enemy camp either during the night or at the latest at first light.

The Roman army felt no less impatient, but was kept in check by the commander's orders. It was about the tenth hour of the day when the consul instructed the men to take their meal, and he ordered them to be armed and ready for the signal, at whatever hour he gave it, day or night. He made a short address, extolling the Samnite wars and disparaging the Etruscans—the one enemy could not be compared with the other, he said, or the one's numbers with the other's. He added that he had another, secret weapon—they would know about it in due course, but for the moment he should say nothing about it. By these vague suggestions he was implying—and this was to restore the men's confidence, discouraged as they were by the enemy's superior numbers—that betrayal of the enemy was under way; and as the enemy had encamped without fortifications the implication was all the more plausible.

After taking food the men slept. Awakened without noise at about the fourth watch, they took up their arms. Pickaxes were distributed amongst the attendants for demolishing the rampart and filling in the ditches. The battle-line was arranged inside the fortifications, and specially selected cohorts were stationed at the gateways. The signal was given shortly before daylight—the time of the deepest sleep on summer nights—and the men, already formed up, flung down the stockade, charged out, and attacked the enemy who were stretched out everywhere. Some were motionless when death struck them, and others half-awake where they lay, but most were fumbling for their weapons in terror. Few were spared the time to arm themselves, and these, too, with no sure standard and no leader to follow, were routed by the Romans and pursued in their flight. Scattered, they headed for their camp and the woods. The woods offered more protection: the camp lay on the plain and was captured the same day. Instructions were given for gold and silver to be brought to the consul; the rest of the spoils went to the men. About sixty thousand of the enemy* were killed or taken prisoner that day.

Some authors have it that this battle, famous as it was, took place on the other side of the Ciminian Wood, in the area of Perusia.* Rome, they say, was in a state of panic, afraid that the army might be cut off in that wood that was so perilous, and wiped out by a general uprising of the Etruscans and Umbrians. Wherever the battle was fought, however, it was Rome that emerged as victor. The result was that from Perusia, Cortona, and Arretium, probably the major cities of the peoples of Etruria in those days, delegates came requesting a peace treaty with Rome and were granted a thirty-year truce.

38. In the course of these events in Etruria, the other consul Gaius Marcius Rutulus took Allifae from the Samnites by force. Numerous other fortresses and villages were completely destroyed or fell into Roman hands intact.

At this same time, too, a Roman fleet commanded by Publius Cornelius, whom the Senate had put in charge of the coastline,* was driven towards Campania and put in at Pompeii. From there the crews set off to pillage the farmlands of Nuceria, but after hurriedly plundering the closest parts (from which they could have safely returned to the ships) they were carried away, as happens, by the joy of the raid and, advancing too far, brought out the enemy. No one confronted them as they sauntered through the fields, although they could have been completely wiped out at that point. It was as they came back in a body and off their guard that some peasants overtook them, not far from the ships, relieving them of their booty and even killing a number. The group that survived the deadly attack was driven back to the ships in panic.

Quintus Fabius' departure to traverse the Ciminian Wood had caused great alarm in Rome, and just as great was the joy brought to the enemy in Samnium by a report that the Roman army was cut off and under siege. They evoked the Caudine Forks as a mirror-image of the disaster. It was the same foolhardiness that had brought a race ravenous for ever further gains into those impassable woods, they said, where they were trapped by the difficulty of the terrain, not the enemy's weapons. Presently, their joy became tinged with envy at the thought that Fortune had diverted the glory of the war with Rome from the Samnites to the Etruscans. Accordingly, they hurriedly assembled with all their weaponry and manpower in order to crush the consul Gaius Marcius, and were intending to head directly to Etruria through the lands of the Marsi and Sabines, if Marcius did not give them the opportunity to fight. The consul confronted them. The battle was savagely fought on both sides, and the outcome uncertain. Although the losses were equal, rumour nevertheless attributed defeat to the Romans,* and this was because their

casualties included members of the equestrian order, military tribunes, and one legate, and most of all because the consul himself had
been wounded.

As a result—and rumour, as usual, also exaggerated things—
sheer terror gripped the senators, who decided that a dictator should
be appointed; and there was no doubt in anyone's mind that the
appointment should go to Papirius Cursor, who was considered the
leading military man of the time. However, they could not be at all
confident that a message could be safely taken through to Samnium,
given the general insecurity of the area, or that the consul Marcius
was still alive. The other consul, Fabius, had personal differences
with Papirius and, so the bad blood between them should not stand
in the way of the public good, the Senate voted that a delegation of
former consuls should be sent to him. These men were to use their
personal authority, as well as that of the state, to induce him, for the
good of his country, to forget their quarrels. The delegates set off to
see Fabius, delivered the Senate's resolution, and added some words
apposite to their commission. The consul lowered his eyes to the
ground and withdrew from the delegates, who were left in the dark as
to what he would do. But then—in the silence of night, as is customary—he named Lucius Papirius dictator. The delegates thanked him
for his self-possession. Fabius, however, maintained an obstinate
silence and dismissed the delegation with no response or comment on
his action, making clear the pain he was suppressing in his great heart.

Papirius appointed Gaius Junius Bubulcus as his master of horse.
However, when he put forward to the *curiae** the bill conferring
office, a bad omen brought adjournment to the proceedings. The
curia with the first vote* was the Faucia, which was notorious for two
disasters, the capture of the city and the Caudine peace, both having
occurred in a year when that *curia* had the first vote. According to
Licinius Macer, this *curia* was also ill-omened for a third disaster,
that of the Cremera.*

39. The following day the dictator retook the auspices and had the
bill passed.* He set off with the legions recently conscripted during
the panic over the army's expedition through the Ciminian Wood,
and reached Longula.* There he took over the veteran troops from
the consul Marcius and marched his force out to form a battle-line.
The enemy, too, seemed not reluctant to engage. But then, though
they were under arms and ready for action, neither initiated battle

and night came upon them. For some time they remained inactive, encamped close to each other, and while they did not lack confidence in their own strength they did not underestimate the enemy, either.

†...†* Meanwhile, under a sacred law,* the Etruscans had raised an army in which each soldier had selected another, and they fought with greater forces, and greater courage, than ever before. The engagement* was marked by such a furious antagonism that weapons were hurled by neither side. The battle started with swords, the clash was ferocious, and the fact that the result long hung in the balance served only to further inflame it, making it look like a struggle not with the Etruscans that they had so often defeated but with some new race of men. There was no step towards flight taken on either side; the front-rank troops fell, and so the standards should not be left bare of defenders the first line was reconstituted from the second. Then men were brought in from the reserves, the last line of defence, and the exertion and danger became so extreme that the Roman cavalry abandoned their mounts and clambered over weapons and clambered over corpses to reach the front ranks of the infantry. It was this virtu-ally new line* springing up amongst the exhausted soldiers that threw the Etruscan troops into disorder. Then, following up the charge of these men, the rest of the infantry, for all their fatigue, broke through the enemy ranks. The enemy's determination began to give way, and a number of units began to be pushed back; and once these turned tail all the rest also took flight. That was the day that first broke the power of the Etruscans after long years of prosperity. Their might was struck down in the battle, and their camp was cap-tured and sacked with the same assault.

40. The war with the Samnites that immediately followed this involved as much danger and had as glorious a result. Apart from their other preparations for war, the Samnites saw to it that their battle-line was agleam with splendid new armour.* There were two armies. The shields of the one they chased with gold, those of the other with silver, and the shape of the shield was as follows. The top, by which the chest and shoulders are protected, is quite wide, with a level rim, and the lower part, to allow for movement, was somewhat narrower. There was a sponge to protect the chest, the left leg was covered with a greave, and the helmets had crests, to make the body look taller. The tunics of the 'gold' soldiers were of many colours, those of the 'silver' were of white linen. It was to these latter that

the right wing was assigned, and the others took their position on the left.

The Romans already knew that the enemy was equipped with splendid armour, but they had been told by their officers that soldiers should have a rough-and-ready look, and instead of being decked out with gold and silver should rely only on iron and courage. That equipment of the enemy was spoils rather than arms, they said— gleaming before the engagement but then disfigured amidst the blood and wounds! Courage was the decoration of a soldier; all that other stuff followed the victory, and a rich foe was the reward of the victor, no matter how poor he be.

His men galvanized by such remarks, Cursor led them into battle. He himself took up his position on the right wing, setting his master of horse on the left. As soon as the sides clashed, the contest with the enemy was furious, but no less fierce was the contest between the dictator and his master of horse over which division of the army would initiate victory. It was Junius who happened to push back the enemy first, the left wing charging the enemy right. This was where the soldiers were deployed who, after the Samnite practice, had 'devoted' themselves, and for that reason stood out by virtue of their white clothing and equally white armour. Junius kept declaring that he was sacrificing these men to Orcus,* and with his charge he caused disorder in their ranks and quite clearly drove back their line.

When he saw this, the dictator exclaimed: 'Is the victory going to start on the left wing, and will the right, the dictator's sector, follow the attack of another and not take the greater share of the victory?' The men were excited by this, and the cavalry proved themselves not inferior to the infantry in courage and the legates not inferior to the generals in ardour. Two ex-consuls, Marcus Valerius on the right and Publius Decius on the left, rode out to the cavalry stationed on the wings, encouraged them to join them in seizing a share of the glory, and then charged the flanks of the enemy at an angle. This was a new source of fear, which swept through the line at both ends, and in reaction to the enemy's fear the Roman legions renewed the war-cry and pushed forward, precipitating flight by the Samnites. The fields were now becoming covered with fallen men and dazzling armour. Initially, the fearful Samnites took shelter in their camp, but then even that could not be held. It was captured, pillaged, and set on fire before nightfall.

By senatorial decree the dictator celebrated a triumph, in which by far the greatest spectacle was the captured armour.* It presented such a magnificent sight that the gilded shields were distributed amongst the bank-proprietors for decorating the Forum. This, it is said, was how the practice began of the aediles decorating the Forum when the ceremonial chariots of the gods were brought through. So the Romans, at least, made use of the splendid armour of their enemies to honour the gods. The Campanians, by contrast, because of their contempt and hatred for the Samnites, used that equipment for arming their gladiators—a show put on during feasting—and called them 'Samnites'.

That same year, in the vicinity of Perusia* (which had also broken the truce), the consul Fabius fought what remained of the Etruscan forces in a battle in which his victory was neither inconclusive nor difficult. He would have captured the city itself—he did come up to the walls after his victory—had a deputation not come out to surrender the town. He imposed a garrison on Perusia, and sent ahead to the Senate in Rome Etruscan delegations who came seeking friendly relations. The consul then rode into the city in triumph for a victory even more outstanding than the dictator's. In fact, the distinction of defeating the Samnites was for the most part redirected to the legates Publius Decius and Marcus Valerius, and at the next elections the people declared these men returned for the consulship and praetorship respectively with overwhelming majorities.

41. Because of his outstanding conquest of Etruria Fabius saw his consulship prolonged,* and he was given Decius as his colleague. Valerius was elected praetor for a fourth term. When the consuls divided their responsibilities, Etruria fell to Decius and Samnium to Fabius. Fabius left for Nuceria Alfaterna, where he refused its people's request for peace on the grounds that they had earlier declined such an offer. He then blockaded the town and forced it to surrender. There was a pitched battle with the Samnites, in which the enemy were defeated with no great effort (and, in fact, there would have been no record of that engagement had it not been the first time that the Marsi had fought the Romans in a war). The Paeligni followed the Marsi* in defecting, with the same result.

Military success also attended Decius, the other consul. He had intimidated the Tarquinienses and had forced them into providing grain for his army and seeking a forty-year truce. He reduced a number of strongholds of Volsinii, demolishing some to prevent their becoming safe havens for the enemy; and by extending hostilities over a wide area he engendered such fear of himself that the entire Etruscan league petitioned the consul for a treaty. They had no success with this, but were granted a year's truce. The enemy supplied the Roman army with a year's pay and two tunics per soldier—such was the price of the truce.

The peace that now reigned in Etruria was disrupted by the sudden insurrection of the Umbrians, a race that had been spared all the misfortunes of war, apart from having experienced an army pass through its territory. They had mobilized all their fighting men and pushed most of the Etruscans into resuming hostilities.* So strong was the army they had formed that, speaking very highly of themselves and contemptuously of the Romans, they boasted that they would simply leave Decius behind them in Etruria and march off from there to attack Rome.

When news of the Umbrians' undertaking was brought to the consul Decius, he proceeded to Rome from Etruria by forced marches and established a position in the territory of the Pupinia tribe,* on the alert for news of the enemy. At Rome, too, the prospect of war with the Umbrians was not taken lightly, and the very threats they had made had brought fear to people who, after the experience of the Gallic disaster, were aware of the weakness of the city in which they lived. A delegation was therefore dispatched to the consul Fabius instructing him to march his army into Umbria at the double should there be any pause in the war with the Samnites. Obeying the order, the consul employed forced marches to head for Mevania,* where the troops of the Umbrians were then located.

The sudden arrival of the consul, whom they had believed to be busy with another war in Samnium, far away from Umbria, so frightened the Umbrians that some felt they should withdraw to their fortified cities, and some that they should abandon the war altogether. One region, however, for which their own name is Materina,* not only kept the others under arms but pushed them into battle immediately. They attacked Fabius as he was building his palisade. When the consul sighted them making a disorderly charge at his defence-works, he called the men back from their building and deployed them as well as the terrain and the circumstances permitted. He then encouraged them with a truthful account of the glory they had won in

Etruria and in Samnium, and ordered them to finish off this trifling addendum to the Etruscan war and make the enemy pay for the impious threat he had made to attack the city of Rome. Such was the enthusiasm of the men on hearing this that a spontaneous shout went up, interrupting the commander as he spoke. Then before the command was given, and before the horns and trumpets sounded, they made a wild charge at the enemy. It did not look as if they were attacking men or armed warriors. Incredibly, it began with the standards being snatched from the enemy standard-bearers; then the standard-bearers themselves were being dragged before the consul; and then armed soldiers were being brought over from one battle-line to the other. Wherever there was any struggle, the fighting was with shields rather than swords; the enemy were brought down with shield-bosses and shoulder-buffeting. More men were taken prisoner than killed, and the single cry to lay down arms echoed along the enemy line. The result was that surrender came while the battle was still in progress, and came from those originally responsible for the war.

The next day and on those that followed the other peoples of Umbria also surrendered. The people of Ocriculum* were admitted to friendship with Rome on the strength of a solemn pledge.

42. Fabius, victor in a war allotted to another, now withdrew his army into his own designated area. The previous year the people had kept him in the consulship; and in recognition of his great success the Senate now likewise extended his command into the following year, the consulship of Appius Claudius and Lucius Volumnius. Appius was very strongly opposed to this measure.

In some annalistic works I find that Appius was censor at the time he stood for the consulship, and that his candidacy was blocked by the plebeian tribune Lucius Furius until he resigned the censorship.* After his election as consul, a new war (in which the Sallentini were the enemy*) was assigned by decree to his colleague, and Appius remained in Rome,* intending to increase his power by his political skills since military distinction remained in others' hands.

Volumnius had no regrets about his commission. He had many successes in battle and took by storm a number of enemy cities. He was open-handed with spoils, and by his affability increased the popularity that generosity brings anyway; and by these qualities he had made his men eager for danger and hard work.

As proconsul, Quintus Fabius* fought a pitched battle with the

Samnite army near the city of Allifae. There was no doubt about the result: the enemy were routed and forced back to their camp. The camp would not have been held, either, had there not been little daylight remaining. It was, however, surrounded before dark, and kept under guard at night to prevent any possibility of escape. Before it was truly light the next day the surrender began, and it was agreed that the Samnites amongst them would be sent out with one article of clothing each—and these were all passed under the yoke. For the allies of the Samnites there was no provision made, and almost seven thousand were sold off at auction. Anyone declaring himself a Hernican citizen* was kept under guard apart from the others. All these Fabius sent off to the Senate in Rome. An enquiry was there held into whether their military service for the Samnites against the Romans had been through conscription or choice, after which they were distributed amongst the various Latin peoples to be kept in confinement. The new consuls, Publius Cornelius Arvina and Quintus Marcius Tremulus (who had been elected by this time), were then instructed to refer the entire matter back to the Senate. The Hernici were angry at this. The people of Anagnia then held a council of all the Hernican peoples in the so-called Maritime Circus* and, with the exception of the populations of Aletrium, Ferentinum, and Verulae, all of the Hernican race declared war on the Roman people.

43. In Samnium, too, there were fresh upheavals occasioned by Fabius' leaving. Caiatia and Sora,* and the Roman garrisons within them, were taken by storm, and outrageous physical abuse was inflicted on the captured soldiers. Publius Cornelius was therefore sent out with an army, and the new enemies (by now war had been authorized against the people of Anagnia and the other Hernici) were assigned by decree to Marcius. At first the enemy captured all the vantage-points between the camps of the two consuls,* making passage impossible even for a messenger travelling light. Thus for a number of days the consuls were without sure information on anything, each of them on tenterhooks with regard to the other's situation, and the fear this raised permeated to Rome. The result was that all younger men had the oath administered to them and two armies with a full complement were enrolled to meet any sudden emergencies. However, the war with the Hernici did not live up to the fear it immediately inspired and the age-old glory of that people. Never did they show any enterprise worthy of mention; three camps were taken

from them in a matter of days; and they negotiated a thirty-day truce—at the cost of providing two months' pay and grain-rations for the army, plus a tunic per soldier—in order to send spokesmen to the Senate in Rome. The spokesmen were referred back to Marcius, who by senatorial decree was granted authority to deal with the Hernici, and Marcius accepted that people's surrender.

In Samnium the other consul was also superior in strength, but he was disadvantaged by his position. To remove any possibility of supplies being brought in, the enemy had blocked all roads and captured the viable passes; and Cornelius could not lure them into a confrontation, despite bringing his troops up to battle-stations every day. It was clear enough that the Samnite would not accept immediate battle and that the Roman could not accept a prolonged campaign. Then the arrival of Marcius, who had brought the Hernici to heel and lost no time in coming to his colleague's aid, removed from the enemy his ability to delay the encounter. They had not considered themselves up to facing one army in battle, and now they certainly did not believe they had any hope left after allowing the two consular armies to join forces. They therefore launched an attack on Marcius as he approached with his troops out of formation. The baggage was hurriedly thrown together in the centre while the line was formed as well as time would allow.

At first the war-cry wafted to the base camp, and then the sight of dust in the distance created a stir among the other consul's troops. Cornelius immediately ordered his men to take up their weapons and he swiftly deployed them in line of battle. He then launched an attack on the flank of the enemy while they were preoccupied with another fight, all the while crying out that it would be utterly shameful if they allowed the other army to take both victories while they themselves failed to claim the glory of a war that was theirs. He broke through just where he had made the attack and headed for the enemy camp through the middle of their line. It was undefended, and Cornelius took it and burned it down. Then Marcius' men caught sight of the flames, as did the enemy when they looked back, and with that the Samnites began to flee in all directions. But slaughter faced them everywhere, and there was no way to safety anywhere.

Thirty thousand of the enemy* had been killed, and the consuls had given the signal to withdraw and were starting to bring together the troops, who were now congratulating each other, into a single body. Then, suddenly, fresh cohorts of the enemy, enrolled as reinforcements, were seen in the distance, and this renewed the carnage. The victors waded into them with no order given by the consuls, and without receiving a signal, crying out that these Samnites needed to be given a hard apprenticeship. The consuls gave free rein to the men's fervour, knowing full well that, rubbing shoulders with veterans in disheartened flight, the raw enemy soldiers would not be capable of even entering the fray. And they were not wrong. All the troops of the Samnites, veteran and new alike, took to their heels for the closest mountains. The Roman column was marched up them, too, and there was no safe haven for the vanquished, who were driven from the heights they had occupied and now were all begging for peace with one voice. Three months' supply of grain was requisitioned from them, plus a year's pay and a tunic for each soldier, in return for which spokesmen were sent to the Senate to sue for peace.

Cornelius remained behind in Samnium. Marcius returned to Rome, entering the city in a triumph over the Hernici; he was decreed an equestrian statue in the Forum, and this was erected before the temple of Castor. The three Hernican peoples of Aletrium, Verulae, and Ferentinum saw their own laws restored to them because they preferred that over receiving citizenship, and they were allowed intermarriage with each other, a right that for a considerable time only these Hernici enjoyed. The people of Anagnia and others who had fought against the Romans were granted citizenship without right of suffrage.* They were stripped of the right to hold assemblies and to intermarry, and forbidden to have magistrates except for religious functions.

That same year the erection of the temple of Salus was put out for contract by the censor Gaius Junius Bubulcus, who had promised it in a vow during the Samnite war, when he was consul. By this man and his colleague Marcus Valerius Maximus roads were constructed through the countryside* from state funds. In the same year the treaty with Carthage was renewed for the third time* and, as a gesture of good-will, gifts were presented to the ambassadors who had come on this commission.

44. That same year saw Publius Cornelius Scipio as dictator, with Publius Decius Mus as master of horse. Consular elections were held by these men, that being the purpose of their appointment, because neither of the consuls had been able to absent himself from the war.

The consuls elected were Lucius Postumius and Tiberius Minucius. Piso* has these men immediately follow the consulship of Quintus Fabius and Publius Decius, and omits the two-year period in which I have recorded that Claudius and Volumnius were made consuls, with Cornelius and Marcius following them. Whether he forgot these in organizing his *Annals*, or whether he deliberately skipped over the two pairs of consuls because he thought their appearance an error, is unclear.

That same year there were Samnite raids on the Plain of Stella* in Campanian territory. As a result, both consuls were dispatched into Samnium. They headed for different regions, Postumius for Tifernum* and Minucius for Bovianum, and it was at Tifernum, under Postumius' command, that a battle was first fought. Some record that there was no doubt about the defeat of the Samnites, and that twenty thousand of them were taken prisoner. Others, however, have it that the battle ended on equal terms; that Postumius, with a pretence of fear, secretly withdrew his troops into the mountains, marching by night; and that the enemy followed and themselves took up a fortified position two miles from his. The consul wanted to convey the impression that his intention had been to establish a secure base with easy access to provisions—and that was what he had there—and so he fortified the camp and furnished it with an array of useful matériel. Then, leaving behind a strong garrison, he struck out at the third watch* and, by the shortest route possible, led his legions, lightly equipped, to his colleague, who was himself encamped facing other enemy troops.

There, on Postumius' recommendation, Minucius engaged the enemy* and, when the battle had continued inconclusively for much of the day, Postumius made a surprise attack on the now-exhausted enemy line with his fresh legions. Fatigue and wounds stood in the way even of flight, and the enemy were totally wiped out, with twenty-one standards captured. The Romans then proceeded to the camp of Postumius. There the two victorious armies attacked an enemy already shaken by the report they had received, defeated them, and sent them off in scattered flight. Twenty-six military standards were taken, along with the Samnite commander, Statius Gellius, and many other men, and both camps were captured. The next day the city of Bovianum also came under siege and was soon taken, and the great glory of their achievements won both consuls a triumph. Some authorities claim that the consul Minucius was carried back to his camp with a serious wound and there expired, that Marcus Fulvius became suffect consul* in his place, and that it was by him that Bovianum was captured, after he was sent to take over Minucius' army.

In that year Sora, Arpinum, and Cesennia* were recovered from the Samnites. The statue of Hercules the Great was also set up and dedicated on the Capitol.

45. In the consulship of Publius Sulpicius Saverrio and Publius Sempronius Sophus, the Samnites sent a delegation to Rome to discuss peace; they were seeking either an end of the war, or a postponement of it. When the delegates adopted a suppliant pose the reply they were given was that if the Samnites had not often sued for peace while preparing for war, a peace treaty could have been settled after discussions conducted between the two. As matters stood, though, the Samnites' words having proved empty up to that point, the Romans had to make a decision based on actions. Publius Sempronius would soon be in Samnium with an army, they said, and he could not be deceived over whether their inclinations were for war or peace. He would be reporting all his findings to the Senate, and the delegates should follow him when he was leaving Samnium.

That year, after the Roman army traversed Samnium, found it peaceful,* and was generously supplied with provisions, the Samnites had their treaty of old restored to them.*

Roman arms then turned against the Aequi,* an old enemy but one who had for many years remained calm under the specious cover of a treaty not faithfully observed. While the power of the Hernici remained intact, the Aequi had joined them in frequently sending assistance to the Samnites and, after the suppression of the Hernici, virtually their whole people had defected to the enemy, without concealing that this was state policy. Then, after the treaty with the Samnites was concluded in Rome, the fetial priests had come to demand reparations, and the Aequi insisted that this was an attempt to intimidate them with the threat of war into becoming Roman citizens. Just how much that was to be wished for, they said, the case of the Hernici had made clear: those given the option had chosen their own laws over Roman citizenship—and for those not having the opportunity to choose, obligatory Roman citizenship would be a punishment!* In the light of such assertions openly made in their council meetings, the Roman people ordered war to be declared on the Aequi.

The two consuls left for the new war and established a position four miles from the enemy camp.

The Aequi had fought no war independently for many years, and their army, looking like a makeshift force, without established commanders and without a command structure, was feeling rather nervous. Some felt that they should take the field, others that they should just guard their camp, and most were disturbed by the thought of the ruin that their farms would face, and the subsequent destruction of the cities, which they had left only lightly garrisoned. Then one proposal was heard, amongst many put forward, which ignored regard for the common good in favour of each looking out for his own: they should leave camp and go their separate ways at the first watch in order to transport everything into the cities and there defend themselves behind their fortifications. This suggestion they all accepted with great unanimity.

The enemy were roaming through the fields at first light when the Romans advanced and deployed in battle order. When no one confronted them, they marched to the enemy camp at a brisk pace. When, however, they observed no outposts before the gates, and no one on the rampart, either, and none of the usual hubbub that usually comes from a camp, they halted, worried by the strange silence and fearing an ambush. Then, after crossing the rampart, they found the camp totally abandoned, and they proceeded to track the enemy. But the tracks went off in all directions, as they would when people dispersed here and there, and that had the Romans bewildered. Later, on learning of the enemy's plans from their scouts, they opened hostilities with individual cities in turn, and captured forty-one strongholds in fifty days,* taking them all by assault. Most were demolished and burned, and the Aequi as a people were almost wiped out.* A triumph was celebrated over the Aequi, and their disastrous fate served as an example, prompting the Marrucini, the Marsi, the Paeligni, and the Frentani to send spokesmen to Rome to ask for a peace treaty and friendship.

46. That same year the scribe Gnaeus Flavius, son of Gnaeus, was a curule aedile, a man who, though born into a humble background as the son of a freedman father,* was nevertheless clever and eloquent. In some annalistic works* I find the following details. Serving as an attendant on the aediles, he saw that, while he had support for the aedileship from his tribe, his candidacy was not accepted because he was doing scribal work. He therefore set aside his writing-tablet and swore he would not in future do scribal work. Licinius Macer claims* that he had actually given up scribal work some time before this, since he had earlier held the position of tribune and on two occasions that of triumvir, once for the night-watch,* and once for establishing a colony. But one thing is not in dispute: the determined struggle that Flavius put up against the nobles who had nothing but contempt for his low birth. He made public the articles of civil law that had been hidden away in the inner sanctum of the pontiffs,* and he put the calendar on display on whitened boards around the Forum so that the dates permitted for legal proceedings would be known. He dedicated the temple of Concord in the forecourt of the temple of Vulcan,* to the mortification of the nobles; and the chief pontiff Cornelius Barbatus* was compelled by the unanimous will of the people to dictate the formulae, although he declared that by ancestral custom none but a consul or commander could dedicate a temple. The result was that, on the authority of the Senate, a measure was brought before the people stipulating that no one should dedicate a temple or an altar without the permission of the Senate or a majority of the plebeian tribunes.

I shall report an anecdote which is not notable in itself, but which does illustrate a plebeian assertion of independence in the face of the nobles' arrogance. Flavius had come to visit a sick colleague and, by mutual agreement, the young men at the bedside did not stand up.* Flavius then had his curule chair brought in, and from the seat conferred by his office* fixed his eyes on his opponents who were in paroxysms of envy.

Flavius' election as aedile had been due to the Forum faction,* which had gained strength as a result of Claudius' censorship. It was Claudius who had first debased the Senate through the introduction of freedmen's sons. When nobody ratified his choice, and he had not gained in the Senate house the influence to which he had aspired, Claudius distributed the low-born of the city throughout the tribes and so corrupted* the Forum and the Campus Martius. Such was the indignation that Flavius' election aroused that most of the nobles set aside their gold rings and horse-medallions.*

From that time on the state fell into two parts. The one, made up of honourable citizens who promoted and supported good people, had one political philosophy; the other, the Forum faction, had another.

This lasted until Quintus Fabius and Publius Decius became censors,* and Fabius, for the sake of concord and at the same time to prevent elections remaining in the hands of the lowest-born, sifted out all the Forum crowd, throwing them into four tribes that he called 'urban'.* This, they say, was so warmly welcomed that by such an organization of the orders he gained the *cognomen* 'Maximus' which he had not gained by all his many victories. He, too, is credited with instituting the parade of the knights* on July 15th.

BOOK TEN

1. In the consulship of Lucius Genucius and Servius Cornelius Rome for the most part enjoyed a respite from wars abroad. Colonies were established at Sora and Alba.* For Alba, in Aequan territory, six thousand colonists were enlisted. To Sora, which had been part of the lands of the Volsci, but which the Samnites had taken over, four thousand men were sent. That same year the people of Arpinum and of Trebula were granted citizenship.* The people of Frusino were fined a third of their farmland for having (as was discovered) incited the Hernici to insurrection; when an investigation had been conducted by the consuls, on a directive from the Senate, the ringleaders of the conspiracy were flogged and beheaded. So that Rome should not pass the year without war, however, a minor foray was made into Umbria when reports kept arriving of raids on the countryside being made by armed bands from a certain cavern.* The Romans entered the cavern with their standards, and in it numerous wounds were inflicted on them because of the darkness of the place, especially from stones that were hurled at them. Eventually, the other entrance to the cavern was discovered—it was open at both ends—and wood was heaped up at both orifices and set alight. As a consequence, up to two thousand armed men were killed inside the cave by the smoke and the heat when, eventually, they rushed straight into the flames in their efforts to get out.

In the consulship of Marcus Livius Denter and Marcus Aemilius hostilities resumed with the Aequi. The Aequi were angry at a colony being installed in their territory like a fortress, and they proceeded with an all-out attack on it, only to be repulsed by the colonists themselves. However, this caused great panic in Rome (it was scarcely to be believed that the Aequi should have independently opened hostilities from such a position of weakness), so much so that Gaius Junius Bubulcus was appointed dictator* to deal with the crisis. Bubulcus set off with his master of horse, Marcus Titinius, and crushed the Aequi in the first engagement. A week later he returned to the city in a triumphal procession and, as dictator, dedicated the temple of Salus which he had promised in a vow as consul and put out for contract as censor.

2. That same year a Greek fleet under the Spartan Cleonymus landed on Italian shores and captured the city of Thuriae in the land of the Sallentini.* The consul Aemilius was sent to deal with this enemy, and he put him to flight in a single battle,* driving him back to his ships. Thuriae was restored to its previous inhabitants, and peace was brought to the Sallentine lands. In some annalistic works I find that the dictator Junius Bubulcus was dispatched to the Sallentini and that Cleonymus left Italy before he was obliged to clash with the Romans.

After sailing from there around the promontory of Brundisium, Cleonymus was swept along by the winds while in the midst of the Adriatic gulf. The harbourless coastline of Italy to his left caused him great fear, as did the Illyrians, Liburnians, and Histrians to his right—savage races notorious for their piracy for the most part—until he came to a point deep within the shores of the Veneti.* He set ashore a few men for reconnaissance and was told that there was, stretching before them, a narrow strip of land, but that, after one crossed this, there were behind it lagoons that were flooded by tidal waters. Not far off, he was told, some flat fields could be seen, and hills were visible beyond them; and there was also in that area the mouth of a very deep river, where the ships could be brought around into a safe anchorage (this was the River Meduacus*). Cleonymus then gave the order for the fleet to sail in and proceed upstream. But the riverbed was not deep enough to take the heaviest of the ships, and large numbers of the soldiers crossed over to the lighter vessels and thus reached some densely populated land (there were three Patavian villages situated there on the bank of the river). They disembarked at that point and, after leaving a meagre force to guard the ships, stormed the villages, set fire to the buildings, and drove off men and cattle as their booty, the joy of plunder making them advance ever further from their ships.

News of this reached Patavium, where having the Gauls as neighbours kept the population on a constant war-footing, and the Patavians split their fighting men into two divisions. One was marched into the area where widespread pillaging was being reported, and the other—to avoid meeting any of the raiders—was taken by another route to the ships' anchorage, fourteen miles from the town. The men on guard were taken by surprise and killed, and the ships were attacked and the terrified crews forced to steer them over to the other bank of the river. On land the fight with the roaming looters had proved equally successful, and when the Greeks were trying to withdraw to their anchorage the Veneti barred their way. Thus the enemy was caught between two forces and cut to pieces. Some who were taken prisoner divulged the information that the fleet and King Cleonymus were three miles away. The captives were then deposited in the closest village for safekeeping, and the Patavians filled with armed men some river-boats (which were custom-built with flat bottoms for negotiating the shallows) or else ships that they had captured. They headed for the fleet and surrounded the ships, which lay at anchor, and were more in fear of the strange surroundings than the enemy. As these were more eager to escape to the open sea than to resist, the Patavians chased them right to the river-mouth, whence they returned victorious, after capturing and burning a number of the enemy vessels that panic had driven onto the shoals. Cleonymus departed with barely a fifth of his ships intact, having gained success in no area of the Adriatic that he had touched. There are many alive today who have seen in Patavium the ships' prows and the Laconian spoils nailed to the wall in the old temple of Juno. As a memorial to that sea battle, a naval contest is regularly held every year, on the date on which it was fought, on the river flowing through the town.

3. That same year a treaty was struck at Rome with the Vestini when they petitioned for friendly relations, and following that there were numerous alarms. A fresh outbreak of hostilities in Etruria was reported following internal strife in Arretium. The disturbance here began with an attempt to remove by force of arms the very powerful Cilnian family,* which was envied for its wealth, and there were at the same time reports of the Marsi vigorously defending their territory after a colony, with four thousand men enrolled, had been established at Carseoli.* In the light of these insurgencies Marcus Valerius Maximus* was appointed dictator, and he chose Marcus Aemilius Paulus as his master of horse. (I am inclined to believe this rather than that Quintus Fabius, at his age and with such offices in his career, should have been under Valerius' orders, though I would not reject the idea that the error arose from the *cognomen* 'Maximus'.)*

The dictator set off with his army and routed the Marsi in a single battle. Then, driving them back into their fortified cities, he captured Milionia, Plestina, and Fresilia* in a few days and renewed the treaty with the Marsi after confiscating some of their territory as punishment. Operations were then shifted to the Etruscans. The dictator thereupon left for Rome to retake the auspices, and meanwhile his master of horse went out to forage and was caught in an ambush. A number of the standards were lost, Aemilius' men were disgracefully put to flight with heavy losses, and he was driven back into the camp. (Such a dreadful reverse cannot be attributable to Fabius. If he lived up to his *cognomen* in any respect it was in his military pre-eminence, but there is also the further point that he remembered Papirius' ruthlessness and could never have been drawn into fighting without the dictator's order.)

4. When this defeat was reported in Rome the panic it generated* was out of proportion to the facts. It was as though the army had been wiped out: a suspension of business was declared; guards were posted at the gates and night-watches in the streets; and arms-caches were gathered together on the walls. All younger men were made to take the oath, and the dictator was sent out to the army where, thanks to the thoroughness of his master of horse, he found everything more peaceful than he had expected and in good order. The camp had been drawn back to a safer location; the cohorts that had lost their standards had been left outside the palisade and been deprived of their tents; and the army was eager to engage, the sooner to have its disgrace expunged. And so he lost no time in advancing the troops into the territory of Rusellae.*

The enemy followed him there. After their success, they had supreme confidence in their ability to fight even in the open, but even so they also tried to catch their enemy with an ambush, which they had already used to effect. Not far from the Roman camp were the partially demolished ruins of a village that had been burned during the raids on the fields. There they set some men in hiding, and drove forward some cattle within sight of a Roman outpost, which was commanded by the legate Gnaeus Fulvius. When no one from the Roman position made a move towards this bait, one of the shepherds advanced right up to the fortifications and shouted to the others who were driving their cattle with some hesitation from the ruins of the village. Why, he asked, were they dawdling when they could safely drive the animals through the centre of the Roman camp? Some citizens of Caere translated these words for the legate, and a great wave of anger spread throughout the maniples which, however, dared not move without being given the order. The legate instructed some men with fluency in the language to observe whether the diction of the shepherds was closer to that of a peasant or a city-dweller, and these reported that their accent, bearing, and neat appearance were all too refined for shepherds. 'Go then,' he said. 'Tell them that they can lay bare their ambush, and that they have set it in vain—the Romans are fully aware of it and can be no more caught by trickery than they can be defeated by weapons.'

When this message was received and passed on to those lying in ambush, the enemy suddenly emerged from the hiding-place and advanced, battle-ready, into the plain, which was open to view on all sides. The legate thought the force to be too great to be repelled by his own detachment, and so he hastily sent to the dictator to ask for help, in the meantime countering the enemy attacks on his own.

5. When he was brought the message, the dictator ordered the standards to be advanced and his men to follow under arms. But all his commands were carried out almost before the order was given— standards and weapons were immediately snatched up, and the men could barely be held back from attacking at running pace. Anger over their recent defeat galvanized them, and so too did the shouting that rang in their ears ever more intensely as the fighting grew hotter. And so they urged each other on and encouraged the standard-bearers to pick up the pace. However, the more the dictator saw them rush ahead, the more determined he was to hold back the column and he gave the order for a gradual advance. The Etruscans, however, were there in full force, all brought onto the field at the start of the battle. Messenger after messenger reported to the dictator that all the Etruscan legions* had joined the battle, and that resistance by his men was now impossible; and from his elevated position the dictator could also see for himself how critical the detachment's situation was. He was nevertheless sufficiently confident that his legate was even at that juncture capable of keeping up the fight, and that he himself was close enough to extricate him from danger; and he wanted the enemy to be as fatigued as possible so that he could attack with his own forces fresh while they were exhausted.

However, despite their measured advance, there was by now little space for making a charge, especially for the cavalry. The legionary standards were moving forward at the front to allay any fear on the enemy's part of a covert or surprise manoeuvre, but the dictator had left gaps in the infantry ranks through which horses could pass with room to spare. The fighting line raised a shout, and at the same moment the cavalry were released. These charged the enemy at a full gallop and suddenly filled with terror men in disarray before riders who were bearing down on them like a hurricane. The result was that, although help had been almost too late in coming for the Romans, who were virtually surrounded, they were now all given a break. The fresh troops took over the fight, and the fight was neither long nor indecisive. Routed, the enemy headed back to their camp, and when the Romans mounted their attack they buckled and crowded together at the far end of it. Fugitives packed the narrow gateways, and large numbers of them clambered up the mound and palisade hoping to gain protection from a higher position, or to climb over at some point and make good their escape. As it happened, the earthwork had been inadequately compressed at one point and it collapsed into the ditch under the weight of the men standing on it. Thanks to that these men got out, shouting that the gods were opening a path for their escape, but more emerged without their weapons than with them.

By this battle the strength of the Etruscans was broken for the second time. After agreeing to provide a year's pay and two months' grain rations for the Roman soldiers, they were granted permission by the dictator to send representatives to Rome to sue for a peace treaty. They were refused the treaty but granted a two-year truce. The dictator returned to Rome in triumph. (I have sources that claim that it was not by any notable battle that Etruria was pacified by the dictator, but only by his settling of the discord in Arretium and his reconciliation of the Cilnian family with the plebs.*) Marcus Valerius was made consul straight after his dictatorship. Some have recorded that he was elected although he was not a candidate and, indeed, when he was even absent from Rome, and that the election was held by an *interrex*. One thing is incontrovertible, however: he held the consulship with Appuleius Pansa as his colleague.

6. In the consulship of Marcus Valerius and Quintus Appuleius, things were relatively peaceful abroad. Military failure and the truce kept the Etruscans inactive; and the Samnites, intimidated by defeats over many years, had not yet tired of their new treaty. At Rome, too, the plebeians were kept at peace thanks to the off-loading of large numbers of them into colonies. But so that there should not be tranquillity in all quarters,* antagonism was instilled amongst the state's leading men, both patrician and plebeian, by the tribunes of the plebs,

Quintus and Gnaeus Ogulnius.* These looked everywhere for opportunities to discredit the senators before the plebs. Finding their other
efforts to be fruitless, they adopted a course of action designed to
spur on not the lowest members of the plebeian order but its leading
men, plebeians who had held consulships and celebrated triumphs,
and whose lists of offices held lacked nothing other than priesthoods,
which were not yet open to all. There were at the time four augurs
and four pontiffs, and there was support for increasing the number of
priesthoods to twelve. The tribunes now put forward a bill for the
appointment of four new pontiffs and five new augurs, all to be drawn
from the plebs.* How that college could have been reduced to four
augurs I am unable to ascertain, unless it was by the death of two
of its members.* It was established practice amongst the augurs for
their number to be uneven, and this was to ensure that the three
ancient tribes—the Ramnes, Titienses, and Luceres*—each had its
own augur. If there were need of more, they would increase the
priests by a number preserving equality, and this was what happened
now, when five new ones were added to the four, making a total of
nine, that is, three for each of the tribes.

However, because these priests were selected from the plebs, the
patricians were just as upset as they had been when they saw the consulship opened up. They pretended that the matter concerned the
gods more than it did themselves. The gods, they said, would ensure
that their worship would not be defiled; they personally hoped
only that it would not mean some catastrophe befalling the state.
However, their resistance was slight: they were now used to being
losers in struggles of that kind. Furthermore, they could see that their
adversaries—something these could scarcely have hoped for at one
time—were no longer hankering after the great offices, but had now
attained all the things for which they had striven with little prospect
of gaining them: multiple consulships, censorships, and triumphs.

7. Even so, they say there was a very heated dispute between
Appius Claudius and Publius Decius Mus over whether the law
should be passed or rejected. These more or less revisited the arguments* about the rights of patricians and plebeians that had earlier
been made for and against the Licinian law, when approval of the
consulship for plebeians was at issue. Then, it is said, Decius recalled
the spectacle of his father as many who were at the assembly had seen
him, wearing his Gabine clothing and standing over his weapon—the

figure he had cut when he devoted himself on behalf of the Roman people and its legions. At that time, he said, the immortal gods had found the consul Publius Decius to be just as pure and pious as if it had been his colleague, Titus Manlius, who was being offered for sacrifice. Could that same Publius Decius not have been duly appointed to offer the public sacrifices of the Roman people? Was there a danger, the consul asked, that the gods would give his own prayers less of a hearing than those of Appius Claudius? Was Appius more pure in the performance of his private devotions and more scrupulous in his worship of the gods than he was? Who felt any qualms about the vows that so many plebeian consuls, and so many plebeian dictators, had made on behalf of the state either when they were going to join their armies or were in the throes of war? Let them simply list the commanders during the years since campaigns were first conducted under plebeian leadership and auspices, and then let them list the triumphs. Now the plebs had no regrets even about their own nobility. He was completely sure that, should a war suddenly arise, the Senate and people of Rome would have no greater confidence in patrician leaders than they would in plebeian.

'That being so,' Decius continued, 'what god or man can think it improper for those men also to assume the insignia of pontiffs and augurs? These are men whom you have honoured with curule chairs, with the *toga praetexta*, with the tunic with the palm-motif and the embroidered toga,* along with the triumphal crown and laurel wreath! Men to whose homes you have given distinction above those of others by affixing to them enemy spoils! If, wearing the attire of Jupiter Optimus Maximus, a man has ridden through the city in the gilded chariot and then mounted the Capitol, should he not be seen with the bowl and curved staff when, his head veiled, he slaughters the sacrificial animal or takes an augury from the citadel? If people will calmly read of the man's consulship, his censorship, and his triumph in the inscription on his ancestral mask,* will their eyes not be able to bear reading of his augurate or pontificate, if you add these to his honours? In fact—and may my words not offend heaven!—I do hope that, thanks to the favour of the Roman people, we have by now reached a point where we may, by the esteem we enjoy, impart to the priesthoods as much distinction as we may receive from them; and where we may, for the sake of the gods more than ourselves, formally request to worship in an official capacity the gods we worship in private.

8. 'But why have I proceeded thus far as though the patricians enjoyed a total monopoly on the priesthoods and as though we were not already in possession of one very important priesthood? We see plebeians as decemvirs in charge of sacred rites,* men who interpret the prophecies of the Sibyl and the fates of this people and who also act as high priests of the cult of Apollo and the ceremonials of other gods. The patricians were not wronged in any way on that occasion when, to accommodate the plebeians, the duumvirs for sacrifices had their number increased. Now, too, when our courageous and vigorous tribune is for adding five augural and four pontifical positions to which plebeians may be appointed, the aim is not to drive you people from your places, Appius, but to have members of the plebs assist you in the management of religious rites as they already assist you, to the best of their ability, in other, secular areas. Feel no embarrassment, Appius, to have as colleague in your priesthood a man whom you could have had as your colleague in your censorship or consulship—and *you* being master of horse and *he* dictator is as likely a scenario as you being dictator and he the master of horse!

'It was a Sabine newcomer who first had the noble rank you enjoy, whether you prefer Attius Clausus or Appius Claudius* as his name. The patricians of old accepted him into their number; don't you now disdain to accept us into the number of priests. We bring many marks of distinction with us, indeed all those that have given you people your airs and graces. Lucius Sextius was the first consul to come from the plebs, Gaius Licinius Stolo the first master of horse, Gaius Marcius Rutulus the first to be both dictator and censor, and Quintus Publilius Philo the first praetor. It is always the same story we have been hearing from you people: the auspices are your prerogative, you alone have a clan,* and you alone have true *imperium* and right of divination at home and in war (though up to now plebeian and patrician have been equally successful in these areas, and will continue to be so). Look, have you never heard it said that those who became the first patricians were not sent down from heaven but were simply those people who could call on a father by name, that is, nothing more than freeborn persons? Already I can call a consul my father, and my son will presently be able to call one his grandfather. All this means, citizens, is that everything we are denied we do eventually secure. The patricians only want a fight; they don't care about how their fights turn out. My vote is for ratifying this law as proposed, and may it bring success, good fortune, and prosperity to you and the state.'

9. The people wanted to have the tribes summoned right then, and it looked as if the law was as good as passed, but that day's business was suspended because of a veto. The next day the tribunes were intimidated* and the law was passed with massive support. The pontiffs elected were: Publius Decius Mus, the law's advocate, Publius Sempronius Sophus, Gaius Marcius Rutulus, and Marcus Livius Denter. The five augurs, also taken from the plebs, were: Gaius Genucius, Publius Aelius Paetus, Marcus Minucius Faesus, Gaius Marcius, and Titus Publilius. Thus the pontiffs became eight in number, and the augurs nine.

The same year the consul Marcus Valerius proposed a law of appeal that was more carefully enacted than its predecessors. This was the third proposal of such a law since the expulsion of the kings, and each time it was made by the same family.* The reason for its multiple revisions was in my opinion only the fact that the wealth of the few triumphed over the liberty of the plebs. The Porcian law,* however, seems to have been unique in that it was passed to protect the backs of citizens, since it prescribed severe punishment for beating or killing a Roman citizen. The Valerian law forbade the flogging or beheading of anyone who had made an appeal, but added only that contravention be considered 'an improper act'. This, I think, appeared to provide strong enough enforcement of the law's provisions, such being people's sense of propriety at the time. These days hardly anyone would seriously make such a threat.

A campaign that was by no means memorable was conducted by the same consul against the Aequi who, despite having nothing left of their fortunes of old except their ferocious spirit, were up in arms again. The other consul, Appuleius, besieged the town of Nequinum in Umbria.* This was on a steep slope that was sheer on one side (it was where Narnia is now located), and it could be taken neither by assault nor by siege-works. As a result, the operation was still in progress when the new consuls, Marcus Fulvius Paetus and Titus Manlius Torquatus, took charge.

According to Licinius Macer and Tubero, the centuries were all for declaring Quintus Fabius consul for that year although he was not a candidate for the office, but Fabius himself urged them to put off his consulship to a year when there was the prospect of more warfare.

In that upcoming year, he said, he would be of greater service to the state holding a city magistracy. So it was that Fabius, who did not try to hide his wishes but did not stand for the post, either, was elected curule aedile along with Lucius Papirius Cursor. What prevents me from declaring this as a fact* is that Piso, one of the earlier annalists, states that the curule aediles for that year were Gnaeus Domitius Calvinus, son of Gnaeus, and Spurius Carvilius Maximus, son of Quintus. I think that it was the *cognomen* that occasioned the error in the identity of the aediles and that a version then emerged to accommodate the error, by putting the elections of the aediles and consuls together. This year the census purification was performed by the censors Publius Sempronius Sophus and Publius Sulpicius Saverrio, and there were two tribes added, the Aniensis and the Terentina.* Such were events in Rome.

10. At the town of Nequinum, meanwhile, time dragged on as the siege made little progress. Then two of the townsmen, who had houses adjacent to the wall, made a tunnel, by which they came secretly to the Roman outposts. Conducted from there to the consul, they gave him their assurance that they would admit an armed detachment within the fortifications and city walls. It seemed that the proposal should not be rejected, but not accepted without circumspection, either. Two scouts were sent through the tunnel with one of the men, the other being detained as a hostage and, when the facts were well enough established by them, three hundred armed men, led by the turncoat, entered the city by night and seized the closest gate. When this was broken down, the consul and the Roman army occupied the city without a fight, and Nequinum came under the control of the Roman people. A colony was sent there as a safeguard against the Umbrians, and it was called Narnia, after its river.* The army was marched back to Rome with large quantities of plunder.

In that same year preparations for war were made by the Etruscans, in violation of the truce, but while they were taking these steps a huge Gallic army crossed their borders, briefly distracting them from their undertaking. Relying then on the great strength of their financial reserves, they tried to convert the Gauls from enemies to friends so that they could fight the Romans with the Gauls' army added to their own. The barbarians had no objection to the partnership; only the price was in question. When this was negotiated and handed over, and when everything else was ready for the campaign, the Etruscans instructed the Gauls to follow them. The Gauls, however, protested that attacking the Romans had not been part of their bargain, that what they had been given was the price for not raiding Etruscan land and making armed forays against the farmers. They added, however, that they would still fight, if the Etruscans really wanted them to, but for one price only, that they be accepted into some part of Etruscan territory where they would finally have a settled abode. There were frequent gatherings of the Etruscan peoples to consider the question, but nothing could be worked out, not so much because of the loss of territory involved, but because they all shuddered at the prospect of taking on men of such a savage race as neighbours. So the Gauls were sent packing, carrying off a huge sum of money gained without any work or risk. At Rome word of a Gallic uprising, added to war with Etruria, brought panic, and there was all the less hesitation about concluding a treaty with the people of Picenum.*

11. Responsibility for Etruria was allotted to the consul Titus Manlius. After barely entering enemy territory, Manlius was training with his cavalrymen when he was thrown from his horse while wheeling around after a swift gallop. The consul almost died on the spot, and his life did end two days after the fall. The Etruscans saw this as an omen for the war and they took heart, declaring that the gods had opened the hostilities taking their side. In Rome the death was sad news, both because the man was missed and because of the bad timing. The senators were deterred from ordering the appointment of a dictator because, in accordance with the opinion of the house leaders, an election was held for a substitute for the consul. Marcus Valerius* was unanimously voted in as consul by the centuries, and he was the man the Senate would have named as dictator.

The Senate then ordered Valerius to set off immediately to the legions in Etruria. His arrival there crushed the spirit of the Etruscans, to the point where none dared step outside the fortifications and their own fear had the effect of a siege. The new consul could not entice them into battle by destroying the countryside and burning buildings, either, although smoke was rising in every quarter, not just from farmhouses in flames, but from a large number of villages, too.

The war was proceeding more sluggishly than Valerius had anticipated. Meanwhile there was talk of another war, which arose from information supplied by Rome's new allies, the people of Picenum, and this aroused well-grounded fear because of the defeats earlier inflicted on each other by both sides. According to this information, the Samnites were considering war and a reopening of hostilities, and the people of Picenum had been approached to join them. The Picentes were thanked,* and the Senate's concern was now mostly turned from Etruria to the Samnites.

The high price of grain also kept the citizens in a state of anxiety. According to those authors who want to see Fabius Maximus as aedile that year, there would have been a disastrous shortage had not Fabius demonstrated the same application* in the distribution of grain, by stockpiling and importing wheat, as he had demonstrated many times in his military career.

This year saw the employment of an *interregnum*, though the reason for it is not recorded. The *interreges* were Appius Claudius, and then Publius Sulpicius. Sulpicius held the consular elections and declared Lucius Cornelius Scipio* and Gnaeus Fulvius consuls elect.

At the start of this year spokesmen for the Lucanians approached the new consuls with a grievance. The Samnites, they said, unable to induce them to accept an armed alliance, had entered their country with a hostile force and were laying waste their territory and by such acts of war forcing them into war. The Lucanian people had, in the past, made mistakes enough and more than enough, they said, but they were now fully determined to bear and endure anything rather than ever again show disrespect to the Roman people. They begged the senators to take the Lucanians under their protection and to defend them against the violent outrages of the Samnites. The fact that they had undertaken a war against the Samnites was itself bound to be taken as a guarantee of their loyalty to the Romans, they added, but even so they were prepared to give them hostages.

12. The discussion in the Senate was brief: the vote for concluding a treaty with the Lucanians and demanding reparations from the Samnites was unanimous. The Lucanians were given a positive answer, the treaty was struck, and fetials were sent to order the Samnites to leave the farmlands of the allies of Rome and withdraw their army from Lucanian territory. The fetials were met by men sent by the Samnites to warn them that if they approached any assembly in Samnium they would not get away unharmed. When news of this was heard in Rome, the Fathers voted for war with the Samnites, and the people ratified their decision.

The consuls divided their responsibilities between them. Etruria fell to Scipio and the Samnites to Fulvius,* and each set off for his respective theatres of war. Scipio, who was anticipating a sluggish campaign, like the previous year's operation, was met near Volaterrae by an enemy column ready for battle. The battle took up most of the day, with casualties heavy on both sides, and when nightfall broke it off the combatants were unsure which army had been granted victory. Dawn the next day revealed the victor and the vanquished, since the Etruscans had abandoned camp in the silence of the night. When the Romans emerged to form up for battle, they saw that victory had been ceded to them by the enemy's departure, and they advanced on the Etruscan camp. Finding it unoccupied, they captured it and along with it (since it had been a base camp and had been hastily abandoned) a rich store of booty. The troops were then marched back into Faliscan territory. Scipio left his baggage at Falerii with a small detachment and, with his column only lightly armed, set off to plunder the enemy's lands. There was wholesale destruction by fire and the sword, and booty was accumulated from all parts. It was not only a matter of the enemy being left with bare soil; fortresses and villages were also put to the torch. Scipio, however, refrained from attacking cities into which fear had driven the Etruscan civilians to seek shelter.

A famous engagement was fought near Bovianum in Samnium by the consul Gnaeus Fulvius, and the victory was certainly not indecisive. Fulvius then went on to take Bovianum by storm,* and not much later Aufidena, as well.

13. In that same year a colony was established at Carseoli* in the territory of the Aequicoli, and the consul Fulvius held his triumph over the Samnites.

As the consular elections drew near, a rumour arose that the Etruscans and Samnites were enrolling huge armies. The Etruscan leaders were reportedly being attacked openly at all their assemblies for not having brought the Gauls to join their war effort on any condition whatsoever, while the magistrates of the Samnites were being reproached for having employed against the Romans an army recruited to face the Lucanian enemy. Thus, the rumour went, their enemies were preparing for war with their allies' forces as well as their own, and the Romans would have to cope with a struggle on terms far from equal.

There were distinguished men standing for the consulship, but the prevailing fear focused everyone's attention on Quintus Fabius Maximus, who was initially not a candidate and who subsequently, when he saw where sympathies lay, also declined to be one.* Why would they bother an old man, he asked, one who had come to the end of his career and the rewards of that career? Neither his physical nor his mental powers remained as they were, he said, and he also feared Fortune herself—one of the gods might think that she had been more generous and steadfast towards him than the human condition required. He had risen to match his elders' glorious records, and was happy to see others rise to match his. There was no shortage of high offices for brave men in Rome, he concluded, and no shortage of brave men for those offices.

By such restraint Fabius only increased the well-deserved support he enjoyed and, thinking that support should be cooled by deference to the laws, he ordered a law read out* by which re-election of a consul within a ten-year period was disallowed. The law was barely audible over the uproar from the attendance, and the plebeian tribunes insisted this would be no obstacle, that they would bring before the people a measure to extricate him from the legal difficulty. Fabius, however, persisted with his refusal, asking what the point was in passing laws that could be circumvented by those who passed them. That meant the laws being ruled instead of doing the ruling. Nevertheless, the people began the election, and as each century was called in it quite clearly designated Fabius as its choice for consul. Then finally, overwhelmed by the general consensus of the community, Fabius said: 'May the gods approve of what you are doing, and what you are going to do, citizens. But since in my case you will have what you want, allow me to use my influence with you in the choice of my colleague. Publius Decius is a man known to me from our good relationship in office, and he is a credit to you and a credit to his father. Please, make him consul along with me.'

Fabius' advocacy seemed fair, and all the remaining centuries declared for Quintus Fabius and Publius Decius as consuls.

That year several people were indicted by the aediles for possession of land beyond the legally prescribed limit.* Hardly anyone was exonerated, and a severe restriction was placed on rapacious greed.

14. The new consuls, Quintus Fabius Maximus and Publius Decius Mus, were serving for their fourth and third times respectively. They discussed together the modalities of the campaign: how

one should take on the Samnite enemy and the other the Etruscan; how large a body of troops would suffice for the one sphere of action and for the other; and which commander would be more suitable for each theatre of war. Meanwhile, envoys arrived from Sutrium, Nepete, and Falerii announcing that assemblies of the peoples of Etruria were being held to discuss peace overtures, and they thus deflected towards Samnium the entire thrust of the war. The consuls then set out, and marched their legions into Samnium; and to facilitate provisioning and to keep the enemy unsure of where the attack would come, Fabius came through the land of Sora, and Decius through that of the Sidicini.

On reaching enemy territory, each commander advanced with raiding parties spread out on a broad front. Their scouts, however, ranged more widely than the raiders, and as a result the enemy did not take them by surprise near Tifernum when, posted in a secluded valley, they prepared to attack from a higher position when the Romans entered it. Fabius removed his baggage to a safe location and left a small detachment to protect it, and then, warning the men that a fight was imminent, he moved up in battle formation to the enemy's concealed position mentioned above. The Samnites now had no hope of making a surprise attack and, since the issue was anyway going to be decided in the open, they also opted for a pitched battle. They accordingly descended to level ground, and trusted to fortune with more courage than hope. Nevertheless, whether it was because they had brought together the entire strength of all the Samnite peoples or because an all-or-nothing confrontation was adding to their courage, they aroused some fear in the Romans even in an open engagement.

When he saw the enemy was being dislodged at no point, Fabius called on his son Maximus* and Marcus Valerius, the two military tribunes with whom he had sped forward to the front line. He ordered them to approach the cavalry and urge them on by telling them to strive that day to keep untarnished the glory of their arm of the forces, if they remembered any occasion when the state had felt the assistance of the cavalry. In the infantry engagement, they were to say, the enemy could not be moved, and all remaining hope lay in a charge by the cavalry. He addressed the two young men by name, and with equal warmth, lavishly alternating praise and promises. However, †in the event of such an attack failing†, Fabius thought he should employ a stratagem, in case sheer strength proved unhelpful, and so he ordered his legate Scipio to withdraw from the battle the *hastati* of the first legion* and, with all possible stealth, to lead them around to the closest mountains. The troops were to climb these (the ascent being kept out of sight) and suddenly make an appearance to the rear of the enemy.

Led by the tribunes, the cavalry suddenly charged out before the standards, but they generated little more panic in the enemy than they did in their own side. The Samnite line stood unmoved before the charging horses. They could not be driven back or broken at any point, and when the attempt proved fruitless the Roman horsemen fell back behind the standards and left the battle. The enemy's morale increased as a result, and the Roman front could not have held out when facing so long a struggle, with the violence increasing as a result of the self-confidence of the foe, had not the second line, on an order from the consul, moved up to relieve the first. There the newly acquired strength halted the Samnites as they now surged forward, and the timely sighting of the standards coming from the mountains, together with the war-cry that went up, filled the hearts of the Samnites with a fear not warranted by the true situation. Fabius shouted out that his colleague Decius was approaching, and every soldier took up the cry with joyful eagerness, saying that the other consul was coming, that the legions were coming. The mistake proved profitable for the Romans, filling the Samnites with dread and thoughts of flight, since their worst fear was that of being over-whelmed while they were exhausted by the other army that was fresh and intact. Because they became widely dispersed in flight, the car-nage was less than one might expect from so crushing a victory. Three thousand four hundred were killed and some eight hundred and fifty taken prisoner,* with the capture of twenty-three military standards.

15. The Apulians* would have united with the Samnites before the battle but for the consul Publius Decius, who barred their way with his encampment at Maleventum, and then drew them into a fight and routed them. In this sector, too, there was more flight than slaugh-ter—only two thousand Apulians were killed. With scant respect for this enemy, Decius led his legions ahead into Samnium. There the two consular armies, ranging widely in different sectors, pro-duced complete devastation in the space of five months. There were forty-five locations in Samnium in which Decius' camp had been

established, and in the case of the other consul the number was eighty-six. It was not just vestiges of the ramparts and ditches of these that were left behind; much more striking monuments than these remained in the devastation all round and whole regions laid waste. Fabius also captured the city of Cimetra,* where two thousand nine hundred soldiers were taken prisoner, and about nine hundred and thirty killed in action.

Fabius then left for Rome for the elections, and he lost no time in holding them. The centuries that were called first all voted for Fabius as consul. Thereupon Appius Claudius, who was a candidate for the consulship, and an energetic and ambitious man, devoted his own influence, and that of all the nobility, to having them name him consul along with Quintus Fabius. (This was not so much for his personal advancement as to have the patricians recover both consular positions.) Fabius at first voiced his objections* in connection with his own candidacy, giving much the same reasons as he had the previous year. All the nobles stood about his chair and implored him to take the consulship out of the plebeian filth it was in and to restore to the patrician families both the office and their dignity of old. When he had obtained silence, Fabius allayed the men's concerns with a measured speech. He said he would have accepted the names of two patricians who were elected if he had seen someone other than himself become consul. As it was, he would not accept his own nomination since that was against the law and would set a bad precedent. As a result Lucius Volumnius, from the plebs, was elected consul along with Appius Claudius (the two had also been put together in an earlier consulship). The nobles criticized Fabius for having avoided Appius Claudius as a colleague saying that it was because the man was clearly his superior in oratory and political ability.

16. When the elections were finished, the old consuls were instructed to prosecute the war in Samnium, for which they received a six-month extension of their *imperium*. Thus, the following year (the consulship of Lucius Volumnius and Appius Claudius), Publius Decius who, while still consul, had been left behind in Samnium by his colleague, did not stop pillaging the farmlands as proconsul until he finally drove the Samnite army—which would not commit itself to pitched battle anywhere—out of the region.

Driven out, the Samnites made for Etruria. They then thought that, with an army of such a size and with threats added to their pleas, they would more effectively gain what they had often unsuccessfully failed to gain by diplomacy, and so they demanded a meeting of the leaders of Etruria. When this was convened, the Samnites emphasized the number of years they had been fighting against the Romans for their freedom. They had tried everything, they said, hoping they could bear the great weight of the war with their own strength alone, and they had also put the assistance of neighbouring peoples to the test, but it proved of little use. Unable to keep up the fight, they had sought peace from the Roman people, but had then recommenced hostilities on finding peace as slaves harder to bear than war as free men. The one hope left to them lay in the Etruscans, they said, as they knew that these were the people in Italy with the greatest resources in arms, manpower, and money. They also knew that the Etruscans had as their neighbours the Gauls who, born amidst armed warfare, were by nature ferocious and hostile to the Roman people, and when they told of how Rome had been captured by them and ransomed for gold, that was no idle boast! If the Etruscans had the spirit once seen in Porsenna* and their ancestors, there was nothing to stop them from driving the Romans out of all the land north of the Tiber and making them fight for their very lives rather than for an intolerable dominance over Italy. They ended by saying that the Etruscans now had at their disposal a Samnite army that had come prepared and equipped with arms and pay, and that the Samnites would follow them in an instant even if they should lead them to the city of Rome itself.

17. While the Samnites were making these boasts and stirring up trouble in Etruria, the Roman campaign was causing them distress at home. Publius Decius had learned from his scouts that the Samnite army had left, and so he had summoned a council of war and said: 'What is the point of our wandering around the countryside taking the war from village to village? Why do we not attack the cities and fortified towns? There is no army standing on guard over Samnium— their forces have left their lands for a self-imposed exile.'

All were in agreement and Decius led the army to launch an attack on the powerful city of Murgantia.* Such was the fervour of the men, both from affection for their leader and the hope of winning more spoils than they had from their raids on the countryside, that they took the city by force of arms in a single day. There two thousand one hundred Samnite combatants were surrounded and taken prisoner, and other forms of plunder were also acquired in massive quantities. Not to burden his army on the march with heavy baggage, Decius had the men summoned to an assembly.

'Are you going to be satisfied with just this victory or this booty?' he asked them. 'Have hopes as great as your courage! All the Samnite cities and the fortunes within them belong to you—you have defeated their legions in so many battles and finally driven them from their lands. Sell that stuff and use profit as an incentive for merchants to follow the army. I shall supply you with goods to sell from time to time. Let us go from here to the city of Romulea where the effort that awaits you is no greater, but the plunder is!'

The booty was sold off and, with the men actually spurring on their commander, they proceeded to Romulea.* There, too, there was no use of siege-works or catapults. As soon as they had advanced on the town, they could be discouraged by no amount of force from taking it, and after swiftly bringing ladders up to the walls at the points closest to them, they climbed over them. The town was taken and looted, and almost two thousand three hundred men were killed and six thousand taken prisoner. The rank-and-file took possession of a huge amount of plunder, which they were obliged to sell, as before, and from there, though given no rest, they were led to Ferentinum* at an extremely rapid pace. There, however, they faced greater hardship and danger: the walls were defended with the utmost vigour, and the place was protected both by fortifications and its topography; but the soldiers, who had grown used to plunder, surmounted all the difficulties. Nearly three thousand of the enemy were killed near the walls, and the plunder went to the men.

The credit for storming these cities* goes mostly to Maximus in some annalists, who record that Murgantia was stormed by Decius, and Ferentinum and Romulea by Fabius. There are some who give the glory to the new consuls, and some who give it not to both but only to one, Lucius Volumnius (to whom, these authors say, Samnium fell as his area of responsibility).

18. Whoever had command and held the auspices in Samnium, in the course of these events a war of massive proportions was being fomented against Rome in Etruria by many nations, its prime mover being Gellius Egnatius, a Samnite. Nearly all the Etruscans had decided on war; the spreading infection had drawn in the closest Umbrian peoples; and offers of money were being made to attract

Gallic mercenaries. The entire body of these forces was gathering at the Samnite camp.

By the time that news of this sudden insurgency was brought to Rome, the consul Lucius Volumnius had already set out for Samnium with the second and third legions and fifteen thousand allies;* and it was now decided that Appius Claudius should proceed to Etruria at the earliest possible moment. Two Roman legions were with him, the first and the fourth, as well as twelve thousand allies, and camp was established not far from the enemy.

In fact, more was achieved by the consul's swift arrival, by which fear of the Roman name restrained some Etruscan peoples already contemplating war, than by any brilliant or opportune enterprise in the area under the consul's leadership. Many battles were fought in the wrong place or at the wrong time, and the enemy's rising hopes made them each day more formidable, to the point where the men were almost losing confidence in their leader and the leader in his men. In three annalistic works I find it said that a letter was sent by Appius asking his colleague to come to his aid from Samnium. I am, however, reluctant to record this as certain since that very point was a matter of dispute between these consuls of the Roman people who were now holding the same office together for the second time. Appius denied that a letter had been sent, and Volumnius strongly maintained that he had been sent for by a letter from Appius.

Volumnius had by this time taken three strongholds in Samnium,* and in them up to three thousand of the enemy had been killed and about half that number taken prisoner. He had also, to the great satisfaction of the patricians, put down some insurrections amongst the Lucanians that had been fomented by leaders who were impecunious plebeians; and for this he used the services of Quintus Fabius, whom he sent to Lucania as proconsul with his seasoned army. Volumnius then left the pillaging of the enemy's agriculture to Decius while he himself headed off with his own troops to his colleague in Etruria. There everybody welcomed his arrival with joy. As for Appius, his reaction, I think, is to be gauged from whatever he knew in his heart to be true: he was justifiably angry if he had written no letter, but putting on a mean-spirited and ungrateful pretence if he had actually stood in need of help. Appius came out to meet his colleague and, when the two had scarcely exchanged greetings, said: 'Is all well, Lucius Volumnius? How are things in Samnium? What has induced you to come away from your province?'

Volumnius replied that all was well in Samnium, and that he had come in response to Appius' letter. If, however, the letter was a forgery and he was not needed in Etruria, he would turn around and go back.

'Go back, then,' said Appius, 'no one is stopping you. It's certainly not right for you to boast about coming here to bring help when you can barely cope with your own campaign!' Volumnius' reply was that he hoped Hercules would make things turn out well,* that he preferred to have had his time wasted than that anything should have happened to render one consular army insufficient for Etruria.

19. As the consuls were parting company the legates and tribunes from Appius' army gathered around them. Some begged their commander not to reject his colleague's assistance, which he should have actually requested and which had now been offered spontaneously; more stood in Volumnius' path as he left, and implored him not to let down the state over a petulant spat with his colleague. If any misfortune occurred, they said, the blame would lie with the man leaving rather than with the one who was left—things had now reached the point where credit or disgrace for success or failure in Etruria would go entirely to Volumnius. No one would ask what it was that Appius had said, only how the army had fared. Yes, he was being dismissed by Appius, but he was being asked to stay by the state and by the army, and he should just try to find out how the serving men felt about it.

With such warnings and entreaties they more or less dragged the reluctant consuls before a general assembly. There speeches were delivered at greater length, but expressing the same views as in their dispute in the small gathering. Volumnius had the stronger case, and he appeared not to lack eloquence, either, before his colleague's superb oratorical ability. This led Appius to comment by way of a joke that the troops should give him the credit for their now having an articulate consul, not one who was dumb and incapable of public speaking. In his earlier consulship, said Appius, at least in his first months, Volumnius had been unable to open his mouth, but now he was giving speeches that had popular appeal.

'How I would prefer you to have learned strength in action from me instead of me learning clever speaking from you!' Volumnius replied. Finally, he said, he was making a proposal that would decide not which of them was the better speaker—that was not what the state needed—but which was the better leader. Etruria and Samnium were their areas of responsibility. Appius should choose which of the two he wanted, and Volumnius would carry on his campaign with his army either in Etruria or in Samnium.

A cry then went up from the soldiers that they should both take on the Etruscan operation together. Observing their unanimity, Volumnius said: 'Since I blundered in my understanding of my colleague's wishes, I shall not let your wishes remain in the dark. Make it clear by a shout whether you want me to stay or go.' With that such a noisy shout went up that it brought the enemy out of his camp; they grabbed their weapons and deployed for battle. Volumnius, too, ordered the signal given on the trumpet and the banners to be carried forward from the camp. Appius, they say, hesitated: he could see that the victory would go to his colleague whether he fought or took no action, but then, fearing that his own legions would follow Volumnius, they say that he too gave the signal to his men, who were demanding it.

The troops had not been properly marshalled on either side. The Samnite leader Gellius Egnatius had gone on a foraging expedition with a few cohorts, and his men proceeded to engage on impulse rather than under anyone's guidance or command, while the two Roman armies were not led out together and had insufficient time to deploy. Volumnius joined battle before Appius actually reached the enemy, with the result that they clashed with the front of their line uneven. Furthermore, it was as if some lottery were switching the usual enemies of each man: the Etruscans now confronted Volumnius, and the Samnites (after some hesitation occasioned by the absence of their commander) confronted Appius. Right at the critical moment of the battle Appius reportedly made the following prayer, and was seen amongst the front ranks with his hands raised toward the sky: 'Bellona, if you vouchsafe us victory today, then I make the vow of a temple to you.'

After uttering this prayer, just as if the goddess were urging him on, Appius found courage equal to his colleague's and his army found courage equal to their commander's. Now the two leaders performed their duties as generals and the soldiers of each did their best to prevent victory starting with the other army. The enemy found it no easy matter to withstand a force greater than that which they had regularly encountered, and the Romans defeated and routed them. By keeping the pressure on them as they gave ground, and chasing them when they fled, they drove them to their camp, and there, with the arrival on the scene of Gellius and the Samnite cohorts, fighting briefly resumed. These troops, too, were soon routed, and the camp came under attack from the victors. Volumnius personally led the charge on the gate; Appius fired his men's courage by repeatedly invoking Bellona the victorious; and they forced their way through the palisade and the ditches. The camp was captured and ransacked, with huge quantities of booty taken and turned over to the men. Seven thousand eight hundred of the enemy were killed, and two thousand one hundred and twenty taken prisoner.*

20. While the two consuls and all the might of Rome remained more focused on the Etruscan war, new armies arose in Samnium to raid lands under Roman authority. They crossed into Campanian and Falernian territory by way of the country of the Vescini,* and made off with huge quantities of plunder. Volumnius was returning into Samnium by forced marches, since the end of Fabius' and Decius' extension of *imperium* was now approaching, but talk of the Samnite army and its raids on Campanian territory made him turn aside to offer protection to the allies. On reaching the territory of Cales, he saw with his own eyes the fresh traces of the devastation, and the Calenians also told him that the enemy were now hauling off so much plunder that they could barely keep their column moving. So, they told him, the Samnite leaders were openly saying they should immediately return to Samnium in order to leave their plunder there and come back to their raiding, and thus not expose their heavily laden column to battle. Plausible though this information was, Volumnius felt that further investigation was warranted, and he sent horsemen to intercept some looters who were drifting at large in the countryside. Interrogating these, he learned that the enemy were encamped at the River Volturnus, that they would be moving off from there at the third watch, and that they were bound for Samnium.

Now having sufficient intelligence, Volumnius set off and encamped at a distance from the enemy such that his arrival could not be detected through his being too close, but also such that he could take them by surprise when they left their camp. Some time before dawn he approached the camp and sent forward men familiar with the Oscan language to find out what was afoot. Blending in with the enemy was easy in the disorder of the night, and the men learned that the standards had gone ahead with few soldiers accompanying them, and that the plunder and those guarding it were now leaving. The main column, however, remained at a standstill, and everybody was looking out for his own business, with no unified plan of action among any of them and no fixed chain of command.

It seemed the most appropriate moment to attack, and by now dawn was also coming on; and so Volumnius ordered the trumpet-call to be given and launched the attack on the enemy column. The Samnites were encumbered with their plunder; few had their weapons; some picked up the pace, driving their animal spoils before them; others just stood there, not knowing whether it was safer to proceed or return to camp. As they hesitated they were overwhelmed, and after the Romans surmounted the palisade carnage and uproar reigned in the camp. The Samnite column was thrown into confusion not only by the attack of their enemy but also by the sudden uprising of their prisoners of war. Some of these, after breaking free, began freeing the men still in bonds, while others proceeded to seize weapons that were tied up in the soldiers' packs; and after that, merging into the column, they all created a fracas more fearful than the battle itself. They then brought off a memorable coup. The enemy leader Staius Minatius was riding up to the ranks and giving encouragement when these men charged at him. They scattered the cavalrymen at his side, surrounded Staius himself, and rushed him to the Roman consul as a prisoner, while he was still on his horse.

The Samnites out ahead were brought back to the fight by the attack, and the battle was renewed when it was practically over. However, holding out much longer was impossible. The dead numbered as many as six thousand; two thousand five hundred were taken prisoner, including four military tribunes;* and thirty military standards were captured. What made the victors particularly happy was the recovery of seven thousand four hundred prisoners of war along with a huge amount of spoils taken from the allies. Owners of these articles were called in by an edict to identify and reclaim them on a specific date. Items for which no claimant was forthcoming were turned over to the men, who were obliged to sell their spoils so they should have nothing on their mind but their military operations.

21. The devastation of Campanian territory had produced great agitation in Rome, and it so happened that during that same period disconcerting news had also been brought from Etruria.* After the withdrawal of Volumnius' army, the country had been roused to insurrection; and the Samnite leader Gellius Egnatius was calling on the Umbrians to revolt and making overtures to the Gauls with large sums of money. Alarmed by such reports, the Senate ordered a suspension of business to be declared, and a levy held of men of all classes. It was not merely the free and those of military age who were made to take the oath; there were also cohorts of older men enlisted, and centuries made up of freedmen.* Ideas for the defence of the city were also being discussed, and the praetor Publius Sempronius* assumed overall command.

The Senate's concern was somewhat alleviated by a dispatch from the consul Volumnius from which it was learned that the marauders in Campania had been killed or driven off. They therefore decreed a period of thanksgiving for this success in the consul's name and the suspension of business, which had lasted eighteen days, was lifted. The thanksgiving was celebrated with great joy.

The next item discussed was defence of the region that had been subjected to Samnite raids, and it was decided that two colonies be established in the territory of Vescia and Falernum. One, called Minturnae, was to be located at the mouth of the River Liris, and the other in the Vescine Wood, which borders on the territory of Falernum. (This is where a Greek city, Sinope, had reportedly stood, and subsequently it was called Sinuessa by the Roman colonists.) The plebeian tribunes were charged with securing a plebiscite by which the praetor Publius Sempronius would be commissioned to appoint triumvirs for conducting the colonists to these areas. However, people to enroll for the project were not easily found, because they thought that they were not being sent to farm the land but to serve as a quasi-permanent garrison in hostile territory.

The Senate was diverted from such concerns by the escalating war in Etruria and by frequent dispatches from Appius warning them not to disregard the upheavals in that region where four peoples—the Etruscans, the Samnites, the Umbrians, and the Gauls—were forming an armed coalition. They had already established two separate camps, he said, because one place could not hold such great numbers. In the light of these problems, and also because of the approaching elections, the consul Lucius Volumnius was recalled to Rome. Before summoning the centuries to vote, Volumnius called the people to an assembly where he made a long address on the gravity of the war in Etruria. Even at the time that he had campaigned in the area together with his colleague, he explained, the war was so great that it could not be conducted by only one leader and one army—and since then it was said that the Umbrians and a huge army of Gauls had joined the enemy! They should bear in mind, he told them, that the consuls were on that day being chosen as leaders to face four peoples. Personally, he added, he was confident that the man undoubtedly considered the foremost commander of his day was going to be declared consul with the unanimous support of the Roman people. Had he not been confident, he would have straightaway named that man dictator, he said.

22. No one doubted that Quintus Fabius was going to be elected with everyone's support, and the leading centuries* and all those centuries called on first after them chose him as consul with Lucius Volumnius as his colleague. Fabius' observations were as they had been two years earlier but, when he found himself overwhelmed by the consensus, they finally changed into a request for Publius Decius as his colleague. That, he said, would be a support for him in his advanced years. After partnership with Decius as censor and twice as consul, he explained, experience had shown him that for the protection of the state nothing was more effective than harmonious relations with one's colleague. It was no longer possible at his age, he added, to become habituated to a new partner in office; he would find it easier to share his thinking with a character that was known to him.

Fabius' words were supported by the consul, who added some well-deserved praise of Publius Decius. He also reflected on the advantages that came from harmony between consuls in directing military operations, and the disadvantages that came from disharmony, calling to mind how close they had come to extreme danger through the quarrels between his colleague and himself. Decius and Fabius, by contrast, were of one spirit and one mind; they were, moreover, men born for the military career, with great records, but they had little experience in battles of words and the tongue. These were the qualities of a consul, he said; shrewd and clever men, men who like Appius Claudius were experts in the law and oratory, should be retained to oversee the city and the Forum, and be elected praetors to administer justice.

The day was taken up with such discussions. On the day that followed, both the consular and praetorian elections were held, and they followed the consul's prescription: Quintus Fabius and Publius Decius were elected as consuls, and Appius Claudius as praetor,* all three *in absentia*. Furthermore, Lucius Volumnius had his *imperium* extended for a year, following a decree of the Senate and its ratification by the people.

23. There were many prodigies that year,* and to avert any misfortune from following them the Senate decreed two days of prayers, with wine and incense provided at state expense. Men and women both went in crowds to offer prayers. What made the prayer-giving remarkable was a quarrel that arose between the married women in the shrine of Patrician Chastity,* which is located in the Forum Bovarium near the round temple of Hercules. Verginia, daughter of Aulus,* was a patrician lady married to a plebeian, the consul Lucius Volumnius, and the married ladies had barred her from their rites for having married outside the patrician body. A short spat flared up into a fierce quarrel thanks to their female irascibility, with Verginia justifiably asserting with pride that she had entered the temple of Patrician Chastity both as a patrician and a chaste woman and that she had been married only to the man to whom she had been given as a virgin bride. Nor, she added, did she feel any embarrassment about her husband, or about his honours or his career.

Verginia then crowned her proud words with a remarkable act. She lived on Vicus Longus,* and there she separated off, at the far end of her house, enough space for a small shrine. She placed an altar in it and called together the married plebeian women. She then condemned the insulting behaviour of the patrician women and said: 'This altar I dedicate to Plebeian Chastity. I urge you to make sure that, while competing for manliness occupies men within the state, there may also be competition in chastity among married women, and that you do your best to see that this altar is reported to receive greater reverence, if that is at all possible, than that other one, and by women of greater chastity.' This altar, too, received much the same ritual as the older one, with no woman having the right to sacrifice unless she was of proven virtue and also had been married only to one man. Subsequently the cult was opened up to impure women, and not only those who were married but women of all sorts, and eventually it sank into oblivion.

In that same year the curule aediles Gnaeus and Quintus Ogulnius indicted a number of moneylenders.* Their possessions were confiscated, and from the sum paid into the public purse the aediles set in place the following: bronze thresholds for the Capitol; silver vessels for the three tables in the cella of Jupiter; a statue of Jupiter with his four-horse chariot on the temple roof; and, by the Ruminal fig-tree, statues of the city's founders as infants beneath the wolf's udders.* They also laid down a path of dressed stone from the Porta Capena to the temple of Mars.* Moreover, games were staged, and golden bowls acquired for the temple of Ceres, by the plebeian aediles Lucius Aelius Paetus and Gaius Fulvius Curvus, and these expenses were also covered by fines, which the aediles exacted after prosecuting livestock-breeders.*

24. Quintus Fabius then entered his fifth consulship and Publius Decius his fourth. They had been colleagues three times as consuls, and once as censors, and were renowned not so much for the eminence of their achievements, great though that was, as for their harmonious relations. To render these impermanent, some contention arose,* more, I think, between the orders than between the individuals themselves. The patricians were bent on seeing Fabius have Etruria as his area of responsibility without following standard procedure, and the plebeians were advising Decius to insist on sortition. There was certainly a dispute in the Senate, where Fabius had the greater influence, and then the matter was taken to the people.

At the assembly words were few, which was natural among military men who set more store by action than talk. Fabius said that when a person has planted a tree it was unfair for someone else to gather the fruit under it; and that it was he who had opened up the Ciminian Forest and made a way for the Romans to take their wars through the remote woodlands. Why had they bothered him at such an age, he asked, if they were going to conduct the war under another man's leadership? He then gradually intensified his criticism by observing that he had evidently chosen an opponent, not an associate in command, and that Decius was resentful over the three offices they had amicably shared. He ended by saying that he insisted on one thing only, that if they thought him worthy of that area of responsibility they should send him to it—he had deferred to the judgement of the Senate and would defer to the power of the people.

Publius Decius began by complaining about the injustice of the Senate, arguing that as far they could the patricians had tried to block plebeian access to the high offices. After merit had of itself succeeded in winning respect amongst all classes of men, they were now trying to nullify not only the votes of the people but even the decisions of fortune, and to have everything put under the power of a few. All consuls before him, he said, had drawn lots for their areas of authority; and now the Senate was giving Fabius his area without sortition. If this was to honour the man, he continued, the service that Fabius had rendered both to him and to the state was such that he would support exalting him provided that such distinction carried no insult for himself. Now, when you had one bitterly fought and difficult war, and that war was given to one of the consuls without sortition, who could doubt that the other consul was being regarded as redundant and good for nothing? Fabius took pride in his military successes in Etruria, and Publius Decius also wanted to feel such pride. And perhaps, Decius added, he would himself put out that fire that Fabius had suppressed, but left in such a state that it was time and again flaring up anew without warning. To sum up, he said, because of the respect he had for Fabius' age and dignity, he would grant him honours and privileges, but when they faced danger and conflict, he made, and would make, no concession to him of his own free will. And, he added, if he gained nothing else from that confrontation, he would at least gain one thing, namely seeing the people give the order about what belonged to them, not the patricians making a gift of it. He now made a prayer to Jupiter Optimus Maximus and the immortal gods, he said, asking them to grant him an equal chance with his colleague, but on condition that they also grant him the same courage and good fortune in conducting the campaign. It was certainly fair in its nature, and useful as a precedent, one in keeping with the reputation of the Roman people, that its consuls should be such that the war with Etruria could be successfully conducted by either of them.

Fabius asked of the Roman people only that, before the tribes were called in to vote, they listen to the letter brought to him from Appius Claudius in Etruria, after which he left the Comitium. Etruria then was granted by decree to Fabius, without sortition, and with no less unanimity amongst the people than there had been in the Senate.

25. Following that nearly all men of military age flocked to the consul, all of them giving their names—so great was the desire to serve under that particular commander. Surrounded by this crowd, Fabius declared: 'I intend to enlist a maximum of four thousand infantrymen and six hundred cavalrymen, and I shall take with me those of you giving me their names today and tomorrow. I am more concerned about bringing everybody back rich than I am about fighting the campaign with a lot of soldiers.'

He set off with an army appropriately sized for the operation, and one which had more confidence and optimism because he had not wanted large numbers, and proceeded to the camp of the praetor Appius near the town of Aharna,* from which the enemy were not far distant. A few miles before reaching there he was met by some wood-gatherers accompanied by an armed escort. When these saw the lictors at the front of the force, and learned that the consul was Fabius, they happily and fervently thanked the gods and the Roman people for having sent him as their commander.

Then, as they milled around the consul and greeted him, Fabius asked where they were going. When they replied that they were going for wood, he retorted: 'Do you mean to say that you do not have your camp surrounded with a palisade?' In reply the shout went up that it was in fact surrounded by a double palisade and a ditch, too, but that they were still in mortal fear. 'Well, you have enough wood, then,' he said. 'Go back and tear up your palisade.'

The men returned to camp and tore up the palisade, striking terror into the soldiers who had been left behind there, as well as into Appius himself; but then they all passed the word along to one another that they were acting on the orders of the consul Quintus Fabius. The next day they struck camp, and the praetor Appius was sent off to Rome. After that the Romans had no base camp anywhere. Fabius claimed that it was not to their advantage for the army to remain in one place; they gained more in terms of mobility and health by marching and changing locations. Such marches took place to the extent permitted by winter, which was not yet over.*

In early spring Fabius left the second legion near Clusium (which once they called Camars)* and, giving Lucius Scipio command of the camp as propraetor, he himself returned to Rome for discussions* on the war. This he did either of his own accord, because he could see before him war on a greater scale than reports had led him to believe, or because he had been recalled by senatorial decree; both versions are found in the sources. Some want to give the impression that he was brought back to Rome by the praetor Appius Claudius with his exaggerated reports, given in the Senate and before the people, about the threat posed by the Etruscan war, like those he had persistently made in his dispatches. Neither one leader nor one army, he is supposed to have said, would suffice to counter four peoples. Whether these peoples united to put pressure on him, or made war as individual units, there was a danger that one man could not meet all eventualities. He himself had left two Roman legions in Etruria, and the troops that had come with Fabius numbered fewer than five thousand infantry and cavalry. His own preference was to have the consul Publius Decius leave* at the earliest possible moment to join his colleague in Etruria, with Lucius Volumnius being given Samnium as his area of responsibility. Should the consul prefer to go to his own area of responsibility, then Volumnius should leave to join the other consul in Etruria with a full consular army.

The praetor's words persuaded most people. They say, however, that Publius Decius recommended leaving everything open and free for Quintus Fabius to decide when he came to Rome. Fabius would either come in person (if that was consistent with the interests of the state) or else send one of his legates from whom the Senate could learn the magnitude of the war in Etruria, and the number of forces and generals needed to conduct it.

26. On his return to Rome, Fabius delivered a balanced speech both in the Senate and when he came before the people. He wished to appear to be neither exaggerating nor underestimating reports on the war, but also, in accepting a co-commander, to seem to be taking account of the fears of other people rather than seeing any danger to himself or the state. But if they were for giving an assistant in the war who would share his *imperium*, how, he asked, could he possibly forget the consul Publius Decius, whose qualities he knew from the many times they had been colleagues? There was no one at all he would prefer to have as a partner: alongside Publius Decius he would have enough strength in his own troops, and the enemy's would never be too great. But if his colleague preferred something else, then they could give him Lucius Volumnius as his helper. Fabius was left to decide on everything by the people, by the Senate, and by his colleague himself. When Publius Decius made it clear that he

was ready to leave either for Samnium or for Etruria, the rejoicing and satisfaction suggested that victory was anticipated and that it was thought that the consuls had been given by decree not a war but a victory.

In some sources I find that Fabius and Decius set off for Etruria as soon as they entered their consulship, and that there is no mention of sortition for the provinces or of the wrangling between colleagues that I have recounted. For some authors, even giving an account of such wrangling was not enough. They have also added accusations which, while Fabius was absent, were made against him by Appius before the people, as well as the praetor's persistent antagonism towards the consul when he was present, and another quarrel between the two colleagues when Decius insisted that they should each look after the area they were allotted. Consistency in the sources begins from the time that both consuls set out for the war.

Before the consuls could reach Etruria, however, the Senonian Gauls advanced in a great horde on Clusium in order to launch an attack on the Roman legion and its camp. Scipio, the camp commander, felt that his men's inferior numbers should be helped by some topographical advantage. He therefore marched his army up a hill between the city and the camp but, as often happens in a crisis, he did not reconnoitre adequately* and headed for a ridge that had been occupied by the enemy, who had approached it from a different direction. As a result the legion was attacked from the rear and surrounded, the enemy putting it under pressure on all sides. A number of authors also say that the legion was wiped out there, with no one surviving to carry away the news. They add that no word of that disaster was brought to the consuls, who were by now not far from Clusium, before some Gallic horsemen came in view carrying heads dangling from the front of their horses or fixed on their spears, and celebrating their victory in song, as they do. There are some who record that they were Umbrians, not Gauls, and that the defeat was not so crushing. Some foragers, these authors say, led by Lucius Manlius Torquatus, had been surrounded, and when the propraetor Scipio brought help from the camp and renewed the battle, the victorious Umbrians were defeated and relieved of their captives and their plunder. It is more likely that the defeat came at the hands of a Gallic foe rather than an Umbrian: dread of a Gallic uprising, present on many other occasions, gripped the state especially strongly that year.

Both consuls, then, had set off for the war with four legions, a strong force of Roman cavalry, a thousand elite Campanian cavalry (sent specifically for this campaign), and with an army of Latin allies greater than that of the Romans.* In addition, there were two other armies* stationed not far from Rome as a safeguard against Etruria, one in Faliscan and the other in Vatican territory. Gnaeus Fulvius and Lucius Postumius Megellus, both propraetors,* were instructed to keep a base camp in those districts.

27. The enemy had crossed the Apennines and the consuls reached them in the area around Sentinum,* where they pitched camp, at a distance of about four miles from them. Meetings were then held amongst the enemy at which it was agreed that they would not all unite in a single camp or take the field together; and the Samnites were joined by the Gauls, and the Etruscans by the Umbrians. A day was appointed for the battle; and the actual battle was assigned to the Samnites and Gauls, while the Etruscans and Umbrians were instructed to attack the Roman camp while the fighting was in progress. This strategy was thwarted when three deserters from Clusium came over to the consul Fabius under cover of night. They apprised Fabius of the enemy's plans, and were sent off with rewards on the understanding that they would at intervals report to him any new decision that they discovered the enemy had reached. The consuls then sent a dispatch to Fulvius and Postumius instructing them to advance their armies respectively from the Faliscan and Vatican regions towards Clusium,* and to lay waste the territory of the enemy with all possible force. The news of this devastation took the Etruscans and Umbrians away from the area of Sentinum to protect their own lands, and this prompted the consuls to try to bring off a battle in their absence. For two days they provoked the enemy with skirmishes, but in those two days there was no action to speak of: there were a few casualties on both sides, but the upshot was merely to whet appetites for a regular engagement rather than to produce any decisive result. The third day saw them go into the field with all their troops.

The battle-lines were standing in position when a deer,* running away from a wolf that had chased it down from the hills, scampered across the plain between the two armies. The animals then separated, the deer turning towards the Gauls and the wolf towards the Romans. The wolf was allowed free passage between the ranks;

the deer the Gauls struck down. Then one of the Roman front-rank soldiers exclaimed: 'That's the side on which there's flight and bloodshed, where you can see the sacred animal of Diana lying dead. On this side, safe and sound, you have the victorious wolf of Mars, who has reminded us that we are the people of Mars and that he is our founder.'

The Gauls made up the right wing, the Samnites the left. Quintus Fabius deployed the first and third legion on the right wing facing the Samnites, and against the Gauls on the left Decius drew up the fifth and sixth. Legions two and four were engaged in operations in Samnium under the proconsul Lucius Volumnius. At the first clash the fighting was so equally matched that, had the Etruscans and Umbrians been present, either in the actual battle or the camp, it would have been catastrophic for us wherever they brought their force to bear.

28. Although the dangers of war were still even for both sides, and fortune had not yet decided on which side to apply her might, the fighting was by no means the same on the left and the right wings. The Romans in Fabius' sector were fighting defensively rather than going on the attack, dragging out the engagement till as late in the day as they could. Their leader was sure that the Samnites and the Gauls were both ferocious fighters only at the first onset, and that it was enough to withstand their attack. As a battle went on, he believed, the Samnites' morale gradually sank, and the Gauls, physically incapable of tolerating strain and heat, lost their strength—more than men at the start of their battles, by the end they were less than women. Thus Fabius was preserving his men's strength as best he could for that time when the enemy usually began to lose their battles.

Decius, more headstrong because of his age and dynamic personality, expended whatever strength he had at the start of the struggle. In fact, because the infantry fighting seemed rather sluggish, he urged his cavalry into battle and, personally joining a squadron of his most intrepid soldiers, pleaded with his leading young noblemen to accompany him in charging the enemy. They would have twice the glory, he told them, if the Roman victory started with the left wing and the cavalry. On two occasions they drove back the Gallic cavalry. On the second occasion they rode out further and were soon urging on the fight in the midst of units of enemy infantry, but then a new kind of fight filled them with alarm. Standing high in chariots and wagons, enemy soldiers came at them with a deafening roar of horses and wheels, terrifying the Romans' horses, which were unused to such commotion. And so a kind of frenzied panic scattered the victorious cavalry, and then brought down horses and riders as they were rushing off in heedless flight. This wrought chaos even in the legionary units, and many front-line soldiers were trampled down by the horses and chariots charging through the ranks; and as soon as they saw their enemies gripped by fear, the Gallic infantry piled on the pressure, allowing them no time to catch their breath or pull themselves together.

Decius shouted to them, asking where they were running to, and what hope they thought they had in flight. He tried to block those giving ground, and to call back those scattered in flight, but finding himself unable, for all his efforts, to hold them in check, he cried out, invoking his father Decius' name: 'Why bother delaying our family's destiny any longer? Such is the fate that has been given to our house—we are expiatory offerings to avert dangers to the state. Now I shall give to Earth and the Shades of Death the enemy legions, to be slaughtered in sacrifice, and myself with them.'

So saying, he turned to the pontiff Marcus Livius,* whom he had ordered, when he was going into battle, not to leave his side, and he commanded him to utter aloud the words with which he would devote himself and the enemy legions, 'for the sake of the army of the Roman people, the Quirites'. He was then pledged, making the same prayer and wearing the same clothing as his father had ordered for his own devotion at the Veseris in the Latin war. In addition to the customary formulae, Livius also added that he was driving before him terror and defeat, slaughter and bloodshed, and the wrath of the gods above and below; that he would 'smite with deadly curses the standards, spears, and weapons of the enemy'; and that the place of his own destruction would also be that of the Gauls and the Samnites. After uttering these curses on himself and on the enemy, he spurred his horse towards what he saw to be the thickest section of the Gallic lines, and charging forward he fell beneath the enemy projectiles.

29. From that point on, the battle could hardly be seen as being directed by mortal power. A leader had been lost, something that in other circumstances would produce panic, but the Romans halted their flight and were intent on starting the battle over again. As for the Gauls, and especially the group around the consul's body, it was

as if they had lost their minds—they were hurling their spears aimlessly and to no effect, some so stupefied that they gave no thought
either to fighting or to fleeing. On the other side, however, stood the
pontiff Livius, to whom Decius had transferred his lictors, and whom
he had ordered to act as propraetor—and he was crying out that the
Romans had prevailed and that they were freed from danger by the
consul's death. The Gauls and the Samnites now belonged to Mother
Earth and the gods of the underworld, he shouted: Decius was dragging towards him, and calling to him, the army that he had devoted
along with himself, and on the side of the enemy all was overtaken by
the Furies and panic. Then, as the Romans were reviving the fight,
Lucius Cornelius Scipio and Gaius Marcius appeared on the scene,
sent on the consul Quintus Fabius' orders to assist his colleague, and
with them were reserve troops taken from the back line.* There they
were told of Publius Decius' fate, and that was a huge incentive for
them to face any challenge on behalf of the state.

The Gauls were standing in close formation, their shields tightly
linked before them, and hand-to-hand fighting did not seem a viable
option. So, on an order from the legates, javelins that were lying
on the ground between the two armies were gathered up and hurled
at the enemy's tortoise-formation.* A number lodged in the shields of
the enemy, and only the odd one in their bodies, but the wedge-shaped
formation was brought to the ground, most of the Gauls collapsing in
a daze* though they were physically unimpaired. Such was the change
in fortune that had occurred on the left wing of the Romans.

On the right wing, as noted above, Fabius had initially drawn out
the day with delaying tactics. Then, when he felt that there was no
longer the same vigour in the enemy's shouts or their attacks or their
spear-throwing, he ordered his cavalry commanders to lead their
units around to points on the Samnite flanks so that, on a given signal, they could attack them at right angles with maximum force. His
own men he ordered to move forward gradually and push back the
enemy. When he saw that there was no resistance and that there was
no doubt about the Samnites' fatigue, he brought together all the
reserve troops that he had been holding back for that moment, roused
the legions to action, and gave his cavalry the signal to attack the
enemy. The Samnites failed to stem the assault and, leaving their
allies to the fighting and actually moving past the Gallic troops, made
for their camp in disordered flight.

The Gauls remained in close order in their tortoise-formation,* and then Fabius, on hearing of his colleague's death, ordered a Campanian cavalry squadron (which numbered about five hundred) to leave the front, ride around the Gallic line, and attack it from the rear. He next ordered the *principes* of the legion to follow these, to apply pressure where he saw the enemy lines disrupted by the cavalry charge, and cut them down while they were terror-stricken. Fabius himself made a vow of a temple and the spoils from the enemy to Jupiter the Victorious,* after which he headed for the Samnite camp, to which the entire horde of the enemy was being driven in panic. As the camp gates could not accommodate such numbers, there was an attempt at making a stand right before the palisade by those shut out by the mass of their comrades, and it was there that the Samnite commander Gellius Egnatius fell. The Samnites were then driven within the palisade, and after a brief engagement the camp was taken, and the Gauls cut off at the rear.

On that day twenty-five thousand of the enemy were killed* and eight thousand captured. It was not a bloodless victory, either: seven thousand of Publius Decius' army were killed, and seventeen hundred of Fabius'. Fabius sent out men to search for his colleague's body, and then he threw the enemy spoils into a heap and burned them in honour of Jupiter the Victorious. The consul's body could not be found that day because it was buried beneath heaps of Gauls who had been felled over him. The following day it was found and brought in, the soldiers shedding many tears. Setting everything else aside, Fabius then celebrated his colleague's funeral, to which he accorded every honour and well-deserved tributes.

30. In those same days the campaign in Etruria under the propraetor Gnaeus Fulvius had proceeded satisfactorily. Apart from the enormous damage the enemy suffered from his raids on their lands, there was also a superb battle in which there were more than three thousand men of Perusia and Clusium killed, with the capture of up to twenty military standards. The Samnite army tried to flee through Paelignian country but were surrounded by the Paelignians, and of their five thousand as many as a thousand were killed.

The fame of that day on which the battle was fought in the territory of Sentinum is considerable, even if one adheres to the truth. Some, however, have gone too far, straining the limits of credibility, in recording that there were in the enemy army six hundred thousand infantry, forty-six thousand cavalry,* and a thousand chariots (naturally this includes the Umbrians and Tuscans, whom they also claim participated in the battle). To boost the numbers of the Roman forces, as well, they have Lucius Volumnius, the proconsul, as a general alongside the consuls, and his army serving alongside the legions of the consuls. In most annalists that victory belongs exclusively to the consuls, with Volumnius meanwhile campaigning in Samnium (and there he made the Samnite army retreat up Mount Tifernum where, undeterred by the difficult terrain, he defeated them and put them to flight).

Quintus Fabius left Decius' army to hold Etruria and led his own legions off to Rome, where he celebrated his triumph over the Gauls, the Etruscans, and the Samnites. His men followed him in his triumphal procession, and in their coarse soldiers' banter* Quintus Fabius' victory figured no more prominently than did the glorious death of Publius Decius. The memory of the father was revived by this, and now it was matched by the renown of the son, both in his contribution to the state and in his own fate. From the plunder the soldiers were each awarded eighty-two bronze *asses*, a cloak, and a tunic, rewards that, in those days, were not to be looked down upon.

31. Despite such successes there was still no peace either with the Samnites or in Etruria. After the withdrawal of his army by the consul, there had been a fresh outbreak of hostilities, for which the Perusians had been primarily responsible,* and the Samnites had proceeded to conduct raids on the lands of Vescia and Formiae and, elsewhere, on Aesernian territory and the country lying alongside the River Volturnus. The praetor Appius Claudius was sent out with Decius' army to counter these insurgencies. In Etruria, which was again up in arms, Fabius killed four thousand five hundred Perusians, and took about one thousand seven hundred and forty prisoners.* These were ransomed at a price of 310 *asses* each, and the rest of the booty was all turned over to the soldiers. The legions of the Samnites, some pursued by the praetor Appius Claudius, and others by the proconsul Lucius Volumnius, came together in the area of Stella.* There they all encamped near Caiatia, and here Appius and Volumnius also combined their troops. The battle was marked by vicious animosity, anger inciting the one side against peoples so often in revolt, the other seeing their last hope in battle. The result was sixteen thousand three hundred Samnites killed, and twenty-seven hundred taken

prisoner, while from the Roman army the fallen numbered twenty-seven hundred.*

The year, while successful militarily, was also one beset by plague and troubled by portents. There were reports of earth falling as rain in many areas and of a considerable number of men being struck by lightning in Appius Claudius' army, and because of these events the Books were consulted. That year Quintus Fabius Gurges, son of the consul, fined several married women* who had been convicted before the people of sexual offences, and from the money exacted from them he had the temple of Venus built that stands near the Circus.

There remain, even now, still more Samnite wars, although I have already been dealing with them without a break for four books and through a period of forty-five years, starting with the consulship of Marcus Valerius and Aulus Cornelius, who were the first to bear arms against Samnium. Instead of rehashing now the defeats sustained over many years by the two sides and the hardships they suffered, but by which their firm hearts could not be crushed, I mention only this. In the year just passed the Samnites had been slaughtered in the land of Sentinum, in Paelignian territory, at Tifernum, and in the plains of Stella at the hands of four armies and four Roman commanders, suffering these losses sometimes on their own and with their own legions, but sometimes also in company with those of other peoples. They had lost their people's most famous general; they could see that their allies in the field—the Etruscans, the Umbrians, and the Gauls—were in the same straits as they were themselves; and they were unable to hold out under their own power or with the help of others. But still they would not renounce war. So far were they from tiring of the liberty that they had defended with unhappy consequences, and they preferred defeat to not attempting to gain victory. Who indeed would be the man who could be wearied by the length of the wars, whether writing or reading about them, when they did not tire out the men fighting them?*

32. Quintus Fabius and Publius Decius were succeeded as consuls by Lucius Postumius Megellus and Marcus Atilius Regulus. Both were assigned Samnium as their province because of a rumour of three enemy armies having been raised there, one for a return to Etruria and the second for resumption of raids into Campania, while the third was being made ready for defending their borders. Poor health kept

Postumius in Rome. Atilius set off immediately, in conformity with the Senate's wishes, in order to crush the enemy before he left. As if by arrangement, the Romans met the enemy at a point where* they themselves could be prevented from entering Samnite territory but where, at the same time, they could prevent the Samnites from heading out for pacified country and lands belonging to allies of the Roman people. The two camps lay close to each other, and the Samnites ventured to take a gamble that the Roman, though so often the victor, would hardly have ventured to take—such is the recklessness that sheer desperation produces—and that was to attack the Roman camp. Such a foolhardy undertaking did not achieve its end, but it was not entirely ineffective. There was a fog that remained thick for most of the day, so thick as to remove visibility, not only cutting off from view what lay beyond the rampart but even preventing people from recognizing each other at close quarters when they met. The Samnites used this as cover for a surprise attack. When it was barely dawn and the fog obscured such light as there was, they came forward to a carelessly guarded Roman outpost at one of the camp gates. The guards, taken by surprise, had neither the spirit nor the strength to resist. The Samnites then attacked through the decuman gate at the rear of the camp,* and the quaestor's quarters* were seized and the quaestor Lucius Opimius Pansa was killed. After that the alarm was sounded.

33. Awoken by the uproar, the consul ordered two cohorts of the allies* that happened to be closest (they were from Lucania and Suessa respectively) to keep watch on the *praetorium*, and he took some legionary maniples along the main road of the camp. The men had scarcely put on their armour when they took up their positions and, since it was from the noise rather than from observation that they became aware of the enemy presence, they were unable to estimate the numbers involved. Initially, they fell back, unsure of their circumstances, and allowed the enemy to advance into the very centre of the camp. Then the consul yelled at them, asking if they were going to be driven out beyond the rampart, and if they would then attack their own camp. At this they raised a shout and, with a great effort, first made a stand, and then advanced and put pressure on the enemy; and, after once forcing them back, they kept driving them on, without letting them recover from their initial terror, and pushed them beyond the gate and beyond the rampart. They did not dare go further and give chase, as the dim light raised fears of an ambush,

and they fell back within the palisade, satisfied with having cleared the camp. About three hundred of the enemy had been killed. Roman dead, both at the first outpost and amongst those taken by surprise around the quaestor's quarters, numbered almost seven hundred and thirty.

The enemy's not unsuccessful act of bravado raised their morale and they began to prevent the Romans not only from advancing but even from foraging in the Samnite fields; the foragers were now going back to the peaceful lands of Sora. Rumours of these events, more alarming than the events themselves warranted, then reached Rome, and they forced the consul Lucius Postumius, although he had barely recovered, to set out from the city. Before leaving, however, he issued a proclamation for his men to muster at Sora and then dedicated to Victory a temple* that he had had built, when he was curule aedile, with money taken as fines. After that he left to join his army, and from Sora made for his colleague's camp in Samnium. With that the Samnites withdrew, lacking confidence in their ability to resist two armies, and the consuls moved off in different directions to raid their farmlands and attack their cities.

34. Postumius proceeded with an attack on Milionia,* which he initially attempted to take by storm, but when that met with little success he finally captured it by bringing siege-works and sheds up to the wall. Although the city was now captured, fighting continued in all areas of the city, from the fourth hour until almost the eighth, the outcome long remaining uncertain. Finally, the Romans took the town. Of the Samnites, three thousand two hundred were killed and four thousand seven hundred prisoners were taken, along with other plunder.

From Milionia the legions were marched to Feritrum, but the townspeople had quietly left the place during the night by the rear gate, taking all such possessions as could be carried or driven off. When the consul arrived, he approached the walls in formation and ready for action, anticipating the same sort of struggle as at Milionia. Then he observed that a desolate silence reigned in the city, and that there were no arms or men on the towers and the walls. He restrained his soldiers who were eager to mount the deserted fortifications, however, in case they rushed blindly into some hidden trap, and he ordered two squadrons of Latin allies to ride around the walls and conduct a thorough investigation.

The horsemen caught sight of one gate and then a second close by in the same area, both of them open, and they also saw on the roads leading from the gates vestiges of the enemy's escape in the night. They then rode cautiously up to the gates, and from a safe distance viewed the city, which could be crossed on straight roads. They reported to the consul that the city had been deserted, and that this was evident from the palpable desolation, and the fresh vestiges of flight, with objects left behind in the panic of the night scattered everywhere.

On hearing this, the consul led his army around to the part of the city that the horsemen had approached. He brought the troops to a halt not far from a gate and commanded five cavalrymen to enter the city and advance a little way into it. If it seemed safe, three were to remain on the spot, and two were to bring back to him word of what they had found. On their return, the men reported that they had reached a point from which there was a view to be had in every direction, and that they had observed that there was silence and desolation the length and breadth of the city. The consul thereupon immediately led some light-armed cohorts into the city, and ordered the rest of the men to build a camp in the meantime. On going in and breaking down a number of doors, the soldiers came upon a few people who were of advanced age or ill, and objects that were left behind as being difficult to move. These latter were taken, and from the prisoners it was learned that a number of cities round about had formed a joint plan to make their escape. Their own people, they said, had left at the first watch, and they thought the Romans would find the other cities similarly abandoned. The prisoners' words proved to be true, and the consul took over deserted towns.

35. For the other consul, Marcus Atilius, the war was nothing like as easy.* When he was leading his legions towards Luceria, which he had been told was going to be attacked by the Samnites, the enemy confronted him on the Lucerian border. Here anger equalized the strength of the two sides. The battle fluctuated and remained indecisive, but in its outcome was more dispiriting for the Romans. This was because they were unused to being losers and also because, as they withdrew, they became more aware than they had been in the actual battle of how heavier the casualties were on their side, both wounded and dead. As a result panic broke out in the camp, to such an extent that it would clearly have meant defeat had it overtaken them when they were in battle. Even as things were, it was a night

fraught with anxiety: they believed the Samnites would soon overrun the camp, or that they would have to do battle with the victors in the morning.

On the enemy side there was less damage but no more fighting spirit. When dawn broke, their fervent wish was to get away without fighting; but there was only one path, and that took them past the enemy. When they set out on it, the impression they gave was that they were heading straight for the camp to make an attack. The consul then ordered the men to take up their arms and follow him outside the palisade, and he issued commands to his legates and tribunes and to the prefects of the allies, explaining what needed to be done in each case. These all promised that they, at least, would do all that was necessary, but added that their soldiers' morale was low, and that they been kept awake all night by their wounds and the groans of the dying. If the enemy had come before dawn, they said, there would have been such panic that the men would have deserted the standards. Even now, they added, it was only by shame that they were kept from flight—that apart, they were like beaten men.

When he heard this, the consul thought he should do the rounds of the men in person and talk to them. He then proceeded to berate any that he approached who were slow in taking up their weapons. Why were they dawdling and hanging back, he would ask. The enemy would come into the camp if they did not go out of it, he said, and they would be fighting in front of their tents if they were reluctant to fight in front of their palisade. When men were armed and fighting, victory was still in doubt, but anyone waiting for an enemy without armour or weapons had to accept either death or slavery. In reply to his reprimands and censure the men said they were exhausted from the previous day's battle, that they had no more strength or blood to spare, whereas the enemy horde appeared larger than the day before.

Meanwhile the enemy column was drawing near, and soon, as the gap between them narrowed and the Romans had a clearer view, they cried out that the Samnites were carrying palisade-stakes and that there was no doubt that they were going to raise a barrier around the camp. It was at that point that the consul shouted that it was truly a disgrace for them to be the object of such a humiliating affront from a cowardly enemy.

'Are we even going to be blockaded in our camp,' he asked, 'to die of hunger in dishonour rather than, if need be, with courage by the sword?' May the gods grant a good outcome, he added, and they should act as they all thought became them! He, the consul Marcus Atilius, was going to confront the enemy and would do so alone if no one else followed him, and he would die amongst the standards of the Samnites rather than see a barrier raised around the Roman camp. The consul's words met with the approval of the legates, tribunes, and all the cavalry squadrons and first-rank centurions.

The soldiers were then overcome by shame. Listlessly they took up their weapons, and listlessly they left the camp in a long, straggling column. Downcast and almost accepting defeat, they moved towards the enemy, whose own hopes or spirits were no higher than theirs. Thus, as soon as the Roman standards were sighted, a murmur ran from the front to the back of the Samnite line that what they had feared was happening: the Romans were coming out to block their passage. There was no escape route open to them, they said, and they had either to die there or else bring down their enemies and get away over their dead bodies.

36. The Samnites piled up their baggage in their midst, took up their weapons, and formed their battle-line with each taking his place in the ranks. By now there was little space between the armies as both stood waiting for the attack and the war-cry to proceed first from the enemy. Neither had the will to fight, and they would both have gone off safe and sound in opposite directions but for the fear that the other would hound them in retreat. Some unenthusiastic fighting then started up, with battle-cries fitful and unsteady, between sides that were half-hearted and reluctant; and no one moved from where he stood.

To get things moving, the consul then sent into the fight some cavalry squadrons detached from the main body. Most of these men fell from their mounts and others were thrown into disarray, which prompted a rush from the Samnite line to dispatch those who had fallen, and from the Roman side to protect their own men. The battle was invigorated a little by this. The Samnites, however, had run forward with a bit more energy and in greater numbers; and the disoriented Roman cavalrymen, with their startled horses, trampled down their own forces who were coming to their aid. The flight started here, prompting the entire Roman army to turn and run, and soon the Samnites were facing in battle only the backs of the fugitives. Then the consul advanced to the camp gate on his horse, posted a detachment of cavalry there to face the men, and gave them the order that anyone making for the rampart was to be regarded as an enemy, whether he be Roman or Samnite; and he also delivered this threat in person to his men, standing in their way as they came streaming to the camp.

'Where are you off to, soldier?' he said. 'Here too you are going to find weapons and men, and while your consul lives you will not enter the camp unless you are victorious. So decide whether you'd prefer to fight with a fellow-citizen or an enemy.'

While the consul was saying this, the cavalry executed a circling movement with spears levelled, and commanded the infantry to return to the fight. It was not only the consul's courage that helped him, but so too did fortune: the Samnites did not follow up their advantage, and there was time for him to turn the troops around and have his line face the enemy rather than the camp. At that point the men started encouraging each other to resume the battle; and the centurions took the standards from the bearers and made the men see that the enemy was coming at them in small numbers and in disorder, with ranks poorly formed. Amidst all this, the consul, his hands raised towards the heavens, called out in a loud voice, making himself clearly audible, and promised a temple to Jupiter Stator* in a vow should the Roman army abandon its flight, renew the battle, and cut down and defeat the Samnite legions. Now all the Romans in every sector—officers and men, cavalry and infantry forces—struggled to restore the fight. It looked as if even the will of the gods had shown consideration for the Roman name, so easily were the tables turned, with the enemy repelled from the camp and driven back to the spot where the battle had started.

There they had to stop, finding their way blocked by the heap of baggage they had piled together; and they placed a circle of armed men around it, to prevent their possessions being filched from them. That was when the Roman infantry charged them in front, while the cavalry rode around to do so at the rear; and caught in the middle, they were cut down or captured. The prisoners numbered seven thousand eight hundred, and they were all sent naked under the yoke. Reports of the dead reached four thousand eight hundred. Even for the Romans it was not a joyous victory. When the consul tallied up the losses incurred over the two days the number he arrived at was seven thousand eight hundred men.*

During these events in Apulia, the Samnites tried to seize Interamna*—a Roman colony on the Latin Way—with a second army, but they failed to hold the town. They devastated the farmlands but, when they were driving off from there an assortment of plunder comprising both humans and animals, along with some colonists that they had captured, they ran into the victorious consul as he was returning from Luceria. Not only did they lose the plunder, but they were themselves cut to pieces as they proceeded, out of order, with their long, overburdened line. The consul then called owners back to Interamna by proclamation to identify and recover their property, after which, leaving his army behind, he set off for the elections in Rome. When he raised the matter of a triumph, the honour was refused him, because of his loss of so many thousands of soldiers and also because he had sent his captives under the yoke without a formal settlement of terms.*

37. The other consul, Postumius, finding no occasion for war in Samnium,* had led his army over into Etruria, where he had first laid waste the territory of Volsinii. Then, when the inhabitants came out to defend their lands, he fought a battle with them not far from the walls of their city. Two thousand eight hundred Etruscans were killed, and the rest owed their safety to the proximity of the city. The army was then led over into the territory of Rusellae, where not only was the farmland subjected to depredations, but the town was also captured, more than two thousand people taken prisoner, and fewer than two thousand killed around the walls. However, the peace that was obtained* was more famous and important than the war that had taken place in Etruria that year. Three very powerful cities, Volsinii, Perusia, and Arretium, the capitals of Etruria, sued for peace, and they negotiated with the consul that, in return for supplying clothing and grain for his troops, they be allowed to send spokesmen to Rome. They then succeeded with their request for a forty-year peace. An indemnity of 500,000 *asses*, payable immediately in cash, was imposed on each of the cities.

Because of these successes, the consul sought a triumph from the Senate,* more as a matter of form than from hope of having the request granted. He could see that some were for denying him the triumph because he had been slow to leave the city, and others because he had crossed from Samnium into Etruria without the Senate's authorization; that a number were his personal enemies, and that a number, being friends of his colleague, wanted to console Atilius for his rejection by refusing Postumius as well.

Postumius therefore said: 'Conscript Fathers: I shall not bear your dignity in mind to the point of forgetting that I am a consul. Relying on the same rights conferred by the authority with which I fought my campaigns, I shall celebrate a triumph since the campaigns have been successful, Samnium and Etruria brought to heel, and victory and peace achieved.' With that he left the Senate.

There then arose disagreement amongst the plebeian tribunes, some stating that they would oppose Postumius gaining a triumph in this unprecedented manner, and others that they would support the triumph in the teeth of their colleagues' opposition. The issue was raised before the people and the consul was summoned to appear. He made the point that the consuls Marcus Horatius and Lucius Valerius, and in recent times Gaius Marcius Rutulus, the father of the current censor, had all celebrated triumphs not by senatorial fiat but on the orders of the people. He then added that he, too, would have brought the matter to the people but for the fact that he knew that some tribunes who were lackeys of the nobility would block the law. For him, he concluded, the will and support of the people when they stood together superseded and would in future supersede all other decrees. And so, the following day, with the support of three plebeian tribunes, and facing the attempted veto of seven tribunes and the united opposition of the Senate, Postumius held his triumph, and the people made it a day of celebration.

For this year, too, there is little consistency in the record. Postumius, according to Claudius, captured a number of towns in Samnium, but was then defeated and put to flight in Apulia and, himself wounded, was forced to find shelter in Luceria with a few of his men. It was by Atilius, Claudius says, that the campaign in Etruria was conducted and he celebrated a triumph for it. In Fabius' account, the two consuls campaigned together in Samnium and at Luceria, and the army was taken over into Etruria, though he does not add by which consul. At Luceria there were severe losses on both sides, and in that battle a vow was made of a temple of Jupiter Stator. Such a vow had earlier been made by Romulus, but only the *fanum*, that is, the temple site,* had been consecrated. However, in that year, religious concern on the part of the state, now twice under obligation from the same vow, finally resulted in an order by the Senate that the temple also be erected.

38. The following year saw Lucius Papirius Cursor as consul, a man famous for his father's glorious record as well as his own. It also saw a huge war in which victory over the Samnites was of an order that no one had achieved down to that day, with the exception of Lucius Papirius, the consul's father. As it happened, the Samnites had invested as much effort and preparation in that war as before, equipping their men with a rich panoply of fine armour, and had even tried to bring in the help of the gods by, as it were, initiating the soldiers through an oath of loyalty administered in an ancient ritual. The levy was held throughout Samnium with new regulations: if any man of military age failed to present himself when notice was given by the generals, or if he left without permission, his life would be sacrificed to Jupiter. Then the announcement was given for the entire army to muster at Aquilonia,* and as many as forty thousand soldiers, which constituted the military strength of Samnium, assembled there.

At Aquilonia, roughly in the middle of the camp, a spot was fenced in with hurdles and screens and roofed over with linen cloth, and it measured about two hundred feet in both length and breadth. There a sacrifice was carried out following instructions from an old scroll made of linen, and a certain priest, Ovius Paccius, officiated.* Ovius, an old man, maintained that he drew this rite from an ancient Samnite religious ceremony that their ancestors had employed after forming clandestine plans to take Capua from the Etruscans.

On the conclusion of the sacrifice, the commander would issue an order through an orderly for all those most distinguished for their noble birth and their exploits to be summoned, and they were each introduced in turn. There were in evidence various pieces of sacrificial paraphernalia that might well fill the mind with fear of the gods, and not the least of these were some altars, in a spot completely enclosed, with slaughtered sacrificial animals lying about them, and centurions standing around with drawn swords. The man would be brought before an altar, looking more like a sacrificial victim than a participant in a sacrifice, and there he was bound by oath not to disclose whatever he saw or heard in that place. Then they made him take a vow, in some ghastly formulaic language, which invoked curses on his own head, and his household and his descendants, if he did not go into battle wherever his generals led, or if either he himself fled from the battle-line or failed to kill immediately anyone else he saw in flight. At first a number of men refused to take the vow, and they were butchered around the altars, and lying there amid the slaughtered victims they provided an object lesson for others not to refuse.*

After the foremost Samnites were bound by this curse, ten were called upon by the commander. Each was told to pick a man, and that man would pick another until they had reached a total of sixteen thousand. That body was called the Linen Legion after the roof of the enclosure* in which the noblemen had been bound by oath. They were issued spectacular weaponry, and helmets with crests so that they stood out amongst the others. The rest of the army numbered slightly more than twenty thousand men, and was not unlike the Linen Legion in physical appearance, military honours, and equipment. Such was the number—the strength of the Samnites—who encamped at Aquilonia.

39. The consuls now left Rome. First to go was Spurius Carvilius, who had been assigned the veteran legions that Marcus Atilius, consul the previous year, had left in the territory of Interamna. Carvilius set off for Samnium with these troops and, while the enemy was engaged in his superstitious practices in secret meetings, he took the town of Amiternum* by force from the Samnites. In the battle roughly two thousand eight hundred were killed, and four thousand two hundred and seventy taken prisoner. Papirius, who had, in accordance with a decree of the Senate, raised a new army, stormed the city of Duronia,* where he took fewer men prisoner than his colleague but killed considerably more. In both cases there were rich pickings in plunder. The consuls subsequently traversed Samnium conducting raids, which focused mainly on the farmlands of Atina, after which Carvilius reached Cominium* and Papirius Aquilonia, the centre of Samnite operations. For some time there was no respite from hostilities at Aquilonia, but no all-out confrontation, either. The day was spent in harassing the enemy when he was inactive, and falling back when he resisted—posing a threat rather than going on the attack. Reports of the outcome of all initiatives taken or abandoned here, even those of little consequence, were taken from there to the other camp, which was twenty miles away, and the plans of the absent colleague also played a part in the direction of all operations in this sector. Indeed, Carvilius was concentrating more on Aquilonia, where events were more critical, than on Cominium, which he had under siege.

Lucius Papirius was now in all respects well enough prepared for the confrontation. He sent a message to his colleague to say that, the auspices permitting, he intended to engage the enemy the following day. He added that it was also necessary for Carvilius to mount as forceful an attack as he could on Cominium so that the Samnites would have no leeway for sending assistance to Aquilonia. The messenger had a day for the journey, and he returned during the night with the news that his colleague was in agreement with Papirius' decision.

After sending off the messenger, Papirius immediately held an assembly. He talked at length about the war in general, and at length, too, about the equipment currently used by the enemy which was, he said, an empty display that was useless for gaining results. Crests delivered no wounds, he said, and a Roman javelin would pass through the painted and gilded shields, while the battle-line agleam with white tunics would be covered with blood when it came to fighting with the sword. A Samnite army in gold and silver had been totally wiped out by his father, he added, and their weapons had brought more distinction to the victors as spoils than they had to the Samnites as arms. It had perhaps been the privilege granted to his name and his family to stand as leaders against the Samnites' greatest efforts, and bring back spoils to be striking embellishments even for Rome's public spaces.

The immortal gods were there to help them, he continued, because of so many treaties that had been concluded, and so many broken. Moreover, if one could divine the thoughts of the gods, never were they more hostile towards any army than they were towards this one which was bespattered with a mixture of human and animal blood from its unspeakable sacrifices. It was an army twice doomed to the wrath of heaven, shuddering first at the realization that the gods were witnesses to the treaties struck with the Romans, and secondly at the thought of the curses invoked by the oath taken to break those treaties. It had sworn reluctantly, hated the oath it had taken, and now at one and the same time lived in fear of the gods, of its fellow-citizens, and of the enemy.

40. Information on this had come from deserters, and when Papirius now informed his men, who were themselves already in fits of rage, they were filled with hopes of divine and human aid, and they called for battle with one voice. They were annoyed at the

engagement being delayed till the next day, and hated the thought of waiting a day and a night. At the third watch of the night, Papirius, who had by now received his colleague's reply, arose quietly and sent the keeper of the chickens* to take the auspices. Now there was no class of men in the camp unaffected by the itch for battle: the highest and the lowest were equally eager, and the commander observed the ardour of the men, and the men that of the commander. That omnipresent ardour even reached those involved with the auspices: when the chickens would not eat, the keeper of the chickens had the temerity to lie about the omen and report to the consul that they ate greedily. Delighted, the consul announced that the auspices were excellent and that they would fight with the support of the gods, and he put up the signal for battle.

It so happened that a deserter reported to Papirius, just as he was going into battle, that twenty Samnite cohorts, each about four hundred strong, had left for Cominium. So his colleague should not remain unaware of this, Papirius immediately sent him a message, and he himself gave the order for the standards to be taken forward. He had already assigned the reserve troops to their respective positions and allocated them their commanders. On the right wing he put Lucius Volumnius in command, and on the left Lucius Scipio; and charge of the cavalry he gave to two other legates, Gaius Caedicius and Titus Trebonius. Spurius Nautius he ordered to remove the pack-saddles from the mules and then, with three allied cohorts, take the animals promptly around to a prominent hill where, in the midst of the fighting, he was to make his presence known by raising all the dust he could.

While the commander was preoccupied with all this, a quarrel arose amongst the keepers of the chickens over that day's auspices. This was overheard by some Roman cavalrymen who, thinking it was not a matter to be disregarded, reported to Spurius Papirius, the son of the consul's brother, that there was some uncertainty about the auspices. Spurius was a young man born before that form of education that slights the gods,* and after investigating the matter, so he would not be reporting unsubstantiated rumour, he brought it to the consul's attention.

'God bless your integrity and your vigilance,' said the commander. 'But if the man who takes the auspices makes any false report, he brings down that sin upon his own head. As far as I am concerned,

I was told the chickens ate greedily, and that is an excellent omen for the Roman people and the army.' Papirius then ordered the centurions to place the keepers of the chickens in the front line.

The Samnites also brought forward their standards, and there followed the line with the decorative armour, providing what even for their enemy was a magnificent sight. Before the first shout was raised and the armies clashed, the keeper of the chickens fell dead before the standards, struck down by a carelessly thrown spear. When news of this was brought to the consul, his comment was: 'The gods are present at the battle; the guilty party has his punishment.' As the consul uttered these words a crow cawed out clearly in front of him, and he was delighted with the omen, declaring that never had the gods so palpably helped in human affairs. He then gave the order to sound the trumpets and raise the war-cry.

41. It was a fiercely fought battle, but morale was very different on the two sides. In the case of the Romans, who were thirsting for their enemies' blood, anger, hope, and ardour for the fight swept them into the fray. For most of the Samnites it was a case of necessity and religious fear compelling them, reluctant as they were, not so much to go on the attack as to fight defensively. They would not have resisted even the initial war-cry and onslaught of the Romans—for they had now, for many years, been used to defeat—but for another, deeper fear in their hearts that kept them from running away. They pictured all the accoutrements of that secret rite, along with the armed priests, the carcasses of men and animals heaped together, the altars spattered with blood—the permissible mixed with the abominable—and the frightful imprecations and hellish incantations, worded to bring curses down on one's household and offspring. Such were the chains that held them where they stood, more in fear of their own countrymen than of the enemy. The Romans, however, pressed ahead, coming from both wings and the centre, and they cut down enemy soldiers paralysed with fear of gods and men. Resistance was half-hearted, as one would expect from men whom only fear kept from flight.

By now the slaughter had almost reached the standards when, off to the side, a dust-cloud appeared, apparently raised by a huge army approaching. This was Spurius Nautius (some record that it was Octavius Maecius) who had arrived leading the allied cohorts, and they were raising more dust than one might expect from such numbers—orderlies mounted on the mules were trailing leafy branches over the ground. Through the haze, arms and standards began to appear at the front, while at the back a cloud of dust rising higher and denser gave the impression that it was cavalry bringing up the rear, and this tricked not just the Samnites but the Romans, too. The consul compounded the error by calling out in the front lines, loudly enough for his words also to reach the enemy, that Cominium had been taken and that this was his victorious colleague arriving. They should now make every effort to win the day, he said, before the glory went to the other army. This he said astride his horse, and he then gave the order to his tribunes and centurions to open up a way for the cavalry (he had already directed Trebonius and Caedicius to have their cavalry make as violent a charge as they could against the enemy when they saw him raising his spear and shaking it). At his signal everything went off according to the prearranged plan: the lanes opened up in the ranks; and the cavalry charged out and, with spears levelled, attacked the enemy centre, bursting through his ranks wherever they struck. Volumnius and Scipio followed up their charge, striking down the terrified Samnites.

So now the power of gods and men was overcome:* the Linen Cohorts were routed, and those who had taken the oath, along with those who had not,* were in flight, now fearing no one but their enemy. Whatever infantry survived the battle was driven back to their camp or to Aquilonia, and the nobles and the cavalry sought refuge in Bovianum.* Cavalry pursued cavalry, and infantry pursued infantry. The Roman wings headed in different directions, the right towards the Samnite camp, and the left towards the city. Volumnius took *his* objective, the camp, considerably earlier. At the city, however, Scipio faced stiffer resistance, not because the defeated enemy had more spirit, but because walls are more effective than a palisade at warding off armed men. From there they repelled their enemy with stones.

Scipio reckoned that an assault on a fortified town would take quite some time unless it was brought off in the first moments of panic, before the enemy pulled themselves together. He therefore asked his men if they were content to see the camp taken by the other wing while they, though victorious, were driven back from the gates of the city. Receiving a resounding 'no' from them all, he took the lead and, raising a shield over his head, advanced to the gate. The others followed in tortoise formation, burst into the city, swept away the

Samnites, and seized sections of the wall on both sides of the gate. They did not dare make their way into the central area of the city because of their very small numbers.

42. The consul was initially unaware of the situation and was focusing on withdrawing his forces, as the sun was now quickly setting and the onset of night was starting to make everything dangerous and suspect, even for the victors. As Scipio advanced, he saw on his right that the camp had been taken, while to the left he heard shouts in the city mingled with the noise of men fighting or screaming in terror— and that was just when the fighting was going on around the gate. He then rode up closer and, seeing his own men on the walls, realized he now had no option. Through the pluck of a few men he had been provided with an opportunity for a great achievement, and so he gave the order for the troops he had withdrawn to be called back and for the standards to be carried forward into the city. They entered the city on the side closest to them and, as night was coming on, halted there. During the night the town was abandoned by the enemy.

On that day twenty thousand three hundred and forty were killed at Aquilonia, and three thousand eight hundred and seventy were captured,* along with ninety-seven military standards. It is on record that there has hardly ever been a commander who appeared happier in the fighting line, whether this was due to his natural inclinations or confidence in his success. Thanks to the same firmness of resolve, he could not be recalled from the battle by the dispute over the auspices. In addition, in the thick of the fighting, when temples are usually promised in vows to the immortal gods, he had made a vow to Jupiter Victor in which he promised that, should he rout the enemy's legions, he would make the god a thimbleful of honeyed wine before he took a stiff drink himself.* The gods were pleased with the vow and made the auspices turn out favourably.

43. The operation at Cominium under the other consul was equally successful. At dawn Carvilius brought all his troops up to the walls and cordoned off the city, stationing some powerful detachments before the gates to prevent any sortie. He was already in the process of giving the signal when the messenger from his colleague arrived in a state of agitation with the news of the coming of the twenty enemy cohorts. This delayed the assault, and also obliged Carvilius to recall some of his troops who were by then deployed and ready for the attack. He ordered his legate Decimus Brutus Scaeva to take the first

legion, ten auxiliary cohorts, and the cavalry to confront the enemy detachment. Wherever he encountered it, Brutus was to obstruct and delay it, engaging if circumstances so required, at all costs making sure that those troops could not be brought to Cominium.

Carvilius himself had ladders carried up to the walls at all parts of the city and approached the gates in tortoise-formation; and then the gates were broken down and an attack launched on the walls at one and the same time. Before they saw armed men on their walls, the Samnites had had courage enough to block their enemy's access to the city; now, however, the battle was no longer conducted at a distance and with projectiles, but was being fought hand-to-hand. In addition, the enemy had, with difficulty, mounted from even ground to the walls and, having mastered the difficulty of the terrain, which was what they had feared most, were now finding it easy to fight on the level against an inferior enemy. The Samnites therefore abandoned their towers and their walls and, when they were all forced back into their forum, for a brief moment tried their luck in battle as a last resort. Then, flinging down their weapons, some eleven thousand four hundred men threw themselves on the consul's mercy. About four thousand eight hundred had been killed.

Such was the action at Cominium and at Aquilonia. In the area between the two cities, where a third battle had been anticipated, the enemy could not be found. When they were seven miles from Cominium, they had been recalled by their own people and had participated in neither battle. Around dusk, they had the camp in sight first, and after that Aquilonia, when shouting came to their ears, equally loud on both sides, and this had brought them to a halt. Then, in the area of the camp, which had been put to the torch by the Romans, the broadly spreading flames gave a clearer sign of defeat and stopped any further advance. On that very spot they unthinkingly threw themselves to the ground here and there, still wearing their fighting gear, and spent an entire night without sleep as they waited for, and dreaded, the arrival of dawn.

At first light, uncertain of which direction to take, they were spotted by Roman cavalrymen—these had pursued the Samnites when they left town during the night and had found their large force defended by neither a palisade nor guard-posts—and were immediately thrown into panic-stricken flight. The large detachment had also been sighted from the walls of Aquilonia, and presently there were legionary cohorts pursuing them as well. The infantry were unable to overtake the fugitives; however, about two hundred and eighty at the end of the column were killed by the horsemen. In their panic they left behind large numbers of weapons and eighteen military standards. The others reached Bovianum,* the rest of the column relatively unharmed given the extent of their confusion.

44. In both cases, the success of the one Roman army also increased the jubilation of the other. With the agreement of his colleague, each consul gave over the city he had captured to be pillaged by the rank-and-file, and put the buildings to the torch when they had been cleared. On the same day Aquilonia and Cominium were burned to the ground, and amid mutual felicitations between the legions, and between themselves, the consuls united their camps.

In the sight of both armies Carvilius lauded his men and rewarded them according to the merits of each. Papirius, too, who had seen action in a number of locations—on the battlefield, around the camp, and around the city—presented Spurius Nautius, Spurius Papirius (his brother's son), four centurions, and a maniple of *hastati* with armbands and gold crowns. Nautius' presentation was for the operation on which he had intimidated the enemy with what appeared to be a large army; the young Papirius' was for his service with the cavalry in the battle, and also during the night when he made retreat dangerous for the Samnites on their clandestine departure from Aquilonia; and the centurions' and soldiers' was for having been the first to take the gate and wall at Aquilonia. Papirius also presented miniature horns and armbands of silver to all the cavalrymen for their outstanding performance in numerous locations.

A council of war was then held to discuss whether it was now time to withdraw both armies from Samnium, or at least one or other of them. Their conclusion was that, given the great damage already inflicted on Samnite power, they should be all the more determined and aggressive in carrying through the work that remained to be done, so that a thoroughly subdued Samnium could be handed on to the incoming consuls. Since there was now no army of the enemy that seemed likely to engage them in pitched battle, they also concluded that only one form of military operation remained for them, namely assaulting cities. They noted that by destroying these they could enrich their men with plunder and also finish off their enemies as they fought for their altars and homes. They therefore sent a dispatch to the Senate and people of Rome listing their achievements, and then they separated, Papirius leading off his legions to attack Saepinum,* and Carvilius taking his to attack Velia.

45. The consuls' dispatch was received with great joy in both the Senate house and the assembly, and in four days of official thanksgiving the public rejoicing was matched enthusiastically on the private level. And for the Roman people that victory was not only great but also very timely, because news of an Etruscan uprising happened to arrive at the same time. The question that arose in people's minds was how Etruria could possibly have been handled if there had been any setback in Samnium. Etruria had been roused to action by the intrigues of the Samnites and, while both consuls and all the strength of Rome had been diverted to Samnium, it had taken the Roman people's involvement there as an opportunity for reopening hostilities.

Delegations from the allies,* brought into the Senate by the praetor Marcus Atilius,* lodged a complaint that their farmlands were being burned and destroyed by the neighbouring Etruscans because they refused to desert the Roman people, and they begged the senators to shield them from the violent outrages of an enemy common to the two of them. The delegates were given the reply that the Senate would make sure that the allies had no regrets about their loyalty, and that the Etruscans would soon find themselves in the same situation as the Samnites. In the case of Etruria, however, the problem would have taken longer to resolve had not news arrived that the Faliscans, who had enjoyed many years of friendly relations with Rome, had also joined forces with the Etruscans. The proximity of this people intensified anxiety amongst the senators, leading them to vote for sending fetials to demand satisfaction. When this was not forthcoming, war was declared on the Faliscans by a resolution of the Senate and on the order of the people, and the consuls were instructed to proceed to sortition to decide which of the two would cross over with his army into Etruria from Samnium.

Carvilius had by now captured Velia, Palumbinum, and Herculaneum* from the Samnites, Velia within a few days and Palumbinum on the same day as he advanced against its walls. At Herculaneum, however, he actually fought a pitched battle in which the issue remained in doubt, and he left the field with heavier losses than did the enemy. Nevertheless, he then pitched camp, pinned down the enemy within his walls, and stormed and took the town.

In these three cities as many as ten thousand men were captured or killed, the number of the captured being higher by a very slight margin. When the consuls drew lots for their provinces, Etruria came to Carvilius, and this was in accord with the wishes of his men who were by now finding the biting cold in Samnium unbearable. Papirius met stiffer resistance at Saepinum: there were many encounters in the field, many on the march, and many around the city itself, where he faced sorties by the enemy. It was less of a siege than an evenly matched campaign, with the Samnites protecting their walls with their arms and their men as much as the walls protected them. Finally, his fighting forced them into a regular siege, and by mounting a blockade with vigour and with siege-works he took the city. The result was that, because of the Romans' anger, the bloodshed in the captured city was greater: seven thousand four hundred men were killed, and fewer than three thousand taken prisoner. Because the Samnites' property had been concentrated in a few cities, the plunder was very large; and it was turned over to the soldiers.

46. Snow had by now covered everything, and staying outside was impossible, so the consul led his army from Samnium. On reaching Rome Papirius was granted a triumph, for which the support was unanimous, and he held it while still in office,* and in magnificent style, by the standards of those days. Infantry and cavalry marched or rode past, cutting fine figures with their military gifts, and there were on view many civic crowns, and many rampart and mural crowns.* The Samnite spoils were examined, and comparisons were made with the spoils of Papirius' father—well known because they were regularly used to decorate public places—for their lustre and beauty, and a number of noble captives were led along who were famous for their own and their fathers' exploits. Two million five hundred and thirty-three thousand bronze *asses* were carted along, and it was said that this was realized from the sale of captives. The silver taken from the cities amounted to 1,830 pounds.* All the bronze and silver was deposited in the treasury, and no award was made to men from the plunder. Resentment over this was increased among the plebs because a tax was gathered for the soldiers' pay; and had Papirius forgone the prestige of bringing the captured money to the treasury, the soldiers could have been presented with a donative from the plunder as well as being provided with their pay.

Papirius also dedicated the temple of Quirinus.* I find it stated in no ancient source that this was offered in a vow in the actual fighting, and in fact Papirius could not have completed it in such a short time. Rather, the son, as consul, dedicated, and decorated with enemy spoils, the temple that had been promised in a vow by his father when the latter was dictator. Such was the abundance of these spoils that not only were the temple and Forum embellished with them, but they were also distributed amongst the allies and nearby colonies for decorating temples and public areas. After the triumph Papirius led his army into winter quarters in the territory of the Vescini because that region was threatened by the Samnites.

Meanwhile, in Etruria, the consul Carvilius proceeded with an attack on Troilum* where he released four hundred and seventy of its richest citizens whom he allowed to depart for a huge sum of money. He took the rest of the population by force along with the town itself. After that he stormed five strongholds in well-defended positions. Two thousand four hundred of the enemy were killed there, and fewer than two thousand were taken prisoner. He also granted the Faliscans a year's truce,* when the Faliscans sued for peace, in return for a hundred thousand bronze *asses* and pay for his men for that year. All this completed, Carvilius left to celebrate his triumph which, though of less distinction than that of his colleague over the Samnites, was its equal when the Etruscan war was factored in.* Of bronze *asses* he brought 380,000 to the treasury, and with the remainder of the money he put out for contract, from his personal spoils, the building of a temple of Fors Fortuna* near the temple of that goddess that was dedicated by King Servius Tullius. He also presented each of the soldiers with 102 *asses*, and the centurions and cavalrymen he presented with double that amount. These were gifts all the more gratifying to the recipients because of the niggardliness of Carvilius' colleague. The good-will that the consul enjoyed protected his legate Lucius Postumius* from the people. Postumius had been impeached by the plebeian tribune Marcus Scantius but had avoided judgement before the people, it was said, through being Carvilius' legate. The charge was able to be brought against him, but not seen through to its conclusion.

47. The year was now over, and the plebeian tribunes had entered office,* but they were themselves replaced by others five days later because of a flaw in their election.* The census-purification ceremony* was performed that year by the censors Publius Cornelius

Arvina and Gaius Marcius Rutulus, and the count of the census was 262,321. These were the twenty-sixth censors since the first ones, and this was the nineteenth purification ceremony.* In that same year those with good conduct in military action watched the Roman Games for the first time wearing their crowns, and they were also presented with palms, a practice taken from the Greeks. Also in that year a number of livestock-breeders were convicted by the curule aediles who put on those games, and this financed the paving of the road from the temple of Mars to Bovillae.*

Lucius Papirius supervised the consular elections, and declared Quintus Fabius Gurges, son of Fabius Maximus, and Decimus Junius Brutus Scaeva elected as consuls. Papirius himself became praetor.

Many things contributed to making that a prosperous year, but not enough to provide adequate solace for one misfortune, a plague that wreaked havoc on both the city and the countryside. It was a disaster that looked ominous, and the Books were consulted to see what remedy might be provided by the gods for the affliction. It was discovered in the Books that Aesculapius had to be brought to Rome* from Epidaurus. However, the consuls' preoccupation with the war meant that no action could be taken on it during that year, apart from the holding of one day of prayers to Aesculapius.

APPENDIX 1

LIST OF VARIATIONS FROM THE OXFORD CLASSICAL TEXT OF WALTERS AND CONWAY

Note: Square brackets [...] indicate editorial excisions from the text, and angled brackets <...> editorial additions, while obeli † show that the text is unsound and that the translation gives only an opinion of what Livy might have been saying at that point. The list is longer than might be expected because Walters–Conway is now dated, and in need of revision. Those interested in the history of the variations should consult the important commentary of S. P. Oakley (see Select Bibliography), where they are all discussed.

	OCT	OWC
6.5.7	Licinium† Menenium	Licinum Menenium
6.6.4	iuventutem suam summisisse	iuventutem suam misisse
6.6.8	[eius ordinis]	eius ordinis
6.21.1	L. Lucretio	L. Lucretio <tertium>
6.23.6	instruentem	instruendis
6.27.2	Licinio† Menenio	Licino Menenio
6.27.3	adgravantibus summam etiam invidiae eius	adgravantibus summam eius invidiosius
6.29.4	ex fuga dissipati	ex fuga dissipata
6.31.1	Licinio† Menenio	Licino Menenio
6.40.3	Claudiae gentis	Claudiae genti
7.14.1	censebat tamen facturum	†cernebat, censebat tamen facturum†
7.17.6	ad Salinas	ad salinas
7.20.8	in senatus consultum referri	in aes referri
7.22.9	censuram	censurae
7.25.9	adeo in quae laboramus	adeo laboramus in quae
7.26.9	inter primos	in primos
	mare inferum	mare superum
7.30.11	†omnes†	[omnes]
7.32.2	[ab urbe]	ab urbe
8.7.19	nec te quidem	ne te quidem
8.9.7	feroque	oroque
9.1.9	[placari nequeant]	<qui> placari nequeant
9.4.14	deserimus [ac prodimus]	deserimus ac prodimus

9.6.12	non reddere salutem [non salutantibus dare responsum]	non dare salutem, non salutantibus reddere responsum
9.8.13	laudibus modo prosequentes	laudibus sine modo prosequentes
9.9.9	nec pro vobis	[nec] pro vobis
9.10.10	[fetialem]	fetialem
9.11.10	†oblactam†	obligatam
9.11.11	[fetialem]	fetialem
9.16.1	Ferentanis	Frentanis
9.16.13	virium vi	crurum vi
9.19.4	†Samnites†	[Samnites]
9.24.9	defendite, ite	defendite [ite]
9.39.4–5	ante [censuram] et longinquitate potestatem	ante censuram et longinquitate potestatis
	†nam et cum Vmbrorum exercitu acie depugnatum est; fusi tamen magis quam caesi hostes, quia coeptam acriter non tolerarunt pugnam; et ad Vadimonis lacum†	*Omitted*
9.39.10	\<ceteri\>	\<ceteri omnes\>
9.41.17	ante imperium deinde concentu	ante imperium, ante concentum
9.43.1	Calatia	Caiatia
9.44.16	Herculis magnum simulacrum	Herculis magni simulacrum
9.45.17	triginta	quadraginta
10.2.15	in oppidi medio	in flumine oppidi medio
10.5.14	Apuleio	Appuleio
10.10.6	alia	talia
10.14.3	concilii . . . †haberi†	concilia . . . haberi
10.14.9	angebat animos	augebat animos
10.14.18	et tempore †inprovisa†	et \<in\> tempore visa
10.15.5	multo alia illis insigniora	multo illis insigni\<it\>iora
10.19.18	†imperatoria opera exsequuntur et milites†; ne ab . . .	Iam et duces imperatoria opera exsequuntur, et milites ne ab . . .
10.20.3	Calenum [agrum]	Calenum agrum
10.21.2	vocari . . . sollicitari	vocare . . . sollicitare
10.22.1	quin Fabius quintum omnium consensu	quin Q. Fabius omnium consensus
10.23.6	ex parte aedium	ex \<extrema\>parte aedium
10.26.6	sunt \<qui\>, quibus ne haec quidem [certamina] exponere satis fuerit, adiecerint et . . .	sunt quibus ne haec quidem certamina exponere satis fuerit; adiecerunt et . . .
10.27.1	†transgresso Appennino†	transgressos Appenninum
10.27.6	Etruscos	Etruscos \<et Umbros\>

10.29.7	raris in corpora . . . fixis	rarisque in corpora . . . fixis
10.31.6	ab ultima . . . spe	[ab] ultima . . . spe
10.39.7	Quodcum<que Comini> inciperetur . . . proferebatur in dies. Altera Romana castra [quae] . . .	Quodcum<que>inciperetur . . . perferebatur in [dies] altera Romana castra quae . . .
10.41.3	iis vinculis fugae obstricti	iis vinculis [fugae] obstricti
10.41.5	dux alaribus cohortibus erat	dux <cum> alariis cohortibus <ad>erat
10.41.10	Tum, iam . . . victa vi, funduntur . . .	tum iam . . . victa vis; funduntur . . .

APPENDIX 2

LIVY ON THE MANIPULAR LEGION

LIVY's description of the mid-fourth-century legion (8.8) is not as clear as it could be. All the same, his basic outline is sound. In the fourth and third centuries a legion did form three main infantry lines—the *hastati*, *principes*, and *triarii*, in that order—with each group subdivided into maniples (*manipuli*, literally 'handfuls'). It also had a body of light-armed fighters, originally called *rorarii*, later on *velites*. Livy is correct, too, in stating that each maniple of *triarii* was termed a *pilus*, and in describing the fighting methods of the three lines. There was also an attached body of Roman cavalry, although the Romans relied more on the large cavalry forces that their allies had to provide.

Livy's controversial features are these:

He gives the *hastati*, *principes*, and *triarii* fifteen maniples each (he terms the *triarii* maniples *vexilla*, as he also does their flags), whereas other evidence gives them ten each.

He assigns twenty 'light-armed soldiers' to each maniple of the *hastati*, together with the maniple's regular soldiers; he does not say how many men were in the maniple altogether.

Behind the *hastati* and *principes* he places not only the *triarii* but two other bodies of men, the *rorarii* and *accensi*.

He tells us that these three bodies formed fifteen 'companies' (he calls them *ordines*), each consisting of one *vexillum* of *triarii*, then behind it one of *rorarii*, and finally one of *accensi* at the back. A *vexillum* unit here is clearly another term for maniple. Arithmetically this means a total of forty-five *vexilla*, arranged in the fifteen *ordines*.

Each of these *vexilla* consisted of sixty men plus two centurions and the flag-bearer (*vexillarius*), and so, he says, each of the *ordines* totalled 186 men. This is arithmetically correct only if he is counting the *vexillarius* as one of the sixty ordinary soldiers—or if we amend his Latin text to read '189' ($= 63 \times 3$), as some editors do.

According to Livy the fourth-century legion was 5,000 strong (infantry) with 300 cavalry.

These features clash with other evidence—some of it in Livy's own history—or with one another. If there were thirty maniples of *hastati* and *principes*, and then forty-five *vexilla* for the *ordines* behind, this would mean a total of seventy-five units per legion. This figure is not backed by any other evidence; nor is his description of the three-part *ordines* supposedly positioned behind the first two lines.

Just as unsupported is his notion that some of the *hastati* themselves were light-armed fighters. In Polybius' description of the legion of 200–150 BC (*Histories* 6.24), the light-armed troops are assigned among all three infantry lines (*hastati*, *principes*, and *triarii*) but plainly are not part of each maniple. They acted in support of these, or independently as skirmishers ahead of the whole army. When Livy narrates the battle at the Veseris (8.9), he mentions the *rorarii* acting to support the *hastati* and *principes*, very much in line with Polybius' description—and with no word of the supposed light-armed *hastati*.

The *accensi*, in turn, were not soldiers at all but the legion's servant-attendants: this is why they were stationed in the rear. Livy's idea that it was because they were unreliable is mere imagination. Though he brings them into battle later, this is not a plausible report either (8.10 note). It follows that his picture of fifteen 'companies', each of three 'detachments', behind the *hastati* and *principes* must be rejected. The only fighting line behind the first two was the *triarii*.

The numerical details, too, are controversial. Livy is probably correct that already in the fourth century each maniple of *triarii* (he calls it a *vexillum*, as just noted) held sixty soldiers and two centurions. He says nothing of the size of those in the first two lines, so we cannot tell whether he views all the legion's maniples as sixty-two or sixty-three strong, or thinks that the *hastati* and *principes* had 120 men per maniple plus two centurions, as they did in Polybius' time. Since in Polybius' day all three lines consisted of ten maniples each, this meant 1,200 men forming each of the first two lines and 600 *triarii* forming the third: Polybius' legion therefore had 3,000 regular infantry. In turn, its light-armed *velites* numbered another 1,200.

Livy, by contrast, gives the fourth-century *hastati*, *principes*, and *triarii* fifteen maniples or *vexilla* each. If the first two lines' maniples were each 120 strong, and if he was right about the three-unit 'companies' behind them, each 'company' comprising 186 men, then the size of a fourth-century legion would be huge: 1,800 *hastati* + 1,800 *principes* + 2,790 or 2,835 in the 'companies' (= 15 × 186 or 15 × 189), adding up to a total of well over 6,000 men. Livy himself states that at this time a legion amounted to 5,000 infantry, so something is amiss. Even if we scale down the number of maniples to sixty by striking out the imaginary fifteen of *accensi*, the total would still be well over 5,000 (1,800 *hastati* + 1,800 *principes* + 1,860 or 1,890 *triarii* and *rorarii*).

Two alternative solutions to the problem look possible. One—the most widely accepted—judges his fifteen maniples/*vexilla* in each fighting line as a mistake, and pronounces ten each as the right number. It treats the *hastati* and *principes* as having 120 men per maniple (leaving open the question of whether the *hastati* maniples included twenty light-armed men), and views the light-armed *rorarii* as a separate element. With sixty in each maniple of *triarii*, the total for the three lines would be 3,000 plus centurions, just as in Polybius' time. Similarly, the *rorarii* could be estimated at about 1,200.

The other solution is, arguably, more attractive. This solution accepts Livy's fifteen fourth-century maniples/*vexilla* per line, infers that each of them comprised sixty men plus two centurions, but rejects the supposed twenty 'light-armed' in each *hastati* maniple. If all forty-five units were indeed of this size, then *hastati*, *principes*, and *triarii* together totalled 2,700 plus ninety centurions. To this figure must be added a body of *rorarii*—perhaps 900, as this could account for Livy supposing that they too formed fifteen *vexilla* (*rorarii* had no centurions). The legion would thus consist of something like 3,700 infantry. The advantages of this solution are: (1) there is no need to puzzle over how Livy could offer a false fifteen-maniple figure instead of ten; and (2) it is plausible that a fourth-century legion was smaller than one of later times.

There is no great difficulty in hypothesizing that the legion's formations were modified at some date: from fifteen to ten maniples per line, and from sixty to 120 soldiers per maniple in the first two lines. After all, the *hastati* and *principes* bore the brunt of a battle, as Livy goes on to tell, and after about 300 BC Rome had the manpower for an increase. Some time after 340 and before 280, moreover, the main fighting weapon of both hastati and *principes* changed from the thrusting-spear to the sword, and the 'Samnite' shield was adopted. These need not have been the only changes made.

Livy reports legionaries using swords in 310/9, though this may be imaginative reconstruction (9.35 and note; also 9.39). By 225, certainly, they were using the 'Spanish' sword with its two straight and lethal cutting-edges. Eventually the *triarii* followed suit. Still later, during the Second Punic War or perhaps some decades after, a unit called the cohort (*cohors*) was formed by combining a maniple from each of the three lines into one operational body, and cohorts became the legion's main tactical subdivision.

Some time between 340 and 225 BC, then, the legion developed into the form described by Polybius, including the increased total of 4,200 infantry. This may have been done to meet the much more demanding warfare of the 290s and 280s, though a later date such as the First Punic War is also possible.

If this solution is correct, it limits Livy's errors essentially to three:

that behind the *triarii* were two other *vexilla* of troops (*rorarii*, *accensi*);
that each maniple of *hastati* itself included twenty light-armed men;
and that the legion in the fourth century had as many as 5,000 infantry.

All these errors may be linked. If his source expressed itself opaquely about where the light-armed *rorarii* were positioned, Livy might well have tried to clarify the matter himself—only to get muddled. That he depicts the *accensi*, too, as fighters is surely due to another mistaken effort to clarify things. Having got that far, his calculation of the legion's total strength would make it 4,650 (with sixty-two per maniple) or 4,725 (with sixty-three), a figure that could readily be rounded off to 'five thousand'.

As a partial defence of Livy, it should be noted that early Roman historians—Fabius Pictor included—wrote not in their own language but in Greek. When writing rather involved technical descriptions in a foreign language, they may not always have been crystal clear. Moreover, we cannot assume that Livy himself is responsible for these errors, rather than his source. It remains true that, these errors apart, his account of the fourth-century Roman legion is coherent and acceptable.

EXPLANATORY NOTES

THE numbers in the left-hand column refer to chapter numbers set in bold type in the text. In references to Livy, 'ch. 20' refers to a chapter in the same Book; '6.20' refers to Book 6, ch. 20; '21.20' to Book 21, ch. 20, and so on. For the abbreviations of Roman first names, see Glossary, 'Names'.

References to 'Oakley' are to S. P. Oakley, *A Commentary on Livy, Books VI–X*, 4 vols. (Oxford: Oxford University Press, 1997–2008).

BOOK SIX

1 *destroyed when the city burned down*: that is, in the sack of Rome by the marauding Gauls in 390 BC—the traditional date, but wrong by at least three years. Evidence from Greek sources like Polybius, and some possible hints in Roman ones including Livy himself (cf. note to ch. 35), point to 387 or 386, with adjustments for ensuing years down to 368 or 367. The traditional dates will be kept in these notes, however, for convenience. Livy's acknowledgement of the scarcity of reliable sources for the period from 753 to 390 was not as plainly enunciated as this in his first five books.

Marcus Furius: M. Furius Camillus, the hero of Book 5, whom Livy here names in the old-fashioned way, by *praenomen* and *nomen* alone (see Glossary, 'Names').

in the hands of the tribunes: military tribunes with consular power, not consuls, had held office in 390.

Quintus Fabius: his *cognomen* was Ambustus. Sent with his two brothers in 391 to dissuade the marauding Gallic army from attacking Rome's Etruscan ally Clusium (Chiusi), he had fought against the Gauls and had slain one of their chieftains (Livy 5.35–6), thus violating the sanctity of ambassadorship, a provocation that incited the Gauls to switch their attention to Rome.

were cut down at the Cremera: in 477 the extended clan of the Fabii, three hundred strong, had undertaken a private campaign against the Etruscan city of Veii, only to be wiped out at the River Cremera (Livy 2.48–50). Supposedly one boy, too young to fight, remained at Rome and became the ancestor of all later Fabii.

battle of the Allia: another stream not far north of Rome, where the Roman army was crushed by the Gauls on 18 July 390, thus leaving the city defenceless.

the Kalends and the Nones: see Glossary, 'Calendar'.

2 *the Volsci*: a central Apennine people who around 500 had taken over the mountains overlooking southern Latium (the Monti Lepini) and nearby valleys and coastal lowlands, even mastering Antium (Anzio) 30 miles

south of Rome. For over a century they fought constant wars with Rome and the Latins, at one time (around 490) threatening Rome herself under the leadership of the famous renegade Roman aristocrat, Coriolanus. Eventually conquered, they were completely assimilated in later times—the most famous of all Volscians was Cicero.

2 *Voltumna*: an Etruscan goddess, whose shrine apparently stood near Volsinii (Orvieto); the League of the Etruscan cities met here for religious ceremonies.

Lake Regillus: here in 496 the Romans had defeated their former Tarquin rulers and the Tarquins' Latin allies to end any chance of a monarchic restoration. Reportedly the victors were aided by the gods Castor and Pollux, the last divine intervention in Roman tradition. The Hernici, a small upland people between the Latins and the Volsci, dwelling in the Trerus (Sacco) river valley and the Monti Ernici alongside, had become allies in about 486.

a suspension of all business: see Glossary.

in centuries: see Glossary, 'Century (army)'.

after seventy years of conflict: Livy is probably thinking of the strife with both the Volsci and the Aequi that began in 459 (3.22). The Aequi were another hardy people dwelling in highlands and valleys north of Latium.

3 *Camillus, the mainstay of Rome*: a striking phrase, unique in Livy.

Sutrium: a small city in Etruria (modern Sutri), on a strong site north of Rome, near Lago di Bracciano (ch. 5 note). A few years later it received Roman colonist-settlers along with Nepete, though Livy mentions only the latter (ch. 21) and later describes Sutrium as an allied city as late as 311 (9.32).

with a Roman army: this is not the only sudden appearance by Camillus on a desperate scene. Earlier (5.49) Livy told of him interrupting the ransom payment which the Romans besieged on the Capitol were making to the Gauls to free the city; Camillus instead called the enemy out to battle and destroyed them—pretty certainly a later Roman invention. Whether the scene at Sutrium is any more likely remains doubtful.

undamaged and spared all the devastation of war: a rather unexpected claim, given that Sutrium's Etruscan captors had ransacked it a few lines above.

4 *auctioned off*: the normal fate of prisoners of war, unless ransomed by their home town or kinsmen.

before the burning of the Capitol: Livy means the great fire of 83 BC which completely destroyed the temple of Jupiter Optimus Maximus ('Best and Greatest') built in the late sixth century on the Capitoline hill; it was of course rebuilt.

Veii, Capena, and Falerii: Capena and Falerii were two cities north of Rome and west of the Tiber, which had been defeated in the 390s. Veii had been captured by Camillus in 396 after a famous siege.

capital punishment: not the death penalty, but the loss of civil rights, for in law a person's *caput*, literally 'head', meant his civic status.

Lucius Julius Iulus: this family must be the same that later produced Caesar the Dictator, for third names (*cognomina*) were not fixed. The Julii were prominent in the fifth and fourth centuries but played minor roles thereafter, until a resurgence around 100 BC.

Tarquinii: a great Etruscan city north of Rome, on a plateau 5 miles from the coast; today a major archaeological site. Rome's fifth and seventh kings, the Tarquins, originated there.

dressed stone blocks: in Latin *saxum* (or *opus*) *quadratum*—squared blocks cut from the quarry and dressed to provide smooth and even structures; the method dated from at least the fifth century.

5 *agrarian legislation*: a recurrent theme in Rome's Republican history. Demands and disputes over proposed land laws crop up so regularly in Livy's first ten books that many scholars are sceptical of them, believing them inventions by the early Roman annalistic historians inspired by the actual agrarian struggles from the 140s on. Livy's depiction of this controversy in 388 does use language redolent of late Republican quarrels (below). He himself is disdainful of the recurrent agitations, seeing them, as did other conservative Romans including Cicero, as populist and rabble-rousing efforts by unscrupulously ambitious leaders.

The Pomptine area: a flat region by the coast of south-eastern Latium, much of it unhealthy marshland but with cultivable sectors near the mountains.

the nobility: see Glossary for Livy's anachronistic use of this term.

declared the following appointed: only five names are given, but consular tribunes otherwise come in fours or sixes, so Livy—or a later copyist—probably missed a sixth name. L. Papirius Cursor may have been the grandfather of the famous general in the later part of the century (cf. 8.12 note). This ancient patrician family, originally Papisii, had held consulships and consular tribunates since 444.

the addition of four tribes: these were in the recently annexed areas of southern Etruria; Livy lists them from east to west. The Stellatina lay directly north of Rome in the eastward bend of the Tiber close to Falerii (cf. 7.16); the Tromentina comprised the territory of Veii; the Sabatina lay around the Lacus Sabatinus (Lago di Bracciano); and the Arnensis along the coast of Etruria between that lake and Caere. The annexations marked a major increase in Roman territory, now over 600 sq. miles in area.

6 *discussion was deferred*: although vague, in ch. 2 and here, about why the Latins and Hernici had turned against Rome, Livy probably means us to infer that the Gallic sack had had the same effect on them as on Rome's foes.

Antium: an old Latin city, it had been seized by the Volsci around 500.

personally thanked them: in this scene—with Camillus modestly but manfully accepting the onerous duties of guiding the state in its emergency, then dispensing encouragement and practical advice—it is hard not to see implicit resemblance to the political scene when Livy was writing his first ten books in the 20s BC, after Augustus, while professing modesty, had agreed to continue guiding the state (see also Oakley, i. 378–9).

6 *this state council*: the Senate. The term 'state council', *publicum consilium*, was not official but had a solemn and historic ring.

7 *Satricum*: a town and religious centre just inland from Antium in southern Latium, and especially renowned for its temple to Mater Matuta, a deity revered throughout Latium (cf. ch. 33 and 7.27).

8 *'Standard forward, soldier!'*: the legionary standard (*signum*) was a sacred religious object, and thus even more meaningful to its soldiers than a regimental standard in modern armies. For it to be captured by enemies was the ultimate military disgrace.

Camillus' age: he had been a censor in 403 and then held his first consular tribunate in 401; according to Plutarch (*Camillus* 40), in 367 he was nearing eighty, and this would make him about sixty in 386.

9 *Nepete and Sutrium*: Nepete or Nepet, probably an Etruscan name (Nepi today), lay a little to the east of Sutrium in another strong position. Although this is its first mention in Book 6, the rescue of nearby Sutrium reported here (in 386) is suspiciously similar to the one (in 389) that Livy has narrated in ch. 3: one or other episode is probably fiction.

10 *a demand for reparations*: a formal act (*rerum repetitio*) which called on an offending state to give compensation to Rome, with the threat of war if this was refused. Livy implies that the Latin and Hernican response was disingenuous or worse, but the decision to take the matter no further may suggest that the Senate did judge their response plausible.

11 *The next year*: Livy now narrates, at considerable length (chs. 11, 14–20), the treasonous ambitions of M. Manlius Capitolinus, the recent hero of the Gallic siege of the Capitol in 390 (see 5.47). The Manlii were an ancient patrician 'clan' (*gens*); M. Manlius was wealthy, distinguished, and popular. That he was tried and put to death in 384, for alleged offences obscure to Livy (ch. 20), seems authentic; but everything else is debatable. Livy's account may be influenced by the fevered final decades of the Republic and especially by the Catiline affair of 63 BC. That patrician senator espoused a wholesale cancellation of debts and was accused by the consul Cicero and others of plotting a *coup d'état*.

the plebeian magistrates: Livy is inexact, for the plebeian tribunes were not technically magistrates since they represented only the plebs, but it was often a convenient term for Roman writers.

which had always been the stuff of sedition: Livy's ingrained conservative outlook is plain. Because richer citizens often and perhaps regularly made use of state land for themselves, at times even coming to think of their holdings as personal property, laws to give parcels of state land to poor Romans aroused bitter opposition and, in later centuries, sometimes physical violence.

So did proposals to ease the burden of debt, which often involved heavy interest-rates (ch. 14).

fetters and imprisonment: although by now a Roman unable to repay his debts could no longer be sold into slavery, he was still a debt-bondsman (*adductus*). His creditor could use him virtually as a slave until he somehow repaid what he owed (see ch. 34, and 8.28).

master of horse: see Glossary.

12 *I do not doubt*: a famous statement by our historian (Introduction, pp. xxiv–xxv) that illustrates both his efforts to create a reliable history and his own limitations.

keep from lapsing into desert: the city of Rome grew huge in later centuries, draining many parts of Latium and central Italy of their once large populations. So did the attractions of settlement in other, wealthier regions. Yet the most likely explanation for what seem inexhaustible numbers of Volsci and Aequi (and Rome's other hardy foes) is that early Roman historians grossly exaggerated them, a point not canvassed by Livy at all even though, elsewhere in his history, he often notes—and deplores—such distortions.

Circeii . . . Velitrae: Circeii stood on a promontory at the south-eastern end of Latium, beyond the infamous Pomptine marshes; Velitrae lay nearer to Rome, on the southern slopes of the Alban Hills.

arm ourselves only with swords: the classic Roman infantryman, the legionary, was armed with two javelins (*pila*) for hurling at the enemy before the armies clashed, and with a sword (*gladius*) for close fighting. Livy assumes that this was already the standard equipment in the early fourth century, but the scanty available evidence indicates that then legionaries fought with thrusting-spears (*hastae*), using swords only as a last resort, much like contemporary Greek hoplites (8.8 notes).

14 *A centurion*: Livy told a similar but more elaborate story much earlier (2.23), setting it in the year 495—there, the plebeian citizens take up the cause of an aged centurion crushed by debt. That almost the same event recurred in 385 is suspicious; one or both stories could be inventions for dramatic effect.

put his hand on him: a Roman had the legal right to rescue a wrongly enslaved fellow-citizen in this way, to launch a case arguing his innocence. Livy extends the image to Manlius freeing the centurion from his debt-bondage, without suggesting that the man had been wrongly treated.

with scales and bronze: a ceremony (*per aes et libram*) formally symbolizing the restoration of the centurion's freedom. It reflected the fact that before regular coinage was introduced around 269 (ch. 20 note, and 10.23 note), Romans used lumps or pieces of bronze (*aes*) as currency, determining their value by weighing them.

the main part of his family fortune: Oakley (i. 523) notes the oddity that Manlius, member of an ancient aristocratic family, supposedly had his ancestral estate in newly annexed Veientane territory. This obviously makes the item look suspect. Yet for the same reason the claim is a strange one for Livy's source, or Livy, to invent. Arguably, Manlius had acquired a sizeable property there which later was carelessly assumed to be 'the main part of his family fortune'.

14 *Manlius made speeches at home*: another detail often viewed as borrowed from much later turmoils. Catiline and his supporters held gatherings allegedly to plan seditious action (Cicero, *Against Catiline* 1.8, 3.10; Sallust, *Conspiracy of Catiline* 20, 27), and so Manlius' meetings, like various other conspiratorial ones reported in these times (e.g. 2.32, 4.13), are usually judged as invented by authors using the Catilinarians as their model.

15 *the Comitium*: the large open space before the Senate house (*curia*); originally the citizens had met there when formally assembled (the word's basic meaning is 'gathering place').

16 *prison*: the prison (*carcer*) was on the southern side of the Capitoline hill, beneath the church of San Giuseppe close by the Senate house. The earliest surviving elements of it date to the third century BC, but it existed well before then.

let their hair and beards grow long: part of the outward gestures of mourning, along with dark and ragged garments.

taken along before his chariot: as captured foreign enemies were. The statement is rhetorical only, for a Roman citizen would not be a triumphal exhibit even had there been a military battle.

two and a half iugera: about one-and-a-half acres, or 0.65 hectares. At colonies founded by Rome and also at 'Latin colonies' (those founded by her and the Latin League together), 2–4 *iugera* were the norm per colonist, but to support his family a colonist also needed access to the state-owned land (*ager publicus*) assigned to the colony.

17 *Spurius Cassius*: in 486 one consul, Sp. Cassius, had put forward the first recorded agrarian law, but was accused by the patrician oligarchy of aiming at making himself king and was executed in 485 (Livy 2.41). Sp. Maelius was a wealthy plebeian who, during a food shortage in 440, relieved the sufferings of the poor by buying grain and distributing it free to them. His aristocratic enemies denounced him as aiming at monarchy, and when he refused a summons in 439 he was slain out of hand by C. Servilius Ahala, the master of horse of the famous dictator Cincinnatus (Livy 4.12–15). In ch. 18 Livy more evocatively gives the deed to Cincinnatus, who was a famous symbol of patriotism.

half-pound measures of grain: for his exploit on the Capitol, Manlius had been rewarded with small gifts of grain and wine by each of his fellow-soldiers (5.47).

18 *So how long*: the same Latin words, *Quo usque tandem*, launch the most famous speech in Roman oratory—Cicero's first invective against Catiline, delivered in November 63 BC to the Senate in the alleged plotter's presence: 'So how long, Catiline, are you going to exploit our tolerance?'

(*Against Catiline* 1.1). The Latin phrase became something of a rhetorical proverb (there is even a Wikipedia entry for it). Livy, however, has Manlius use it to his own followers, as Sallust's Catiline does (*Catiline* 20; cf. Oakley, i. 545–6). Sallust's work had made a strong impact when it appeared *c*.41 BC; if Livy is echoing him, it may be a literary compliment rather than a symbolic characterization of Manlius as a proto-Catiline.

Is this great people's spirit so small: this rhetorical question is complex— not to say convoluted—both in Latin and in translation (in Latin it does not even open in question-form, but as a statement, to heighten the effect). Manlius is referring to the role of the tribunes of the plebs, who existed to protect plebeians from oppression. He sarcastically asks whether the plebs looks to them for help only in private disputes because, in political disputes with the patricians, the plebs strives only to subject itself more thoroughly to the oligarchs.

patron of the plebs: a unique phrase in Latin literature, but based on the relationship of high-ranking Romans to their social dependants (the former were termed *patroni*, the latter *clientes*). Manlius thus designates himself *patronus* of the entire plebeian citizen body—which comprised well over 90 per cent of Rome's citizenry. Perhaps Livy is also recalling Manlius' sarcastic description in ch. 15 of the dictator Cornelius as 'patron of the moneylenders'.

there is no clear account: Manlius' speech grows noticeably more and more revolutionary, with him by its end demanding the overthrow of existing political institutions and his own elevation as sole ruler. Yet the historian at once admits that he has no firm evidence for any of this, only that 'it is said', and he reinforces this in ch. 20. Ironically, in his day it was the 'first citizen' Augustus who, in practice though not in name, fulfilled precisely the role that Livy makes Manlius claim (note Tacitus, *Annals* 1.2).

19 *in the citadel*: Manlius, along with some of his kinsmen, dwelt on the Capitoline hill. That the entire plebs, or even a sizeable fraction of it, was in or even around his house is rhetorical hyperbole; on the cry for another Ahala see ch. 17 note.

that the state suffered no harm: this is the terminology of the much later emergency decree of the Senate (the so-called 'final decree'), first attested in 121 when used against the ex-tribunes C. Gracchus and M. Fulvius Flaccus. There is no possibility that any such language was used in the fourth century, still less in the fifth (as Livy 3.4 claims). But some decree against the real Manlius is quite believable once the authorities decided to move against him.

the authority of the Senate: a specific function performed by the patrician senators (see Glossary).

the plebeian tribunes: this sudden volte-face is remarkable—Livy has said nothing of how any plebeian tribunes felt about Manlius until the previous paragraph. To reveal that two of them were now planning to prosecute him, virtually as surrogates for the patricians, is clumsily abrupt.

20 *When Appius Claudius was imprisoned*: in Book 3 Livy told the story of how Ap. Claudius, one of the ten Decemvirs appointed to codify the laws, took the lead in 450–449 in trying to make their rule permanent, only for his increasingly tyrannical actions to bring about his and his colleagues' downfall. Imprisoned by the plebeian tribunes, he was defended by his hitherto hostile brother Gaius (3.58), but took his own life.

mural crowns … civic crowns: 'crowns' (*coronae*) were wreaths of oak leaves or grass presented to soldiers who had been first to scale an enemy town's wall (the mural crown) or had saved a fellow-citizen's life in battle and been thus acknowledged by that man (the civic crown). Manlius had no fewer than twenty-three battle-scars (Pliny the Elder, *Natural History* 7.103), further honourable marks of valour.

to vote in the Campus Martius: the Campus Martius ('Field of Mars') is the broad level area between the Capitoline hill and the westward bend of the Tiber, originally an open plain. In the early Republic it was the assembly-ground for Rome's citizens in arms, and this gathering in turn evolved into the political *Comitia Centuriata* (see Glossary).

a people's assembly: this is another of the opaque features in Livy's account of Manlius. Plebeian tribunes could summon the plebeian citizens as a body called the *Concilium Plebis*, 'council of the plebs'. But this had no power of capital punishment, while the two *Comitia*, *Centuriata* and *Tributa* (see Glossary), could not be summoned by the tribunes.

no view of the Capitol: it is not clear where either the Porta Flumentana ('River gate') or the Peteline Wood lay, and—more to the point—not clear that Livy himself knew. The likeliest site for the Flumentana gate seems to have been by the Tiber between the Capitol itself and the Palatine hill just to its south (Oakley, i. 563), thus in the area where the famous round temple stands. This does not fit the claim that there was no view of the Capitol. But Livy's narrative, in spite of its seeming detail, is questionable in any case as a piece of history, while the sudden change of heart in Manlius' followers in their new venue is psychologically childish. So all the colourful details may simply be imaginative elaborations by earlier writers whom he used.

the temple and mint of Moneta: these stood on a rise on the eastern side of the Capitol, the original citadel (*arx*) of Rome and now the site of the Museo Capitolino. The temple of Juno Moneta ('she who warns') in Roman tradition housed the workshop where Rome's first coinage would be struck *c*.269 BC (hence the word 'money'), and it was her sacred geese which in 390 had alerted Manlius to the Gauls climbing the steep slope below.

21 *plague was followed by famine*: such ills were sadly frequent in the ancient world. Livy's history registers twenty-nine plagues afflicting Rome between 496 and 293, thirteen of them in Books 6–10 (Oakley, i. 58–9, 733); they will have included smallpox, measles, malaria, and typhus (not bubonic or pneumonic plague until much later times). Because such disasters required religious measures, they were carefully recorded, often together with the measures taken.

Lanuvium: an ancient Latin city on the southern slopes of the Alban Hills, south-east of Rome, with a venerated temple of Juno Sospes ('the saviour').

the tribes voted unanimously for war: 'tribes' is an anachronistic detail, for the war- and peace-making citizen assembly in the early Republic was the *Comitia Centuriata* which voted by centuries. By 200, however, the centuries had been grouped so as to coordinate with the tribes, so from then on the *C. Centuriata* could be described as voting by tribes. Livy's wording here probably stems from this later arrangement.

the Praenestines: Praeneste (Palestrina) was a strong Latin city on the western side of the Alban Hills. Roman troubles in and after the Gallic sack, including wavering loyalties from some Latin cities, presumably tempted the Praenestines to make a bid to replace Rome as hegemon of the Latin League.

22 *Lucius Furius*: not Camillus' son but L. Furius Medullinus, member of a related family within the *gens* of the Furii, and allegedly (ch. 23) a young man.

each four thousand strong: probably Livy's estimate, based wrongly on assuming that fourth-century legions had the same manpower as in later centuries. A passable estimate for a legion in the 380s might be about 3,000 legionaries and 300 cavalry, along with some hundreds of light-armed fighters (see Appendix 2). Whether Camillus did raise as many as four legions, all the same, is debatable.

24 *an attack on the enemy on foot*: a frequent habit of cavalry in early times, or so at any rate Livy believed (e.g. 4.38, 7.7, 9.39), like some other writers.

26 *dictator of Tusculum*: not an emergency supreme magistrate like Rome's, but apparently the equivalent of a consul. Tusculum is today's Frascati.

and Roman citizenship not long afterwards: thus Tusculum became a part of the Roman Republic, the first Latin city to do so, though it kept its local institutions. This was a major step in the extension of the Roman state. The great Roman leader and founder of Latin historiography Cato the Censor (234–149) was from Tusculum.

27 *the military tribunes for the following year*: i.e. for 380. Our ancient sources vary greatly on these. The *Fasti Capitolini* name no fewer than nine, five of which match Livy's. His older contemporary Diodorus (15.50) claims eight and names six, of whom five also match Livy's. These five—the brothers Valerii, Menenius, Papirius, and Cornelius—may therefore be accepted as genuine, but the actual total remains unknown.

the gods seemed to be opposed to a censorship for that year: Sulpicius' colleague Postumius' death is curiously mirrored later at 7.1–2 (365 BC), where a censor who must be another Postumius dies in an epidemic, and the *Fasti Capitolini* name his fellow-censor as another Sulpicius. The parallels have caused some to doubt the abortive censorships of 380, but the early election of fresh censors in the ensuing year (ch. 31) suggests that there was indeed a problem (T. R. S. Broughton, *The Magistrates of the Roman Republic*, 3 vols. (Philadelphia and Chicago: American Philological Association and Scholars Press, 1951–2, 1984), i. 106 n. 2).

27 *become a credit-prisoner*: in Latin an *adductus* ('assigned man'); see ch. 11 note.

28 *Porta Collina*: in the northern wall of the city. Hannibal too, in his famous march on Rome in 211, reached this point, only to retreat just as the Praenestines had.

doom for the city of Rome: because it had been the site of the Roman defeat by the Gauls in 390.

the following day at Gabii: the tradition was that, after cancelling the ransom payment by his sudden arrival (ch. 3 note), Camillus had annihilated the Gauls next day in a great battle east of Rome, at the eighth milestone from Gabii (5.49).

29 *you gods of the treaty*: the treaty of alliance with Praeneste. The gods guarded the good faith (*fides*) of treaties and other sworn agreements, so were expected to punish oath-breakers. The Romans always stressed the importance of *fides* (cf. ch. 33)—naturally insisting that they themselves never violated it.

Jupiter Imperator: 'Jupiter the Commander'; it is not certain that the epithet was in use as early as this, however (cf. 7.38 note).

shrine of Minerva: the Capitol housed the three ancient deities Jupiter, Minerva, and Juno. Quinctius' inscription is one of Livy's rare quotations of an actual document; perhaps he saw it himself.

30 *without sortition or mutual agreement*: a very unusual procedure, and therefore doubted by some scholars, though why such a detail should be invented by any of Livy's sources (or Livy himself) is not obvious. See Glossary for 'sortition'.

Setia: modern Sezze in the Monti Lepini, heartland of the Volsci. The rather later historian Velleius Paterculus, listing early colonies (Velleius 1.14), dates the foundation 'seven years after the Gauls had taken the city', which would make it 382 (a date that most scholars prefer), unless Velleius here follows a source which correctly dated the Gallic sack to 387 (cf. 8.14 note on Aricia).

31 *an explosion of civil discord*: chs. 31–42 are the climax of the internal history element of Book 6, with the persistence of the plebeians under two resolute leaders finally achieving major social and political reforms. Scholars generally agree that the ancient accounts are too worked-up to be accepted without question, but how the events should be reconstructed (or whether they can) remains contentious.

the property tax: i.e. *tributum*. First levied in 406 to fund the innovation of pay for soldiers in the long siege of Veii (Livy 4.59–60), but details are not known.

Ecetra: a Volscian site, not identifiable.

32 *a wall of dressed stone*: the famous wall that later Romans credited to their
sixth-century king Servius Tullius. All public works were contracted out to
private entrepreneurs. The project must certainly have been very
costly: built of large blocks of tufa from quarries near Veii, the 'Servian
Wall' was almost 7 miles (11 km.) around and originally more than 30 feet
high. A few parts of it survive, for instance outside Termini railway station.
The area it enclosed was about 1,052 acres or 426 hectares, marking out
Rome as one of the largest cities in fourth-century Italy and Greece.

two miles away: a Roman mile of 1,000 'paces' (*passus*) measured about
1,618 yards or 1,480 metres.

34 *to compete with patricians*: in 379 three of that year's six consular tribunes
had been plebeians (ch. 30), so either the debt situation had worsened
severely between then and 376 or Livy is exaggerating for effect. But continuing hardship for many plebeians cannot be doubted.

a trivial event intervened: while aware of the social and economic problems
just mentioned, Livy as often cannot resist focusing on a personalized individual case to set the story in motion; cf. Introduction, p. xiii.

unacquainted with the convention: whoever thought up this detail (Fabius
Pictor, perhaps) overlooked that the young woman's father had been a consular tribune himself in 381 and that she, member of an ancient patrician
family, would surely have observed lictors doing their duties from early in
her life.

to form plans with his son-in-law: Fabius Ambustus does not, in fact,
reappear in the narrative except briefly as a consular tribune in 369, so
crediting him as the man whose counsel initiated the great struggle looks
unconvincing—and suggests that Fabius Pictor originated his role in the
story. The claim could have arisen from the marriage between Licinius
Stolo and Ambustus' daughter (Oakley, i. 647).

35 *the bills that they announced*: there is much debate on how accurate, or even
authentic, these bills in Livy are. It seems safe to hold that they achieved
three things. (i) One eased the harsh penalties for debt in various ways.
(ii) Another placed a limit on how much state land any one person could
hold. And (iii) the third abolished the consular tribunate and restored the
consulship, perhaps with a clause expressly recognizing that a plebeian
could hold it (next note).

should . . . be from the plebs: in Livy's own narrative, not to mention other
sources, two patrician consuls occur several times after these bills became
law (in 355, 353, 351, 349, 345, and 343); only from 342 on was one consul
each year always a plebeian—and not until 172 were they both plebeians.
The third bill, then, cannot have been as sweeping as Livy claims; it more
likely permitted, but did not require, one consul each year to be plebeian.

held back the city for five years: i.e., from 375 to 371 inclusive, the so-called
'anarchy' (in its original sense, a lack of proper organs of government). This
claim is beyond serious belief and indeed borders on the farcical. Livy
found almost nothing to report for those years (ch. 36), a further giveaway.

Diodorus (15.61) seems to imply that the 'anarchy' lasted less than one year; and while he is not always reliable on early Roman history, a year or so of political paralysis looks more believable. On the chronological problems in fourth-century Roman history see Introduction, pp. x–xii.

36 *elections were held by an interrex*: this unnamed *interrex* looks invented—needed because Livy has had no regular magistrates for the past five years. The consular tribunes thus elected took office in 370 by the traditional dating.

nothing noteworthy accomplished at Velitrae: the improbable notion that the town was besieged for three or four years (370–367) is bound up with the supposed five-year 'anarchy'.

had by now been re-elected eight times: this ensuing year is traditionally counted as 369.

experts at manipulating the feelings of the plebs: Livy's narrative now starts to turn subtly critical of the radical tribunes, despite his description of the serious social and economic ills that they were attacking. Note the waspish remark (ch. 37) that their description of the ill-treatment of plebeians 'generated more indignation in their hearers than they felt themselves'.

more than 500 iugera: on the meagreness of a 2-*iugera* allocation see ch. 16 note. In later times there existed a law banning anyone from holding more than 500 *iugera* of state land, but wealthy men apparently had little difficulty in getting around it or simply ignoring it (cf. 10.13 and note).

dragged in droves from the Forum: after their cases had been decided against them in court, because proceedings were held in the Forum.

37 *the first man elected from the plebs*: P. Licinius Calvus had been a consular tribune in 400; but the earliest plebeians in that office had been L. Atilius in 444 (the first year of consular tribunes), and in 422 Q. Antonius, for these family names (*nomina*) are not patrician. Moreover Calvus himself had had three other plebeians among his colleagues. Livy compresses the point for rhetorical effect.

quaestors, too: the quaestorship, first created in 447, had been open to plebeians since 409 (Livy 4.54).

38 *the appointee was Marcus Furius Camillus*: many scholars doubt that this appointment occurred, because Livy's narrative involves a number of improbabilities and uncertainties, and because nothing happened in the supposed dictatorship. Yet it can equally be argued that the appointment is unlikely as fiction precisely because nothing came of it.

some flaw in his election: an appointment or election could be declared invalid by state priests if there was an ill omen at that time, or if the auspices taken by the new officials proved unfavourable (8.23 note; Glossary, 'Augurs'). Livy soon suggests that the latter event had occurred, no doubt because his admiration for the aged hero makes him disbelieve any less decorous reason. By contrast, Plutarch (*Camillus* 39) ascribes Camillus' resignation to fear of being exiled again or to belief that he could not win the political struggle.

a fine of 500,000 asses: this threat is almost certainly invented, for it was not legally possible to fine or otherwise coerce a dictator in office.

Publius Manlius: his full name was P. Manlius Capitolinus, and he seems to have been a cousin of M. Manlius Capitolinus (both were grandsons of an A. Manlius, but with different fathers).

39 *Gaius Licinius*: at first sight, this might seem to be Licinius Stolo the current plebeian tribune (as Plutarch, *Camillus* 39, and Dio, fragment 29, claim), but if so it is strange that Livy does not identify him; nor was Stolo mentioned previously as a consular tribune or as a close connection of P. Manlius. Another suggestion is C. Licinius Calvus, but no earlier consular tribunate is known for him either. Possibly 'C. Licinius' is a slip for P. Licinius Calvus, consular tribune thirty-two years earlier, mentioned in ch. 37; the Romans had high regard for aged experience. Despite these appointments, yet another year's delay supposedly ensued: but it is just conceivable that the bills may in fact have been enacted now, rather than a year later. Making them wait a further year allowed the pro-Camillus tradition to credit him—unconvincingly—with yet another dictatorship to set his revered seal on the reforms (ch. 42).

40 *Appius Claudius Crassus, grandson of the decemvir*: on the decemvirs of 451–449 see chs. 1 and 20 notes. The decemvir Appius' grandson had a long career: from consular tribune in 403 to consul in 349 (7.25). The name Appius was used only by his family: it was given to the eldest son in each generation, while the second son was usually named Gaius (cf. ch. 20). This Appius' grandson was the famous Ap. Claudius Caecus, censor in 312 and twice consul later, who plays a busy part in Books 9 and 10.

spoke much as follows: a form of words that indicates an authorial composition, though one supposedly based on some record of the original. Appius' speech is a highly wrought conservative argument, both against allowing committed ideologues to lead political change and against change that undermines the existing elite. He is made to sound a hidebound, not to mention supercilious, reactionary, none of whose gloomy predictions comes true (as the next Books show). The 'arrogant Claudii' theme was something of a cliché in ancient authors (cf. Oakley, iii. 357–61), but it is curious that Livy seconds it, for he was writing when current patrician Claudii were members of Augustus' own family, including his wife Livia.

Tarquinian: an insulting equation of the reforming tribunes with the Tarquin royal family, especially the tyrant L. Tarquinius Superbus and his vicious second son Sextus (Lucretia's rapist), who had been driven out in 509.

when Porsenna occupied the Janiculum: after the Tarquins' expulsion, they were helped for a time by Lars Porsenna, king of Clusium in Etruria. He besieged Rome from his encampment on the Janiculum hill, until the resolute resistance of the new Republic—with champions like Horatius and

Mucius Scaevola—won him over. A different tradition had him capture Rome for a time, although without restoring the monarchy (Pliny the Elder, *Natural History* 34.139; Tacitus, *Histories* 3.72).

41 *make your votes predetermined instead of voluntary*: during the civil wars before Livy began his history, this had been precisely the situation. Even after Augustus achieved sole power, effective if unobtrusive 'guidance' was applied especially at the level of consulships. Livy's readers can hardly have been blind to how Appius Claudius' impassioned comments, supposedly made in 368, could apply to current times.

In the patricians' hands, of course!: in early Republican Rome the patricians alone had the right to 'take the auspices' (see Glossary, 'Auspices')—notably though not solely by observing birds' flight. The original patricians were the *patres* who formed the Senate in regal times; in the absence, or upon the deaths, of both consuls or of all the consular tribunes, the auspices were deemed to 'return to the *patres*', who then nominated an *interrex* (ch. 1). These usages perhaps explain the claim that only patricians could take auspices. Livy seems interested in the claim but does not himself vouch for the truth of it.

if the chickens will not eat: see Glossary, 'Auspices'. A brood accompanied each general on campaign (e.g. 9.14, 10.40). In making Appius complain of plebeian mockery of the sacred chickens, Livy may well want readers to have in mind the irony that Appius' own descendant P. Claudius Pulcher, leading a fleet in 249 against the Carthaginians, likewise mocked his brood's ill-omened refusal of food and continued with his attack, only to suffer disastrous defeat.

the shields: twelve shields, *ancilia*, of antique (figure-of-eight) shape; one had been sent to earth by the war-god Mars, and the other eleven were exact replicas to frustrate enemies or thieves. They were borne by the 'leaping priests', the Salii, who in their ceremonies wore the armament of archaic Italic warriors and whose leapings may have ritually re-enacted early drills.

Tatius: Titus Tatius, king of the Sabines north of Rome, had for a time co-reigned over Rome with its founder Romulus.

42 *Titus Quinctius Poenus*: recorded by Livy as dictator in 361 (7.9) and consul in 351 (7.22), but it is likelier that the real spelling of his *cognomen* was Pennus.

Claudius' account: Claudius Quadrigarius (see Introduction).

at least ten years after this: careless, for Livy later reports it in the year 361, six years after this (7.9–10). He disbelieves Claudius' date and version because 'most of our sources' put the episode later. Thus a simple headcount, so to speak, is about the extent of his own research into the question. Meanwhile his narrative of Camillus' victory is quite compressed compared to those in some other writers, notably Dionysius (14.8–10) and Plutarch (*Camillus* 40–41).

internal strife even more fierce: yet Livy wraps all of it up in half-a-dozen sentences, a striking contrast to his long account of the previous confrontations—another clue that the supposed two-year length for this final stage of the reform struggle was really shorter, and similarly that Camillus' supposed two dictatorships in successive years (chs. 38 and 42) were in reality only one.

the Great Games: the Ludi Magni, also called Ludi Romani, were held in September. *Ludi* had ceremonial and religious status, although they involved competitive events like races, wrestling, and sometimes dancing; over the centuries many others were instituted, including ones at which plays were performed (see 7.2).

the young patricians loudly proclaimed: another touch of aristocratic partiality in our historian. He does not explain the plebeian aediles' refusal—arguably they lacked enough funding, or felt they had enough duties already—and he presents the offer as an act applauded by 'the whole community', with the added implication that the new aediles would pay the cost of the fourth day themselves.

BOOK SEVEN

1 *'new man'*: see Glossary. The consuls of 366 were the first since 392 to hold this office.

from amongst the patricians: or 'from amongst the senators', for Livy at times uses *patres* ambiguously—here and in chs. 6 (at the end), 17, and 21—in the sense either of 'patricians' or 'senators' (cf. 6.41 note; literally the word means simply 'fathers', but in political contexts the other meanings are commoner).

talk about the Gauls: these seem to have consisted of one or more wandering warbands from the north, which plagued the Italian peninsula from time to time until the 340s.

the praetexta, on curule chairs: the *praetexta* was the toga with a crimson (*purpurea*) border worn by magistrates in office, and such magistrates sat on folding-chairs carved in ivory, the *sellae curules*.

so that there should at no point be relief from fear and danger: one of Livy's moralizing comments, linked to the widespread view that Rome's destined greatness had to be challenged by hardships and setbacks to steel the nation's character (similarly ch. 27; 10.1; 10.6). On plagues at Rome see 6.21 note.

a censor: the *Fasti Capitolini* name two censors for this year (365), one Postumius Albinus and C. Sulpicius Peticus. As Sulpicius held five consulships down to 351 (next note), Postumius (not the censor of 380; see 6.27) must have been the casualty. Their abortive censorship explains why two new censors held the office in the following year (M. Fabius Ambustus and L. Furius Medullinus), though Livy equally fails to mention these and some scholars doubt one or both pairs.

1 *Marcus Furius*: Camillus, who was reportedly eighty years old.

2 *Gaius Licinius Stolo*: ancient sources vary on his consulship. The *Fasti Capitolini* (6.27 note) have it three years later in 361, and name this year's consul C. Licinius Calvus; whereas Livy reverses them (see ch. 9). Sulpicius Peticus had been a consular tribune in 380 (6.27), censor in 365 (ch. 1 note), and would hold five consulships (364, 361, 355, 353, 351): he was therefore one of the most successful leaders of mid-fourth-century Rome.

theatrical performances were introduced: one of Livy's few literary disquisitions follows, though he does not explain just how the innovation was supposed to appease the gods. While not certain about the earliest nature of the performances (note the cautious 'they say'), and critical of the moral value of the theatre, as the end of the chapter reveals, he is interested enough in the topic to give a useful sketch of how drama developed at Rome. Whether the sketch is entirely accurate is less clear.

Fescennine verse: songs sung at weddings, often with very obscene words in order to ward off unfriendly spirits. Catullus' Poem 61 includes an example.

It was Livius: Livius Andronicus, from the Greek city of Tarentum (Taranto), settled at Rome around 250 BC, became a Roman citizen, and composed the first serious plays and poetry in Latin, using Greek models and staging his first play in 240. His abbreviated translation of the *Odyssey* was also famous, but only a few quotations from his many works survive. He was no relative of our historian, who all the same may feel pleased at sharing the name.

Atellan farces: drawn supposedly from the town of Atella in Campania, an Oscan-speaking region. Enormously popular at Rome for centuries, they had stock Oscan-named characters like Maccus the clown and Dossennus the scheming glutton, with plots based on farcical versions of everyday life. Stage actors were legally *infames*, 'of ill repute', although in later times some were exempted.

3 *the Circus*: the broad area of the Circus Maximus between the Palatine and Aventine hills.

a dictator to hammer in a nail: Livy confuses two nailing ceremonies at the Capitoline temple of Jupiter. A special, rarely appointed dictator hammered in a nail on the occasion of a disaster like a plague; and one consul in each year hammered in a nail on the Ides (13th) of September for the anniversary of the temple's dedication in 508.

chief praetor: a phrase commonly judged as showing that consuls had originally been so styled (*praetores maximi*), but there is no other ancient evidence for this and Livy's own interpretation of the 'old law' is otherwise inexact, as just noted. Some scholars think that 'chief praetor' was an earlier term for the dictator; debate continues. Livy does not cite wording from the archaic law itself—not the only place where he shows distaste for quoting old Latin.

Nortia: an Etruscan goddess of fate. Cincius was not the early Roman historian (on whom see the Introduction) but a Cincius contemporary with Livy, who wrote books, now lost, on old Roman institutions and customs.

as if he had been appointed for military purposes: it was only a convention—but a powerful one—that a dictator should carry out just the task for which he had been nominated. Cicero writes that it was Manlius' attempt to keep on being dictator past the allotted time that caused resentment (*On Duties* 3.112).

4 *his treatment of his young son*: the story is also told more briefly by Cicero (ibid.) to illustrate, if paradoxically, how deeply Romans had once respected oaths. All the same the tale looks more like fiction than fact, even though both father and son were real persons: it may have been a Manlian family legend.

5 *'Rufuli'*: supposedly a nickname bestowed on the additional military tribunes in memory of the army reformer P. Rutilius Rufus, consul in 105; but the practice began well before his time.

6 *The Curtian Lake*: the Lacus Curtius, once a marshy pond, now a site marked out by a circle of paving-stones near the temple of Vesta. Early Roman history had several stories of *devotio*, a rite under which a patriotic hero sacrificed his own life for the safety of Rome (also 8.9–10, 10.28–29). Curtius' action is unlikely to be true, but the priestly annals (see Introduction) could have recorded a fissure in the ground—although how he came to be linked with it remains unguessable. The Sabine warrior Mettius Curtius, mentioned here with names reversed (a literary conceit), had escaped death in an early battle by riding into the marsh that later became the Forum (Livy 1.12).

7 *were duly enrolled*: Hernican territory (6.2 note) can hardly have had large military manpower, so 3,200 may have been virtually their full strength (but army numbers for early foes of Rome are dubious anyway). On 'cohorts' see Glossary.

began the battle anew: another dubious-looking item, for although cavalry did at times dismount during a mêlée, to dismount and lead the charge would have been dangerously unwise—they lacked infantry shields and heavy armour. Livy's account of the struggle is largely rhetorical.

8 *Signia*: a Latin colony in the upper Sacco valley (today Segni).

9 *Tibur*: one of the original Latin cities (today's Tivoli) but, it seems, no longer a member of the Latin League which was allied with Rome. A strong city, Tibur must have been growing apprehensive about the revival of Roman power since the Gallic sack. Ferentinum (Ferentino) stood on the southern edge of the Monti Ernici.

Licinius Macer: he claimed that his ancestor, the consul Licinius Calvus, checked his colleague's improper ambitions by appointing a dictator to hold elections at the correct time. Livy rightly throws doubt on this bit of familial boasting.

9 *at the third milestone on the Via Salaria*: the Via Salaria was one of the roads leading from the Colline gate in Rome's north-eastern wall (cf. ch. 11 note). The Anio (Aniene) river joins the Tiber just north of Rome.

a suspension of business: see Glossary. This was the worst emergency in thirty years, with memory of the Gallic sack still vivid.

a Gaul of huge build stepped forward: this is the first of two famous duels between a Roman David and a Gallic Goliath; for the other see ch. 26. Whether either occurred is debated. Each gained the victor an evocative name, Torquatus and Corvus respectively. Manlius' duel was dated to 368 by Claudius Quadrigarius, who in turn must have drawn on some earlier account for it. His version is quoted at length by the second-century AD essayist Aulus Gellius (*Attic Nights* 9.13), who admires its unadorned style. Livy—though rejecting 368 as the date—clearly bases his own narrative on it, but with much more rhetorical and emotive colouring; for instance, Quadrigarius does not have the dialogue between Manlius and the dictator.

10 *the Tarpeian rock*: young Manlius was the great-nephew of the hero and traitor M. Manlius Capitolinus.

a Spanish sword: not the short two-edged *gladius Hispaniensis* of later times. Fourth-century swords did include medium-sized stabbing versions, and also a curved single-sided blade which resembled one used in Spain called a *falcata*. All these had a sharp narrow point suitable for Manlius' exploit.

also thought worthy of mention: Quadrigarius has this detail, but the prim comment is pure Livy, who does not also mention the Gaul singing as he advanced.

his multicoloured garb and armour painted and embossed with gold: this vivid description fits a Gallic chieftain, not an ordinary warrior who fought naked or bare-chested. Quadrigarius by contrast has the Gaul 'naked save for his shield and two swords', as well as wearing a torque and armbands (these would be of gold, or gilded), ornaments dear to Celtic warriors. The combat itself differs in various ways from Quadrigarius, who has Manlius unbalancing his opponent by twice striking his own shield against the other's, thus getting under his guard to bring him down. Livy's variants may come from another source.

spared his corpse all other forms of abuse: Livy, again prim, avoids stating the obvious (as Quadrigarius does)—that to take the torque Manlius had to behead the corpse—but uses wording that hints it.

coarse and jocular quasi-poetical banter: to ward off any anger of the gods towards the pride and self-congratulation of a triumphator, his soldiers would sing affectionately mocking and often foul-mouthed verses about him (Suetonius quotes examples from Caesar's triumph in 46 BC: *Divus Julius* 49, 51), though the songs could offer praise too (e.g. ch. 38; 10.30; 39.7).

11 *not far from the Colline gate*: if so, the new Gallic incursion reached much the same spot as the one in the previous year (ch. 9). On the other hand, it

could be that this incursion is a mistaken doublet of the earlier one and that the supposed great battle here is fiction. The fact that both consuls but not the dictator were rewarded for their successes strengthens the sceptical view.

12 *A Tarquinian raiding force*: Tarquinii and Rome had clashed in 388 (6.4), but there was no sequel then. Rome's territory now included Veii's conquered lands (6.15 note).

allowed to lapse: many, though not all, Latin cities had defied Rome since the Gallic sack (6.2, 6.6–8, etc.). Livy has not mentioned them since 6.33 (377 BC), thus leaving unexplained what now made them seek peace. Renewal of the 'old treaty'—the *foedus Cassianum* of 493 (see Glossary)—was an important stage in Rome's recovery.

Gaius Sulpicius: the indispensable Peticus (ch. 2 note).

should make the case on behalf of the army: this episode of an aggressively spirited Roman army berating its over-cautious general is plainly much elaborated by Livy, notably in the centurion Tullius' rhetorical speech. It is not impossible, though, that restiveness towards a commander did occasionally occur. Sixteen years later, in 342, there would be a serious mutiny which achieved a range of political and military reforms (chs. 39–41).

15 *offered in sacrifice by the Tarquinienses*: the small and precise number seems plausible; so does that of 358 Tarquinians later treated in the same way at Rome (ch. 19).

two tribes, the Pomptine and the Publilian: these lay south-east of Rome, the Pomptine consisting of territory taken from the Volsci and the Publilia (sometimes spelled Poplilia) to its north in territory annexed from the Hernici. Rome was now incomparably the largest city-state in Italy, and her growing range of allies made her more powerful still.

a law dealing with electoral corruption: Livy has not mentioned any previous corruption allegations, but that a plebeian tribune was prepared to put such a proposal to the people suggests that concern was felt by more than the still largely patrician Senate. Poetelius had been consul in 360 (ch. 11) and would remain a leading plebeian figure for forty years.

16 *Gaius Marcius and Gnaeus Manlius*: C. Marcius Rutulus, another leading plebeian, would be consul four times and be the first plebeian to hold the dictatorship and censorship (chs. 17, 22). One descendant would be Julius Caesar through Caesar's grandmother. His colleague Cn. Manlius Capitolinus was very probably brother to the valiant Torquatus, for both are listed in the *Fasti Capitolini* as sons of L. and grandsons of A. Manlius Capitolinus.

set the rate of interest at 8¹/₃ per cent: the heavy burden of debt on poorer citizens continued, but the economic reasons are not clear, although Rome's incessant wars on many fronts must have been one factor. In Roman terms the new rate was one-twelfth per pound of bronze money (*aes*, 6.14 note), but it is uncertain whether this was an annual rate or a monthly one

(Oakley, ii. 177–8, views it as monthly). If monthly, it would mean that interest equivalent to the entire debt must be paid over 12 months (together, no doubt, with part-repayment of the debt itself). Even if an annual rate, the repayment under compound interest would still be sizeable and, of course, would take years. This new limitation, whether annual or monthly, shows that the old rate or rates had been still higher.

16 *the Falisci*: the people of Falerii, 30 miles due north of Rome (6.4 note). Camillus had made them accept a treaty in 393 (Livy 5.26–7), but the Falisci like Rome's other neighbours had probably become aggrieved over her recent growth in power.

Privernum: a Volscian city in the hills 10 miles east of Setia (6.30 note; cf. 8.21 note), evidently very close to the new Pomptine tribe—but Livy depicts the campaign as the consul's initiative for his soldiers to acquire booty.

a law proposed in his camp at Sutrium: a unique procedure—which a tribunician law promptly prevented ever happening again. The *Comitia Centuriata* had indeed originated as an army muster, but for one body of citizens (Manlius' army) to act on its own as a legislature was unprecedented.

5 per cent tax on manumitted slaves: this law and the resulting revenue imply that there were already numerous slaves owned by Romans, even if the size of the slave population cannot be known. That 'the senators ratified it' (the law) refers to the *auctoritas patrum*: see Glossary, 'Authority of the Senate'.

releasing the son from his authority: on the *as* see Glossary, 'Money'. Licinius' illegal thousand *iugera* must be state-owned land, *ager publicus* (6.11, 35 notes). Sons remained subject to a father's authority, *patria potestas*, throughout his lifetime, but a legal procedure existed for freeing them. That one of the great reformers should fall foul of his own law is no doubt an intentional Livian irony.

17 *torches and snakes*: symbols of power and mystery. Snakes were generally seen by ancient peoples as sacred animals (the acropolis at Athens was protected by a giant one; see also 10.47 note), though priests bearing snakes into battle was fairly unusual. The Romans took chickens (6.41, etc.).

legates: anachronistic, for not until centuries later were individual legions each commanded by a legate (*legatus*). A consul or dictator, however, could appoint someone as his deputy in his absence, and this man could be termed a legate (see Glossary).

an insurrection of the entire Etruscan race: exaggerated, although some Caeritans joined the men of Tarquinii and Falerii (ch. 19).

reached the salt deposits: probably the important salt-pans, *salinae*, on the northern side of the mouth of the Tiber (so too ch. 19). This seems slightly likelier than the site called Salinae, beside the City walls next to the Tiber, where shipments of salt were warehoused. The new dictator's counterstroke would fit either interpretation, though.

constituted a decree: M. Fabius' rather legalistic argument was, in effect, that voting for two patrician consuls amounted to the people voting to permit this and thus remove the law of 367 that supposedly required one plebeian consul every year. There were indeed two patricians again in both 354 and 353, but this did not, in fact, violate the recent law (6.35 note).

18 *in the four-hundredth year*: Livy's reckoning is slightly out, for 354 BC, not 355, was the four-hundredth. His rather portentous announcement about the consulship is exaggerated; plebeians had not monopolized the office since 366, and plebeian consuls reappeared from 352 on (cf. ch. 24 note).

Empulum: perhaps in the narrow Valle di Empiglione below Tibur. Livy's uncertainty about just where the two consuls operated in this year is not the only case of contradictory Roman traditions. Conceivably, of course, both campaigned against Tibur, while Sulpicius alone operated in Etruria before or after.

I find Marcus Popilius: M. Popilius Laenas had been consul in 359 and 356 (chs. 12, 17), and would hold the office twice more (chs. 23, 26); like C. Poetelius and Marcius Rutulus, he was one of the new plebeian leaders. Livy does not say which historians termed him consul, nor is he listed in any other surviving source.

19 *Tarquinienses and Tiburtines*: Livy does not mention the Praenestines also making peace now, but Diodorus does (16.45) and there is no reason to doubt it. Perhaps 'Tarquinienses' here is a mistake for 'Praenestines'; for despite claiming that the Tarquinienses too were forced to terms this year, a few lines lower down Livy reports continuing warfare against them.

the Samnites: a large group of Oscan-speaking peoples. They comprised the Carricini (sometimes spelled Caraceni), Caudini, Hirpini, and Pentri, in the mountainous heart of central Italy between Campania and Apulia; in Oscan their name was 'Safinim'.

Caere: a rich old Etruscan city, near the coast only 30 miles north-west of Rome and long associated with her.

Titus Manlius: the hero Torquatus. If Livy is right about his youth nine years earlier (chs. 4–5), he must now have been only in his early thirties.

20 *on bronze*: not in any of the MSS., which have *in s c̃*, normally an abbreviation for *in senatus consulto*, 'in a decree of the Senate'. But treaties were not so recorded: since they were made with and ratified by the Roman people, they were engraved on bronze plates set up in temples—some later copies survive. The correction to *in aes*, proposed in the nineteenth century, is persuasive, for a copyist could have confused the two phrases.

21 *Quintus Publilius, and Titus Aemilius*: Q. Publilius Philo (8.12 note) and probably Tiberius (Ti.), rather than Titus (T.)—again despite the manuscripts—Aemilius Mamercinus, who were to be consuls together in 339.

Gaius Julius: he was perhaps a Julius Iullus, otherwise unknown but a member of the patrician *gens* that later produced Caesar.

22 *Manlius Naevius*: in fact Cn. Manlius Capitolinus; *Naevius* is a manuscript error probably due to his *praenomen* Gnaeus.

23 *the temple of Mars outside the Porta Capena*: the Capena gate stood on the south-eastern side of Rome, close to that end of the Circus Maximus. The ancient temple of Mars stood about a mile beyond the gate (cf. 10.23).

hastati and principes: two of the three infantry lines of a legion; see 8.8, Appendix 2, and Glossary.

24 *the front maniples of the Gauls*: Gallic armies never had such units; Livy simply uses a Roman term, as often.

the citadel of Alba: the battle had thus been fought around the western edge of the Alban Hills, 15 miles south-east of Rome.

army rich with Gallic spoils: the Gauls must have taken their booty from the territory they had passed through; ironically, therefore, the Roman army was enriched with spoils looted from their own countrymen and allies (Livy ignores this point).

Lucius Furius Camillus: son of the great leader. Livy is misleading about him restoring patrician monopoly of the consulship, for after Camillus and the aged (6.40 note) Ap. Crassus in 349, there was no patrician pair until 345 (ch. 28), and pairs only intermittently thereafter.

25 *Greek fleets*: if really Greek—Livy notes that their origin was not certain—he is surely right to infer below that they were from Greek Sicily (freebooters from Greek southern Italy may have taken part too). Between 355 and 338 Greek Sicily was distracted by internal dissensions, inter-city hostilities, and more than one Carthaginian onslaught. Piracy against vulnerable neighbours may well have resulted.

the grove of Ferentina: the meeting-place of the Latin League, perhaps near Aricia in the Alban Hills.

ten legions were conscripted: Livy seems doubtful about this total (though more confident of it later: 9.19), and scholars reject it, holding that Rome alone could not field so many troops in the mid-fourth century (Oakley, ii. 234). It may be that only the normal number was levied in 349, for Livy reports operations only against the Gauls. But with a population now of some 150,000 adult male citizens, ten legions may have been recorded at the time as the potential maximum, even if perhaps misinterpreted later as the total levy.

the growth of our power—riches and luxury: this dictum, one of Livy's intermittent moralizing contrasts between the 'good old days' and his own time, is at odds with facts that he must have known. Until recently Rome had had over 300,000 citizen legionaries in service. Even after Augustus' large demobilizations in 29–28 BC, about 150,000 remained in frontier or provincial stations. But that power and empire had degenerated the moral fibre of Rome is a cherished lament in Roman authors.

26 *a Gaul came forward*: the second famous duel between a Roman and a Gallic champion, again providing a new *cognomen* for the victor. That two

such fights happened just a dozen years apart, while often doubted, is not entirely inconceivable. The details of the two duels differ—this Gaul, unlike Torquatus' Gaul, is the Gallic leader; the fight is only briefly told as Livy is more concerned to stress its religious and marvellous aspects; and even the raven may be significant (see below).

Marcus Valerius: another of Rome's exemplary heroes, supposedly attaining six consulships between 348 and 299, and twenty-one curule magistracies in all. According to Cicero (*On Old Age* 60) he lived to a vigorous 100. Livy in this chapter gives his age as twenty-three, which would place his birth in 372. Valerius may have been the youngest consul in the Republic's history, though in 198 T. Quinctius Flamininus would be consul aged twenty-nine.

a raven suddenly landed on his helmet: a *corvus*, so that Valerius afterwards took the word as his *cognomen* (cf. ch. 32 note). The story is of course unlikely as it stands, but it might well have started from the fact that Celtic chieftains' helmets bore a bird or animal effigy (cf. Diodorus 5.30). A fourth-century Celtic helmet of bronze and iron, found in Romania, includes a large raven with outspread wings as a crest; another raven helmet appears on a first-century BC silver cauldron from Gundestrup, Denmark. If such a crest loosened and toppled over its wearer's face in combat, his opponent would certainly have an advantage much like the one Livy ascribes here to a live raven. Even if Valerius merely took such a helmet as his trophy, or just its *corvus*, tradition could eventually produce the more dramatic version.

made for Apulia and the Adriatic Sea: Livy's older manuscripts read *mare inferum*, 'the lower [i.e. Tyrrhenian] Sea', but Apulia is on the other side of Italy, making *mare superum*—the 'upper sea'—a necessary correction.

27 *so things should not be going too well*: for such bits of sententiousness see the Introduction, p. xxii.

a colony was founded at Satricum: the city had been largely destroyed by the hostile Latins in 377 (6.33).

ambassadors from Carthage: Rome and Carthage had struck an earlier treaty, reportedly in 509 BC; Livy does not mention it but Polybius gives a Greek translation and discussion of it and the present one (Pol. 3.22–4). It is noteworthy that Livy says nothing about the contents. Peaceful relations between the two states continued unbroken for another eighty-four years, until replaced quite abruptly by the first of the Punic wars.

from 8⅓ per cent to 4⅙ per cent: for the previous rate see ch. 16. The new rate (half an ounce per pound of bronze), if applied monthly, would be 50 per cent per annum, still a disastrous burden on peasant farmers or workers. By contrast an annual rate of 4⅙ would be a meaningful reduction even at compound interest. On the property tax see 6.31 note.

28 *the Aurunci*: a people, sometimes called Ausones, dwelling around Monte Roccamonfina near the coast between Latium and Campania. Despite Livy's claim, they were not Latins although later they collaborated with

the Latins hostile to Rome (8.1–2). The L. Furius now appointed dictator was either the consul of 348 or, less likely, his son.

28 *a temple to Juno Moneta*: vowing a temple in return for victory happened often between 345 and 265 (nine examples in Oakley, ii. 267–8).

Sora: a Volscian town in the upper Liris (Liri) valley, on a major route into central Italy; the town still bears this name. Its position made it a key contention point in the Second Samnite war (Book 9).

the prodigy of old on the Alban Mount: during the reign of Tullus Hostilius (Livy 1.31).

to establish days of religious observance: an unusual task for a dictator, especially as there was an established ritual to expiate such prodigies (e.g. Livy 1.31, 23.31). To include 'neighbouring peoples' in the observances, presumably the Latins and maybe the Caeritans and Hernici, too, was equally unusual. The Romans were evidently quite alarmed, and if their neighbours complied these too must have felt alarm. The Books were the Sibylline books.

29 *From this point*: Livy opens this chapter with a brief but portentous list of the great wars to come in the next century and a half down to 201. In effect, it closes off the period of painful recovery from the Gallic sack of 390, and introduces an era of challenges to Rome even more stressful and more epic. It is noteworthy that whereas chs. 1–28 in this Book cover the years 366–344 inclusive, chs. 29–42 narrate only 343 and 342. Livy's scale is already enlarging.

against the Samnites: cf. ch. 19 note. Each Samnite canton was self-governing, but the four formed a religious and military confederation headed by an annually elected *meddix tuticus* and a consultative body, which Livy calls a *concilium* and sees as a senate (cf. ch. 31). Relatively populous, with an estimated 450,000 people in this period (*Cambridge Ancient History*, 2nd edn., vii/2. 353), Samnium could field sizeable armies, well-equipped, disciplined, and ferociously tough (9.13; 10.38). In 293 a full levy reportedly totalled 40,000 men (10.38)—and this after decades of damaging wars with Rome (cf. 10.31). Rome's victories over Tarquinii, Tibur, and other foes made her a power about which the Samnites obviously felt some concern.

the Sidicini: a formerly Samnite community now dwelling in north-west Campania; their chief town was Teanum Sidicinum (Teano).

the Campanians: the name applies, in Livy, not to all Campania's communities but to powerful Capua and its subordinate cities like Atella and Casilinum. Capua (S. Maria di Capua Vetere) had been taken over by Samnite invaders between the 440s and 420s, but its wealth and sophistication encouraged Roman writers to complain moralizingly about Campanian self-indulgence, fancy lifestyles, cowardice, and other vices alien to virtuous Rome (ch. 38 note; Oakley, ii. 305).

Tifata: Mt Tifata (Monti di Maddaloni), 1,860 ft. or 604 m., overlooks Capua and much of the Campanian plain from the north.

to seek aid from the Romans: that this appeal did occur is now generally accepted; so too the First Samnite war in 343–341. Livy's account of the Campanians' appeal is highly dramatized; to some moderns, their surrender-formula (ch. 31) looks like an annalistic anachronism.

30 *they spoke very much as follows*: the Campanians' speech has echoes of Corcyra's envoys to Athens, appealing in 431 for help against Corinth (Thucydides, *History* 1.24–45). An evocative literary composition like this was expected to contain appropriate echos of eminent predecessors.

31 *gave the following reply*: the Roman response observes the proprieties, only for the envoys to trump it by performing a formal 'surrender', *deditio*. Similar but not identical to modern 'unconditional surrender', *deditio* was often offered peacefully by a people anxious to avoid a Roman attack or, conversely, hoping for Roman protection. Livy gives the most formal version of the *deditio*-formula at 1.38; a succinct form similar to the present one is Capua's later *deditio* in 211 after supporting Hannibal (26.33).

as subjects who have surrendered to you: the most crucial feature of *deditio* was that those giving it placed themselves and everything they had entirely at the disposal of the Romans. Their hope was that they would be treated mercifully, as could happen if the surrender had not been preceded by military hostilities. In 211, by contrast, the Capuans suffered severe punishment.

those who had surrendered: a voluntary *deditio* did not of course come into effect automatically, despite the Campanians' Livian rhetoric. The Romans were free to reject it if they chose; but Livy depicts the Campanians' emotive arguments as causing the Senate to reverse its views. This dramatic conversion should be doubted. The Campanians dwelt in Italy's richest region, and the Romans may well have calculated that it was better to bring them under Roman hegemony than to let the Samnites take them over. Roman historiography would not, of course, want to stress this point of view.

32 *a formal declaration of war*: Livy writes loosely, for the Senate had no power to declare war and could only recommend this to the people.

near Saticula: Saticula stood on the western edge of the Samnite mountains, east of Capua. Mt Gaurus was one of a line of high volcanic hills in the coastal Campi Flegrei near Puteoli (Pozzuoli), south-west of Capua.

compelled them to run off to the sea and their ships: the only mention of the Gauls having anything to do with sea travel. In ch. 25 it was the marauding Greeks who moved by sea and the Gauls were on land; here Livy seems to confuse the two.

this new cognomen Corvinus: a slip, for Valerius' new name was Corvus; Corvinus was an adaptation by his descendants down to Livy's time. Publicola, 'respecter of the people', had been given to early Valerii because of their measures to benefit ordinary Romans.

33 *No other leader*: it is rare for Livy to give an encomium like this to a historical figure. Papirius Cursor a generation later (9.16), Scipio Africanus

(38.53), Cato the Censor (39.40), and Cicero (in an extract quoted by the elder Seneca) are among the few others so lauded. Valerius embodies the ideal Roman citizen and commander, combining innate dignity with approachability and respect for others. Livy places his praise here in anticipation, perhaps, of the role that Valerius will play during the later mutiny (chs. 39–41).

34 *Publius Decius*: his *cognomen* was Mus ('the mouse'), perhaps originally given as a jest—or after the exploit related here (cf. ch. 38 note). Decius' heroic diversion tactic to save a trapped Roman army is told at rhetorically florid length (chs. 33–7), with the tribune making no fewer than four speeches. Yet the story looks strangely similar to an episode in 258 during the First Punic war, when a heroic military tribune with 400 men seized a Sicilian hilltop to divert the Carthaginians' attention and thus save the main army—though only the tribune, seriously wounded, survived. Around Saticula there are passes and defiles through the hills into Samnium, so a nugget of truth may just possibly underlie Livy's report.

only the hastati and principes of a single legion: perhaps 1,800 men in all (see Appendix 2)—rather a large force for a diversion. Livy may be reinterpreting his source's account in the light of his own stereotyped idea of a fourth-century legion.

35 *when the trumpet-call was given for the second watch*: night was divided into four watches (*vigiliae*) of three hours each, their length varying with the seasons. Livy mechanically envisages Decius' detachment performing the standard military practice of trumpet-calls to announce each *vigilia*, even though it was vital not to wake the surrounding Samnites and Decius himself commands strict silence.

36 *Let us quietly wait here for dawn*: another piece of implausible staginess, for in reality it would be folly to move through open countryside with the aroused Samnite army somewhere behind. Livy wishes to close Decius' heroic venture triumphantly, with the men's comrades seeing and cheering their return. This means that he has to depict the Samnites as still dazed and disorganized hours later.

a triumph in the camp for Decius: the phrase has a more specific import in Latin, as a *triumphus* was a formal victory parade (see Glossary). Livy's phrase is a metaphor, because a real triumph could be celebrated only by the general of an army.

or pull back within their stockade: Livy here envisages the Samnites as having one camp, even though in the previous paragraph they were described as 'scattered around the hill in small camps'.

about thirty thousand of them: needless to say, a fanciful figure. Not only were Roman historians prone to exaggerate enemy losses, but 30,000 is one of Livy's favourites.

37 *a further gift*: Livy's description of the gifts and awards is a mixture of authentic-looking items—oxen, tunics—and anachronistic ones like the golden crown and the permanent double rations. The 'fat and white' ox

would in fact have been a bull, for a castrated animal could not be offered to Mars (Oakley, ii. 353). Gilded horns and a white hide were standard for sacrificial animals.

a 'siege crown' of grass: awarded by the comrades of a soldier who broke a siege to rescue them.

Suessula: on the plain south-east of Capua and close to the Samnite mountains; Puteoli lay some 18 miles away on the bay of Naples, so Valerius' army had not very far to march. All these operations, if genuine, took place in quite a small area of northern Campania.

forty thousand shields: implying that the Samnite army comprised at least that many. Another fanciful figure: added to the '30,000' dead near Saticula, it would mean that the Samnites had mustered 70,000 soldiers—virtually their entire fighting strength (ch. 29 note)—and then lost more than half.

38 *the Paeligni*: a mountain people centred on Sulmo (Sulmona) in the centre of Italy, with Samnium immediately to their south and the Aequi to their east. What grievance the Latins had with them is not stated.

the uncouth jokes of the soldiers: these were about the consuls' names. Mus means 'mouse', Corvus 'raven', and Cossus 'woodworm'; cf. ch. 10 note.

a very unhealthy place for military discipline: Capua's reputation for exceptional moral corruption (cf. ch. 29) is useful to Livy as the way to explain the otherwise unsettling fact that a Roman citizen army mutinied. The cliché is later revisited when he records Hannibal's army wintering there in 216–215 (23.4 and 23.18).

39 *the calm that reigned amongst the Samnites*: Livy does not explain this calm, perhaps assuming that his readers will put it down to the Samnites' previous defeats. Roman victories quite possibly had occurred, despite his narrative's imaginative implausibilities, for the consuls' ensuing triumphs are recorded in the *Fasti Triumphales*. It is equally conceivable that the Samnites were not enthusiastic for the war.

Anxur: the old Etruscan name for Tarracina (Terracina) on the coast. The pass of Lautulae lay just to its north, where the mountains meet the sea.

Titus Quinctius: Livy views him as a separate person, different from known contemporaries like T. Quinctius Poenus or Cincinnatus; if so, he must have been a relative.

hailed as 'imperator': an anachronism, for this courtesy title was first given to Scipio Africanus in 209 (Polybius 10.40; Livy 27.19). It was awarded by the soldiers themselves, by acclamation, after a victory. The men perhaps called Quinctius their *dux*, 'leader', an undramatic term which later tradition might well change. The 'insignia of the office' would be the scarlet cloak of a general and the *fasces*, which symbolized *imperium*.

now the Appian Way: Rome's first all-weather highway, built in 312 by the censor Ap. Claudius (9.29); it ran originally to Capua and eventually to Brundisium on the Adriatic.

39 *Lucius Aemilius Mamercus*: in the *Fasti* his *cognomen* is Mamercinus; see
8.1 note on the relevance of this.

40 *so hardened as to spill citizen blood*: a bitterly sarcastic comment, for Livy
shares the revulsion of his fellow-Romans at the horrors of the intermittent
civil wars that had afflicted the Republic from the 80s to the 30s BC.

the hills of your homeland: Valerius means the Seven Hills of the City, then
much more visible from the countryside.

occupied the Aventine: in the fifth century, the plebeian citizens had twice
'seceded' in a body to force the patrician oligarchy to grant concessions on
debt and civil rights. The first secession in 494 was to the Sacred Mountain
(*Mons Sacer*), a hill outside Rome; the second in 449 to the Aventine. The
secessions symbolized rejection of membership of the body politic, as both
hills lay outside the sacred boundary (*pomerium*) of the city.

41 *on a second occasion to the legions*: the Aventine secession had been by the
plebeian soldiers in arms.

A military sacred law: a resolution passed by the assembly and backed by a
sacred oath sworn by all. This *lex sacrata* seems prompted by Marcius
Rutulus' secretive troop dismissals (ch. 39), but the connection is not clear.
Perhaps Marcius had added ignominy to the dismissals by striking those
soldiers' names from their proper place in the census list, making them
ineligible for further service with its prospects for booty.

because of Publius Salonius: otherwise unknown; the clause implies that he
had alternated in different years between being a legionary tribune and a
chief centurion, but the reason for doing so is opaque.

earning triple that of the infantry: cavalry had been paid at this rate since
401 (Livy 5.12).

42 *Lucius Genucius*: perhaps son of the consul killed in 362 (ch. 6). These
laws, like so much else in Livy's narrative of the fourth century, are debated
(Oakley, ii. 24–5). One aim was no doubt to make magistracies more accessible to non-patricians; plebeians did reach the consulship in some numbers
after 340. By contrast the ban on interest on loans was widely flouted, as
might be expected (cf. 10.23 and note). The point about banning two magistracies in one year is obscure; it did not apply to non-elective offices like
the dictatorship.

In other annalistic works: Livy's rapid summary of the alternative version
of the mutiny shows that he prefers the lengthier one he has narrated. As
he says resignedly, the only secure fact is 'that there was discord and that it
was resolved'. Even this is disputed by some moderns, but overall consensus now seems to favour Livy's conclusion.

with a lightning attack: the Privernates were last heard of in 357 (chs.
15–16). The book ends abruptly and suspensefully, perhaps to encourage
the reader to go on at once to Book 8. Norba, a Latin colony since 492,
stood on the western side of the Monti Lepini near Setia (cf. 6.30).

BOOK EIGHT

1 *Both wars fell by lot to Plautius*: his supposedly successful war with Privernum is suspiciously like that in chs. 19–21 for 329 BC. Here, in 341, C. Plautius' colleague is L. Aemilius Mamercus—actually Mamercinus (7.39 note)—and Plautius defeats the Privernates. There the consul Aemilius Mamercinus' colleague is C. Plautius, who defeats them too, although with a different outcome. The report here may be a later invention or simply a careless doublet by some annalist; on the other hand, the two sets of consuls are genuine (although in 329 it was C. Plautius Decianus). Probably in 341 there was a clash with Privernum that was inconclusive and later embroidered in tradition. If so, the confiscation of Privernate territory is better dated to 329.

against the Antiates at Satricum: here 'Antiates' and 'Volsci' are plainly meant to be the same, though Livy does not say so (and it is not strictly true). The Romans' victory here should imply that they recovered Satricum (cf. 9.12).

Lua Mater: one of the more obscure ancient Roman deities, also called Lua Saturni ('Saturn's Lua'); enemy spoils dedicated to her were burned.

Sabellian territory: 'Sabellian' was a less usual term for central Italian regions and peoples.

2 *the most cowardly of peoples*: this means the Campanians (7.29 note)—but Livy, inconsistently, has just made the Latins the prime actors in the invasion of Samnium.

3 *Thus an interregnum followed*: once the consuls of 341 were bidden to abdicate office early, concern arose that the gods would not favour them conducting the elections with their *imperium* thus diminished.

it was in this year: Livy's chronology is faulty, even though he implies that he had checked a variety of sources. Alexander of Epirus' expedition to Italy began in 334, not now in 341 or 340, while his nephew (and brother-in-law) Alexander the Great became king of Macedon in 336 and crossed to Asia in 334. The older Alexander went to Italy to help the rich Greek city of Tarentum against her southern Italian enemies. Despite early successes he was defeated and killed in 331, as Livy narrates in ch. 24—again with the wrong date of 327. Livy's interest in Alexander the Great, meanwhile, is fully displayed in the famous excursus in 9.17–19.

Both were from Roman colonies: Setia and Circeii were Latin colonies, not Roman (see Glossary, 'Colony'). If not a careless mistake, Livy may have in mind that, like every Latin colony, these had been founded at Rome's initiative.

6 *could also be fiction*: a good example of Livy's common sense rationalism, aware as he was of many earlier writers' proneness to invoke, or invent, portents. He does accept Annius' actual mishap and uses it for a further exercise in rhetoric by the consul Manlius.

6 *through Marsian and Paelignian territory*: in the Apennines north of Samnium—a very roundabout route for reaching Capua, so Livy's report is often judged just another annalistic fancy. Still, it is not implausible. A more direct advance would have had to pass through or near the territories of several Latin states and their allies. Moreover, this longer route would take the Romans into Samnium, which fits their rendezvous with a Samnite army. Besides, if an obvious direct route had been taken, it is hard to see why even a fanciful annalist would invent this one.

gods of the netherworld and Mother Earth: the Di Manes were the gods who ruled the souls of the dead, and therefore are regularly mentioned in Latin epitaphs. *Terra Mater* was of course where the dead were interred (in ch. 9 its other term is used, *Tellus* 'earth').

often in the same maniples: a piece of imaginative rhetoric. In reality, Roman and allied soldiers always served in their own separate units.

7 *a grim example for posterity*: the story of Torquatus the elder executing his son for breach of discipline, famous in Roman times, is generally judged a fiction and as perhaps inspired by the contrasting tale of Torquatus' own victory over the Gallic champion (7.10). That the story is fiction, though, is not certain. Such punishment was not merely a moralistic fancy: in 63 BC a senator Fulvius put his son to death for supporting the revolutionary Catiline (Sallust, *Catiline* 39). Some versions of the present episode, all the same, are overwrought—for instance, that Torquatus first honoured his son with a crown of victory, then immediately beheaded him (Dionysius 8.79; Zonaras 7.26).

8 *In earlier days*: here begins a famous digression on the make-up and fighting methods of Rome's fourth-century legions. Livy seems to have drawn on a well-informed source, perhaps Fabius Pictor or Cincius Alimentus, but either he has misunderstood some features or his source was confused. The chief problems are discussed in Appendix 2.

they manufactured the scutum instead: the *clipeus* was a round shield of bronze or iron, protecting the head and upper body, whereas the *scutum* consisted of two oblong layers of wood glued together, protecting the soldier down to the ground. Army pay dated from 406 (6.31 note), but the *scutum* became the norm only sometime in the fourth century: some ancient writers thought that the Romans copied its design from the Samnites (cf. 9.40).

a phalanx, like that of the Macedonians: archaeological evidence supports the view that the early Roman army was more or less a hoplite phalanx, a close-order infantry force whose main attack weapon was a thrusting spear. The Macedonian phalanx, with very long spears called *sarisae* (9.19), evolved only during the fourth century, just around the time when the Romans adopted the manipular array. The *hastati* and *principes* also had a short sword, initially as a back-up weapon, though by 310/9 Livy reports swords as their main weapon (9.35 and note).

maniple: literally 'handful' (*manipulus*). Roughly equivalent to a company, it was subdivided into two centuries (*centuriae*), each commanded by a centurion.

three vexilla: Livy uses the word *vexillum* in two senses, first for the troop detachment, then for its flag-standard (*vexillum* basically means 'flag'), carried by the *vexillarius*. Since he gives each detachment sixty-three men in all, his total for each group of three *vexilla* should be 189, and some editors amend the Latin numeral accordingly. More likely, though, the *vexillarius* should be counted as one of the ordinary soldiers. His notion that the third section of the legion, behind the *hastati* and *principes*, consisted of fifteen groups ('companies'), each comprising three different detachments for a total of forty-five *vexilla*, is quite mistaken (Appendix 2). It is clear, though, that the fifteen *vexilla* of *triarii*, immediately behind the first two lines, were maniples.

the accensi, the least reliable unit: in reality, *accensi* were not soldiers but the legion's servants, who played no part in battle; the term is properly used in ch. 31. Livy's stab at explaining why they were in the rear is fanciful (also ch. 10 note). The *rorarii*, in turn, were the legion's light-armed force, and he is wrong to place them all behind the *triarii*. In Polybius' time they were assigned to support the *hastati*, *principes*, and *triarii* (Pol. 6.24), a role that Livy implies in his narrative (ch. 9).

they would fall back at a measured pace: ancient battles were not the formless mêlées portrayed in films, which would quickly have degenerated into catastrophic chaos on both sides. After two armies' front lines clashed, if one line did not break quite soon both tended to separate for a space to recover breath and realign ranks; then they clashed again. If one line wavered, fell back, or (worst of all) broke, the second line would come forward in support. The struggle would continue in this way until one army finally retired in defeat or broke up in a rout, or until both armies separated from a drawn combat (see e.g. 9.32). Preserving ranks was vital, for otherwise the enemy could break into the line and initiate a rout.

'the action has reached the triarii': there is no other record of this saying, but the *triarii* were certainly a legion's last resource (although even they needed help in one battle in Samnium: 9.39). Their waiting posture in battle is confirmed by other writers (Oakley, ii. 464).

five thousand infantrymen: Livy's preceding details, including the supposed thirty *vexilla* of servants and light-armed, would add up to 4,725, but his calculations are muddled (Appendix 2). A fourth-century legion probably totalled about 3,700 infantry, plus accompanying cavalry.

two primi pili, one in each army: the term *primus pilus*, later *primipilus*, was given to the chief centurion of the senior maniple of the *triarii* (always positioned on the right-hand side of the line). Selected for his outstanding qualities of leadership and experience, perhaps even as early as this he formed part of a commander's military council.

8 *the Veseris*: apparently a river, but Livy creates a problem in putting it near Mt Vesuvius, for he reports the defeated Latins retreating to Minturnae (Minturno: ch. 10), on the Latium coast 60 miles away. 'Vesuvius' is probably a (copyist's?) mistake for a mountain nearer Minturnae—perhaps Mons Mefineis (M. Roccamonfina) around which the nearby Aurunci dwelt (7.28), or a height connected with the town of Vescia (ch. 11). Diodorus (16.90) does site the battle near Suessa, thus in Auruncan territory.

9 *in the section relating to him*: the sacrificial animal's liver was supposed to convey divine portents in different sections, one relevant to the sacrificing magistrate, another to the enemy, and so on. A natural gash was a bad sign, meaning that the liver was imperfect.

Marcus Valerius: Livy may mean Valerius Corvus, who as consul in 343 had won victories over the Samnites in Campania (7.38) and may well have been a pontiff too.

to devote myself for my legions: ritual self-sacrifice in battle (*devotio*), to gain victory for Rome. In Roman tradition no fewer than three Decii, all consuls, 'devoted' themselves—this one, his son (10.28), and his grandson, the only Romans so remembered. Whether all three *devotiones* occurred is debated, though the battle-deaths of the Decii are undoubted. The ritual details may be authentic: it would be hard to think of any reason why Livy or his source should, for instance, invent that the consul must touch his chin while speaking the prayer. Standing on a spear must be linked to the fact that this was the Roman soldier's original combat weapon.

Janus: as the god of doors, entrances, and beginnings, Janus often stood first in a series of deities invoked in ritual. Quirinus was one of the oldest Roman gods; so was Bellona, whose sole focus was war (*bellum*; cf. 10.19)—unlike Mars who had other functions as well. Her temple was built near the Tiber but outside the sacred boundary of the city. The Lares were the household gods protecting Roman homes, while the Divi Novensiles and Di Indigetes were divine groups so thoroughly obscure that even the meaning of their names was disputed—but Rome's tenaciously conservative religion continued to invoke them.

the Roman people, the Quirites: *Quirites* was the ancient epithet of the *populus Romanus*, and citizens were so addressed when assembled as the *Comitia Centuriata*. How the term originated was uncertain even to Romans.

arranged his toga in the Gabine manner: a ritual practice borrowed from the Latin city of Gabii, near Rome. The toga's lower corner was pulled up over the left shoulder and under the right arm to be girded round the waist, thus leaving both arms free. That Decius was 'fully armed' probably refers to his weapons, for the toga must have precluded armour.

10 *ordered the accensi to move from the rear*: unlikely, and equally so if Livy really means the *rorarii* (ch. 8 note). The Latins would not mistake light-armed *rorarii*, still less *accensi*, for *triarii*; these details look more like some later author's over-enthused reconstruction of the fighting.

who have transmitted an account: no contemporary or near-contemporary accounts of the battle are known of, so at best Livy means family records or traditions that later authors like Fabius Pictor, Cincius, and Cato consulted.

the following information should be added: this virtual footnote cannot be checked against any other evidence. No such substitute *devotiones*, or magistrates' failed *devotiones*, are known, although possibly some did occur without earning a mention in surviving literature.

11 *a preference for the new and foreign*: on Livy's annoyance with modern attitudes and trends see Introduction, pp. xxii–xxiii (but contrast the cheerier statement at the end of 9.19).

Lavinium: an important city and religious centre, near the coast 13 miles south of Rome, renowned as being Aeneas' own foundation. Its people were called Laurentes.

Vescia: just east of Minturnae (cf. ch. 8 note, and 9.25), but the exact site is unknown.

Falernian territory: the fertile *ager Falernus* extended from the River Volturnus north to Mons Massicus (Monte Massico) which separated Latium from Campania; it formally became part of the Roman state in 318 (9.20).

the Campanian knights: that is, the horse-riding upper class (*equites*). Presumably they had opposed the Campanian defection from Rome.

450 denarii: as the *denarius* coin was not struck until the later third century, this item could perhaps be a later invention. Possibly, though, one of Livy's sources converted an earlier figure into *denarii*—accurately or otherwise (cf. ch. 14 note).

12 *Lucius Papirius Cursor*: the first mention of the most prominent military leader of the later fourth century. Many stories were told about him and, in Livy's patriotic opinion (9.16, 17), he was quite equal to Alexander the Great. He may have been a grandson of the like-named consular tribune of 387 and 385 (6.5 and 11) and a cousin of the dictator Papirius Crassus.

Quintus Publilius Philo: despite Livy's sniffy putdown, Publilius was one of the major figures of Rome's fourth-century history, a plebeian leader with bold ideas for reforming politics and social affairs. Ancestors of his had (it seems) been consular tribunes in 400 and 399, but none thereafter. On his colleague Aemilius cf. 7.21 note.

the Latins rose up again in anger: this comes as a surprise after their supposedly decisive defeats the previous year, but Livy's claims of massive losses (three-quarters of their army at the Veseris: ch. 10) are typically uncritical and implausible. The 'Fenectan Fields' are unknown. Pedum was a small place near Tibur and Praeneste; since Aemilius proceeded to besiege it while Philo stayed behind to receive Latin surrenders, the Fields perhaps lay between the Tiber and the highlands of Alba and Praeneste.

12 *Junius Brutus*: probably D. Junius Brutus, consul in 325 and like Philo a plebeian, so that for the first time in history both emergency offices were held by non-patricians.

contrary to the nobles' interests: Philo is depicted in a fashion standard among conservative writers, as an anti-Senate demagogue. Similarly, his laws are automatically treated by Livy as damaging to the state, even though the upshot (as Livy knew) was nothing of the sort.

binding on all citizens: this first law is one of three reported with the same content, the first dated to 449 and the third to 287 (the *lex Hortensia*). The genuineness of the first is much debated, nor is the precise import of Publilius' clear (Oakley, ii. 522–5).

approve before voting began: the Senate's ancient right of granting or withholding approval (*patrum auctoritas*) of a law enacted by the people had grown increasingly irksome. Requiring advance approval weakened senatorial power, though senators might still try to block a proposal by withholding approval. Publilius' law was not as radical as detractors chose to think.

13 *Gaius Maenius*: another important plebeian, notable as the builder of the Rostra, the speakers' platform outside the Senate house (ch. 14). Strikingly, neither he nor the great Publilius Philo (unlike Marcius Rutulus, Decius Mus, or even Plautius Venox) had descendants of similar eminence, though their families did not die out. The Astura river is near Antium.

Conscript Fathers: for this phrase see Glossary. Knowing the outcome of the Latin war, Livy fashions an oration that displays two qualities that Romans most admired in themselves, mercy and moderation.

14 *a decision reached on them individually*: since Livy does not give reasons for individual decisions, some are puzzling—Lanuvium and Antium had shared in the defeat at the Astura, and Pedum had just been stormed, but all were granted Roman citizenship. This status need not have struck the recipients as a benefit, for they were losing their independence, but it was obviously preferable to being enslaved or expelled, and they remained self-governing.

Aricia: Velleius (1.14) dates its citizenship to forty-eight years after the Gallic capture of Rome, thus to 342 and not 338—unless his source dated the capture correctly to 387 (6.30 note).

a thousand asses: an intentionally large sum, meant to be a deterrent.

Their warships: Antium was not only a thriving merchant port but had long been a haven for pirates (the two callings were not always strictly separate). If the Antiates were barred from the sea, however, they soon got round this: Rome received complaints about Antiate pirates over the next half-century (Strabo, *Geography* 5.3, C232).

all the other Latin peoples: in effect Rome abolished the ancient Latin League, though respecting shared religious usages like the Latin Festival.

Latin cities not given Roman citizenship remained her allies, but foreign policy and military initiatives were henceforth directed by Rome alone.

Citizenship without the right to vote: not as severe a punishment as it might look, for the Campanians remained fully self-governing until 211, when the 'voteless' citizenship was abolished. Campania—meaning Capua and its dependent cities—formed almost a joint state with Rome, but its foreign relations were controlled by Rome.

the Fundani and Formiani: Fundi (Fondi) was another Volscian town, 10 miles inland from Tarracina; Formiae (Formia) stood on the coast between Tarracina and Minturnae. Fundi is found at war with Rome only a few years later (ch. 19), so perhaps these towns received voteless citizenship not now but after that.

'the Rostra': the word means 'prows'.

15 *the Aurunci be given protection*: on the Aurunci/Ausones see 7.28 note. The Sidicini were their neighbours (7.29 note). The Romans now had a stronger interest than ever in ensuring stability in those districts, but Livy's narrative again offers problems: a year later the Ausones reportedly were in league with the Sidicini (ch. 16).

Gaius Claudius Inregillensis: probably the father of the famous Ap. Claudius Caecus; the Claudii believed that they had originated from the Sabine village of Inregillum. C. Claudius Hortator (a unique *cognomen*) was perhaps a kinsman.

both abdicated: 'abdicate' was the technical term for a magistrate's resignation from office. Religious concern could arise from ominous signs at sensitive moments (a roll of thunder, even a mouse's squeak).

the Vestal Minucia: though plebeian, her family had consuls as early as 497 and 492. Minucia was not the first recorded Vestal to offend—three others had preceded her in earlier centuries—but the opening charge of wearing over-stylish clothes seems unique to her. Livy indicates, however, that her slave's evidence concerned unchastity.

to maintain her slaves under her authority: lest she set them free, which would make it impossible to compel them to give evidence against her.

the Sinful Field: or 'accursed field'. Even if convicted, a Vestal's person remained taboo to violence, so her death involved being shut in an underground chamber outside the Colline gate, with a lamp and small portions of food and drink, to die of starvation (see Plutarch, *Numa* 10).

Philo was elected praetor: until the mid-third century, many ex-consuls held this office. It too had *imperium*, and there was only one praetor until 241, giving it higher prestige than in later ages.

16 *Cales*: another centre of the Aurunci, overlooking the Falernian plain.

Philo as his master of horse: Publilius Philo's alliance with Aemilius' family was obviously continuing (cf. 7.21, and ch. 12 above).

17 *took over the army from their predecessors*: so had the previous consuls, according to Livy (ch. 16). But it is hard to believe that fourth-century

farmer-soldiers could be kept under arms for three years running: they had to tend their farms as well.

17 *had the force of an insurrection*: 'insurrection' (*tumultus*) had a particular sense where Gauls were involved, akin to 'national emergency'. Normal military arrangements were suspended: for example, exemptions from conscription might not be allowed (ch. 20).

a peace treaty with the Romans: Livy's phrase 'peace treaty' is misleading since the king had not been at war with Rome; it was a rather vacuous treaty of friendship and alliance.

the tribes Maecia and Scaptia: in southern Latium, linking the Pomptine tribe (7.15) to the rest of Rome's territory.

Acerrae: a Campanian city (now Acerra) 11 miles south-east of Capua, but not part of the recent rebellion against Rome.

18 *Marcus Claudius Marcellus*: the first member of this plebeian family to reach the consulship; the plebeian Claudii Marcelli were not related to the patrician Claudii.

the terrible climatic conditions: plague was thought to be caused sometimes by inclement weather, partly because, in low-lying places like Rome, heavy rains and flooding could lead to outbreaks (see also 6.21 note).

Quintus Fabius Maximus: another commanding figure of the age now appears. The son of M. Fabius Ambustus (thrice consul), he was the first to bear the *cognomen* Maximus, and was additionally called Rullus or Rullianus. A fresco in an early tomb on Rome's Esquiline hill may depict some of his military exploits (*Cambridge Ancient History*, 2nd edn., vii/2. 13, fig. 2). He famously did not get on with another grandee, L. Papirius Cursor (chs. 30–5).

a heinous crime perpetrated by women: this extraordinary episode is strongly dramatized by Livy. That there was an accusation of poisoning, followed by investigation and punishment, looks likely, for there was no obvious reason to invent it (no Greek myth as an incentive, for instance). No reason for so much wifely dissatisfaction is offered. The concoctions may have been medicinal—prompted by fear of the plague—which had deadly effects, as ancient medical potions sometimes did.

hammered in by a dictator: see 7.3 note.

Gnaeus Quinctilius: the manuscripts have 'Quinctilius', but the *Fasti Capitolini* call him Cn. Quinctius Capitolinus. If Livy did write these names, 'Quinctilius' might be due to an early copyist clumsily telescoping the second and third. He was probably one of the first curule aediles in 366 (7.1).

19 *Fabrateria and Luca*: Fabrateria stood in Hernican territory, but now counted as a Volscian town; Luca probably lay nearby. As Volscian Privernum remained hostile to Rome, the two towns must have decided to strike out on their own from fear of the Samnites.

The other consul, Plautius: Livy's account of how he forgave Fundi is another opportunity to highlight Roman mercifulness and moderation (cf. ch. 13 note), but he also mentions Claudius Quadrigarius' less flattering version in the next paragraph.

20 *starting-barriers*: for chariot racing, and Livy must mean that these were fixed (wooden) structures instead of previous temporary ones. Such items would have been entered in chronicles like the pontifical annals.

Lucius Aemilius Mamercinus and Gaius Plautius: see also ch. 1 note; see Glossary, 'Date for entering office'.

carrying the caduceus before them: this was an olive-wood staff symbolizing peaceful intent. Often carved to include two coiled snakes, it was also a symbol of the god Mercury (Hermes), and according to one theory may be the origin of the modern dollar sign ($).

Semo Sancus: another of Rome's lesser gods, named in full Semo Sancus Dius Fidius. The name Fidius, derived from *fides*, 'good faith, trust', shows that Semo's responsibilities included sanctioning oaths and contracts, which can explain why the faithless Vitruvius' goods were used to honour him.

21 *who believe themselves worthy of freedom*: the same Privernate reply is given by Dionysius (14.13), but it is made to the consul Marcius Rutulus in 357. Livy briefly reported Marcius' campaign against Privernum (7.16), without the anecdote—which in Dionysius continues with the envoy speaking as spiritedly as here. The dialogue, in other words, is most likely a later invention, and the ultimately respectful response by the Senate (and by Rutulus in Dionysius) is another self-pat on the Roman back. Nonetheless the tale rested on a fact: the incorporation of Rome's former enemy Privernum into the Roman state, just like others in recent years.

the ex-consuls, who expressed their opinions first: hierarchy ruled in the Senate, with a strict order of precedence when the presiding magistrate called for opinions. The ex-consuls had first, and sometimes sole, say.

to colonize Anxur: on Anxur (Tarracina), see 7.39 note. Three hundred men, plus their families, was the regular number for early colonies of Roman citizens.

22 *Fregellae*: a few miles down the valley from Fabrateria; it too commanded an important position, close to the confluence of the Trerus and Liris rivers—and its foundation provoked the Samnites (perhaps intentionally).

Signini: 'Signini', meaning the people of Signia (Segni) not far from Praeneste, may be what Livy wrote; the manuscripts' *Segnini* was not an ancient name. 'Signini', however, would be a mistake—Signia was too distant from Fregellae. Perhaps Livy meant *Samnites* but a copying error occurred.

Palaepolis: sometimes spelled Palaeopolis. Livy abruptly opens a new topic: how Roman power's extension further into Campania had a momentous consequence—the second Samnite war. Palaepolis was in fact Neapolis' (Naples') citadel (cf. ch. 23), though it had begun as an earlier Greek foundation on a nearby hilltop, today's Pizzofalcone: its name means 'old city', Neapolis 'new city'. The *Fasti Triumphales*, too, mistakenly treat Palaepolis as a separate city-state.

22 *a race stronger in speech than action*: one of various barbed digs at Greeks. Other Roman authors too, while admiring the Greeks of classical times, liked to sneer at their descendants.

his base camp: Livy does not state where in fact the camp was, but if the Campanians were thought liable to defect, somewhere near Capua seems plausible. His manuscript in chs. 22–3 presents other difficulties, including an actual loss in the wording, so here too a place-name (Capua?) may have been lost.

23 *where their commanders led them*: there is clearly a lacuna in the text at this point, though the extent of it is uncertain (see Oakley's note).

as 'proconsul': see Glossary. A momentous innovation: by command of the people, Publilius retained his *imperium* despite ceasing to be consul, and would hold it until the war ended. In 295 the same arrangement was made for praetors commanding in the field (9.25–6, 29). Eventually such extensions became a crucial factor in Rome's military and provincial activities, and ultimately would form one element of Augustus' supremacy.

appointed the dictator in silence: darkness and silence were better able to provide favourable auspices. The silence did not apply, of course, to the consul speaking the name of the appointee.

that the dictator was a plebeian?: the Romans took such matters quite seriously. In 215 this Marcellus' eminent descendant and namesake was denied a new consulship because his already-elected colleague was also a plebeian: a peal of thunder was judged a sign from heaven against two plebeian consuls (Livy 23.31). In 327 the resulting *interregnum* lasted more than two months.

Lucius Papirius Mugillanus: it is possible or even likely that Papirius Cursor also bore the extra *cognomen* Mugillanus (Oakley, ii. 664; cf. 9.15 note), so this could have been he.

24 *Alexandrea in Egypt*: Alexandrea was the usual Latin spelling until the first century AD (the Greek form is *Alexandreia*). Livy's date is out by four years, for the city was founded in 332/1 (cf. ch. 3 note).

Dodona: this oracle of Zeus in Epirus was second in importance only to Apollo's at Delphi. Livy's lengthy digression on Alexander of Epirus' doings in Italy is at least partly intended to set the scene for Rome's great war against Tarentum and its ally Pyrrhus of Epirus in 280–272. No doubt another reason for it is the bizarre tale of Alexander's fate.

Sipontum: by the Adriatic over 100 miles north of Tarentum; but as Alexander also fought a battle at Paestum on the Tyrrhenian Sea, far from both Tarentum and Sipontum (ch. 17), 'Sipontum' may be a mistake. 'Consentia' and 'Terina', in turn, are the likeliest solutions to a garbled Latin text.

rightly named Acheros: 'river of woe' in Greek; more commonly spelled Acheron.

Metapontum: a Greek colony (today Metaponto) south of Tarentum; the final home of the philosopher Pythagoras.

25 *Allifae, Callifae, and Rufrium*: Allifae and Rufrium (or Rufrae: 9.31 note) lay in the upper valley of the River Volturnus, on the main route between western Campania and Samnium. 'Callifae', though, looks suspiciously like a copyist's semi-repetition of Allifae.

prove to be auspicious, fortunate, and advantageous: a standard prayer formula (*quod bonum faustum felix sit*, sometimes abbreviated in inscriptions to just *q.b.f.f.*).

had returned to their friendship: Livy has not previously intimated any friendship between Palaepolis-Neapolis and Rome—quite the opposite (ch. 22).

26 *stripped and impoverished*: Livy apparently implies that the Samnites had loaded their arms and weapons aboard the ships, perhaps obeying one of Nymphius' various commands, and were prevented from recovering them afterwards.

sources that are more reliable: Livy fails to say which sources he judged as more reliable, and why (likewise in ch. 30). The treaty with Neapolis was on very favourable terms; the city was not tempted to defect to Hannibal when Capua and much of southern Italy did in 216–215.

27 *Another war*: yet no hostilities are recorded by Livy or anyone else. His ensuing story of how the Tarentines manoeuvred the easily fooled Lucanians into exhanging their brand-new alliance with Rome for one with the Samnites does not inspire confidence either.

enter the Roman camp: Livy does not state where this camp was, and why some young Lucanians should want to enter it. He is equally silent about where the Lucanian assembly and senate were when the young tricksters approached them.

28 *the ending of slavery for debt*: a major event supposedly resulting from a dramatic personal episode is often found in ancient writers—perhaps the most famous Roman example being the rape of Lucretia causing the expulsion of the Tarquins. On the fourth-century form of slavery for debt (*nexum*, 'bond') cf. 6.11 note.

a single moneylender: that the lecherous lender was named L. Papirius and his victim C. Publilius—the same family names as the currently prominent Cursor (then one of the consuls) and Philo—is one oddity. Another is that other sources give a later date for the event, 313, or different names: P. Plotius (Plautius?) and T. Veturius respectively—again aristocratic names. Suspicion must arise that the tale is a later fiction.

given the lash: no Roman citizen could lawfully be so treated (except in the army: ch. 32), for it was a slave's punishment. When St Paul stated to officials that he was a citizen, his threatened flogging was instantly stopped (*Acts of the Apostles* 22: 24–30).

28 *forced to convene the Senate*: this account bears a curious resemblance to ch. 27, where the young Lucanians burst into a public gathering and the resulting outcry impels the Lucanian magistrates to summon their senate.

29 *Vestini*: a small people dwelling around the Gran Sasso massif, east of the Sabine country. Why they should wish to ally with the Samnites is not clear; it must have been linked to the reason—not stated—why the Romans viewed them as deserving punishment.

such anxiety pervaded the senators: on the recurrent image of Roman anxiety or even terror caused by alarming developments, see 10.4 note.

the Marsi, the Paeligni, and the Marrucini: warlike Oscan-speaking Apennine peoples neighbouring the Vestini.

Cingilia: unknown, like Cutina; such upland centres were usually large fortified villages rather than towns.

30 *under dubious auspices*: a technical phrase, not a metaphor. The auspices had not given clear guidance: perhaps some of the sacred chickens ate but others refused (see Glossary, 'Auspices'). A Roman general would err on the side of caution.

they removed the bridles from their horses: Livy also reports this tactic in a battle in 426 (4.33), and later has a Roman general in Spain in 179 declare it a proven way to make a charge irresistible (40.40). Ancient military manuals do not seem to mention—far less recommend—it, but supposedly the horses would gallop faster and thus heighten the enemy's fear. The pugnacious Southern general J. B. Hood in the American Civil War recommended it, too. All the same it must have been an extremely risky tactic.

Twenty thousand of the enemy: certainly another exaggeration; cf. 7.36 note. Such losses would have crippled the Samnites for decades.

I find it in some sources: Livy takes care to show that he has consulted more than one earlier historian, but only after giving the version that he prefers. As he cites Fabius Pictor soon after (his first mention of Pictor in Books 6–10), his 'earliest authors' must include Fabius and perhaps the often-overlooked Cincius.

31 *called an assembly*: although the army forms the assembly, Livy in chs. 31–2 refers to it by the civilian term (*contio*: see Glossary). Nevertheless he views it as standing in ranks, for after a while we find the *triarii* at the back (ch. 32).

under whose leadership and auspices: Rullianus makes a patently false claim, for not only had the auspices been dubious, but anyway they belonged to his superior the dictator.

he was entrusting his life and his fortunes to their loyalty and courage: whatever the rights and wrongs of the case, Rullianus is here, in effect, advocating disobedience to the authority of the supreme commander—in Roman military usage, a crime as base as cowardice.

32 *regal prerogative*: consuls had the powers of the ousted kings, though each could check the other.

the rods and axes brought out: these are the *fasces* (see Glossary).

33 *Then the father, Marcus Fabius, said*: Livy now sets out a sequence of
speeches, carefully alternating from direct to indirect format, in which
first M. Fabius and then Papirius have their say. They enable the historian
to put forward both sides of a serious and complex issue: individual initiative for the public good versus obedience to constituted authority—the
same dilemma portrayed, for instance, in Sophocles' *Antigone* and, indeed,
at the Nuremberg trials.

I appeal to the people: Romans in legal trouble had the right to call for
help on their fellow-citizens, a right termed *provocatio ad populum*.
Originally informal, it came to be recognized as having at least moral force,
though it received legal standing only in 300 (10.9). In addition Livy makes
M. Fabius appeal to the plebeian tribunes—an odder item, since the Fabii
were patricians.

Tullus Hostilius gave way: in legend the first case of *provocatio* (Livy 1.26).
When the young Roman hero P. Horatius slew his unpatriotic sister and
faced execution for it, he appealed successfully to his fellow-citizens, and
Tullus gave way.

extricated the consul Lucius Minucius: one of the most famous stories of
early Rome. In 458 Cincinnatus was summoned from the plough to become
dictator and save Minucius' army trapped by the Aequi in the Alban Hills
(Livy 3.25–9).

35 *to appease his anger with entreaties*: Livy shows that Papirius Cursor's stern
logic has prevailed, leaving Fabius and his father no recourse but to appeal
to his mercifulness and moderation. Their success illustrates another moral
message: law and discipline need always to be tempered with humanity.
Papirius emerges as the grander figure, insisting on strict Roman values yet
prepared to forgive an honest transgression.

he would not further detain the master of horse: the standard statement by a
magistrate discharging an accused person.

36 *authority over the city*: Papirius Crassus was probably Cursor's kinsman
(ch. 12 note). Consuls could appoint a 'superintendent of the city' (*praefec-
tus urbi*) when they were absent for the Latin Festival, but not otherwise.
Since Livy avoids the term here, Crassus may have been left in charge
without a special title, or conceivably was the praetor, the next most senior
magistrate.

37 *Quintus Aemilius Cerretanus*: in the next paragraph Livy mentions that
some annalists gave the *nomen* as Aulius; and for the year 319 he names Q.
Aulius Cerretanus as consul for the second time (9.15). So 'Aulius' was
probably the consul's true name here.

war with the Apulians: these formed a loose confederation, like the Samnites
and Lucanians, while each of their cities—like Arpi, Salapia, and Teanum
Apulum—remained self-governing. In 326 they had made an alliance with
Rome (chs. 25, 27), so it is surprising to read now of hostilities. Nor did the

Apulians offer any resistance. Livy's perfunctory narrative suggests that the campaigning in both Apulia and Samnium was a later fiction to have some warfare in what was really a quiet year.

37 *judgement before the people*: another dubious item, for Flavius' proposal sought to punish Tusculum for events thirteen years earlier, in 338—even though Tusculum had suffered punishment then (ch. 14). L. Fulvius of Tusculum was seeking the consulship for the following year (ch. 38): Flavius may have been trying to block him in some way that later tradition distorted (Oakley, ii. 755).

hardly ever carrying the vote of the Papirian: Tusculum belonged to the Papiria tribe; quite likely, Flavius was in the Pollia.

38 *Quintus Fabius*: Rullianus again, holding the first of his many consulships.

Aulus Cornelius Arvina: the same man as A. Cornelius Cossus, master of horse in 353 and consul in 343. On his and his deputy's supposed exploits see ch. 40 note.

39 *died amongst them*: vivid as this battle narrative is, it seems entirely invented (Oakley, ii. 757–61).

40 *According to some authors*: the *Fasti Triumphales* list Fulvius as triumphing 'over the Samnites' on 19 March 321, and Rullianus over Samnites and Apulians two days later. Since the master of horse was Rullianus' father, thrice consul between 360 and 354, he must have been quite elderly in 322. If he and Cornelius were the generals, we are in the dark about what the two consuls—one of them the energetic Rullianus—did in office and why the *Fasti* commemorate them. Nor does Livy mention Apulia. His version arose perhaps from confusion between the roles of Fabius father and son, combined with the notion that a dictator and master of horse would not be appointed just for starting races.

illegitimately appropriating to themselves military campaigns and public offices: on fictitious magistracies, invented triumphs, and exaggerated exploits distorting the records of earlier times, see Introduction, p. xiv.

no writer contemporaneous with those events: in fact there was no contemporary Latin historian at all, while contemporary Greek authors paid small attention to events in Italy unless these involved Greeks, like Alexander of Epirus.

BOOK NINE

1 *a Roman debacle*: most of Livy's account of this famous episode (chs. 1–11) consists of emotional speeches, some quite long. Much of the rest portrays the emotions of the participants during and after the debacle.

Herennius: Herennius Pontius, according to a tradition at Tarentum, had conversed there in 349 with the visiting Plato (Cicero, *On Old Age* 41). Another member of the family, centuries later, may have been Pontius Pilate (Oakley, iii. 41).

2 *Caudium*: Caudium, the centre of the Samnite canton of the Caudini, lay across the mountains from Campania; Calatia stood on the plain about five miles east of Capua.

Luceria: a strongly sited town (Lucera) overlooking northern Apulia. For Livy to call it a loyal ally is strange, because he has not mentioned it before (strangely, too, he describes it as 'situated on a plain': ch. 26) and it soon reappears as a Samnite centre (ch. 12). Nor were the Apulians on Rome's side, for we saw Rome warring against them as recently as the year before (8.37, 40). Roman tradition probably sought to depict the consuls as over-eager to rescue distressed allies, thus excusing their military carelessness.

the Upper Sea: the Adriatic.

by way of the Caudine Forks: just where these lay is a much-debated question. Livy alone describes the area, but he is not precise enough for it to be readily identified. The site now most widely agreed on is the valley east of Calatia which narrows steadily from today's Arienzo eastward to Arpaia, until, at Arpaia, the broad interior plain of Caudium opens. Still, there are difficulties with this identification too; the much narrower valley of Durazzano, nearby, may be likelier. Wherever the Forks lay, Livy's implication that they led directly to Luceria is misleading: from the western borders of Samnium it is 80 miles at best, across several mountain ranges.

paralysis seized their limbs: such reactions to sudden frightening events are a stereotype that Livy, like other ancient writers, sometimes uses for vividness (cf. 6.40, 7.10, 8.7).

The legates and tribunes: on the improbability of legates at this period see 7.17 note. On Livy's highly implausible addition of two plebeian tribunes to the army see ch. 8.

3 *no plan of action either*: it is hardly plausible that the Samnites planned a skilful entrapment, achieved it, and then had to figure out what to do next. More likely this is a later Roman moralizing fancy—how the Samnites sought good advice, then spurned it, and afterwards were duly punished by fate.

4 *numerous attempts to break free had failed*: Cicero might imply that the Romans were defeated in a battle (*On Duties* 3.109), but his wording could just as well fit such attempts.

to send them under the yoke: a symbolic humiliation. Two spears were fixed upright in the ground, and a third tied horizontally between them, forcing a prisoner to bend double to pass under it. Livy's vivid description may draw on a later notorious disgrace: in North Africa in 111 BC, the Romanized Numidian king Jugurtha sent another surrendered Roman army under the yoke before releasing it. Only in 321, though, were both consuls thus humiliated.

Lucius Lentulus spoke: Lentulus' speech for surrender is paradoxical in Roman terms. Normally, entrapped fighters were expected to force a way out or die trying—but Livy signals approval of Lentulus in advance by favourable comments on his qualities.

5 *by a solemn pledge*: a *sponsio*. Livy emphasises this point because he does not accept that it was a treaty (*foedus*), and he has Rome repudiate the *sponsio* afterwards. It was a treaty not only for Claudius Quadrigarius but also for Cicero (with the detail about striking a pig: *On Invention* 2.91). Moderns mostly agree with them, even though Livy implies that there was a document supporting his view.

their military cloaks: a general wore a distinctive scarlet cloak, the *paludamentum*.

6 *the appropriate insignia for the consuls*: Livy assumes, rather improbably, that the Capuans had consular insignia at hand.

7 *were set aside*: 'broad bands' is shorthand for senators' togas, edged with a broad 'purple' band (i.e. a scarlet one). Gold rings were worn by citizens of high social status. It was customary to don shabby and even squalid garments as a sign of grief, personal or public.

they all hid themselves away in their homes: for further pathetic effect, Livy quite misleadingly depicts all the returned legionaries as City residents. In reality, legions were largely recruited from country-dwellers.

8 *not to honour me but to humiliate me*: a rhetorical but not logical claim, for obviously one of the defeated generals had to speak. Postumius, depicted as a nobly self-sacrificing patriot, completely overshadows his ex-colleague Veturius who, in fact, disappears from the story.

a pledge that was either disgraceful or essential: a rhetorical contrast only, for the pledge was paradoxically both. Postumius' argument is sophistry: as others soon point out, if the claimed 'pledge' was to be renounced, not just the two commanders but the entire army should be handed back. Livy does his best to embroider a weak case by giving Postumius the lengthiest oration of all, a two-part exercise in special pleading (chs. 8 and 9).

their sacrosanct status: plebeian tribunes could not leave the city during their magistracy—a fact that Livy knew, only to disregard it for this tale.

9 *formulae for the surrender of cities*: for the surrender formula (*deditio*) see 7.31; it is also summarized in the next sentence.

a three-day journey: from the Caudium area to Rome by road is about 150 miles, so Livy is thinking of a fast journey on horseback.

10 *Nine legions*: as improbable as the ten claimed for 342 (7.25 note), but here Roman tradition could play as it liked with numbers, since what supposedly followed the surrender is largely invented.

declared that he was a Samnite citizen: a Roman handed over to another state in punishment for a crime legally ceased to be a citizen; if the other state received him, he was regarded as now its citizen. Postumius' charade ignores the Samnites' refusal to receive him. Ancient international law (*ius gentium*)—the universally accepted conventions governing inter-state relations—treated ambassadors' persons as sacred.

11 *Pontius then replied*: even though Livy is essentially in sympathy with Postumius, he gives the Samnite leader an excellent refutation of the flimsy 'pledge' argument.

Go, lictor, and untie: the Samnites are treated as having lictors just as the Romans did, and Pontius' command is in standard Roman fashion (cf. 8.7 and 32; 9.16).

12 *the people of Satricum*: Satricum in southern Latium (6.7 note) was far from Samnium, so this alleged defection, and equally its involvement against Fregellae, are both surprising. Although Oakley (iii. 145–6) thinks that an obscure village near Arpinum also called Satricum is meant, it is hard to see why such a place should earn mention in annalistic records. More likely *Satricani* in Livy's text is an error for *Sidicini* or (better) *Sorani*—Sora stood near Fregellae (7.28 note; cf. below, ch. 16 note).

divided their responsibilities: the sensational Roman victories which Livy goes on to narrate (chs. 13–16) are suspect. The Samnites are repeatedly shattered in battle; Luceria—mystifyingly Samnite-held now, though supposedly a Roman ally in ch. 2—is gloriously captured along with Gavius Pontius; 'Satricum' is punished. Yet Livy finds no agreement in his sources about who was responsible for these redemptive successes. The only (just) believable items are some limited gains in 319 (ch. 16 notes).

14 *arrived from Tarentum*: this item too is doubtful. The envoys disappear, their threat with them, and Tarentum is not mentioned again in Books 9–10. At best a real Tarentine embassy may have been sent to observe the situation after the peace of 321.

the keeper of the chickens: see Glossary, 'Auspices'.

15 *was sent under the yoke*: a blatantly wishful claim, made by Quadrigarius as a surviving excerpt shows (Quadrigarius, fragment 21).

this glorious achievement: Livy almost casually reveals a dictator named L. Cornelius in this year (320), with the consul Papirius as his master of horse, but does not explain the appointment. The *Fasti Capitolini*, meanwhile, list no fewer than three such pairs in 320: C. Maenius dictator and M. Foslius Flaccinator master of horse; L. Cornelius Lentulus and Papirius Cursor; and lastly T. Manlius Torquatus with Papirius again. Livy somehow overlooks this unique event—triple dictatorships in one year—even though all were (presumably) on public record. On Papirius' triumph see below.

Mugillanus: the *Fasti Capitolini* list Cursor; for the possibility that he bore the extra *cognomen* Mugillanus, see 8.23 note.

16 *Frentani*: they have not been mentioned before by Livy, yet supposedly Rome was at war with them. They dwelt beyond Samnium on the Adriatic, their town is not named, and they reappear only in 304 BC (ch. 45). 'Fregellani', therefore, has been suggested as what Livy really wrote. Though Fregellae was captured by the Samnites in 320 (ch. 12), it reappears in 313 on Rome's side (ch. 28).

the Satricans: see above (ch. 12 note) for the possibility that Livy really means Sora. If Papirius Cursor captured Sora with its Samnite garrison, this would account for his triumph, which the *Fasti Triumphales*, too, list as 'over the Samnites' and in 319.

16 *his cognomen*: *Cursor* means 'runner'. Livy then uses this encomium as a link to his famous discussion of how Alexander the Great would have fared, had he lived to invade Italy.

capacity for food and wine: Cassius Dio (fragment 36.23–4) has a story of Papirius accused of being a drunkard but replying that he was on the go from dawn till late every night, and drank wine only to sleep.

pat your horses when you dismount: this seems such a pointless concession that some commentators suggest Livy means 'rub down'—in other words, the riders could leave that task to their servants.

A praetor from Praeneste: this title of Praeneste's two chief magistrates is confirmed by later inscriptions. Like Roman consuls, one or both could lead their city's forces on campaign, but, like all Rome's allies, they were under the absolute authority of the Roman commander.

17 *gives rise to reflections*: it is rare for Livy to insert non-narrative digressions like this, apart from character-appraisals like those for Camillus (7.1) and Papirius (ch. 16), but we can compare his descriptions of the origins of drama at Rome (7.2), and of the fourth-century legion (8.8). His lost Book 16 introduced the First Punic war with an account of Carthage's people and history. Alexander had died in 323, but Livy places his essay after the events of 319: as he himself says, his praise of Papirius forms a suitable bridge. Possibly, too, he follows a faulty chronology (cf. 8.3 note). On the digression see Oakley, iii. 184–206.

fortune, a dominant force in all human activity: a commonplace among ancients, and one of the dominant themes of Livy's great Greek predecessor Polybius. Livy's phrasing perhaps deliberately echoes his older contemporary Sallust's famous aphorisms about fortune (*Conspiracy of Catiline* 8 and 10; *Jugurthine War* 102). The role of fortune in warfare is also a commonplace, noted for instance by the experienced general Julius Caesar (*Gallic War* 6.30; *Civil War* 3.68).

Cyrus: founder of the Persian empire, who reigned from about 559 to 530. Livy must be thinking especially of Herodotus' famous account (in *Histories*, book 1) and Xenophon's lengthy historical novel *Cyropaedia*. Cyrus perished in battle in central Asia and his body was maltreated by the victors: the head was cut off. So was Pompey's after his murder by the Egyptian authorities in 48, following his defeat by Caesar at Pharsalus. In his lost account of the late Republic, Livy reportedly favoured Pompey over Caesar.

Curius: he, Volumnius, and the younger Decius were generals at the close of the century and early in the next. M'. Curius Dentatus' most famous victory was the defeat of Pyrrhus of Epirus in 275, which forced the king to leave Italy.

witnessed by the young men: an exaggeration, for Camillus' wars had been fought fifty to eighty years earlier.

an accurate picture: Cineas, Pyrrhus' envoy to Rome in 280, uttered this pronouncement when the Senate proudly refused the king's peace demands.

partying with his drunken army: Livy's discussion grows increasingly excitable. In reality Alexander had to fight hard in India, and nearly got himself killed. Reportedly he and his army held a grand carousal after their near-disastrous return march (Plutarch, *Alexander* 67; Quintus Curtius, *History of Alexander the Great* 9.1): Livy distorts this to make a rather snide rhetorical point.

18 *the change of personality*: a standard—and accurate—ancient judgement was that success turned Alexander into an increasingly capricious tyrant, much like his Persian predecessors.

I am reluctant to mention: the habits and actions Livy now mentions are well attested; they all date to the second half of the reign.

even the Parthians: Romans unwisely looked down on the Parthians, who had taken over the old Persian and Seleucid empire beyond the Euphrates. In fact, on their own ground the Parthians were a match for Rome: they had destroyed an invading army in 53 BC, overrun Rome's eastern provinces in 40–39, and then wrecked Mark Antony's invasion in 36—only a decade or so before Livy wrote these dismissive words.

even from hearsay: Livy writes with enthusiasm rather than care. There is plausible, though not decisive, evidence of a congratulatory Roman embassy to the king (Pliny the Elder, *Natural History* 3.57, cites Cleitarchus, an early Greek biographer of Alexander, for it). Other sources report embassies to him from as far west as Gaul and Carthage, making Livy's claim about Roman ignorance of him quite unconvincing.

ruins of Thebes close by: in 335 Alexander had razed to the ground Thebes in Boeotia, which had made the mistake of going to war against him on its own.

conform to their strategy: Livy skilfully turns around one clichéd contrast of republican institutions versus monarchical ones—that republics lack the focused control that a monarchy has—to show that, despite the regular changes in leadership and military forces, Rome always had generals who transcended such limitations.

19 *250,000*: Livy oddly does not mention that in 319 and again in 318, according to the *Fasti Capitolini*, censors were elected. The first pair had probably failed to complete their tasks. Those in 318, L. Papirius Crassus and C. Maenius, must have registered these citizens. Other sources give much lower totals, 130,000 and 150,000. Since census totals are not easy to evaluate, especially as manuscript numerals risked being miscopied, it could be argued that Livy actually wrote 150,000 (*milia CL* mis-copied as *milia CCL*). Besides her own citizens, of course, Rome levied further forces from her ever-expanding roster of allies.

all the way to Antium and Ostia: Livy is over-enthusiastic again, for not all the states and peoples named were yet Roman allies—some would be hostile for a long time yet. Thurii became attached to Rome only years later, in 302 (10.2), and stood not on the Tyrrhenian coast but on the Ionian gulf.

19 *stationary fighters who maintained ranks*: Livy completely ignores Alexander's use of cavalry, even though it was with cavalry that the king won all his battles. Alexander's phalanx was also more flexible than those of later times.

Antiochus, Philip, and Perses: these wars were fought between 200 and 167. Philip V and his son Perses (or Perseus) ruled Macedon, Antiochus III (self-styled the Great) was the Great King ruling the Seleucid empire from Asia Minor to the Indus. In each war, Rome won a decisive battle which ended enemy resistance, but Livy exaggerates in denying that there were any defeats or dangers.

never have we been hard pressed: fresh exaggeration—Cannae in 216 (to name one disaster) was lost through Hannibal's cavalry, even though the ground could not have been more favourable to the Romans.

20 *renewal of their treaty*: what treaty Livy means (and which Samnite tribes) is not clear. Since the alleged victories of 320–319 are fairly certainly invented (ch. 12 note), this request in 318—if factual—could be for an extension of a post-Caudine peace: that Livy narrates no warfare against them in 318–317 supports this. The picture of Samnite envoys prostrating themselves before the Senate is a ludicrous fancy; it is what many Greeks and Romans wrongly thought Persian *proskynesis* involved (grovelling obeisance: ch. 18).

Teanum and Canusium in Apulia: the two leading Apulian cities, yet in recording earlier Roman activities there (8.37, 9.2 notes) Livy has not named them; nor does he name them again after this, apart from the following paragraph—even though Apulia occasionally returns (e.g. 10.15). If this mention is genuine, possibly the Romans during the post-Caudine peace were trying to dominate regions beyond Samnium, anticipating fresh hostilities.

prefects being sent to Capua: Livy implies that these were sent regularly or even annually, but in reality Capua remained self-governing. The prefects in 318, and probably on later occasions, were sent to settle political strife between Capuan politicians.

the Ufentina and the Falerna: these new tribes brought the total to thirty-one (four in the city, twenty-seven outside). The Ufentina (usually spelt Oufentina) comprised the land south of Privernum down to Tarracina (now a Roman colony: 8.21). The Falerna was formed on the 'Falernian land' occupied since 340 by Roman settlers (8.11).

the Apulian Teates: Teate was the Oscan form of the name Teanum and its citizens were called Teates. The city was usually called Teanum Apulum to distinguish it from Campanian Teanum. Livy is simply repeating the item from the previous paragraph with variant details, probably having found it in separate sources under the two different names and in different years.

Forentum: if this name is correct, a fortress somewhere in Apulia. Nerulum, the other place mentioned, is unknown.

the patrons of the actual colony: the three commissioners (*triumviri*) appointed to found a colony became its patrons, an honour usually passed on to their descendants.

21 *a dictator*: Livy fails to say why one was appointed, or how he could take over command from outgoing consuls—i.e. at the beginning of a new consular year—and then stay in command until the start of the next consular year (ch. 22). Perhaps Aemilius and Folius were appointed for a civil purpose, ignored by later tradition so as to give them a prestigious military victory.

an attack on Saticula: for the years 316 (here) and then 315 (ch. 22) Livy records a suspiciously parallel sequence of events. Each year a dictator attacks Saticula; the Samnites come or (in 315) come back to its aid; they are driven off, and instead attack Plistica, an unknown site. The parallels strongly suggest that some of Livy's sources put the events in 316, others in 315, and he uncritically accepted both. The narrative for 315 is fuller and ends with the Romans taking Saticula and the Samnites taking Plistica, so 315 is probably the right year. If so, the war with Samnium was renewed then, not in 316 as Livy claims. Even on his own showing, renewing it was a deliberate choice by the Romans.

22 *the dictator Quintus Fabius*: Rullianus again, in another narrative distorted by later colouring, for he cannot have been dictator all year as Livy has it. In Diodorus' shorter report (19.72), he was appointed dictator later in 315 against the Samnites, and was the general at the battle of Lautulae—not a detail that admirers of the great man would like to bring out.

The new consuls: extraordinarily, Livy does not name them. They were none other than Papirius Cursor and Publilius Philo, both for the fourth time. Yet to face the Samnites, Fabius Rullianus was appointed dictator. Political machinations (cf. ch. 26)—or, just conceivably, illnesses—may be suspected for the consuls' eclipse.

The Samnites' cavalry charges: the sudden appearance of strong Samnite cavalry is another clue that much of the detail here is later invention (cf. ch. 27). On all other evidence, the mountain-dwelling Samnites had limited cavalry at any time.

Quintus Aulius Cerretanus: cf. 8.37 note. He was very probably killed in battle not at Saticula but later at Lautulae.

23 *over to Sora*: Livy last clearly mentioned Sora under the year 345 (7.28), though his 'Satricans' in chs. 12 and 16 above may be a mistake for it. Nor has he mentioned Roman colonists before. Following the dubious details here, we find the opposing armies marching for Sora but clashing at Lautulae, the pass near Tarracina (7.39 note)—about 50 miles to the south. A cautious surmise is that the Romans started for Sora but changed direction because the Samnites made a bold advance towards Latium, so that the two armies then clashed near the strategically vital pass.

23 *proved inconclusive*: a shameless claim by later tradition, for the upshot of the battle, seconded by Diodorus' brief account (19.72), reveals a serious defeat—as Livy himself implies (ch. 25), reporting 'total upheaval' in Campania and surrounding districts. The Aurunci/Ausones defected, some Campanians sought to do the same, and the Samnites apparently ravaged Latium as close to Rome as Ardea, 20 miles south-east of the city.

laden with spoils: this smashing victory, compensating for Lautulae, is a later fiction probably copied from the likelier victory in 314 (ch. 27; 28 note).

24 *returned to Sora*: Livy gives the recapture to the consuls of 314, but the *Fasti Triumphales* to M. Valerius Maximus, consul in 312. Even if Livy is right—a debatable point—his vivid account of how the feat was achieved is surely fiction.

25 *was wiped out*: this would be genocide if true, but rhetorical exaggeration is at work—though likely enough there were massacres, typical of ancients' treatment of rebels. When the Teretina tribe was created in Ausonian territory in 300 (10.9), the surviving Ausones apparently became Roman citizens (Oakley, iii. 301).

26 *situated on a plain*: a foolish error. Livy perhaps assumes that being 'taken with the first assault' meant flat ground (Oakley, iii. 317); in any case he obviously did not think of checking on Luceria's position. Luceria became another Latin colony, with a firm history from then on of loyalty to Rome even during Hannibal's invasion.

Ovius and Novius Calavius: members of one of the dominant Capuan families. Despite their fate, the family remained powerful there, with close ties to the Roman aristocracy. Livy downplays the crisis to focus on the political ructions that ensued at Rome.

formed for gaining magistracies: this unflattering image of late fourth-century internal politics (emphasized at the close of this chapter) contrasts with Livy's usually positive picture. The rise of new plebeian leaders no doubt sharpened political rivalries, not necessarily just patricians versus plebeians although Livy presents it thus (established elite vs. 'new men', i.e. plebeians). The factions were more complex—for instance, the master of horse Folius, prosecuted along with Maenius, belonged to a very old patrician family.

27 *level terrain*: Livy is unclear about the battle-site, whereas Diodorus has it at 'Cinna' (19.76) which some moderns think a slip for Tarracina. The manuscripts actually have 'to level terrain, the Campanian plains' (*in loca plana Campanos campos*): unlike most editors, Oakley (iii. 324) thinks the second phrase genuine, too. In any case, a site in Campania would be credible. Livy's vague account can fit the consuls coming to Capua but—no doubt remembering the Forks—hesitating before the various passes over to Caudium (cf. ch. 2 note). This would allow the Samnites to move into Campania.

the reserve cohorts: Livy means the maniples of *triarii;* 'cohorts' is anachronistic for the Roman army (see Glossary).

Beneventum: Samnite Mal(e)ventum was renamed when it became a Latin colony in 268, because in Latin *maleventum* would have the ill-omened meaning 'evil result'.

28 *a splendid victory*: although Livy exaggerates its scale, the victory was real. As the consul Sulpicius celebrated a triumph on 1 July, Diodorus' briefer account seems correct to put the battle early in the year. If so, the events of chs. 24–6 did not precede but followed it.

assumed command of their army: it is, to say the least, odd to find the experienced Papirius Cursor replaced in command by this obscure Poetelius. In reality, as Livy soon shows, ancient sources were at odds over who was dictator in 313 and who commanded in the field. Diodorus (19.101) even makes Fabius Rullianus the dictator, but this must be a confused memory of his appointment in 315.

recover Nola by force: Livy has not mentioned Nola since 327 BC (8.26); now we find it again allied with its kinsmen the Samnites.

Atina and Calatia: Atina lay 50 miles to the north-west, near Fregellae; Livy (10.39) reports Atina's territory being ravaged in 293 by Papirius Cursor's son and namesake. These facts suggest that Livy is wrong about it being taken in 313; perhaps the Romans took Atella, near the Campanian coast south of Calatia (cf. 7.2 note). Atella and Calatia might have turned against Rome after Lautulae.

Suessa and Pontiae: Suessa lay in Ausonian territory (8.15 note) and Pontiae was on the island of Ponza, south of Tarracina. An offshore colony was unusual; the aim must have been to safeguard the sea lanes between Latium and Campania (cf. ch. 30 note).

Interamna Sucasina: in the Liris river valley just north of the Ausonian mountains. With Latin colonies and a range of allies on both sides of Samnium, the Romans were in effect caging their enemies within their mountains while strengthening Rome's own dominance across central Italy. These advances, not surprisingly, had begun to cause alarm elsewhere, notably among the Etruscans.

Marcus Valerius and Publius Decius: bearing the old family *cognomen* Maximus, Valerius was son of the redoubtable Corvus (still active in affairs himself: 10.3 note). Decius was the son of the hero of the battle of the Veseris; he was a firm ally and friend of Fabius Rullianus, his colleague in all his later consulships—though Livy tells of a brief spat in the final one (10.24)—and both were censors in 304.

29 *the Etruscans*: peace had prevailed with them since 351 (7.22), but the leading Etruscan cities could not help being worried at Rome's resurgence and what it could mean for them.

what remained of the war in Samnium: see ch. 24 note, on the possibility that Valerius captured Sora in this year (312).

29 *to name Gaius Sulpicius Lóngus dictator*: the manuscripts have simply 'to name Gaius Junius Bubulcus dictator' and end the sentence there, but the *Fasti Capitolini* list Sulpicius as the dictator and Junius as master of horse. Oakley (iii. 348–50) shows that a copyist's slip probably dropped Longus out.

Appius Claudius: the first mention of one of the most famous Romans of olden times, the builder of the Appian Way. Originally Ap. Claudius Crassus, he was later nicknamed Caecus, 'blind', because he lost his sight. In 312 he probably was in his thirties, and was not yet consul. Besides his public career, he wrote on Roman law, left behind a famous collection of axioms ('each man is the maker of his own fortune', the best known, is still popular for school mottoes), and in 280 in old age delivered his famous speech denouncing negotiations with Pyrrhus. Despite his lasting reputation, Livy portrays him as essentially another 'arrogant Claudius', repeatedly emphasizing his arrogance and high-handedness—the cliché-view of the patrician Claudii that Roman tradition cherished. He reports Appius' important censorial reforms in minimal detail, some only when annulled later (ch. 46).

resigned his office from embarrassment: implicitly contradicted in ch. 33, where C. Plautius simply retires when his censor's term ends.

the Potitii clan: in legend (Livy 1.7; other sources include Vergil, *Aeneid* 8.268–75), they and the Pinarii clan, both patrician, had been entrusted with the cult of Hercules by that hero himself. Patrician clans did, or could, have their own family cults (as the Fabii did: Livy 5.46, 52). In one view of Appius' action, he aimed to make the Hercules cult open to all citizens. Another view, turning Livy's story on its head, is that the Potitii had already died out and he came to the cult's rescue—although the Pinarii remained very much alive.

30 *equipping and servicing a fleet*: as the Greek pirates affair of 349 shows (7.25, 26), the Romans had had no naval forces before now, despite their large-scale foreign commerce. Still, the fleet apparently comprised only ten ships per duumvir, and after a less than glorious outing a year later (ch. 38) it is not heard of until another inglorious episode in 282.

The flute-players: these musicians (*tibicines*) were a formally instituted college or guild, with the monopoly of performing at important public ceremonies.

in ceremonial dress: according to Ovid, who also tells the story (*Fasti* 6.651–92), and Plutarch (*Roman Questions* 55), the flute-players wore women's garments for their three-day party every 13–15 June to commemorate this incident.

31 *Cluviae*: a town not mentioned anywhere else by Livy, in northern Samnium inland from the Adriatic. When and how a Roman garrison could have occupied it, with enemy territory on every side, Livy does not say. 'Cluviae' looks like a mistake, perhaps for Rufrae in the Volturnus valley, taken by the Romans in 326 (8.25).

Bovianum: Boiano, on the northern side of the lofty Monti del Matese (cf. ch. 44 note). Rufrae (previous note) lay about 37 miles away by road around the northern slopes of the Matese.

lightly equipped, on a raiding expedition: yet in the next sentence we find that the army has its baggage and equipment at hand; Livy can hardly have it both ways. It looks as though he is working up an ambush report with imaginative details, such as the consul dismounting and uttering highly rhetorical remarks. Some scholars prefer Zonaras' report (Zon. 8.1, from Cassius Dio) of an annihilating Roman defeat, but Junius Bubulcus' triumph 'over the Samnites' in the *Fasti Triumphales*, and later his temple to Salus, goddess of health and safety (ch. 43 and 10.1), indicate that he was victorious, whether or not this followed a near-disastrous ambush.

twenty thousand men were killed: spectacular exaggeration again (cf. 7.36, 8.30, 9.27), and Livy kills another 30,000 only five years later (ch. 43). Were such statistics accurate, these losses would have crippled if not almost annihilated Samnium's male population (7.29 note).

32 *Arretini*: at Arretium (Arezzo). They later became friends of Rome (ch. 37) and later the Romans settled their internal strife (10.3 and 5).

tablet sent around: a wooden tablet (*tessera*) with the daily security password chosen by the general and circulated to each unit commander in turn. Here Livy seems to mean that Aemilius used it to issue the order to eat and then ready for battle.

withdrew in the dark: whether this clash occurred at all is debated. After a lull, next year the Etruscans attack Sutrium anew and are badly defeated (chs. 33, 35). The *Fasti Triumphales* do accord Aemilius a triumph, but if not just invented it must mark a difficult—and perhaps overstated—success.

33 *Quintus Fabius*: Rullianus once more, consul for the second time with the younger Decius Mus.

the Aemilian law: enacted in 434 by the dictator Aemilius, to the chagrin of the then censors Furius and Geganius (Livy 4.24, and below).

could not be brought to resign by any pressure whatsoever: whether this really happened or was invented later (the patrician Claudii always had plenty of enemies) is also debated. Sempronius' efforts at unseating Appius, even if they occurred, consist here almost entirely of one elaborate speech which nevertheless fails. No doubt Livy composes it partly to re-emphasize the traditional theme of Claudian extremism; but another motive may be to stress that Rome needs binding political conventions, limited-term magistracies, and moderation in office-holders. The political free-for-all of the civil wars had only recently ended, in which these principles had been mercilessly flouted. Nor can it have been certain that the new ruler, Augustus, would always observe them either.

34 *poll-tax payer*: an *aerarius*, the lowest class of taxpayer; they also increased Aemilius' taxes eight times over.

34 *in that five-year period*: the earlier Papirius Cursor and his colleagues had been elected censors in 393, and Rome had been captured by the Gauls in 390 (traditional date). Sempronius' point is that by not abdicating office when his first colleague died, Papirius had acted wrongly and the capture was a form of divine punishment.

alone in the censorship: though Livy insists that Sempronius had the approval of plebeians and patricians alike, by his own account three plebeian tribunes protected the censor. Appius' measures—he complains later (ch. 46)—had won much popular support.

35 *already under siege from the Etruscans*: arguably this siege renewed that of the previous year, which had ended after a drawn battle (ch. 32). Livy's ensuing narrative, though, crams improbably many events into Fabius Rullianus' consulship. Fabius wins victory after victory, for example (chs. 35, 37, 39, 40), receives two different senatorial delegations (36, 38), and forces Perusia (Perugia) and other Etruscan cities to terms (37), yet Perusia is soon at war again without explanation, and again is forced to terms (40). Probably many events are narrated twice over because Livy, as often, draws on sources giving varying accounts. One victory at Sutrium is likely, then a more decisive one near Perusia.

drew their swords, and charged: if this is accurate, Roman legionaries by 310/9 were using swords as their main battle weapon. The battle details, unfortunately, could be annalistic or Livian imagination (see Appendix 2).

Ciminian Wood: on the Monti Cimini surrounding Lago di Vico, near Sutrium.

36 *born of the same mother as the consul*: after the death of Rullianus' father, his mother presumably married a (no doubt patrician) Claudius. Possibly, then, Rullianus and his bitter political foe Ap. Claudius were relations by marriage.

some guest-friends: aristocrats commonly had friendly relations with their counterparts in other cities and states, even overseas, and when visiting those places would be welcomed as a guest (*hospes*). On Caere see 7.19 note.

the Umbrian Camertes: of Camerinum on the far side of the northern Apennines—an implausible information centre for men scouting an invasion-route into Etruria. Livy is dubious ('it is said'), nor are the Camertes heard of again as allies. Perhaps 'Camertes' is a mistake for 'Tudertes': Tuder (Todi) was an important and strategically sited city in southern Umbria.

37 *the neighbouring parts of Umbria*: a not very precise description, and these bellicose Umbrians very promptly disappear. They may be the same as, or perhaps a mistaken doublet of, the Umbrians in the following year (ch. 41).

sixty thousand of the enemy: an exaggeration extreme even for Livy, more than the 48,200 Roman and allied dead he reports at Cannae in 216 BC (22.49), one of history's bloodiest battles.

the area of Perusia: if genuine, this victory took Roman arms well into the heart of Etruria, but Livy reports another victory there later on (ch. 40) and yet more Etruscan peace-overtures. Probably the battle here is a mistaken doublet of the second (cf. ch. 35 note).

38 *put in charge of the coastline*: what caused Cornelius' appointment Livy does not say, but the new fleet cannot have been large (ch. 30 note). This may have been a trial run; the episode is too inglorious to be invented.

rumour nevertheless attributed defeat to the Romans: a neat example of Livy's unwillingness to admit the fact outright. This battle, too, surely occurred, for Roman tradition did not invent defeats.

the curiae: see Glossary, 'Comitia Curiata'.

curia with the first vote: voting order in the *Comitia Curiata* was chosen by lot, as in the other citizen assemblies; this was seen as giving the choice to the gods.

the Cremera: 6.1 note.

39 *had the bill passed*: Livy does not state whether Papirius solved the problem through a fresh casting of lots; perhaps the auspices assured him that all was well.

Longula: this must be a place in Samnium, although the only known Longula lay in Latium.

†...†: three lines at this point are obelized in the OCT. They are 'one of the most desperate cruces in L's first decade' (Oakley iii. 497) and we have, following the Loeb edition, decided to omit them.

under a sacred law: not used at Rome, this seems to have been a ritual form of military levy (cf. 4.26, 10.38, 36.38), to gather a force utterly devoted to its people's cause.

The engagement: serious difficulties in the Latin text (Oakley iii. 497–500) make it unclear who commanded the Roman army. To judge from the next stage of the war (ch. 40), most likely it was still Rullianus.

virtually new line: here for once the *triarii* fail to turn the tide, and the cavalrymen have to improvise as foot-soldiers. This unusual occurrence may be genuine.

40 *splendid new armour*: Livy's vivid description (for a similar but more concise one see 10.38) combines accurate details, such as crested helmets and linen tunics (shown in surviving Samnite artworks), with items used by 'Samnite'-type gladiators, like the shield broader above than below and the chest sponge (to absorb blood). The gold and silver shield-chasings, in turn, would have been too costly for almost any Samnite except aristocrats. Conceivably Livy's description relied partly on ornate artworks, which of course need not be realistic.

Orcus: the Roman name for both the netherworld of the dead and its god.

the captured armour: in Book 10, Papirius Cursor's son and namesake defeats another gleaming Samnite army and uses a huge haul of spoils to adorn not only Rome but allied cities (10.38–42, 46). Livy voices no suspicion that the one may be a doublet of the other, though in Book 10 he does note the similarity.

40 *vicinity of Perusia*: probably the genuine battle this time (chs. 35, 37 notes). The 'friendly delegations' from Etruscan cities, too, look like a doublet of those reported earlier (37), though Livy thinks they were different. The powerful cities of Tarquinii and Volsinii, however, remained hostile.

41 *Fabius saw his consulship prolonged*: that is, he was re-elected; he must have been exempted from the law banning two magistracies within ten years (7.42; cf. 10.13).

The Paeligni followed the Marsi: on these peoples see 8.29, where Livy mentions them allowing Roman forces in 325 to pass through their territory. Their hostility in 308 suggests alarm at Rome's recent successes in Etruria and Samnium. Diodorus (20.44) mistakenly has the Marsi fighting on Rome's side.

into resuming hostilities: this is very dubious. The Etruscans had just come to terms, and Livy treats the ensuing hostilities as purely versus the Umbrians.

the Pupinia tribe: one of the fifteen oldest rural tribes of Rome, a small and narrow tract of land outside the city's eastern wall on the road to Gabii (cf. 6.28 note).

Mevania: north of Tuder and south-east of Perusia. Wherever Rullianus was in Samnium, he had a long distance to cover.

Materina: possibly a district in northern Umbria by the River Metaurus and between Tifernum and Urbinum, about 45 miles north of Mevania. Inscriptions there of later date name its inhabitants 'Mataurenses', perhaps a variant spelling.

Ocriculum: Umbria's most southerly town. Seemingly it had not taken part in the Umbrian war effort, or else had soon changed sides.

42 *until he resigned the censorship*: another item from the same anti-Claudian tradition (ch. 29 note). Livy does not trust the story, mentioning it quite tersely.

the Sallentini were the enemy: these folk dwelt in the heel of Italy, so a Roman expedition against them in this period is peculiar and untrustworthy; likewise the one Livy has in 302 (10.2 and note). If Volumnius' exploits are not entirely fictitious—Livy is very vague about them—they must have involved some other people less distant.

Appius remained in Rome: yet his eulogy from Augustus' forum credits him with victories in Samnium, which must have been won in this first consulship because in his second he operated in Etruria (in 296: 10.18–22). The anti-Claudian tradition that Livy prefers may have transferred exploits of Appius to his political enemy Fabius Rullianus.

As proconsul, Quintus Fabius: Livy leaves it to his readers to infer that, after his victory over the Umbrians, Fabius Rullianus returned to Samnium.

a Hernican citizen: for the Hernici see 6.2 note. Livy does not explain why Hernici were fighting alongside the Samnites; they seem few, but how the Romans treated them provoked a full Hernican defection.

the so-called Maritime Circus: an unknown site at or near Anagnia, with a puzzling name since the sea is far away across the mountains. The refusal of the three important Hernican cities made the defection of the others much easier for the Romans to crush.

43 *Caiatia and Sora*: Livy's manuscripts have 'Calatia', but Oakley (iii. 357 n. 2) argues that Caiatia (Caiazzo), in the hills between Campania and the Volturnus valley, is likelier than Calatia, close to Capua (9.2 note). Sora (7.28 note) was almost 60 miles north-east of both, which suggests two separate Samnite armies in action—or else serious Roman inattention.

between the camps of the two consuls: Livy implies that the two were not far apart, but the ensuing narrative suggests otherwise.

Thirty thousand of the enemy: virtually the standard figure for enemy dead (7.36 note). Livy is studiously vague on where the victory was gained, only that it was 'in Samnium'.

citizenship without right of suffrage: the same kind of citizenship that Capua held, but with the extra restrictions mentioned. The magistrates of the loyal Hernican cities apparently now exercised authority over the defeated ones.

roads were constructed through the countryside: thus the example of the much-maligned Ap. Claudius was followed by the next censors, with no complaint (and no details) from Livy. One of the roads was the Via Valeria, linking Rome with the Adriatic via Tibur and Alba Fucens (cf. 10.1).

renewed for the third time: just what this treaty's terms were is much debated. 'Renewed' should imply that they were the same as in the treaty of 348 (7.27), but Livy may not be precise: the political situation in Italy was very different forty-two years on. As usual, he ignores the treaty's content.

44 *Piso*: the mid-second-century annalist (see Introduction). His list of consuls for these years differs from other extant sources, and Livy is right to doubt it.

the Plain of Stella: a small area along the north bank of the Volturnus, renowned for its fertility. As the Samnites probably held Caiatia, just to the east (ch. 43 note), raiding was easy.

Tifernum: the name for the Monti del Matese massif between central Samnium and Campania; Livy seems to think it a town or village. Bovianum lay on its Samnite side. Another Tifernum lay in Umbria: 10.31.

at the third watch: i.e. in the dead of night (7.35 note).

Minucius engaged the enemy: it is strange that the Samnites should choose to fight one Roman army while another stood nearby, clearly awaiting its opportunity. If Livy envisaged Postumius' troops hiding until then, he should have made this clear.

44 *Marcus Fulvius became suffect consul*: see Glossary, 'Suffect consul'. The *Fasti Triumphales* list him, not Minucius, as triumphing late in the year 'over the Samnites'. This is the first attested appointment of a suffect consul.

Arpinum, and Cesennia: Arpinum, the birthplace of Cicero, was a strongly fortified Volscian city in the Liris valley, but neither place had been Roman-controlled hitherto. 'Cesennia' (with varying manuscript spellings) is unknown and may be a manuscript mistake, e.g. for Cisauna, which the Romans captured, or recaptured, some years later (10.12 note).

45 *found it peaceful*: by contrast the *Fasti Triumphales* register Sulpicius triumphing 'over the Samnites', presumably utilizing other sources that told of further fighting. A one-sentence report in Diodorus (20.101) agrees with Livy.

restored to them: Livy means the treaty of 354 (7.19), but, far more likely, the new treaty recognized Roman control over Campania and other regions.

the Aequi: on this highland people see 6.2 note.

Roman citizenship would be a punishment: certainly it was not always a boon in this era. Voting required travelling to Rome, seeking office needed support from Roman aristocrats, and communal benefits like roads and aqueducts were rare if the community lay off the beaten track. Moreover, every community had its own religious cults and sanctuaries, reinforcing feelings of local identity which a wider citizenship might weaken.

captured forty-one strongholds in fifty days: some manuscripts have 'thirty-one'. The Aequi were quite a small people by 304; if not mere fiction, these 'strongholds' must have included villages, fortified lookouts, and even strongly walled farms.

almost wiped out: standard historiographical exaggeration, for in 302 (10.1) we find the Aequi back in arms and an Aequan army on the attack.

46 *the son of a freedman father*: a Roman's legally freed slave became a citizen, though subject to some restrictions including inability to hold office. None applied to sons born after he became free, but social acceptability was still hard to gain. Livy soon implies that Cn. Flavius was supported by Ap. Claudius.

some annalistic works: one account that survives is Piso's, quoted by the later author Aulus Gellius. It is in a (deliberately?) bald, unsophisticated style: for instance, almost every sentence begins 'Gnaeus Flavius, son of Annius'. Annius is also the father's *praenomen* in Cicero and Pliny the Elder; Livy's 'son of Gnaeus' looks like a copyist's error, *An. filius* becoming the better-known *Cn. filius* (Oakley, iii. 604)—or perhaps just a careless repetition of Cn. Flavius' own *praenomen*.

Licinius Macer claims: the extensive career he gave Flavius is not corroborated by the other writers on the aedile's doings, and looks invented (cf. next note).

the night-watch: probably meaning the *triumviri capitales*, junior magistrates whose duties included patrolling the city by night—but the office was not introduced until after 293, for Livy recorded it in his lost Book 11. Triumvirates for establishing colonies, on the other hand, were frequent (e.g. 8.16, and ch. 28 above; see Glossary, 'Boards').

hidden away in the inner sanctum of the pontiffs: presumably in the Regia, the official residence of the Pontifex Maximus beside the Forum. The 'articles of civil law' were, it seems, the rules for the procedures governing civil litigation. The Roman calendar, a complex affair (see Glossary, 'Calendar'), showed on which days legal cases could and could not be heard, and those when the Senate and the various *Comitia* could assemble. When such documents could be consulted only by magistrates and priests (largely, of course, members of Rome's elite), the ordinary citizen—even if well-to-do— was at their mercy over correct procedures and dates.

temple of Vulcan: this and Flavius' temple of Concord seem to have stood in or near the Forum; neither survives. Concord, goddess of civil harmony, was chosen no doubt to emphasize that Flavius' actions promoted the well-being of society, whereas the aristocracy's attitudes did not—hence their mortification.

Cornelius Barbatus: probably a Scipio, several of whom were prominent in this period. Before a temple could be dedicated, the pontiff had to grasp its door-post and recite the proper formula; only then could the magistrate performing the dedicatory rites proceed.

did not stand up: rising, then and now, showed respect for a magistrate or a senior citizen.

the seat conferred by his office: Piso makes the added point, glossed over by Livy, that Flavius placed his curule chair in the doorway so that no one could leave the room.

the Forum faction: cf. ch. 26 note. Even if such a faction existed, it is not obvious how strong it really was. Cn. Flavius is the only magistrate reported as a member. Livy's added claim that henceforth the state 'fell into two parts' has no real supporting evidence—the contests between patricians and plebeians were already almost two hundred years old. It resembles, and surely reflects, the equally stereotyped view that the late Republic's party-politics pitted Optimates against Populares.

corrupted: educated and well-to-do Romans almost invariably believed that the more influence poorer people had on political life, the more the state became prey to corruption and risked anarchy.

set aside their gold rings and horse-medallions: to signify deep grief (ch. 7 and note). Horse-medallions (*phalerae*) were often embellished with gold or silver by wealthy cavalrymen, and might also be awarded as prizes for valour.

became censors: in 304–303; taken literally, then, Livy's alleged 'Forum faction' operated for under two years.

called 'urban': the city itself had been allocated four tribes long ago, as Livy himself recorded (1.43). So—unless he has simply forgotten this—here he must mean that Fabius now named these the 'urban' tribes. Yet it is not easy to see what else they could have been called during the previous centuries.

46 *the knights*: the cavalrymen (*equites*) who rode warhorses supplied by the state; they rode in splendid array through the city on the 15th (Ides) of July in honour of the Heavenly Twins, Castor and Pollux. Livy's contemporary Dionysius, though, dates the the parade to 496 (Dionysius 6.13).

BOOK TEN

1 *Alba*: in full Alba Fucens, 60 road miles east of Rome, a strategic site on the Via Valeria through the central Apennines and on the northern edge of the Fucine Lake (now a broad plain) below the impressive 2,487-metre M. Velino.

were granted citizenship: citizenship without the vote—Arpinum became a full citizen town only in 188. Of the five cities named Trebula, Livy probably means Trebula Suffenas just east of Tibur. Frusino acquired voteless citizenship too, on other evidence. The grants may have been as much for closer control as for a reward.

a certain cavern: a strange story, involving a cavern apparently big enough to admit one or more military units in regular array. Where the brigands came from is not stated, nor is the Roman commander named.

Bubulcus was appointed dictator: the consul Aemilius was supposedly in the south of Italy (ch. 2), but Livy does not say why his colleague did not take command; perhaps he was ill. The *Fasti Triumphales* also list Bubulcus as triumphing 'over the Aequi', in late August.

2 *Thuriae in the land of the Sallentini*: there was no such city; Livy probably mislays the Greek colony Thurii, south of Tarentum.

in a single battle: it is very unlikely that Cleonymus fought against the Romans. Diodorus in a fairly detailed account (20.104–5) mentions no such clash, despite claiming—wrongly—that Tarentum was at war with both Rome and the nearby Lucanians. The circumstantial story of Cleonymus then being worsted in northern Italy by Livy's countrymen, the Patavians, is equally hard to believe. Perhaps some of his forces were blown off course and had these adventures, which Patavian memories afterwards amplified.

the Veneti: they dwelt around the head of the Adriatic. Their name would be taken by the city founded on offshore islands there in the early Middle Ages.

the River Meduacus: the Brenta, which flows from the Alps to the Adriatic below Padua.

3 *Cilnian family*: Augustus' famous friend C. Maecenas, the poet Horace's patron, was of this family on his mother's side.

Carseoli: 40 miles east of Rome on the road to Alba Fucens. Carseoli lay not in the territory of the Marsi but of the Aequicoli, as Livy himself later states when reporting its foundation, more reliably, in 298 (ch. 13).

Marcus Valerius Maximus: in the *Fasti Triumphales* he is called M. Valerius Corvus. This was probably the famous Corvus (7.26), though some scholars think that he was the son, consul in 312 (9.28). The elder Corvus, aged twenty-three in 348, would now be seventy, but he had two further consulships to come.

the error arose from the cognomen 'Maximus': as masters of horse the *Fasti Capitolini* list both Fabius Rullianus and, after he abdicated, Aemilius Paulus. Livy's point about the *cognomen* is not clear, for the question was not whether Valerius Maximus or Fabius Maximus Rullianus was dictator but whether Fabius or Aemilius was master of horse.

Milionia, Plestina, and Fresilia: unknown places, probably hilltop forts.

4 *the panic it generated*: Livy repeatedly depicts terror gripping Rome when bad news arrives (also 8.29, 39; 9.38, 39, 43; 10.1, 10, 11, 13, 26). There would be little reliable evidence for this, except perhaps in ch. 26, and as a literary cliché it wears thin. The defeat can be cautiously believed but, as Livy himself hints, it was probably just a skirmish.

Rusellae: near the Tyrrhenian coast 90 miles north-west of Rome. That the Romans could advance so far before meeting Etruscan forces suggests that these came from central and northern Etruscan cities—e.g. Rusellae, Vetulonia, and Volaterrae. Volsinii, Perusia, and Arretium had made peace with Rome, as had Tarquinii (9.37, 41).

5 *the Etruscan legions*: on Livy's use of Roman military terms for non-Roman armies, cf. 7.31, 32.

with the plebs: this much less dramatic version of events in Etruria may look more plausible than the exciting battle just narrated. Yet the two-year truce should have been on record, like other pacts, and Valerius in the *Fasti Triumphales* celebrates a triumph 'over the Etruscans and Marsi'.

6 *not be tranquillity in all quarters*: on this literary trope see 7.1 note, and ch. 1 note above.

Quintus and Gnaeus Ogulnius: brothers and young men—Quintus was consul thirty-one years later, and dictator in 257 (no doubt a venerable figure by then). Despite opening membership of the two chief priestly colleges to plebeians, they were no friends of Ap. Claudius Caecus, if indeed he opposed their law (ch. 7). Livy's remark about their political opportunism shows that he dislikes them almost as much as he dislikes Appius.

from the plebs: the proposal did mark a telling stage in the long struggle between patricians and plebeians. With most legal and economic restrictions on ordinary citizens now eased or abolished, the ruling elite was joined by more and more plebeians: Publilius Philo, Decius Mus father and son, Junius Bubulcus, and Sempronius Sophus were merely the most obvious examples. Purely patrician priesthoods were now clearly anachronistic.

the death of two of its members: Livy's point is opaquely put. He means that six augurs might be expected to be in office, but at this time there were only four. Apparently at all times the number of augurs should be divisible by three, a feature for which Livy's explanation seems as good as any. What evidence he had for four augurs at this time he does not say.

6 *Ramnes, Titienses, and Luceres*: according to Roman legend, the first Romans were divided into these tribes by Romulus.

7 *revisited the arguments*: put by Ap. Claudius Crassus in 6.40–1. Despite disliking the Ogulnius brothers, Livy admires Decius Mus and—in essence—the principle that Decius defends, so he gives him a lengthy speech.

the embroidered toga: this and the palm-motif tunic, together with the triumphal crown and laurel wreath, were worn by a triumphator (see Glossary, 'Triumph'). As Decius implies, the Romans held that in these garments the triumphator represented Jupiter himself.

ancestral mask: wax busts portraying an eminent Roman's ancestors, each with an inscription listing the forebear's offices and other achievements, were displayed in the atrium of the eminent man's house and in public at his funeral.

8 *decemvirs in charge of sacred rites*: see Glossary.

Attius Claudius or Appius Claudius: Attius or Attus Clausus, a grandee from the Sabine country north of Rome, had migrated to Rome with 5,000 followers in 504, Romanized his name, and became consul in 495 (Livy 2.16, 21). In another version, his *praenomen* was Atta and he migrated in Romulus' time.

you alone have a clan: i.e., belong to recognized clans (*gentes*).

9 *tribunes were intimidated*: Livy means the tribunes who had vetoed summoning the tribes (the Council of the Plebs), but he neither names them nor explains why they had used their veto.

by the same family: the earlier 'Valerian laws' of 508 and 449 establishing *provocatio*, the right of appeal, are dubious (Oakley, iv. 120–34). Livy recognizes this, but tries to account for the repetitions.

Porcian law: enacted in the early second century BC by a tribune or praetor named Porcius Laeca (not by M. Porcius Cato the Censor). A descendant of Laeca who was a mint-master in 110 or 109 struck coins lauding *provocatio*.

Nequinum in Umbria: since all Umbria had supposedly surrendered in 307 (9.41), Livy should but does not explain why this operation was needed. It looks an aggressive act, aimed at strengthening Rome in relations with her not entirely friendly Umbrian neighbours.

from declaring this as a fact: another instructive example of Livy's problems with his sources and with assessing them. He clearly prefers the accounts of Macer and Tubero, as he can use them to depict Fabius Rullianus' exemplary civic modesty (cf. ch. 13 note), but he is scrupulous about including Piso's too. His own effort to explain the contradiction is flimsy (another 'mixup' due to the shared *cognomen* Maximus: cf. ch. 3), and this time Piso may have been right (Oakley, iv. 139–44).

the Aniensis and the Terentina: the latter, officially spelt Teretina, lay along the coast between Minturnae and the Volturnus, incorporating Auruncan/ Ausonian territory and connecting the Oufentina to the north with the Falerna to the south (cf. 9.20). The Aniensis lay east of Rome, along the River Anio (Aniene).

10 *called Narnia, after its river*: for Romans, 'Nequinum' sounded unattractively similar to *nequam*, 'worthless'. The River Nar (Nera) flows below Narnia's spectacular cliffs.

Picenum: the region between Umbria and the Adriatic. To its north lay Gallic territory, which no doubt explains the Picentes' readiness for a treaty with Rome.

11 *Marcus Valerius*: Livy fails to say whether this was Corvus again or Corvus' son, but the *Fasti Capitolini* register the elder man, who would now be seventy-two and who thus attained his sixth consulship.

Picentes were thanked: they later fell out with their Roman allies, lost a war in 269–268, and suffered serious confiscations of territory.

the same application: Livy seems to imply that the grain problem was mentioned only in the sources who had Fabius Rullianus as curule aedile (ch. 9 note), a version that probably began with his descendant Fabius Pictor.

Lucius Cornelius Scipio: great-grandfather of Scipio Africanus. His extra *cognomen* Barbatus appears in the oldest surviving Scipio family epitaph, inscribed on the tomb of the Scipios beside the Appian Way (next note).

12 *Etruria fell to Scipio and the Samnites to Fulvius*: Scipio Barbatus' own surviving epitaph (H. Dessau, *Inscriptiones Latinae Selectae* (Berlin, 1882– 1916), no. 1) states that he captured *Taurasia Cisauna Samnio* ('Taurasia, Cisauna in(?) Samnium') and took hostages after subduing *Loucana* (Lucania). This obviously puts in question Livy's accuracy. Scholars, on the whole, prefer the epitaph—believing that it reports Scipio's actions when consul in 298. Yet if in reality Scipio, not Fulvius, campaigned in Samnium, it is strange to find his epitaph ignoring the capture of Aufidena, a much more important prize than two obscure places. In Livy's account, his activities as consul are modest: a de facto 'victory' in Etruria, and raids on Faliscan territory. But in 297 the consul Rullianus left Scipio as his legate in Samnium (ch. 15): conceivably the epitaph lists successes—still rather minor ones—that he perhaps gained there, ignored by Livy. In 296 Fabius as proconsul quelled 'insurrections' in Lucania (ch. 18); he may have had Scipio as legate again (as he did when consul in Etruria in 295: ch. 25). Although Fabius legally had title to any such successes, by the time of the epitaph both men were dead. Fulvius' triumph in 297 'over the Etruscans' in the *Fasti Triumphales* contradicts Livy's 'over the Samnites' (ch. 13); but the *Fasti* need not invariably be right (9.39 note and ch. 37 note).

take Bovianum by storm: Livy has the Romans capture Bovianum no fewer than four times between 311 and 293, which seems excessive (9.31, 44; here, and ch. 41). The cursory mention here, after a 'famous engagement' also mentioned cursorily, prompts suspicion. Later family tradition might want to have him take Bovianum to match M. Fulvius' achievement in 305 (9.44).

13 *Carseoli*: this is the likelier occasion for the Latin colony (ch. 3 note). The Aequicoli were a branch of the Aequi.

declined to be one: once more (as in ch. 9) Livy depicts Fabius as public-spiritedly modest in the face of universal admiration. Nor is this the last occasion (chs. 15, 22). As Rullianus was certainly elderly—his career went back to 331—perhaps he did decline office once (ch. 15 note), whereas thrice looks like embroidery. Livy uses the stories to underline how patriotically incorrupt the heroes of earlier times were, and to assert the supremacy of law over political convenience, themes highly relevant in his own day.

ordered a law read out: one of the Genucian laws of 342 (7.42 and note).

legally prescribed limit: one of the Licinian-Sextian laws of 367 forbade anyone from leasing more than 500 *iugera* of state-owned land (6.35).

14 *Maximus*: Q. Fabius Maximus, for some reason nicknamed Gurges ('wastrel'). He would be consul in 292 and 276.

of the first legion: ch. 18 note.

some eight hundred and fifty taken prisoner: as Oakley notes (iv. 193), this is the first of many itemized reports, down to ch. 46, of prisoners' numbers. These figures, like those for captured standards (from 9.42 on) and even the number of campsites (ch. 15), suggest that Livy's sources were becoming more detailed and less hyperbolic. Still, over the years 297–293 they add up to a startling 69,000 men, mostly Samnites and Etruscans. Prisoners, except those who could afford ransom or had guest-friends at Rome, would be sold as slaves. If correct (but cf. chs. 31, 36 notes), this total shows how calamitous these campaigns were for the populations of Samnium, Etruria, and other regions.

15 *The Apulians*: Livy suddenly introduces these on the Samnites' side, even though when last mentioned (9.20) Apulia was totally under Roman control. The Apulians probably feared what a Roman victory over the Samnites might mean for them, but Livy unhelpfully returns them to his narrative without even a minimal explanation. Since they then pose virtually no problem to the Romans, we may suspect an annalistic fiction here.

Cimetra: as so often, unknown.

his objections: this could be the one genuine occasion when Fabius refused election, for successful refusal of a deserved honour brought its own renown to an already distinguished Roman.

16 *Porsenna*: Lars Porsenna had besieged Rome in 508 (and in one Roman tradition, had captured the city—though not in Livy's account; cf. 6.40 note). He was admired as one of Rome's noblest enemies.

17 *Murgantia*: this 'powerful city' has left no obvious traces. Possibly it was the small and very ancient hilltop town of Morra de Sanctis, some 36 miles

south-east of Benevento. A Roman army moving from west to east across southern Samnium would reach Morra's site before Romulea or Forentum.

Romulea: perhaps the place recorded much later as Sub Romula, 46 Roman miles east of Beneventum.

Ferentinum: not the Hernican city (7.9); it may be Forentum in western Apulia (cf. 9.20), identified with modern Lavello 25 miles east of Lacedonia.

The credit for storming these cities: if Livy means what he says, he must have consulted six or more earlier accounts—at least two for each of the three different versions that he outlines. The credit here may well have belonged to Volumnius and Decius (ch. 18 note).

18 *fifteen thousand allies*: if the legions were each about 3,700 strong (see Appendix 2) and Livy's figure for allies is right, Volumnius commanded over 22,000 troops, as well as cavalry; Ap. Claudius will have had about 19,000; meanwhile Rullianus as proconsul had his own army. It should be noticed that Livy, here for the first time, ascribes numbers to each consul's legions (though he mentions a 'first legion' of Fabius in ch. 14). The numbers were assigned simply in the order that legions were recruited.

three strongholds in Samnium: this looks like a repeat of the captures of Murgantia, Romulea, and 'Ferentinum' (ch. 17), which 'some' of Livy's sources credited to Volumnius with different prisoner numbers.

turn out well: an echo of the common prayer or wish 'so help me Hercules' (*ita me Hercules iuvet*). Livy's telling of what ensued is hostile to Ap. Claudius, as usual. Appius is patronizingly arrogant to Volumnius; his soldiers, not he, have the true interests of Rome at heart; and in the battle Volumnius is more heroic, though Appius is briefly inspired to act like a proper Roman general.

19 *two thousand one hundred and twenty taken prisoner*: despite this supposedly splendid victory—which indeed was commemorated by the temple to Bellona—serious war continued (ch. 21 and note), and neither consul celebrated a triumph.

20 *Vescini*: the people of Vescia, a town of the Aurunci/Ausones (cf. ch. 21), though some of the manuscripts offer the topographically impossible 'Vestini' (for them, see 8.29 note).

four military tribunes: perhaps the Samnites had adapted their military organization to the efficient Roman model, but see also 7.32 note.

21 *brought from Etruria*: the third announcement of such news (cf. chs. 16, 18). Each time, Livy writes as though the great war was just being launched, and this time despite the consuls' recent victory: rhetorical over-enthusiasm, at best.

centuries made up of freedmen: the context shows that these centuries were military units, not electoral ones as in ch. 22. The older men also conscripted were those over forty-five, normally exempt from army service.

21 *Publius Sempronius*: Sophus, tribune in 310 (9.33).

22 *the leading centuries*: Livy's wording (*'praerogativae centuriae'*) is untechnical, for only one century was chosen by lot to vote first of all, and was therefore called the *praerogativa* ('asked first'). He seems to mean the eighteen centuries of senators and 'knights' which then voted, ahead of the five 'classes' (see Glossary, 'Comitia Centuriata'). All the same, the only sound details in this election narrative may be that Fabius and Volumnius were nominated and Volumnius then stood aside for Decius.

Appius Claudius as praetor: in this period, several consuls were elected praetor for the following year. Other examples in this Book are M. Atilius Regulus, consul in 294, praetor in 293 (ch. 45), and the younger L. Papirius Cursor (293, 292: ch. 47). It was an alternative to extending their consular *imperium* as proconsuls.

23 *many prodigies that year*: Livy omits details—blood seeping from the altar of Capitoline Jupiter, and a bronze statue of Victory found standing on the ground in the Forum instead of on its pedestal, among others (Zonaras 8.1).

Patrician Chastity: there seems no firm evidence for such a shrine; one suggestion is that a veiled statue thought to represent Patrician Chastity stood in the temple of Fortune in the Forum Bovarium or Boarium ('cattle market') beside the Tiber, near the famous round temple of Portunus.

Verginia, daughter of Aulus: Aulus Verginius perhaps was descended from L. Verginius, a consular tribune in 389 (6.1). This tale, of the personal grievance of a plebeian leader's patrician wife having wider consequences, recalls the tale of Licinius Stolo's patrician wife Fabia (6.34–5).

Vicus Longus: running from south-west to north-east between the Viminal and Quirinal hills, to the Colline gate.

moneylenders: from time to time henceforth, Livy records details like this (e.g. 23.30, 25.2), though he does not indicate why he chooses items from some years and not others.

as infants beneath the wolf's udders: silver coins of the third century BC depict this statuary group. The coins, Rome's earliest true monetary issues, were probably minted when Q. Ogulnius was consul in 269. The *ficus Ruminalis* stood by the Lupercal cave at the edge of the Palatine hill, where the twins Romulus and Remus had been suckled by the she-wolf.

from the Porta Capena to the temple of Mars: cf. 7.23 note.

prosecuting livestock-breeders: for illicitly appropriating public land.

24 *some contention arose*: Livy plainly finds it distasteful to record any form of disagreement between these two veteran colleagues, yet he yields to the sources—they must have been the majority—who told of it. Those without it are only briefly mentioned (ch. 26). The disagreement should therefore be genuine, though not necessarily all its details.

25 *Aharna*: a town about 5 miles east of Perusia across the Tiber. This item suggests that Perusia had not yet changed sides—otherwise Appius would have risked extreme peril by camping nearby.

winter, which was not yet over: Livy's chronology is opaque. If Fabius Rullianus was exercising his army during winter, he and Decius must have been elected consuls before then, but that is quite at odds with the norm (see Glossary, 'Date for entering office'). Fabius as the incoming consul in 295 cannot have taken command before the spring. This affects unfavourably Livy's version of events, which has other difficulties too (below).

Clusium (which once they called Camars): Clusium never bore such a name—its old Etruscan name was Clevsins. 'Camars' looks akin to 'Camertes', as the people of Camerinum in Umbria were named (9.36 and note). Indeed Polybius (2.19), in a brief summary of Rome's wars with the Gauls, locates the defeat in ch. 26 'in the territory of the Camertes'. This should be accepted; the mistaken identification could be Livy's own, if not his sources.

returned to Rome for discussions: an odd development, wherever Fabius had left the second legion. In effect, he was handing the initiative over to the enemy, and his doings at Rome (ch. 26) hardly justify his action. The trip to Rome and then his return north with Decius look like an effort to absolve him from the disaster and blame L. Scipio for it instead (cf. Oakley, iv. 287).

to have the consul Publius Decius leave: Livy implies that Decius had not yet left the city, even though Fabius supposedly had done so earlier. The version in some of his sources—both consuls leaving for Etruria together on entering office (ch. 26)—is much more convincing.

26 *not reconnoitre adequately*: even making Scipio the scapegoat was too much for some patriotic annalists, who converted the Gauls' victory into him defeating Umbrians. Livy rightly disbelieves them.

greater than that of the Romans: the forces put into the field by Rome and her allies in 295 must have been the greatest so far in her history. The four consular legions would total 12,800 to 16,800 men (see Appendix 2). Cavalry and allied infantry would total at least as many. The propraetors' forces probably consisted of one legion each, again with allies. Meanwhile the proconsul Volumnius had two legions near Samnium (ch. 27).

two other armies: Faliscan territory was north of Rome (6.4 note), while the Vatican territory lay across the Tiber from the city, covering the Vatican hill and its neighbourhood. Such reserve forces underscore the crisis: had the consuls been defeated, the city itself would have been exposed to the enemy.

propraetors: so Livy similarly terms L. Scipio (ch. 25) and M. Livius (ch. 29). None of the four men had been praetors in 296, so if the term is accurate they were the first independently appointed propraetors in history.

27 *Sentinum*: near modern Sassoferrato in Umbria. All of Rome's major enemies, Samnites as well as Etruscans, Umbrians, and Gauls, were now in alliance to destroy her power. The future of the Republic hung in the balance; but the intelligent distraction by the propraetors was enough to draw away perhaps half the coalition forces.

towards Clusium: here Livy does mean Clusium in Etruria (contrast ch. 25 note).

a deer: omens and portents in Livy are rare at the outset of a battle. This one may be fictitious, but its point is to underline the significance of the battle. The wolf, Rome's emblematic animal (cf. ch. 23), is given free passage through the Roman ranks; the Gauls make the mistake of slaying the deer, a creature under the protection of the goddess Diana.

28 *Marcus Livius*: Livius Denter, consul in 302/1, and elected pontiff in 300 (ch. 9); another reminder that no Roman general campaigned without the necessities of religion in attendance (6.41 and note). For the *devotio* of Decius' father see 8.9–10.

29 *from the back line*: Fabius, even though his own struggle was not over, transferred some (not all) of his *triarii*—and no doubt their allied counterparts—to reinforce Decius' wing.

enemy's tortoise-formation: Livy calls it a *testudo*, which technically describes legionaries' shields held above their heads to ward off missiles (e.g. ch. 41). The Gauls, however, have theirs fixed in the ground before them, like the English shield-wall at Hastings in 1066.

collapsing in a daze: Livy seems to envisage the Gauls' upright shields as locked together, so that when some warriors fell they dragged the rest down. That this scene is realistic may be doubted.

their tortoise-formation: if this had just collapsed, the Gauls cannot still have been holding it. Oakley (iv. 327) suggests that Fabius attacked their rear at the same time as Decius died. More likely, Livy envisages only the first rank of the formation collapsing under the rain of javelins, but those behind standing firm until attacked by Fabius.

Jupiter the Victorious: the temple seems to have been built, for there are later references to it, including that it was dedicated on the Ides (13th) of April (Ovid, *Fasti* 4.621–2).

twenty-five thousand of the enemy were killed: this figure looks too high, both because of its size and also because warfare continued in Samnium itself, with further massive slaughter alleged (ch. 31). Livy's figure for Fabius' dead may be nearer reality, but his narrative of the fighting by Decius' wing scarcely suggests that as many as 7,000 Romans and allies were killed—a mortality of over 20 per cent (cf. ch. 26 note)—not to mention the wounded.

30 *six hundred thousand infantry, forty-six thousand cavalry*: Livy rightly disbelieves both totals. Gross inflations were current even from the start, for Diodorus (21.6) cites the Greek historian Duris, who was ruler of Samos in this period, for 'ten myriads' of enemy troops—100,000 men—being slain

in the war. The Christian historian Orosius (3.21) wildly misreports Livy as giving 140,330 enemy infantry and 46,000 cavalry.

coarse soldiers' banter: see 7.10 note.

31 *Perusians had been primarily responsible*: Fabius triumphed 'over the Samnites, Etruscans, and Gauls' on 4 September 295 (*Fasti Triumphales*). Yet only the Samnites and Gauls had fought at Sentinum. Possibly Cn. Fulvius' victory over Perusia and Clusium (ch. 30) had been indecisive—Livy does not claim otherwise—and Fabius then struck another and final blow before returning to Rome. Tradition could then have misdated this to after his triumph.

about one thousand seven hundred and forty prisoners: this number seems based on an actual record of the ransoms, so it may be trustworthy. The 4,500 slain look less so, especially as Perusia was in arms again the following year (ch. 37).

the area of Stella: the Plain of Stella in northern Campania (9.44 note); on Caiatia see 9.43 note.

numbered twenty-seven hundred: a suspect statistic. Livy gives the same number for the Samnite prisoners and the alleged 16,300 Samnite dead is a far higher total (like the Perusian figure). Copying errors may be at work.

married women: Livy does not state Gurges' office, but the fines indicate that he was curule aedile. How the offences had been discovered Livy again does not state, or why the cases were put before the people—probably, that is, before the *Comitia Centuriata*.

the men fighting them?: these are remarkable, obviously strongly felt sentiments. Livy admires the heroic Samnites' doomed devotion to liberty, as he does one individual enemy, Hannibal, praising his indomitable leadership against ever darker odds (28.12, 39.51).

32 *a point where*: unusually Livy does not offer a place-name, but from ch. 33 it seems the site lay somewhere beyond Sora.

at the rear of the camp: the *porta decumana* was on the side of the camp opposite the *porta praetoria*.

quaestor's quarters: on campaign the quaestor paid the soldiers and kept charge of booty.

33 *two cohorts of the allies*: here 'cohorts' seems accurate, for Livy is differentiating between them and legionary maniples (see Glossary).

dedicated to Victory a temple: this stood on the southern side of the Palatine hill, overlooking the Forum Boarium (ch. 23 note) and the Tiber. The temple and its surrounds were built on an imposing scale (Oakley, iv. 357–8), and it was dedicated on 1 August. This means that Postumius began campaigning only later in the summer of 294.

34 *Milionia*: in ch. 3 Livy located a Milionia among the Marsi; perhaps a town in Samnium bore the same name, but his account of warfare in 294–293 has many dubious place-names. Feritrum, mentioned next, is unknown.

35 *nothing like as easy*: the details of Atilius' second battle (chs. 35–6) cannot come from any reliable source. If correct in outline, it might be an Atilian family memory that found its way into Fabius Pictor's and Cincius' histories. Livy embellishes it greatly, including the slightly comical picture of both armies, Roman and Samnite, too frightened of each other to want to fight.

36 *a temple to Jupiter Stator*: the site is not known for certain, but it was not far from the Forum. In 63 BC it was the venue for Cicero's famous denunciation of Catiline (6.18 note).

seven thousand eight hundred men: this figure, again the same for Roman losses and Samnite prisoners (cf. ch. 31), is an emendation. The manuscripts' numerals for the hundreds in both totals make no sense (*ACCC* and the like). *DCCC* ('800') is the widely accepted correction; yet for all three totals to end in *DCCC* looks too much of a coincidence. The numeral at least for Roman losses must be wrong.

Interamna: the colony on the River Liris established in 312 (9.28). The Latin Way (*Via Latina*), which led to Capua via the Trerus and Liris valleys, may have been built in 306/5 by the censors (9.43).

formal settlement of terms: apparently the objection was that Regulus should have forced the Samnites—not just the captives but their whole army— to make a formal surrender. Such an objection looks fairly specious, but as usual we cannot be sure how well based Livy's account is.

37 *no occasion for war in Samnium*: Postumius must have been operating in western Samnium, but now moved to Etruria—which we now learn was far from pacified, despite Fulvius' and Rullianus' victories. Volsinii had made a truce with Rome in 308 (9.41) and had not renewed hostilities since then, but Roman successes against the Samnites probably alarmed the Volsinians.

the peace that was obtained: Livy's narrative conflicts again with the *Fasti Triumphales*. These list Postumius and Atilius each triumphing over both Samnites and Etruscans, on 27 and 28 March 293, respectively. Moreover *FT* have Atilius triumphing 'over the Volsinians and Samnites', Postumius 'over the Samnites and Etruscans'. This does not necessarily overrule Livy, for we cannot be sure that the compilers of the *Fasti* used sources invariably superior to his (see Introduction).

sought a triumph from the Senate: Postumius Megellus is depicted as an assertive character willing to defy the Senate, and happy to insult opposing tribunes as 'lackeys of the nobility'. Ironically, the Postumii were themselves one of the most ancient patrician *gentes*. His contentious style would continue unabated in later years, as the epitome of Book 11, and other sources, record.

the fanum, that is, the temple site: Livy's definition does not correspond to ordinary Roman usage, in which the *fanum* is the sacred shrine or temple itself. On this temple see ch. 36 note.

38 *Aquilonia*: ancient evidence registers an Aquilonia at or near today's Lacedonia (cf. ch. 17 note), 40 miles by road east of Beneventum. But Lacedonia is some 75 miles by road from ancient Bovianum (cf. 9.31 note), to which Livy says the surviving Samnite cavalry fled after defeat (ch. 41). Some scholars therefore hypothesize an Aquilonia in northern Samnium closer to Bovianum (cf. Oakley, iv. 383–90, who remains agnostic). The question is relevant to locating Cominium, the city attacked by the consul Carvilius, because this lay only 20 Roman miles from Aquilonia (ch. 39).

Ovius Paccius, officiated: it is credible that the Samnites were making a maximum effort and did have an elite corps called the 'Linen Legion' or a Samnite equivalent; moreover Ovius and Paccius are authentic Samnite names. Logically, such a significant effort should have occurred more than once before 293; but Livy presents it as a unique and fearful scenario to underline the drama of the occasion.

not to refuse: here the Samnites are fanatical, almost barbaric foes, a paradoxical contrast to the sympathy that Livy expressed in ch. 31. In reality, many of his details—the old linen roll, the procedure of enrolment, the instant execution of backsliders, and so on—are mere imagination.

the roof of the enclosure: unconvincing again, for a name derived from the soldiers' linen tunics makes much more sense.

39 *Amiternum*: the only known Amiternum stood in Sabine country, near today's L'Aquila at the foot of the Gran Sasso range. This does not fit an opening move into any part of Samnium, and some scholars posit, instead, an Amiternum (otherwise unknown) within Samnium. The problem recurs with other Samnite place-names in Livy's ensuing narrative.

Duronia: location unknown (not today's Duronia, so renamed only in 1875).

Cominium: a Cominium Ocritum lay near Beneventum (Livy 25.14), and so would lie reasonably close to Aquilonia if this stood at or near modern Lacedonia (ch. 38 note). By contrast, moderns hypothesizing an Aquilonia in northern Samnium have to postulate another Cominium nearby: for example, in the Val di Cómino just east of Sora and at the foot of the lofty Monti della Meta. But it strains probability that this campaign should repeatedly involve places—some very obscure—that shared the same names as known places elsewhere. More likely, obscure Samnite names were confused with better-known ones by Livy's sources, by Livy himself, or by later copyists.

40 *the keeper of the chickens*: see Glossary, 'Augurs'. On this occasion at least, Livy shows that there was more than one keeper (*pullarius*); the untruthful *pullarius* must have been the senior one. Normally, a falsified omen brought divine wrath on all the people it concerned (here Papirius and his army), but Livy prepares us for the opposite with Papirius' rousing speech emphasizing the godless treachery of the Samnites. Then the keeper's death at the very start of the battle shows that divine wrath fell on him alone.

40 *slights the gods*: Livy means the culture of his own day, which traditionally minded Romans invariably viewed with much suspicion, as being
over-sophisticated and sceptical to the point of atheism (cf. Introduction,
pp. xxii–xxiii).

41 *the power of gods and men was overcome*: that is, the power of the Samnites
and their gods.

   those who had not: whereas Livy's description of the levy (ch. 38) might
   suggest that all the Samnites had taken the oath—except the few who
   refused and were executed—this phrase indicates that the oath had been
   exacted only from the warriors of the Linen Legion.

   refuge in Bovianum: if Aquilonia lay near Lacedonia, Bovianum might seem
   an implausible or impossible refuge (ch. 38 note). But according to Livy,
   only the Samnite nobles and cavalry fled there. Nobles, almost by definition, would be riders too. Seventy-five miles through their own countryside
   could be covered in three or four days by desperate riders. In 1745 Sir John
   Cope, routed at Prestonpans near Edinburgh, by next day was 50 miles
   away at Berwick-upon-Tweed.

42 *three thousand eight hundred and seventy were captured*: the disproportion
   between this figure and the alleged 20,340 dead recalls earlier suspicious
   totals (chs. 29, 36 notes).

   before he took a stiff drink himself: a grateful offering of honeyed wine (*mul-
   sum*) to a god was a regular practice, but Livy clearly means to portray
   Papirius as being so confident of the gods' favour that he feels able to make
   just a small gesture of thanksgiving.

43 *reached Bovianum*: these Samnite cohorts would have been infantry, who
   after scattering across the countryside would take some days to reach
   Bovianum. Clearly they were no longer being pursued.

44 *Saepinum*: about 10 miles south-east of Bovianum.

45 *Delegations from the allies*: Livy does not name these allies, but the only
   hostile Etruscan city that he names is the unknown Troilum (ch. 46), which
   suggests that the 'uprising' was not a major affair.

   the praetor Marcus Atilius: ch. 22 note.

   Velia, Palumbinum, and Herculaneum: these cannot be Velia, on the coast
   near Paestum, or Herculaneum near Pompeii, which make no sense in
   Samnite warfare. 'Velia' is actually a modern suggestion for *Vella, Veletia*,
   and the like in the manuscripts. Both are probably sources' or copyists'
   mistakes for less recognizable Samnite place-names. For instance, a town
   existed at 'the shrine of Hercules Ranus', apparently with the same or a
   similar name, between Saepinum and Bovianum (though Oakley, iv. 388
   n. 1, is dubious that this is the solution). Palumbinum is unknown.

46 *still in office*: the *Fasti Triumphales* list Papirius triumphing on the Ides
   (13th) of February, Carvilius on the Ides of January, thus in 292. Livy narrates Papirius' triumph first, because of its magnificence and because it
   recalled that of his famous father (9.40).

rampart and mural crowns: on the 'mural' crown see 6.20 note. The 'rampart' crown (*corona vallaris*) was similarly awarded to the first man to scale the rampart (*vallum*) of an enemy camp.

1,830 pounds: this is the first time that Livy gives a detailed breakdown of the funds brought back to Rome by a triumphator. From Book 30 on he will make this a fairly regular feature.

temple of Quirinus: on Quirinus see 8.9 note. This temple stood appropriately on the Quirinal hill, perhaps replacing an older one.

Troilum: unknown, but hardly a major centre like Volsinii or Perusia.

a year's truce: this was later extended to fifty years; perhaps in 291 because, fifty years afterwards, Falerii again went to war with Rome—only to be razed to the ground.

was factored in: even so, the *Fasti Triumphales* do not list Carvilius triumphing over Etruscans, another clue that the fighting there was not rated as major.

Fors Fortuna: Fors was the older name of Fortuna; though the second name became preferred, the older was kept with it out of religious scruple. The new temple, dedicated on 24 June (presumably in 292), stood across the Tiber.

Lucius Postumius: the feisty consul of the year before. His impeachment may have been on a charge similar to the one threatened then, of insisting on an unauthorized triumph.

47 *had entered office*: plebeian tribunes did so on 10 December, so these tribunes' ensuing abdication took place on the 15th. Although the consuls triumphed afterwards (ch. 46 note), Livy reports their triumphs first in order to round off Papirius' and Carvilius' eventful year.

flaw in their election: cf. 6.38 note and Glossary, 'Augurs'.

census-purification ceremony: the censors completed their term of office with a religious rite, the *lustrum*, which marked the successful completion of their tasks and, therefore, the purification of the city and state.

nineteenth purification ceremony: the *lustrum* dated to the time of the kings (supposedly it was instituted by Servius Tullius), but not all censors had performed it. The citizens' numbers given here should be more or less reliable, but there is always the risk of numerals being corrupted by copyists ancient or medieval.

Bovillae: an ancient Latin town some miles south-east of Rome.

Aesculapius had to be brought to Rome: that is, an effigy of Aesculapius (in Greek, Asclepius) the god of healing. The temple was built not long after, on the Tiber island where San Bartolomeo's church now stands.

GLOSSARY

aediles two plebeian magistracies created in 494 originally for looking after the shrines (*aedes*) of Ceres and Diana, divinities particularly reverenced by the plebs. Their duties expanded to supervising markets and traders, the fabric of city streets, and public order in Rome; they also had power to prosecute for certain offences. In 366 a second, curule pair was created for patricians, although very soon these were opened to plebeians as well.

allies other Italian city-states and communities allied with Rome; the number and range grew immensely in the fourth century BC, eventually covering all of peninsular Italy save for the areas that formed the Roman state itself. The Latin allies (*nomen Latinum*) consisted originally of the other Latin League cities, then also of colonies founded jointly by these cities and Rome; after about 290, with most old Latin cities incorporated into the Roman state, the growing number of Latin colonies formed the bulk of the *nomen Latinum*. The term 'Italian allies' (*socii Italici*) was used of all other Italian states in alliance with Rome.

annalists Latin historians before Livy, whose histories of Rome narrated events year by year, as his does (see Introduction).

annals see PONTIFFS.

as, asses see MONEY.

assemblies see COMITIA CENTURIATA, COMITIA CURIATA, COMITIA TRIBUTA, *CONTIO*, COUNCIL OF THE PLEBS.

augurs one of the four chief priestly colleges. Their number, originally three patricians, was increased to nine in 300 BC so as to have five plebeian and four patrician augurs. Augurs were senators, chosen by co-optation and for life. They interpreted omens, drawn sometimes from the flight of birds but also from other occurrences that indicated the will of the gods. As a college, or individually, augurs could be consulted by magistrates or the Senate on matters of religious duty, and could announce their own opinion if necessary—for example, an omen that vitiated the election of a magistrate.

auspices the signs (*auspicia*) provided by heaven to guide the state and its magistrates in decisions. One method of seeking divine guidance for a proposed action was for an augur to observe how a brood of sacred chickens responded when food was offered to them, or if they would not leave their coop. Refusal to eat or come out revealed the gods' disapproval of the proposal; whereas if the birds not only ate but spilled some food from their beaks, the omen was especially favourable.

authority of the Senate (*auctoritas patrum*) approval conferred by the patrician members of the Senate on a measure enacted by one of the assemblies. Whether the approval was purely formal or could be withheld (and thus invalidate the law) was a divisive issue in the fourth century.

boards mostly ad hoc panels of senators created for specific tasks, such as founding colonies, overseeing construction work, or organizing a small fleet; these generally consisted of two or three members, though sometimes of more (see TWELVE TABLES). A 'duumvir' was a member of a two-man board, a 'triumvir' one of a board of three; 'quinquevirs' and 'decemvirs' were members of five-man and ten-man boards respectively. The Latin terms are *duumvir*, plural *-viri*; *triumvir*, *-ri*; *quinquevir*, *-ri*; and *decemvir*, *-ri*. The board of two (*duumviri*) for sacrifices, later enlarged to ten (*decemviri sacris faciundis*), was different, a lifetime priesthood (see PRIESTS).

calendar (*fasti*) the fourth-century Roman calendar had four months of thirty-one days (March, May, July, October), seven months each of twenty-nine, and one (February) of twenty-eight. To keep the years in line with solar years, an extra twenty-eight-day month was added by the pontiffs biennially between 26 and 27 February. Every month had three fixed days: Kalends (the 1st), Nones (the 5th for the shorter months, 7th for the four longer ones), and Ides (13th and 15th respectively). Other days were counted backward from these, using inclusive counting: e.g. 13 March was 'three days before the Ides of March'.

censors, census censors were instituted in 443, at five-year intervals and holding office for eighteen months, to maintain the registers of male citizens aged sixteen and over, keep membership of the Senate and other public bodies in order, and arrange building contracts and the leasing of state-owned lands. They acquired a moral function, penalizing any citizen (senators included) whom they judged morally deficient; offending senators could be demoted in rank or even expelled from the Senate. The census registered citizens liable for military service, and entitled them to vote in the Comitia and to seek elected office. It also registered their economic and financial resources and, on this basis, assigned to them membership of appropriate units in the Comitia Centuriata and other assemblies.

century (army) the *centuria* was the basic unit of the infantry legion, originally composed of 100 men but, by the fourth century BC, of sixty plus their centurion; centuries of *triarii* were half this size. Two centuries formed a maniple.

century (political) see COMITIA CENTURIATA.

citizenship without voting rights *civitas sine suffragio* was an innovation of the fourth century, enabling Rome to bring Capua and its dependencies into the Roman state on a semi-autonomous basis.

clan see GENS.

cognomen see NAMES.

cohort in the fourth century BC, a unit of Italian infantry, especially one of allies in a Roman army. By the late third century if not earlier, it was also applied to a Roman legionary unit made up of one maniple each of *hastati, principes*, and *triarii*. This more flexible force became the legion's standard tactical unit.

coinage see MONEY.

colony, colonist an urban settlement founded at a strategic or economic site by an existing state. A Roman colony (*colonia Romana*) was a small settlement consisting of citizens with their families. A Latin colony (*colonia Latina*) was larger, comprising both colonists from Latin cities and others who were Roman citizens; in time, the Roman element in such foundations predominated. Latin colonies, like the original Latin cities allied to Rome, enjoyed special privileges: for example, Latins visiting Rome could vote in the Comitia Centuriata and C. Tributa, and they enjoyed full reciprocal rights of inheritance and intermarriage with Roman citizens.

Comitia Centuriata the assembly of citizens which legislated, elected consuls, censors, and praetors, declared war, ratified treaties, and judged trials of persons on capital charges. It was summoned by a consul or praetor, and could vote only on matters laid before it by the presiding magistrate. Citizens could not debate or amend a proposal, though they could call for a specific person to be elected to an office even if he had not put his name forward. Developing from the early citizen army assembled in its military centuries (see above), the C. Centuriata met on the Campus Martius, then a broad meadow between the Tiber and the city walls. Its centuries were fixed at 193, arranged in five 'classes' of unequal numbers: a majority vote of each century's members counted as one vote in the Comitia. Citizens were assigned by the censors to centuries in the classes according to the value of their property. Senators, and the knights (*equites*) who were eligible to serve as Rome's cavalry, were enrolled in eighteen special centuries. Then the 'first class' (eighty centuries) was reserved for the other wealthiest citizens, while the remaining four classes had descending levels of property qualifications. Romans with no property at all (possibly a majority of all citizens) were assigned to a single century which voted last—and sometimes never, because voting went class-by-class and stopped as soon as a majority of centuries had voted the same way. Thus the structure of the C. Centuriata guaranteed the predominance of aristocratic and upper-class Romans.

Comitia Curiata an ancient assembly consisting of thirty *curiae*, the earliest communal units to which all citizens belonged. In historical times, only thirty lictors attended, with the chief priest presiding. The C. Curiata alone could confer *imperium* on magistrates, ratify priestly appointments, and validate wills and adoptions.

Comitia Tributa another assembly of all citizens, in which they met and voted by tribes (see TRIBE); the C. Tributa elected curule aediles and quaestors, and could pass laws. A majority vote of each tribe's members counted as one vote in the Comitia. In the third century BC the centuries of the C. Centuriata were grouped, in each of its 'classes', to match the number of tribes, which by then totalled thirty-five; in practice, therefore, the two assemblies became almost identical.

Conscript Fathers the formal term (*patres conscripti*) used in addressing the Senate as a body. Its origin and precise meaning were, and are, debated.

consular tribunes see TRIBUNES, CONSULAR.

consuls the highest regular magistrates of the Roman Republic, elected annually, holding *imperium*, and ultimately responsible for matters of peace and war. On all questions, however, they were expected to consult the Senate and, when appropriate, to put proposals to the people assembled as the Comitia Centuriata. (See also DATE FOR ENTERING OFFICE; *IMPERIUM.*)

contio an assembly of citizens summoned by a magistrate to hear news or listen to a policy discussion, but not to vote on any matters.

Council of the Plebs a voting assembly open only to plebeians on the summons of a plebeian official, usually a tribune or tribunes. Voters were grouped in their tribal units (see TRIBE), and a majority vote of each century's members counted as one vote in the Council. Its resolutions, called plebiscites (*plebiscita*), eventually became (in practice) binding on all citizens; this was enshrined in law in 287.

curule (chair) a magistrate sat on a folding chair made of ivory (a *sella curulis*), which thus symbolized his office.

date for entering office the calendar date for consuls and praetors varied over time. In the fourth century, it seems to have been some date towards the middle of the year. By the last two decades of the third century it had moved to the Ides (15th) of March; in 153 BC it was changed to 1 January. Tribunes entered their office on 10 December.

decemvirs in charge of sacred rites one of the four chief priestly colleges; they began with two members (*duumviri sacris faciundis*), but in the fourth century numbered ten (*decemviri s.f.*), and later on fifteen. New decemvirs were co-opted by the existing ones, held their priesthood for life, and were always senators. They had charge of the Sibylline Books, which only they could consult as directed by the Senate.

dictator an emergency magistrate with supreme civil and military power (*imperium*), appointed by a consul to take charge in a crisis, or to perform certain ancient rituals which were seen as too important even for consuls. The dictator was always an ex-magistrate; he in turn appointed another as his deputy, called the master of horse; they laid down their offices as soon as the crisis, or ritual, had been dealt with, and were not allowed to exceed six months' tenure in any case. Archaic conventions required that the dictator be named by a consul in the dead of night, and that he must not ride a horse. The principal dictatorial functions were: to conduct military operations, to hammer a nail into the temple of Jupiter on the Capitol (a ritual against plague, efficacy unknown), and to supervise elections if neither consul could do so.

'dictator years' a peculiarity of the *Fasti Capitolini*, which mark the years 333, 324, 309, and 301 BC as having not consuls but only dictators as magistrates with their masters of horse. These items are inventions of the late first century BC, taken over if not in fact thought up by the Augustan-era compilers of the *Fasti*. Greek and Roman historians, Livy included, have no such anomalous years: Livy records the dictators being appointed, for the normal brief term, during the previous years (334, etc.). The reason for these intrusions must be linked to debated questions like the date of Rome's founding—Roman scholars canvassed several years from 755 to 728—and that of the Gallic sack in 390/387/386. Moderns keep the conventional BC numbering of the years but use the forms '334/333', '325/324', and so on, to show that the alleged 'dictator years' did not exist.

duumvir see BOARDS.

duumvir for sacrifices see DECEMVIRS IN CHARGE OF SACRED RITES.

equites see KNIGHTS.

fasces a tied bundle of rods and axes, carried by each lictor attending a consul or praetor, and symbolizing—or, at times, applying—their power to inflict punishments of flogging or execution on offenders. The two consuls took it in turn, month by month, to be attended by twelve lictors; the praetor had six.

Fasti Capitolini inscribed lists on marble giving the names and dates of the consuls of the Roman Republic from 509 BC down to the time of Augustus. They were set up in his temple to Mars the Avenger, dedicated in 2 BC. The large fragments that survive are now in the Palazzo dei Conservatori Museum on the Capitoline hill.

Fasti Triumphales inscribed lists of the magistrates, from Romulus down to 19 BC, who celebrated triumphs over enemies of Rome; preserved with the *Fasti Capitolini*.

fetial priests a body of priests (*fetiales*) who performed the rites required for declaring war and concluding peace. Declaring war involved a preliminary stage in which a pair of fetials formally demanded from the opposing state a satisfaction of Roman grievances; if these were not satisfied, the rite of declaring war took place.

flamens a priest called a *flamen* (plural *flamines*) served each of Rome's three most ancient gods, Jupiter, Mars, and Quirinus. The flamen of Jupiter (*flamen Dialis*), always a patrician, was subject to a remarkable range of restrictions that reveal very ancient horrors of ritual pollution: for instance, his hair when trimmed and his nail-clippings must always be gathered up and buried beneath a sacred tree; he could not wear rings unless they were cut through, or have knots in his garments; nor was he permitted to see a dead body. He wore a conical cap when out of doors, and was attended by a lictor. His wife, the *flaminica*, also performed rites, and the couple could not divorce; if she died, the flamen had to resign office. Unlike most Roman priests, this flamen—and perhaps the other two—could not participate fully in public and political life because of his duties and taboos.

Foedus Cassianum a treaty made in 493, reportedly by the consul Sp. Cassius, allying Rome and the cities of the Latin League; its purported text still existed in Cicero's day.

freedman the slave of a Roman citizen, when formally set free, became a citizen himself, though certain duties and restrictions were imposed on him (e.g. he could not hold office); these did not pass on to his sons.

gens a group of families with the same family name, *nomen* (e.g. Cornelius, Valerius), supposedly descended from the same forebear. Patrician *gentes* shared particular religious rituals, and liked to claim that such ritual tasks marked them out as the only true *gentes*—a piece of exclusivism which aimed to put plebeian families at a moral disadvantage and so was contested by these. Some plebeian families may have had equally ancient ancestry (9.29 and 10.8 notes). Note that there were two leading *gentes* of Claudii: the patricians descended from Attius Clausus the Sabine, and the plebeians, who almost always bore the *cognomen* Marcellus.

hastati see *PRINCIPES*.

imperium the 'power to command', conferred by a *lex curiata* (see COMITIA CURIATA) on incoming consuls and praetors, and on a dictator by the nomination of a consul. Holders of *imperium* summoned and put proposals to the Senate and to the people; judged legal cases (consuls often passed these over to the praetor or other officials); commanded Roman forces in war; and could celebrate a triumph. Consular *imperium* was superior to that of praetors, while the dictator's was superior to all. Originally the king's absolute power, *imperium* incurred checks and balances in the Republic. One consul could prevent the other from taking an action (a rare event), a consul could give orders to a praetor, and a dictator likewise to the consuls. In civil life, a Roman convicted on a capital charge could appeal either to the people directly (i.e. to a hearing by the Comitia Centuriata) or to any of the plebeian tribunes, whose veto-power even consuls had to respect.

interregnum, interrex if no consul or dictator was available, the Senate had the power to declare an *interregnum*, a function that obviously dated back to the time of the kings, so as to have new magistrates elected. An *interrex* must be a patrician and his tenure was limited to five days. Each first appointee could not hold elections but had to nominate a successor, and he in turn a further *interrex* if elections still could not be held; the sequence continued until satisfactory elections took place.

iugerum the basic unit of land measurement (plural *iugera*), equivalent to about 0.62 acres or 0.25 hectares.

King of Sacrifices the *rex sacrorum* performed sacred rites which originally had been the preserve of the Roman king. He had to be a patrician, held the office for life, and could hold no other office.

kings of Rome traditionally the seven rulers from 753 to 509, from Romulus to the evil Tarquin the Proud. Servius Tullius, the sixth king, was credited with extensive progressive reforms and innovations, including creation of the Comitia Centuriata and of the census. The historicity of the kings is widely debated.

knights *equites* (horsemen) were Roman citizens who had the duty to serve as cavalry in the legions, an expensive task because most of the costs of upkeep and presentation had to be paid by the cavalryman himself. The term 'knights' also came to be unofficially applied to all Romans whose wealth could meet such expenses. Senators, though also able to serve in the cavalry, were not covered by the term.

Latin colony see COLONY.

Latin Festival one of Rome's chief religious festivals, originally a cult of the ancient Latin League (see ALLIES). It was celebrated on the Alban Mount on a date in spring that was determined each year by the consuls, who presided over it.

Latin League see ALLIES.

lectisternium a public ceremony in times of stress, in which images of twelve important gods were set up on couches (*lecti*) with offerings of food and drink, to appease their supposed anger against the community.

legate the deputy to a consul or proconsul on campaign, always a senator of military experience and almost always an ex-magistrate. In Livy's time, commanders of individual legions were likewise called legates, and he repeatedly but anachronistically applies this to the fourth century.

lictor see *FASCES*.

magistrate the term for an elected executive official of the Roman state. The chief magistrates were the two consuls; others were the censors, praetors, curule aediles, and quaestors. Plebeian tribunes and plebeian aediles technically were not magistrates because they were elected by only the plebs, but the widening range of their activities led to them—especially the tribunes—often being included in the term.

master of horse the deputy to a dictator, who appointed him and told him what to do.

money the bronze *as* (plural *asses*) was Rome's earliest monetary value, although Roman coinage itself did not exist until around 269 BC. The *as* was a unit of value, one-tenth of a pound of bronze (*aes*). Actual transactions were made by weighing out bits or pieces of bronze, silver, gold, or other valuable items, or through barter.

names a Roman man had a first name (*praenomen*), a family name equivalent to our surname (*nomen*); and often but not always a third name (*cognomen*), which could come from almost any source. *Cognomina* were usually, but not always, passed from father to son. Women bore only the feminine form of the *nomen*, such as Fabia, Verginia, or Minucia. The small number of *praenomina* led to them being quite commonly abbreviated: A. (Aulus), Ap. (Appius, used only by patrician Claudii), C. (Gaius, abbreviated before the letter G had been devised), Cn. (Gnaeus), D. (Decimus), K. (Kaeso, used only by Fabii and Duillii), L. (Lucius), M. (Marcus), M'. (Manius), Mam. (Mamercus, used only by Aemilii), N. or Num. (Numerius, used solely by Fabii), P. (Publius), Q. (Quintus), Sex. (Sextus), Sp. (Spurius), T. (Titus), Ti. (Tiberius).

'new man' the unofficial term for a consul who had no consular ancestors (see NOBLEMEN). Though it was probably not used before the second century BC, Livy has no other term available for fourth-century newcomers. Such men would necessarily be plebeians.

noblemen, nobles, nobility the word *nobilis*, originally meaning 'notable', in later times took on the unofficial sense of 'illustrious' and was applied to the families of men who held magistracies with *imperium*. As these were effectively monopolized by the patricians in the early Republic, applying the later terms to them came naturally to authors like Livy.

nomen see NAMES.

patricians, plebeians the earliest status rankings at Rome, subject to continuous scholarly debate. Basically, patricians were the original ruling elite, which until the fifth century BC might still accept new members (like the Claudii), but increasingly they tried to close their ranks even though these began to diminish. Plebeians in practice were all the other citizens—except that in some scholars' view the 'clients' (social dependants) of patrician families were neither the one nor the other but formed a special intermediate, if nameless, caste. Many plebeians were also wealthy and some could claim equally ancient Roman lineage. As plebeian numbers grew, including those of the plebeian elite, struggles for social, political, and economic reforms repeatedly broke out. During the fourth century, plebeians gradually achieved most of their demands, but political life continued to be run by a patrician–plebeian aristocracy. This grew greatly in size, but the remaining patrician families would always enjoy disproportionate influence and respect.

patron the senators appointed to establish a new colony would afterwards continue to enjoy influence there, and would support the colonists if these later found need to petition the authorities at Rome for help or redress. Descendants of the original patrons would maintain these links. Another type of patron was the former master of a freed slave; the freedman, though now a citizen, legally owed a variety of duties to his patron as a return for being set free.

plebiscite see COUNCIL OF THE PLEBS.

plebs see PATRICIANS, PLEBEIANS.

pontiffs Rome's chief priestly college, headed by the Chief Priest (*Pontifex Maximus*) and responsible for the most important religious duties and rites of the state. In 300 BC their number was doubled from four to eight by the addition of four plebeians (all previous pontiffs were patricians). The King of Sacrifices and the three great flamens of Mars, Quirinus, and Jupiter were also members. The pontiffs supervised festivals and state games, the calendar, the Vestal Virgins, the major ceremonies and sacrifices, and various other matters. The Chief Priest's official residence was the Regia—'royal house' in the time of the kings—that stood beside the sanctuary of Vesta and next to the Forum. He also saw to the regular chronicling of noteworthy religious events, including omens and portents, and over time came to add events of state that had religious relevance, such as the making of treaties. Eventually these Pontifical Annals, or Greatest Annals, were published (see Introduction).

praenomen see NAMES.

praetor a magistracy with *imperium* instituted in 366 to relieve the consuls of some duties, especially judicial ones. As holder of *imperium* the praetor could command an army, too. His *imperium* was theoretically inferior to that of the consuls, but many consuls after their year of office are recorded as holding the praetorship in its turn. In the later third century, more praetors were created to handle the widening tasks of administration and war, which put the office definitely one grade below the consulship.

prefect in the army, an officer in command of a cavalry force or a contingent of allied troops. In civil administration, a Roman appointed for a special purpose—a rare appointment in the fourth century, perhaps limited to the 'prefects sent to Capua' mentioned at 9.20.

priests pontiffs, augurs, and other sacred officials were not a separate body of clergy, but could also hold public office, with a few exceptions such as the King of Sacrifices and the Flamen Dialis.

principes in a legion, the second line of infantry, standing behind the *hastati* and before the *triarii*; see Appendix 2.

proconsul *pro consule*, literally 'in place of/acting as a consul'. From 327 on, a consul still on campaign when his year of office expired might have his *imperium*, though not his consulship itself, prolonged by a Senate decree. As the range and complexity of Rome's military efforts grew, this became an important way of keeping up continuity in a war theatre, or of making commanders available on more fronts than there were consuls and praetors.

propraetor a praetor on campaign might also have his *imperium* prolonged to enable him to finish his work (see PROCONSUL), but this did not happen often until the great wars of the third and second centuries.

province a specific field of responsibility (*provincia*) assigned to a consul or praetor. It could be civil or military, but over time its commonest use was to designate the region assigned to a magistrate for his campaign. This eventually led to the term being applied to the territory under Roman rule that a magistrate or promagistrate was assigned to govern.

quaestor a lesser-ranking magistrate whose task was to administer the state's financial accounts, or at times to accompany a consul on campaign and see to the army's financial needs.

Sibylline Books three scrolls kept in the temple of Jupiter on the Capitoline hill in the care of the decemvirs in charge of sacred rites, who consulted them only when authorized by the Senate. The Books apparently gave oracular instructions on dealing with omens, portents, threats to the state, and other critical matters. Their origin and how they came to Rome were told as legends. 'Sibyl' was a Greek term for a type of individual priestess-prophetess, the nearest of whom to Rome dwelt in a cave near Cumae in Campania; the Cumaean Sibyl figures in Vergil's *Aeneid* as the hero Aeneas' guide through the Underworld.

sortition determining how a range of tasks should be assigned to which magistrate or other official was carried out by casting lots (*sortes*) under the eyes of the gods, in the expectation that they would guide the lots.

suffect consul if a consul died in office, a special election could be held to replace him; the new consul, who then held office for the rest of that year, was termed a *consul suffectus*.

suspension of all business a *iustitium*; in emergencies, or for religious purposes, a magistrate could declare a *iustitium*, requiring all ordinary state and public activities to halt while the matter was dealt with.

toga a large, roughly semicircular, white woollen garment worn over the tunic by a Roman citizen on formal occasions. A magistrate's *toga praetexta* was bordered with a scarlet (*purpureus*) band; in later times, senators' and knights' togas also had such bands—broad and narrow respectively—to show their status. A triumphator (see TRIUMPH) wore a scarlet toga embroidered with gold thread.

triarii see *PRINCIPES*.

tribe the territory of the Roman state was parcelled out in districts called 'tribes' (*tribus*: perhaps from the verb *tribuere*, 'to allocate, attribute'), which grew in number as Rome annexed further territories. In the early Republic there were four city tribes and seventeen rural ones, of which those close to Rome were very small. By 241 BC the rural tribes had increased to thirty-one; later territorial annexations, even abroad, were allocated to existing rural tribes. The tribes bore distinctive names, some of the oldest having the names of early aristocratic families (e.g. the Fabia and Papiria).

tribunes, consular their full title was 'tribunes of the soldiers with consular power' (*tribuni militum consulari potestate*); they were a remarkable example of Roman political flexibility. The traditional account, disputed by some moderns, is that the patricians in the mid-fifth century tried to compromise with the plebeians' demands for access to consulships by agreeing to replace consuls from time to time with these magistrates, who could include plebeians—though in practice most consular tribunes were patricians. Their number varied between three and six according to military needs. Consular tribunes were elected intermittently between 444 and 367; then the practice lapsed.

tribunes, military 'tribunes of the soldiers' (to be distinguished from 'tribunes of the soldiers with consular power': see TRIBUNES, CONSULAR) were the four senior officers of a legion, usually younger men of higher social rank. There were no professional military ranks or careers until late Republican times, and to win respect and attract votes for office such men needed to earn military experience. The tribunes of the first two legions levied by each consul were elected by the people; those of other legions could be appointed directly by the consuls or the praetor.

tribunes, plebeian *tribuni plebei* or *t. plebis*, the elected representatives of the Roman plebs, instituted in 494. At first two, but from 457 ten in number, they held office from 10 December for one year. Plebeian tribunes were almost always men of some social status, and some achieved higher office during the fourth century and later. Although technically they were not magistrates and did not have *imperium*, they could be extraordinarily effective because the entire plebeian citizenry was sworn to support them. A tribune was physically and ritually untouchable (*sacrosanctus*) during his term of office—anyone who struck a tribune was liable to instant execution. Plebeian tribunes had the right of veto (*intercessio*) over any action or proposal of any official, and could also intervene on behalf of a plebeian wronged or mistreated by a magistrate. They summoned and put proposals to the Council of the Plebs, whose resolutions (*plebiscita*) came to be binding on the state as a whole; they could declare a suspension of business (*iustitium*); and they acquired the power to judge cases affecting plebeians. Inevitably they also gained the right to convoke and address the Senate. By the early third century they were, in practice, regular magistrates whose interests ranged over all public affairs.

triumph a victory parade through Rome, with strong religious aspects, celebrated by a commander at the head of his army. Only a magistrate with *imperium* and acting under his own auspices (see AUSPICES) could hold a triumph. Borne in a chariot, he wore splendid ceremonial dress with his face painted red, while his captives and booty moved ahead of him and his soldiers followed, with songs and jokes (some of them crude and insulting, to placate the gods' jealousy) about him and the victory. The parade marched through central Rome to the Capitoline hill, where the triumphator entered the temple of Jupiter to make offerings selected from the captured enemy booty, in thanksgiving for the victory. It was one of the proudest days in a Roman leader's life.

Twelve Tables the code of civil law compiled and published in 451–450 by a specially appointed board of ten, the *decemviri*. Roman tradition maintained that before then the laws had not been written down but were orally preserved by the patricians, with resulting manipulation. The Twelve Tables remained the hallowed foundation of all subsequent Roman law. Schoolboys had to memorize them, and substantial excerpts from them survive.

Vestal Virgins Rome's only female priesthood, a college of six unmarried women under the authority of the Chief Priest. The Vestals were highly venerated, for they guarded the rites and sacred fire of Vesta, goddess of fire and of the essence of Rome. After thirty years' service a Vestal was permitted to retire and to marry. If the sacred fire went out in the shrine of Vesta, close to the Forum, or if a Vestal was seduced, it was a serious calamity endangering the state, and had to be expiated with cleansing rites including the death of the offending priestess. Vesta's cult and her college endured until AD 394.

veto see TRIBUNES, PLEBEIAN.

INDEX

Magistrates' names are entered in full according to the lists in T. R. S. Broughton, *The Magistrates of the Roman Republic*, and with the date of their most senior office, or the first of these.

NB *trib. mil.* = military tribune with consular power; *trib. pl.* = tribune of the plebs; *mag. eq.* = master of horse.

For the abbreviations of first names, see Glossary under 'Names'.

*The
Oxford
World's
Classics
Website*

www.worldsclassics.co.uk

- Browse the full range of Oxford World's Classics online

- Sign up for our monthly e-alert to receive information on new titles

- Read extracts from the Introductions

- Listen to our editors and translators talk about the world's greatest literature with our Oxford World's Classics audio guides

- Join the conversation, follow us on Twitter at OWC_Oxford

- Teachers and lecturers can order inspection copies quickly and simply via our website

www.worldsclassics.co.uk

American Literature

British and Irish Literature

Children's Literature

Classics and Ancient Literature

Colonial Literature

Eastern Literature

European Literature

Gothic Literature

History

Medieval Literature

Oxford English Drama

Poetry

Philosophy

Politics

Religion

The Oxford Shakespeare

A complete list of Oxford World's Classics, including Authors in Context, Oxford English Drama, and the Oxford Shakespeare, is available in the UK from the Marketing Services Department, Oxford University Press, Great Clarendon Street, Oxford OX2 6DP, or visit the website at www.oup.com/uk/worldsclassics.

In the USA, visit www.oup.com/us/owc for a complete title list.

Oxford World's Classics are available from all good bookshops. In case of difficulty, customers in the UK should contact Oxford University Press Bookshop, 116 High Street, Oxford OX1 4BU.

THOMAS AQUINAS	Selected Philosophical Writings
FRANCIS BACON	The Essays
WALTER BAGEHOT	The English Constitution
GEORGE BERKELEY	Principles of Human Knowledge and Three Dialogues
EDMUND BURKE	A Philosophical Enquiry into the Origin of Our Ideas of the Sublime and Beautiful Reflections on the Revolution in France
CONFUCIUS	The Analects
DESCARTES	A Discourse on the Method
ÉMILE DURKHEIM	The Elementary Forms of Religious Life
FRIEDRICH ENGELS	The Condition of the Working Class in England
JAMES GEORGE FRAZER	The Golden Bough
SIGMUND FREUD	The Interpretation of Dreams
THOMAS HOBBES	Human Nature and De Corpore Politico Leviathan
DAVID HUME	Selected Essays
NICCOLÒ MACHIAVELLI	The Prince
THOMAS MALTHUS	An Essay on the Principle of Population
KARL MARX	Capital The Communist Manifesto
J. S. MILL	On Liberty and Other Essays Principles of Political Economy and Chapters on Socialism
FRIEDRICH NIETZSCHE	Beyond Good and Evil The Birth of Tragedy On the Genealogy of Morals Thus Spoke Zarathustra Twilight of the Idols